A

NARRATIVE

OF

THE CAPTIVITY AND ADVENTURES

OF

JOHN TANNER,

(U. S. INTERPRETER AT THE SAUT DE STE. MARIE,)

DURING

THIRTY YEARS RESIDENCE AMONG THE INDIANS

IN THE

INTERIOR OF NORTH AMERICA.

PREPARED FOR THE PRESS
BY EDWIN JAMES, M. D.
Editor of an Account of Major Long's Expedition from Pittsburgh
to the Rocky Mountains.

London:

BALDWIN & CRADOCK, PATERNOSTER ROW.
THOMAS WARD, 84 HIGH HOLBORN

1830.

This scarce antiquarian book is included in our special *Legacy Reprint Series*. In the interest of creating a more extensive selection of rare historical book reprints, we have chosen to reproduce this title even though it may possibly have occasional imperfections such as missing and blurred pages, missing text, poor pictures, markings, dark backgrounds and other reproduction issues beyond our control. Because this work is culturally important, we have made it available as a part of our commitment to protecting, preserving and promoting the world's literature.

INTRODUCTORY CHAPTER.

JOHN TANNER, whose life and adventures are detailed in the following pages, is now about fifty years of age. His person is erect and rather robust, indicating great hardiness, activity, and strength, which, however, his numerous exposures and sufferings have deeply impaired. His face, which was originally rather handsome, bears now numerous traces of thought and passion, as well as of age; his quick and piercing blue eyes, bespeak the stern, the violent, and unconquerable spirit, which rendered him an object of fear to many of the Indians while he remained among them, and which still, in some measure, disqualifies him for that submissive and compliant manner which his dependent situation among the whites renders necessary. Carefully instructed in early youth, in all those principles and maxims which constitute the moral code of the unsophisticated and uncorrupted Indian, his ideas of right and wrong, of honourable and dishonourable, differ, of course, very essentially from those of white men. His isolated and friendless situation, in the midst of a community where the right of private warfare is recognized as almost the only defence of individual possessions, the only barrier between man and man, was certainly in the highest degree unfavourable to the formation of that enduring and patient submissiveness, which, in civilized societies, surrenders so great a share of individual rights to the strong guardianship of the law. Accordingly, to a correct sense of natural justice, he unites a full share of that indomitable and untiring spirit of revenge, so prominent in the Indian character. The circumstances into which he has been thrown, among a wild and lawless race, have taught him to consider himself, in all situations, the avenger of his own quarrel; and if, in the better regulated community into which he has been recently drawn, he has, by the consciousness of aggravated insult, or intolerable oppression, been driven to seek redress, or to propose it to himself, we cannot be surprised that he should have recurred to the method, which long habit, and the paramount influence of established custom, have taught him to consider the only honourable and proper one. He returns to the pale of civilization, too late in life to acquire the mental habits which befit his new situation. It is to be regretted, that he should ever meet among us with those so destitute of generosity, as to be willing to take advantage of his unavoidable ignorance of the usages of civilized society. He has ever been found just and generous, until injuries or insults have aroused the spirit of hatred and revenge; his gratitude has always been as ardent and persevering as his resentment. But it would be superfluous to dwell on the features of his character, which are best displayed in his narrative of those events and scenes, to which he might, with so much propriety, apply the hackneyed motto,

quæque ipse miserrima vidi,
Et quorum pars magna fui.

The preceding remarks would not, perhaps, have been hazarded, had not some harsh imputations been made to rest on the character of our narrator, in the district where he has for some time past resided, in consequence of differences growing, as appears to us, entirely out of the circumstance of the Indian character, with many of its prominent peculiarities, being indelibly impressed upon him. However such a character may, under any circumstances, excite our disapprobation or dislike, some indulgence is due where, as in this case, the solitary savage, with his own habits and opinions, is brought into contact with the artificial manners and complicated institutions of civilized men.

In an attempt to aid this unfortunate individual in addressing his countrymen, it seemed desirable to give his narrative, as nearly as possible, in his own words, and with his own manner. The narrator himself is not without a share of that kind of eloquence which we meet with among the Indians; but as this consists more in action, emphasis, and the expression of the countenance, than in words and sentences, he has been followed in the style of the humblest narration. This plainness, it is hoped, will render the history little less acceptable to the general reader, while the philosophic inquirer will undoubtedly prefer to trace, in the simplest possible guise, the operations of a mind subjected for so long a time to the influence of all the circumstances peculiar to savage life. It ought to be distinctly understood, that his whole story was given as it stands, without hints, suggestions, leading questions, or advice of any kind, other than " to conceal nothing." The sentiments expressed in relation to the character and conduct of individuals on the frontiers, or in the Indian country, or on other subjects connected with the condition of the Indians, are exclusively his own. One liberty it has been found necessary to take, namely, to retrench or altogether to omit many details of hunting adventures, of travelling, and other events, which in the simple lives of the Indians have only a moderate share of importance, but on which, in the lack of other matter, they learn to dwell very much at length in those long narrative conversations with which it is their habit to amuse each other. It is probable the narrator might have proved more acceptable to many of his readers, had this retrenchment been carried to a greater extent; but it is to be remembered, that the life of the savage, like that of the civilized man, is made up of a succession of little occurrences, each unimportant by itself, but which require to be estimated in making up an opinion of the character of either.

Some particulars in Mr. Tanner's narrative will doubtless excite a degree of incredulity, among such as have never attended particularly to the history and condition of the Indian tribes. Many will find their confidence in him much impaired, when he tells of prophetic dreams, and of the fulfilment of indications, and promises, necessarily implying the interference of invisible and spiritual beings. He will appear to some, weakly credulous—to others, stupidly dishonest;—so would any one among us, who should gravely relate tales, which the advance of education, and the general intelligence, have, within two centuries, converted from established doctrines, to "old wives fables." To enforce this remark, we need not refer to the examples of Cotton Mather, and others of his times, not less renowned for human learning, than for exemplary piety. The history of the human mind in all ages, and among all nations, affords abundant examples of credulity; closely resembling that which we feel disposed to ridicule or to pity in the savage. It may be of some importance toward a clear comprehension of the Indian character, to be assured that the powerful mind of our narrator, was at all times strongly influenced by a belief in the ubiquity, and frequent interpositions in the affairs of men, of an over-ruling Providence. His may have been a purer and more consistent Theism, than that of many of his untaught companions, but in many important particulars his belief was the same as theirs. If he was less entirely than his Indian associates the dupe of those crafty prophets, who are constantly springing up among them; yet it will be found he had not, at all times, entire confidence in the decisions of his own mind, which taught him to despise their knavery, and to ridicule their pretensions. In all times of severe distress, or of urgent danger, the Indians, like other men, are accustomed to supplicate aid from superior beings, and they are often confident that a gracious answer has been granted to their petitions. This belief need not shock the pious; as it certainly will not appear in any respect remarkable to those who have accustomed themselves to close observance of the workings of the human mind, under all variations of circumstances. We believe there is nothing inconsistent with true religion, or sound reason, in supposing that the *same Lord over all, is gracious unto all* who worship him in sincerity. It will be manifest also, that this inherent principle of religious feeling is made the instrument, by which superior minds govern and influence the weaker. Among the Indians, as among all other races, from the times of the philosophic leader of the Retreat of the Ten Thousand, to the present day, religion has been an engine in the hands of the few, who in virtue of intellectual or accidental superiority, assume the right to govern the many.

Doubtless many of the representations in the following narrative, are somewhat influenced by peculiarities in the mental constitution, and the accidental circumstances of the narrator; yet making all admissible allowances, they present but a gloomy picture of the condition of uncivilized men. Having acquired some idea of those things considered most reprehensible among us, it would be surprising if he should not have felt some reluctance to giving an explicit detail of all his adventures, in a community whose modes of thinking are on many subjects so different from ours. Traits, which must in our estimation constitute great blemishes, he has freely confessed; whether other or greater faults remain undivulged is unknown; but it should not be forgotten, that actions considered among us not only reprehensible, but highly criminal, are among them accounted shining virtues. In no part of his narrative will he probably appear in a more unfavourable light, than when he details his severity to an unfortunate captive girl, through whose negligence his lodge, and all his little property, was consumed by fire, in the midst of winter. This kind of cruelty, as well as the abandonment of the sick, the aged, and the dying, practised so extensively by the Chippewyans, and other northern Indians, and more or less by all the tribes, remind us, how much even in what seem spontaneous and natural courtesies, we owe to the influence of civilization. The conduct of the Indians in all these cases, however we may see fit to call it, is certainly not unnatural, being in strict and implicit obedience to that impulse of nature, which prompts so irresistibly to self-preservation. How admirable is that complicated machinery which in so many instances avails to overcome and control this impulse—which postpones the interest, the happiness, or the life of the individual, to the good of the associated whole!

The sketch which the following narrative exhibits of the

evils and miseries of savage life, is probably free from exaggeration or distortion. Few will read it without some sentiments of compassion for a race so destitute, so debased, and hopeless; gladly would we believe, it may have a tendency to call the attention of an enlightened and benevolent community, to the wants of those who are *sitting in darkness*. In vain do we attempt to deceive ourselves, or others, into the belief that in whatever "relates to their moral condition and prospects, the Indians have been gainers by their intercourse with Europeans."* Who can believe that the introduction of ardent spirits among them, "has added no new item to the catalogue of their crimes, nor substracted one from the list of their cardinal virtues?" Few, comparatively, have the opportunity, fewer have the inclination, to visit and observe the Indians in their remote haunts, or even on our immediate frontiers; all who have done so, must be convinced that wherever, and for whatever purpose, the Indian and the white man come in contact, the former, in all that relates to his moral condition, is sure to become severely and irretrievably a sufferer. Every unbiassed inquirer, who will avail himself of the abundant means of information before the public, will be convinced, that during more than two hundred years, in despite of all the benevolent exertions of individuals, of humane associations, and of governments, the direct tendency of the intercourse between the two races, has been the uniform and rapid depression and deterioration of the Indians.

Among the most active of the extraneous causes which have produced this conspicuous and deplorable change, must be reckoned the trade for peltries, which has been pushed among them from the earliest occupation of the country by the whites. The ensuing narrative will afford some views of the fur trade, such as it formerly existed in the north west, such as it now exists throughout the territories claimed by the United States. These views are certainly neither those of a

* N. A. Review, No. 60. p. 101.

statesman, or a political economist, but they may be relied on as exhibiting a fair exposition of the influence of the trade upon the aborigines. Recently, the Indians in all that wide portion of North-America, occupied by the Hudson's Bay Fur Company, have been, by the consolidation of two rival associations, relieved alike from the evils, and deprived of the advantages, accruing from an active competition in the trade. Among other advantageous results supposed to be attained by this exclusion of competition, one, and probably the most important, is the effectual check it interposes to the introduction of spirits into the Indian country. Even the clerks and agents stationed at the remote interior posts, are forbidden to introduce the smallest quantity of spirit or wine, among their private stores. This one measure, incalculably of more value than all that has been effected in times remote or recent, by the interference of governments, or the exertions of benevolent associations, has originated in the prudent foresight, and well instructed love of gain, of an association of merchants; and while it makes us fully acquainted with the views of those best informed in relation to the effect of the introduction of whiskey among the Indians, it shows the possibility of remedying this great evil.

In former times, when the whole of the northwest of our continent was open to the competition of rival traders, all the evils and all the advantages of the system at present existing in the United States territories, were felt to the remotest and least accessible of those dreary regions. The Indian could probably in all instances realize a higher price for his peltries, than he can hope to do at present. The means of intoxicating himself and his family, were always to be had at some rate, and the produce of his hunt was artfully divided, and disposed of in the manner which seemed to promise him the greatest share of this deadly indulgence. During the times of active competition, it was found accordingly, that the fur bearing animals, and the race of native hunters, were hastening with equal and rapid strides towards utter extinction. The effect of a competitionary trade, managed, as it will always be, in districts for the most part or wholly without the jurisdiction of the governments of civilized countries, upon the animals whose skins constitute the sole object of the visits of the traders, must be obvious. The vagrant and migratory habits of the Indians, would render it impossible for any individual, or any association of men, to interrupt or even to check the destruction of animals, wherever they could be found. The rival trader was ever at hand to take advantage of any forbearance a prudent foresight might dictate. Thus it will appear that districts, where game had existed in the greatest abundance, were in the course of a few years so stripped, that the inhabitants could avoid starvation only by migrating to some less exhausted region. Wherever the Indians went, the traders were sure to follow, as the wolves and buzzards follow the buffaloe. But in the state of things at present existing in the north, the traders are represented to have entire control of the motions of the Indians. The most valuable part of the territories of the Hudson's Bay Company is the forest country. With the Indians of the plains, who subsist almost entirely by hunting the buffaloe, they concern themselves no further than to purchase such robes or other peltries as they may, on their visit to a post, offer for ready pay. The people of the plains having few possessions beside their horses, their bows and arrows, and their garments of skins, are so independent, and the animals they hunt of so little value to the traders, that they are left to pursue whatever course their own inclination may point out, and at present they never receive *credits*. With the forest Indians the case is quite different. Such is their urgent necessity for ammunition and guns, for traps, axes, woollen blankets, and other articles of foreign manufacture, that at the approach of winter, their situation is almost hopeless, if they are deprived of the supplies they have so long been accustomed to receive. A consciousness of this dependance sufficed, even in times of competition, to some extent, but far more at present, to render them honest, and punctual in discharging the debts they had incurred. The practice of the traders now is, whenever they find the animals in any district becoming scarce, to withdraw their trading establishment, and by removing to some other part, make it necessary for the Indians to follow. Regions thus left at rest, are found to become, in a few years, in a great measure replenished with the fur-bearing animals. The two regulations by which the clerks and agents are forbid to purchase the skins of certain animals, if killed before they have attained their full growth, and by which the use of traps, which destroy indiscriminately old and young, is interdicted, doubtless contribute essentially to the attainment of this important result. It cannot be otherwise, than that the moral condition of the hunter population in the north, must be somewhat improved, by the severe discipline which convenience and interest will equally prompt the Company possessing the monopoly to introduce and maintain; but whether this advantage will, in the event, counterbalance the effect of the rigid exactions to which the Indians may be compelled to submit, must be for time to determine.

It is manifest that plans of government adopted and enforced to subserve the purposes of the fur traders, will be framed with the design of keeping the Indians in a state of efficiency as hunters, and must thus in the end be directly opposed to all efforts to give them those settled habits, that attachment to the soil, and that efficient industry, which must constitute the first step in their advance towards civilization. Such are the climate and soil of a great part of the country northward of the great lakes, as to render it extremely improbable that any other than a rude race of hunters will ever be found there; and for them it would probably be in vain to hope for a milder government, than such a kind of despotism as can be swayed by a company of traders. But within the country belonging to the United States, are many rude tribes distributed at intervals through boundless forests, or along smiling and fertile plains, where it would seem that industry and civilization might be introduced. Here it is not probable that the fur trade can ever become a protected and exclusive monopoly;

and since, while conducted as it is, and as it must continue to be, it is the most prolific sources of evil to the Indians, it may be allowed us, to look forward to the time, when many among the remnants of the native tribes, shall escape from its influence, by becoming independent of the means of subsistence it offers them.

Some change may reasonably be supposed to have taken place in the course of two centuries, in the sentiments of the European intruders towards their barbarous neighbours. In relative situation, they have changed places. Those who are now powerful were then weak; those who now profess to offer protection, then looked with anxiety and trembling, upon the superior strength of the race which has so soon perished from before them. In the early periods of our colonial history, the zeal of religious proselytism, and the less questionable spirit of true philanthropy, seem not to have availed, generally, to overcome the strong hatred of the savage race, produced by causes inseparable from the feeble and dependant condition of the colonies, and from the necessity which compelled our forefathers to become intruders upon the rightful possessions of the Indians. In the writings of the early historians, particularly of the Puritanical divines of New-England, we find these people commonly described as a *brutal* and *devil-driven* race, *wild beasts, bloodhounds, heathen demons;* no epithet was considered too opprobrious, no execration too dire, to be pronounced against them.*

---

* "The little *kingdoms* and *glories*," says Cotton Mather, "of the great men among the *Indians*, was a powerful obstacle to the success of *Mr. Elliot's* ministry; and it is observable, that several of those nations who thus refused the gospel, were quickly after so *devil-driven* as to begin an unjust and bloody war upon the English, which issued in their speedy and utter extirpation from the face of God's earth. It was particularly remarkable in Philip, the ring leader of the most calamitous war ever made upon us; our Elliot made a tender of the *everlasting salvation* unto that king, but the monster entertained it with contempt and anger, and after the *Indian* mode of joining signs with words, he took a button upon the coat of the reverend man, sidding, that *he cared for his gospel as much as he cared for that button.* The world has heard what terrible ruins soon came upon that monarch and upon all his people. It was not long before the hand that now writes, upon a certain occasion, took off the jaw from the exposed *skull* of that *blasphe-*

It may be supposed, that in losing the power which made them formidable, they became less obnoxious to the hatred of the whites. Accordingly, we find that it was long since the fashion to profess much good will and compassion towards this ill-starred race. Some efforts have been made, and many more have been talked of, for their civilization, and for their conversion to the true religion. Here and there, a Penn has appeared among our statesmen; an Elliot or a Brainerd among our religionists—some have been incited by motives of pure benevolence, or by a love of natural justice, to labour perseveringly and faithfully in the work of reclaiming and benefitting the Indians. Could we trust implicitly to the statements of many who in our day write and speak on this subject, we might infer, that the only sentiment influencing us, as a people, in our intercourse with our Indian neighbours, is an ardent desire for the promotion of their best interests. But if we estimate public sentiment by the surer criterion of public measures, we must admit that the present generation are seeking, with no less zeal and earnestness than their forefathers, the utter extermination of these *bloody and idolatrous Canaanites*. The truth is, it has been, and still is, convenient to consider this a *devil driven* race, doomed by *inscrutable destiny* to sudden and entire destruction. This opinion accords well with the convenient dogma of the moral philosopher, who teaches that such as will make the best use of the soil, should drive out and dispossess those who, from ignorance or indolence, suffer it to remain uncultivated. It is of little importance to cavil at the injustice of such a course. The rule of *vis major* seems to be with almost equal force obligatory on both parties,

mous leviathan, and the renowned Samuel Lee hath since been a pastor of an English congregation, sounding and showing the praises of heaven upon that very spot of ground where Philip and his Indians were lately worshipping the Devil." Christian Magazine, p. 514. Vol. I. Boston. Many passages, breathing the same spirit, will at once occur to the recollection of those who are familiar with the writings of the early puritans of New-England. When such was the language learned divines chose to record for posterity, it is not difficult to discover what must have been the general tone of feeling toward the Indians.

and it would perhaps be now as impossible for us to avoid displacing the Indians, and occupying their country, as for them to prevent us.

The long agitated subject, of the "melioration of the condition of the Indians," appears therefore to present two questions of primary importance : 1st. Can any thing be effected by our interference ? 2d. Have we in our collective character, as a people, any disposition to interpose the least check to the downward career of the Indians ? The last inquiry will be unhesitatingly answered in the negative, by all who are acquainted with the established policy of our government in our intercourse with them. The determination evinced by a great part of the people, and their representatives, to extinguish the Indian title to all lands on this side the Mississippi—to push the remnants of these tribes into regions already filled to the utmost extent their means of subsistence will allow—manifests, more clearly than volumes of idle and empty professions, our intentions toward them. The vain mockery of treaties, in which it is understood, that the *negotiation*, and the *reciprocity*, and the benefits, are all on one side ; the feeble and misdirected efforts we make for their civilization and instruction, should not, and do not, deceive us into the belief that we have either a regard for their rights, where they happen to come in competition with our interests, or a sincere desire to promote the cause of moral instruction among them. The efforts of charitable associations, originating as they do in motives of the most unquestionable purity, may seem entitled to more respectful notice ; but we deem these efforts, as far as the Indians are concerned, equally misapplied, whether they be directed, as in the south, to drawing out from among them a few of their children, and giving them a smattering of " astronomy, moral philosophy, surveying, geography, history, and the use of globes,"* or as in the north, in educating the half breed children of fur traders and vagabond Canadians, in erecting workshops and

---

* Letter to Col. M'Kenney, from the Principal of the Lancasterian Chocktaw School at the Great Crossings, Kentucky, in the National Intelligencer, July, 1828.

employing mechanics in our frontier villages, or building vessels for the transportation of freight on the upper lakes. These measures may be well in themselves, and are doubtless useful; but let us not flatter ourselves that in doing these things we confer any essential benefit on the Indians. The Chocktaws and Chickasaws will not long retain such a knowledge of *astronomy* and *surveying*, as would be useful to guide their wanderings, or mete out their possessions, in those scorched and sterile wastes to which it is our fixed intention to drive them. The giving to a few individuals of a tribe, an education, which, as far as it has any influence, tends directly to unfit them for the course of life they are destined to lead, with whatever intention it may be undertaken, is certainly far from being an act of kindness. If, while we give the rudiments of an education to a portion of their children, our selfish policy is thrusting back into a state of more complete barbarism the whole mass of the people, among whom we pretend to qualify them for usefulness, of what avail are our exertions, or our professions in their favour? We cannot be ignorant, that in depriving the Indians of the means of comfortable subsistence, we take from them equally the power and the inclination to cultivate any of the branches of learning commonly taught them at our schools. Will the Indian youth who returns from the Mission school, after ten or fifteen years of instruction, be likely to become a better hunter, or a braver warrior, than those who have remained at home, and been educated in the discipline of his tribe? Will he not rather find himself encumbered with a mass of learning, necessarily as uncurrent, and as little valued among his rude companions, as would be a parcel of lottery tickets or bank notes? On this subject, as on many others, the Indians are qualified to make, and often do make, extremely just reflections. To say that they consider the learning of the whites of no value, would be to misrepresent them. On the contrary, they speak in terms of the highest admiration of some branches, particularly writing and reading, which, they say, enables us to know what is done at a distance, to recall with the greatest accuracy, all that we or others have said, in past times. But of these things they say, as of the religion of the whites, " they are not designed for us." " The Great Spirit has given to you, as well as to us, things suited to our several conditions; He may have been more bountiful to you than to us; but we are not disposed to complain of our allotment."

In relation to the other branch of this part of our subject, namely, the practicability of benefiting the Indians by our instructions, a few words may suffice. More than two hundred years have passed, during all which time it has been believed that systematic and thorough exertions were making to promote the civilization and conversion of the Indians. The entire failure of all these attempts ought to convince us, not that the Indians are irreclaimable, but that we ourselves, while we have built up with one hand, have pulled down with the other. Our professions have been loud, our philanthropic exertions may have been great, but our selfish regard to our own interest and convenience has been greater, and to this we ought to attribute the steady decline, the rapid deterioration of the Indians. We may be told of their constitutional indolence, their Asiatic temperament, destining them to be forever stationary, or retrogradent; but while remaining monuments and vestiges, as well as historical records of unquestionable authority, assure us, that a few centuries ago they were, though a rude, still a great, a prosperous, and a happy people; we ought not to forget that injustice and oppression have been most active among the causes which have brought them down to their present deplorable state. Their reckless indolence, their shameless profligacy, their total self-abandonment, have been the necessary consequences of the degradation and hopelessness of their condition.*

---

* " There are no beggars among them, nor fatherless children unprovided for." Roger William's Key, ch. 5.

" *Obs*. They are as full of business, and as impatient of hinderance, (in their kind,) as any merchant in *Europe*. Many of them naturally princes, or else industrious persons, are rich; 'and the poore amongst' them will say they want no-

That there exists, in the moral or physical constitution of the Indians, any insuperable obstacle to their civilization, no one will now seriously assert. That they will ever be generally civilized, those who know them intimately, and who have observed the prevailing tone of feeling of both races towards each other, will consider so extremely improbable, that they will deem it scarce worth while to inquire what system of measures would be best calculated to effect this desirable object.

thing." Williams, ch. 7. " Obs. The women of the family will commonly raise two or three heaps [of corn] of twelve, fifteene, or twentie bushells a heap, which they drie in round broad heaps; and if she have help of her children or friends, much more." Ch. 16. "I could never discerne that excess of scandalous sins amongst them which Europe aboundeth with. Drunkennesse and gluttony generally they know not what sins they be. And although they have not so much to restraine them (both in respect of knowledge of God and laws of men) as the English have, yet a man shall never hear of such crimes among them, of robberies, murthers, adulteries." Ch. 22. Quotations to the the same effect might be adduced from nearly all the early writers. Yet we are told that in all that regards their moral condition, the Indians have been gainers by their intercourse with the whites!

It is probably within the recollection of many persons now living, when the very considerable quantities of corn required for the fur trade in the country about Lake Superior, were purchased from the Indians, by whom it was raised at a place called *Ketchewawe Seebee*, or Garden river, a small stream falling into the strait between Lakes Superior and Huron, about six miles below the Saut St. Marie. "The Indians at the first settlement of the English, performed many acts of kindness towards them: they instructed them in the manner of planting and dressing the Indian corn," and "by selling them corn when pinched with famine, they relieved their distresses, and prevented them from perishing in a strange land, and uncultivated wilderness." *Trumbull's History of Connecticut*, Vol. I. Ch. 3. In another place, speaking of a famine among the colonists, he says, "In this distressful situation a committee was sent to an Indian settlement called Pocomtock, where they purchased such quantities, that the Indians came down to Windsor and Hartford with fifty canoes at one time laden with Indian corn." Vol. I. Ch. 6. The Indians on Block Island, according to the same authority, "had about two hundred acres of corn." This the English, after two days spent on the Island "burning wigwams," and "staving canoes," destroyed, and then sailed for the Pequot country. Ib. Ch. 5. Charlevoix, a less exceptionable authority than most of the early French writers, says, that in an incursion into the country of the Senecas, the French destroyed four hundred thousand minots [1,200,000 bushels] of corn. "They also killed a prodigious number of swine, which caused much sickness." *Hist. de la Nouvelle France*, liv. XI. It is unnecessary to cite passages, hundreds of which might be adduced to prove, what few, except the reviewer above quoted, ever considered doubtful.

3

Of what advantage could any degree of civilization have been to those unfortunate Seminoles, who were a few years since removed from their beautiful and fertile lands in Florida, to those deep and almost impassable swamps in the rear of Tampa Bay, where it has been found not only necessary to confine them by a military force, but to subsist them, from day to day, and from year to year, by regular issues of provisions? Need we give them education, that they may be the better able to estimate our munificence and generosity, in suffering them to roam at large, in cypress swamps, in sandy deserts, or wherever else we may think the soil of no value to us?

The project of congregating the Indians, from the extended portions of the United States, in some place not only *west of the Mississippi*, but westward of the arable lands of Missouri and Arkansaw, in those burning deserts which skirt the eastern base of the Rocky Mountains, is, perhaps, more pregnant with injustice and cruelty to these people, than any other. Such is the inveterate and interminable hostility existing, time out of mind, between the people of different stocks, portions of which are already in too near vicinity, such as the Dahcotah and the Ojibbeways, the Osages and Cherokees, that nothing but mutual destruction could be the consequence of crowding them together into a region already more than filled with warlike and jealous hunters. The region to which Mr. M'Koy, in his pamphlet, proposes to remove the Indians, would, such is its naked and inhospitable character, soon reduce civilized men who should be confined to it, to barbarism; nothing but inevitable destruction could there await a congregation of fierce, subtle, and mutually hostile savages.

Of all plans hitherto devised to benefit the Indians, by far the best, though doubtless attended with great difficulty in the execution, is, *to let them alone*. Were it possible to leave to them the small remnant they still hold of their former possessions, to remove from them all the poisoning influences of the fur trade and the military posts, and the agencies auxiliary to it, necessity might again make them industrious. Industry thoroughly re-established, would bring in its train prosperity, virtue, and happiness. But since we cannot reasonably hope that this plan will ever be adopted, the friends of humanity must continue to wish that some middle course may be devised, which may, in a measure, palliate the misery which cannot be removed, and retard the destruction which cannot be prevented. The first labour of the philanthropist, who would exert himself in this cause, should be to allay or suppress that exterminating spirit so common among us, which, kept alive by the exertions of unprincipled *land jobbers*, and worthless squatters, is now incessantly calling for the removal of the Indians *west of the Mississippi*. Many, and doubtless some of those who legislate, may consider the region west of the Mississippi, as a kind of fairy land, where men can feed on moonbeams, or, at all events, that the Indians, when thoroughly swept into that land of salt mountains and horned frogs, will be too remote to give us any more trouble. But suppose those who now so pertinaciously urge this measure completely successful, let every Indian be removed beyond the Mississippi, how soon will the phrase be changed, to *west of the Rocky Mountains?* We may send them into the sandy wastes, but cannot persuade them to remain there; they will soon become not less troublesome to the settlers in the countries of Red River, White River, and the Lower Arkansaw, than they are now to the people of Georgia, Alabama, Missouri, and Illinois. Is it absolutely necessary, that while we invite to our shores, and to a participation in all the advantages of our boasted institutions, the dissatisfied and the needy of all foreign countries, not stopping to inquire whether their own crimes, or the influence of an oppressive government, may have made the change desirable for them, we should, at the same time, persist in the determination to root out the last remnants of a race who were the original proprietors of the soil, many of whom are better qualified to become useful citizens of our republic, than those foreigners we are so eager to naturalize? It is certainly by no means desirable that any of the aboriginal tribes who have retained; or acquired, or who shall acquire so much of civilization as to be able to increase in numbers, and to gain strength, surrounded by the whites, should be suffered to establish independent governments, which may, in time, acquire such strength as to be highly troublesome to their neighbours. Could the project of colonization be carried into complete effect, the measure, leaving out of consideration its daring and flagrant injustice, would be of as questionable policy as our unavailing attempt to restore to Africa the descendants of her enslaved children. It is believed by many, that national as well as individual crimes, are sure to be visited, sooner or later, by just and merited punishments. Is it not probable, that despite the efforts of the Colonization Society, the African race, now so deeply rooted and so widely spread among us, must inevitably grow to such a magnitude as to requite, fourfold, to our descendants, our own and our forefathers crimes against the aborigines?

The past history and the present condition of the Indians, make it abundantly manifest, that, if any thing is intended on the part of the United States, except their speedy and utter extinction, an immediate change of measures is loudly called for. The most important particulars of the course to be pursued should be, the prevention, as far as possible, of the evils resulting from competition; the introduction of whiskey, and other existing abuses in the fur trade; the encouragement of agriculture and domestic industry, which may at length render them independent of that trade. Donations of horses, cattle, tools, and farming utensils, handsome clothes, neat and tasteful ornaments, bestowed as marks of honourable distinction, and rewards for successful and persevering industry, may, by degrees, overcome the habitual indolence and contempt of labour, so generally met with among the Indians. With the efforts for the promotion of industry, the cultivation of the mind, not in one out of ten thousand, as at present, but in the whole mass of the children; and the introduction of the English language should keep equal pace. No effort should be spared to advance either. We deem it important that they should not only learn the English language, but, at the same time, lay aside and forget their own, and with it their entire system of traditional feelings and opinions on all subjects. Could all this be effected; could, furthermore, the rights and privileges of citizenship be held out as a reward for a prescribed course of conduct, or attach as a right to the possession of a certain amount of property, the effect would doubtless be a great and rapid elevation of the Indian character. By a system of measures of this kind, a portion of the remnants of these people might probably be preserved, by becoming embodied with the whites. As separate and independent tribes, retaining their own languages, manners, and opinions, it is probable they cannot long continue in existence.

TANNER'S NARRATIVE.

CHAPTER I.

Recollections of early life—capture—journey from the mouth of the Miami to Sa-gui-na—ceremonies of adoption into the family of my foster parents—harsh treatment—transferred by purchase to the family of Net-no-kwa—removal to Lake Michigan.

THE earliest event of my life, which I distinctly remember, is the death of my mother. This happened when I was two years old, and many of the attending circumstances made so deep an impression, that they are still fresh in my memory. I cannot recollect the name of the settlement at which we lived, but I have since learned it was on the Kentucky river, at a considerable distance from the Ohio.

My father, whose name was John Tanner, was an emigrant from Virginia, and had been a clergyman. He lived long after I was taken by the Indians, having died only three months after the great earthquake, which destroyed a part of New Madrid, and was felt throughout the country on the Ohio, [1811.]

Soon after my mother's death, my father removed to a place called Elk Horn. At this place was a cavern—I used to visit it with my brother. We took two candles; one we lighted on entering, and went on till it was burned down; we then lighted the other, and began to return, and we would reach the mouth of the cavern before it was quite burned out.

This settlement at Elk Horn was occasionally visited by hostile parties of Shawneese Indians, who killed some white people, and sometimes killed or drove away cattle and horses. In one instance, my uncle, my father's brother, went with a few men at night, and fired upon a camp of these Indians; he killed one, whose scalp he brought home; all the rest jumped into the river and escaped.

In the course of our residence at this place, an event occurred, to the influence of which I attributed many of the disasters of my subsequent life. My father, when about to start one morning to a village at some distance, gave, as it appeared, a strict charge to my sisters, Agatha and Lucy, to send me to school; but this they neglected to do until afternoon, and then, as the weather was rainy and unpleasant, I insisted on remaining at home. When my father returned at night, and found that I had been at home all day, he sent me for a parcel of small canes, and flogged me much more severely than I could suppose the offence merited. I was displeased with my sisters for attributing all the blame to me, when they had neglected even to tell me to go to school in the forenoon. From that time, my father's house was less like home to me, and I often thought and said, "I wish I could go and live among the Indians."

I cannot tell how long we remained at Elk Horn; when we moved, we travelled two days with horses and wagons, and came to the Ohio, where my father bought three flat boats; the sides of these boats had bullet holes in them, and there was blood on them, which I understood was that of people who had been killed by the Indians. In one of these boats we put the horses and cattle—in another, beds, furniture, and other property, and in the third were some negroes. The cattle boat and the family boat were lashed together; the third, with the negroes, followed behind. We descended the Ohio, and in two or three days came to Cincinnati; here the cattle boat sunk in the middle of the river. When my father saw it sinking, he jumped on board, and cut loose all the cattle, and they swam ashore on the Kentucky side, and were saved. The people from Cincinnati came out in boats to assist us, but father told them the cattle were all safe.

In one day we went from Cincinnati to the mouth of the Big Miami, opposite which we were to settle. Here was some cleared land, and one or two log cabins, but they had been deserted on account of the Indians. My father rebuilt the cabins, and enclosed them with a strong picket. It was early in the spring when we arrived at the mouth of the Big Miami, and we were soon engaged in preparing a field to plant corn. I think it was not more than ten days after our arrival, when my father told us in the morning, that from the actions of the horses, he perceived there were Indians lurking about in the woods, and he said to me, "John, you must not go out of the house to day." After giving strict charge to my step mother to let none of the little children go out, he went to the field, with the negroes, and my elder brother, to drop corn.

Three little children, beside myself, were left in the house with my step mother. To prevent me from going out, my step mother required me to take care of the little child, then not more than a few months old; but as I soon became impatient of confinement, I began to pinch my little brother, to make him cry. My mother perceiving his uneasiness, told me to take him in my arms and walk about the house; I did so, but continued to pinch him. My mother at length took him from me to give him suck. I watched my opportunity, and escaped into the yard; thence through a small door in the large gate of the wall into the open field. There was a walnut tree at some distance from the house, and near the side of the field, where I had been in the habit of finding some of the last year's nuts. To gain this tree without being seen by my father, and those in the field, I had to use some precaution. I remember perfectly well having seen my father, as I skulked towards the tree; he stood in the middle of the field, with his gun in his hand, to watch for Indians, while the others were dropping corn. As I came near the tree, I thought to myself, "I wish I could see these Indians." I had partly filled with nuts a straw hat which I wore, when I heard a crackling noise behind me; I looked round, and saw the Indians; almost at the same instant, I was seized by both hands, and dragged off betwixt two. One of them took my straw hat, emptied the nuts on the ground, and put it on my head. The Indians who seized me were an old man and a young one; these were, as I learned subsequently, Manito-o-geezhik, and his son Kish-kau-ko.* Since I returned from Red River, I have been at Detroit while Kishkau-ko was in prison there; I have also been in Kentucky, and have learned several particulars relative to my capture, which were unknown to me at the time. It appears that the wife of

---

* The name of this man Tanner pronounces Gish-gou-ga. He has subsequently been well known in Michigan, and other portions of the north-western frontier, by his numerous murders and depredations. He died in prison at Detroit, as lately as the fall of 1825.

Manito-o-geezhik had recently lost by death her youngest son—that she had complained to her husband, that unless he should bring back her son, she could not live. This was an intimation to bring her a captive whom she might adopt in the place of the son she had lost. Manito-o-geezhik, associating with him his son, and two other men of his band, living at Lake Huron, had proceeded eastward with this sole design. On the upper part of Lake Erie, they had been joined by three other young men, the relations of Manito-o-geezhik, and had proceeded on, now seven in number, to the settlements on the Ohio. They had arrived the night previous to my capture at the mouth of the Big Miami, had crossed the Ohio, and concealed themselves within sight of my father's house. Several times in the course of the morning, old Manito-o-geezhik had been compelled to repress the ardour of his young men, who becoming impatient at seeing no opportunity to steal a boy, were anxious to fire upon the people dropping corn in the field. It must have been about noon when they saw me coming from the house to the walnut tree, which was probably very near the place where one or more of them were concealed.

It was but a few minutes after I left the house, when my father, coming from the field, perceived my absence. My step mother had not yet noticed that I had gone out. My elder brother ran immediately to the walnut tree, which he knew I was fond of visiting, and seeing the nuts which the Indian had emptied out of my hat, he immediately understood that I had been made captive. Search was instantly made for me, but to no purpose. My father's distress, when he found I was indeed taken away by the Indians, was, I am told, very great.

After I saw myself firmly seized by both wrists by the two Indians, I was not conscious of any thing that passed for a considerable time. I must have fainted, as I did not cry out, and I can remember nothing that happened to me, until they threw me over a large log, which must have been at a considerable distance from the house. The old man I did not now see; I was dragged along between Kish-kau-ko and a very short thick man. I had probably made some resistance, or done something to irritate this last, for he took me a little to one side, and drawing his tomahawk, motioned to me to look up. This I plainly understood, from the expression of his face, and his manner, to be a direction for me to look up for the last time, as he was about to kill me. I did as he directed, but Kish-kau-ko caught his hand as the tomahawk was descending, and prevented him from burying it in my brains. Loud talking ensued between the two. Kish-kau-ko presently raised a yell; the old man and the four others answered it by a similar yell, and came running up. I have since understood that Kish-kau-ko complained to his father, that the short man had made an attempt to kill his little brother, as he called me. The old chief, after reproving him, took me by one hand, and Kish-kau-ko by the other, and dragged me betwixt them; the man who had threatened to kill me, and who was now an object of terror, being kept at some distance. I could perceive, as I retarded them somewhat in their retreat, that they were apprehensive of being overtaken; some of them were always at some distance from us.

It was about one mile from my father's house to the place where they threw me into a hickory bark canoe, which was concealed under the bushes, on the bank of the river. Into this they all seven jumped, and immediately crossed the Ohio, landing at the mouth of the Big Miami, and on the south side of that river. Here they abandoned their canoe, and stuck their paddles in the ground, so that they could be seen from the river. At a little distance in the woods, they had some blankets and provisions concealed; they offered me some dry venison and bear's grease, but I could not eat. My father's house was plainly to be seen from the place where we stood; they pointed at it, looked at me, and laughed, but I have never known what they said.

After they had eaten a little, they began to ascend the Miami, dragging me along as before. The shoes I had on when at home, they took off, as they seemed to think I could run better without them. Although I perceived I was closely watched, all hope of escape did not immediately forsake me. As they hurried me along, I endeavoured, without their knowledge, to take notice of such objects as would serve as landmarks on my way back. I tried also, where I passed long grass, or soft ground, to leave my tracks. I hoped to be able to escape after they should have fallen asleep at night. When night came, they lay down, placing me between the old man and Kish-kau-ko, so close together, that the same blanket covered all three. I was so fatigued that I fell asleep immediately, and did not wake until sunrise next morning, when the Indians were up and ready to proceed on their journey. Thus we journeyed for about four days, the Indians hurrying me on, and I continuing to hope that I might escape, but still every night completely overpowered by sleep. As my feet were bare, they were often wounded, and at length much swollen. The old man perceiving my situation, examined my feet one day, and after removing a great many thorns and splinters from them, gave me a pair of moccasins, which afforded me some relief. Most commonly, I travelled between the old man and Kish-kau-ko, and they often made me run until my strength was quite exhausted. For several days I could eat little or nothing. It was, I think, four days after we left the Ohio, that we came to a considerable river, running, as I suppose, into the Miami. This river was wide, and so deep, that I could not wade across it; the old man took me on his shoulders and carried me over; the water was nearly up to his arm pits. As he carried me across, I thought I should never be able to pass this river alone, and gave over all hope of immediate escape. When he put me down on the other side, I immediately ran up the bank, and a short distance into the woods, when a turkey flew up a few steps before me. The nest she had left contained a number of eggs; these I put in the bosom of my shirt, and returned towards the river. When the Indians saw me they laughed, and immediately took the eggs from me, and kindling a fire, put them in a small kettle to boil. I was then very hungry, and as I sat watching the kettle, I saw the old man come running from the direction of the ford where we had crossed; he immediately caught up the kettle, threw the eggs and the water on the fire, at the same time saying something in a hurried and low tone to the young men. I inferred we were pursued, and have since understood that such was the case; it is probable some of my friends were at that time on the opposite side of the river searching for me. The Indians hastily gathered up the eggs and dispersed themselves in the woods, two of them still urging me forward to the utmost of my strength.

It was a day or two after this that we met a party of twenty or thirty Indians, on their way towards the settlements. Old Manito-o-geezhik had much to say to them; subsequently I learned that they were a war party of Shawneese; that they received information from our party, of the whites who were in pursuit of us about the forks of the Miami; that they went in pursuit of them, and that a severe skirmish happened between them, in which numbers were killed on both sides.

Our journey through the woods was tedious and painful: it might have been ten days after we met the war party, when we arrived at the Maumee river. As soon as we came near the river, the Indians were suddenly scattered about the woods examining the trees, yelling and answering each other. They soon selected a hickory tree, which was cut down, and the bark stripped off, to make a canoe. In this canoe we all embarked, and descended till we came to a large Shawnee village, at the mouth of a river which enters the Maumee. As we were landing in this village, great numbers of the Indians came about us, and one young woman came crying directly towards me, and struck me on the head. Some of her friends had been killed by the whites. Many of these Shawneese showed a disposition to kill me, but Kish-kauko and the old man interposed, and prevented them. I could perceive that I was often the subject of conversation, but could not as yet understand what was said. Old Manito-o-geezhik could speak a few words of English, which he used occasionally, to direct me to bring water, make a fire, or perform other tasks, which he now began to require of me. We remained two days at the Shawnee village, and then proceeded on our journey in the canoe. It was not very far from the village that we came to a trading house, where were three or four men who could speak English; they talked much with me, and said they wished to have purchased me from the Indians, that I might return to my friends; but as the old man would not consent to part with me, the traders told me I must be content to go with the Indians, and to become the old man's son, in place of one he had lost, promising at the same time that after ten days they would come to the village and release me. They treated me kindly while we staid, and gave me plenty to eat, which the Indians had neglected to do. When I found I was compelled to leave this house with the Indians, I began to cry, for the first time since I had been taken. I consoled myself, however, with their promise that in ten days they would come for me. Soon after leaving this trading house, we came to the lake; we did not stop at night to encamp, but soon after dark the Indians raised a yell, which was answered from some lights on shore, and presently a canoe came off to us, in which three of our party left us. I have little recollection of any thing that passed from this time until we arrived at Detroit. At first we paddled up in the middle of the river until we came opposite the centre of the town; then we ran in near the shore, where I saw a white woman, with whom the Indians held a little conversation, but I could not understand what was said. I also saw several white men standing and walking on shore, and heard them talk, but could not understand them; it is likely they spoke French. After talking a few minutes with the woman, the Indians pushed off, and ran up a good distance above the town.

It was about the middle of the day when we landed in the woods, and drew up the canoe. They presently found a large hollow log, open at one end, into which they put their blankets, their little kettle, and some other articles; they then made me crawl into it, after which they closed up the end at which I had entered. I heard them for a few minutes on the outside, then all was still, and remained so for a long time. If I had not long since relinquished all hope of making my escape, I soon found it would be in vain for me to attempt to release myself from my confinement. After remaining many hours in this situation, I heard them removing the logs with which they had fastened me in, and on coming out, although it was very late in the night, or probably near morning, I could perceive that they had brought three horses. One of these was a large iron-gray mare, the others were two small bay horses. On one of these they placed me, on the others their baggage, and sometimes one, sometimes another of the Indians riding, we travelled rapidly, and in about three days reached Sau-ge-nong,* the village to which old Manito-o-geezhik belonged. This village or settlement consisted of several scattered houses. Two of the Indians left us soon after we entered it; Kish-kau-ko and his father only remained, and instead of proceeding immediately home, they left their horses and borrowed a canoe, in which we at last arrived at the old man's house. This was a hut or cabin built of logs, like some of those in

---

* *Sa-gui-na*. The word *Sau-ge-nong*, appears to mean, "the town of the Saukees."

Kentucky. As soon as we landed, the old woman came down to us to the shore, and after Manito-o-geezhik had said a few words to her, she commenced crying, at the same time hugging and kissing me, and thus she led me to the house. Next day they took me to the place where the old woman's son had been buried. The grave was enclosed with pickets, in the manner of the Indians, and on each side of it was a smooth open place. Here they all took their seats; the family and friends of Manito-o-geezhik on the one side, and strangers on the other. The friends of the family had come provided with presents; mukkuks of sugar, sacks of corn, beads, strouding, tobacco, and the like. They had not been long assembled, when my party began to dance, dragging me with them about the grave. Their dance was lively and cheerful, after the manner of the scalp dance. From time to time as they danced, they presented me something of the articles they had brought, but as I came round in the dancing to the party on the opposite side of the grave, whatever they had given me was snatched from me: thus they continued great part of the day, until the presents were exhausted, when they returned home.

It must have been early in the spring when we arrived at Sauge-nong, for I can remember that at this time the leaves were small, and the Indians were about planting their corn. They managed to make me assist at their labours, partly by signs, and partly by the few words of English old Manito-o-geezhik could speak. After planting, they all left the village, and went out to hunt and dry meat. When they came to their hunting grounds, they chose a place where many deer resorted, and here they began to build a long screen like a fence; this they made of green boughs and small trees. When they had built a part of it, they showed me how to remove the leaves and dry brush from that side of it to which the Indians were to come to shoot the deer. In this labour I was sometimes assisted by the squaws and children, but at other times I was left alone. It now began to be warm weather, and it happened one day that having been left alone, as I was tired and thirsty, I fell asleep. I cannot tell how long I slept, but when I began to awake, I thought I heard some one crying a great way off. Then I tried to raise up my head, but could not. Being now more awake, I saw my Indian mother and sister standing by me, and perceived that my face and head were wet. The old woman and her daughter were crying bitterly, but it was some time before I perceived that my head was badly cut and bruised. It appears that after I had fallen asleep, Manito-o-geezhik, passing that way, had perceived me, had tomahawked me, and thrown me in the bushes; and that when he came to his camp he had said to his wife, "old woman, the boy I brought you is good for nothing; I have killed him, and you will find him in such a place." The old woman and her daughter having found me, discovered still some signs of life, and had stood over me a long time, crying, and pouring cold water on my head, when I waked. In a few days I recovered in some measure from this hurt, and was again set to work at the screen, but I was more careful not to fall asleep; I endeavoured to assist them at their labours, and to comply in all instances with their directions, but I was notwithstanding treated with great harshness, particularly by the old man, and his two sons She-mung and Kwo-tash-e. While we remained at the hunting camp, one of them put a bridle in my hand, and pointing in a certain direction, motioned me to go. I went accordingly, supposing he wished me to bring a horse; I went and caught the first I could find, and in this way I learned to discharge such services as they required of me.

When we returned from hunting, I carried on my back a large pack of dried meat all the way to the village; but though I was almost starved, I dared not touch a morsel of it. My Indian mother, who seemed to have some compassion for me, would sometimes steal a little food, and hide it for me until the old man was gone away, and then give it me. After we returned to the village, the young men, whenever the weather was pleasant, were engaged in spearing fish, and they used to take me to steer the canoe. As I did not know how to do this very well, they commonly turned upon me, beat me, and often knocked me down with the pole of the spear. By one or the other of them I was beaten almost every day. Other Indians, not of our family, would sometimes seem to pity me, and when they could without being observed by the old man, they would sometimes give me food, and take notice of me.

After the corn was gathered in the fall, and disposed of in the Sau-je-gwun-nun, or Ca-ches, where they hide it for the winter, they went to hunt on the Sau-ge-nong river. I was here, as I had always been when among them, much distressed with hunger. As I was often with them in the woods, I saw them eating something, and I endeavoured to discover what it was, but they carefully concealed it from me. It was some time before I accidentally found some beach-nuts, and though I knew not what they were, I was tempted to taste them, and finding them very good, I showed them to the Indians, when they laughed, and let me know these were what they had all along been eating. After the snow had fallen, I was compelled to follow the hunters, and often-times to drag home to the lodge a whole deer, though it was with the greatest difficulty I could do so.

At night I had always to lie between the fire and the door of the lodge, and when any one passed out or came in, they commonly gave me a kick; and whenever they went to drink, they made a practice to throw some water on me. The old man constantly treated me with much cruelty, but his ill humour showed itself more on some occasions than others. One morning, he got up, put on his moccasins, and went out; but presently returning, he caught me by the hair of my head, dragged me out, rubbed my face for a long time in a mass of recent excrement, as one would do the nose of a cat, then tossed me by the hair into a snow bank. After this I was afraid to go into the lodge; but at length my mother came out and gave me some water to wash. We were now about to move our camp, and I was as usual made to carry a large pack; but as I had not been able to wash my face clean, when I came among other Indians they perceived the smell, and asked me the cause. By the aid of signs, and some few words I could now speak, I made them comprehend how I had been treated. Some of them appeared to pity me, assisted me to wash myself, and gave me something to eat.*

---

* Tanner has much of the Indian habit of concealing emotion; but when he related the above to me, the glimmering of his eye, and a convulsive movement of his upper lip, betrayed sufficiently, that he is not without the enduring thirst for revenge which belongs to the people among whom he has spent his life. "As soon," said he, in connexion with this anecdote, "as I landed in Detroit on my return from Red River, and found a man who could speak with me, I said 'where is Kish-kau-ko?' 'He is in prison.' 'Where is Manito-o-geezhik, his father?' 'Dead two months since.' 'It is well he is dead.'" Intimating that though more than thirty years had elapsed, he intended now to have avenged himself for the injury done him when a boy not eleven years of age.—Ed.

5

Often when the old man would begin to beat me, my mother, who generally treated me with kindness, would throw her arms about me, and he would beat us both together. Towards the end of winter, we moved again to the sugar grounds. At this time, Kish-kau-ko, who was a young man of about twenty years of age, joined with him four other young men, and went on a war-party. The old man, also, as soon as the sugar was finished, returned to the village, collected a few men, and made his preparations to start. I had now been a year among them, and could understand a little of their language. The old man, when about to start, said to me, " now I am going to kill your father and your brother, and all your relations." Kish-kau-ko returned first, but was badly wounded. He said he had been with his party to the Ohio river; that they had, after watching for some time, fired upon a small boat that was going down, and killed one man, the rest jumping into the water. He [Kish-kau-ko] had wounded himself in his thigh with his own spear, as he was pursuing them. They brought home the scalp of the man they had killed.

Old Manito-o-geezhik returned a few days afterwards, bringing an old white hat, which I knew, from a mark in the crown, to be that of my brother. He said he had killed all my father's family, the negroes, and the horses, and had brought me my brother's hat, that I might see he spoke the truth. I now believed that my friends had all been cut off, and was, on that account, the less anxious to return. This, it appears, had been precisely the object the old man wished to accomplish, by telling me the story, of which but a small part was true. When I came to see Kish-kau-ko, after I returned from Red River, I asked him immediately, "Is it true, that your father has killed all my relations?" He told me it was not; that Manito-o-geezhik, the year after I was taken, at the same season of the year, returned to the same field where he had found me; that, as on the preceding year, he had watched my father and his people planting corn, from morning till noon; that then they all went into the house, except my brother, who was then nineteen years of age: he remained ploughing with a span of horses, having the lines about his neck, when the Indians rushed upon him; the horses started to run; my brother was entangled in the lines, and thrown down, when the Indians caught him. The horses they killed with their bows and arrows, and took my brother away into the woods. They crossed the Ohio before night, and had proceeded a good distance in their way up the Miami. At night they left my brother securely bound, as they thought, to a tree. His hands and arms were tied behind him, and there were cords around his breast and neck; but having bitten off some of the cords, he was able to get a pen-knife that was in his pocket, with which he cut himself loose, and immediately run towards the Ohio, at which he arrived, and which he crossed by swimming, and reached his father's house about sunrise in the morning. The Indians were roused by the noise he made, and pursued him into the woods; but as the night was very dark, they were not able to overtake him. His hat had been left at the camp, and this they brought, to make me believe they had killed him. Thus I remained for two years in this family, and gradually came to have less and less hope of escape, though I did not forget what the English traders on the Maumee had said, and I wished they might remember and come for me. The men were often drunk, and whenever they were so, they sought to kill me. In these cases, I learned to run and hide myself in the woods, and I dared not return before their drunken frolick was over. During the two years that I remained at Sauge-nong, I was constantly suffering from hunger; and though strangers, or those not belonging to the family, sometimes fed me, I had never enough to eat. The old woman they called Ne-keek-wos-ke-cheem e-kwa—" the Otter woman," the otter being her *totem*—treated me with kindness, as did her daughters, as well as Kish-kau-ko and Be-nais-sa, the bird, the youngest son, of about my own age. Kish-kau-ko and his father, and the two brothers, Kwo-ta-she and She-mung, were blood-thirsty and cruel, and those who remain of this family, continue, to this time, troublesome to the whites. Be-nais-sa, who came to see me when I was at Detroit, and who always treated me kindly, was a better man, but he is since dead. While I remained with them at Sau-ge-nong, I saw white men but once. Then a small boat passed, and the Indians took me out to it in a canoe, rightly supposing that my wretched appearance would excite the compassion of the traders, or whatever white men they were. These gave me bread, apples, and other presents, all which, except one apple, the Indians took from me. By this family I was named Shaw-shaw-wa ne-ba-se, (the Falcon,) which name I retained while I remained among the Indians.

I had been about two years at Sau-ge-nong, when a great council was called by the British agents at Mackinac. This council was attended by the Sioux, the Winnebagoes, the Menomonees, and many remote tribes, as well as by the Ojibbeways, Ottawwaws, &c. When old Manito-o-geezhik returned from this council, I soon learned that he had met there his kinswoman, Net-no-kwa, who, notwithstanding her sex, was then regarded as principal chief of the Ottawwaws. This woman had lost her son, of about my age, by death; and having heard of me, she wished to purchase me to supply his place. My old Indian mother, the Otter woman, when she heard of this, protested vehemently against it. I heard her say, "My son has been dead once, and has been restored to me; I cannot lose him again." But these remonstrances had little influence, when Net-no-kwa arrived with considerable whiskey, and other presents. She brought to the lodge first a ten gallon keg of whiskey, blankets, tobacco, and other articles of great value. She was perfectly acquainted with the dispositions of those with whom she had to negotiate. Objections were made to the exchange until the contents of the keg had circulated for some time; then an additional keg, and a few more presents, completed the bargain, and I was transferred to Net-no-kwa. This woman, who was then advanced in years, was of a more pleasing aspect than my former mother. She took me by the hand, after she had completed the negotiation with my former possessors, and led me to her own lodge, which stood near. Here I soon found I was to be treated more indulgently than I had been. She gave me plenty of food, put good clothes upon me, and told me to go and play with her own sons. We remained but a short time at Sau-ge-nong. She would not stop with me at Mackinac, which we passed in the night, but ran along to Point St. Ignace, where she hired some Indians to take care of me, while she returned to Mackinac by herself, or with one or two of her young men. After finishing her business at Mackinac, she returned, and continuing on our journey, we arrived in a few days at Shab-a-wy-wy-a-gun. The corn was ripe when we reached that place, and after stopping a little while, we went three days up the river, to the place where they intended to pass the winter. We then left our canoes, and travelling over land, camped three times before we came to the place where we set up our lodges for the winter. The husband of Net-no-kwa was an Ojibbeway, of Red River, called Taw-ga-we-ninne, the hunter. He was seventeen years younger than Net-no-kwa, and had turned off a former wife on being married to her. Taw-ga-we-ninne was always indulgent and kind to me, treating me like an equal, rather than as a dependant. When speaking to me, he always called me his son. Indeed, he himself was but of secondary importance in the family, as every thing belonged to Net-no-kwa, and she had the direction in all affairs of any moment. She imposed on me, for the first year, some tasks. She made me cut wood, bring home game, bring water, and perform other services not commonly required of the boys of my age; but she treated me invariably with so much kindness, that I was far more happy and content, than I had been in the family of Manito-o-geezhik. She sometimes whipped me, as she did her own children; but I was not so severely and frequently beaten as I had been before.

CHAPTER II.

First attempt to hunt—measles—trapping martins—emigration to Red River—death of my foster father and brother—arrival at Lake Winnipek.

EARLY in the spring, Net-no-kwa and her husband, with their family, started to go to Mackinac. They left me, as they had done before, at Point St. Ignace, as they would not run the risk of losing me by suffering me to be seen at Mackinac. On our return, after we had gone twenty-five or thirty miles from Point St. Ignace, we were detained by contrary winds, at a place called Me-nau-ko-king, a point running out into the lake. Here we encamped with some other Indians, and a party of traders. Pigeons were very numerous in the woods, and the boys of my age, and the traders, were busy shooting them. I had never killed any game, and, indeed, had never in my life discharged a gun. My mother had purchased at Mackinac a keg of powder, which, as they thought it a little damp, was here spread out to dry. Taw-ga-we-ninne had a large horse-man's pistol; and finding myself somewhat emboldened by his indulgent manner toward me, I requested permission to go and try to kill some pigeons with the pistol. My request was seconded by *Net-no-kwa*, who said, "It is time for our son to begin to learn to be a hunter." Accordingly, my father, as I called Taw-ga-we-ninne, loaded the pistol and gave it to me, saying, "Go, my son, and if you kill any thing with this, you shall immediately have a gun, and learn to hunt." Since I have been a man, I have been placed in difficult situations; but my anxiety for success was never greater than in this, my first essay as a hunter. I had not gone far from the camp, before I met with pigeons, and some of them alighted in the bushes very near me. I cocked my pistol, and raised it to my face, bringing the breech almost in contact with my nose. Having brought the sight to bear upon the pigeon, I pulled trigger, and was in the next instant sensible of a humming noise, like that of a stone sent swiftly through the sky. I found the pistol at the distance of some paces behind me, and the pigeon under the tree on which he had been sitting. My face was much bruised, and covered with blood. I ran home, carrying my pigeon in triumph. My face was speedily bound up; my pistol exchanged for a fowling-piece; I was accoutred with a powder horn, and furnished with shot, and allowed to go out after birds. One of the young Indians went with me, to observe my manner of shooting. I killed three more pigeons in the course of the afternoon, and did not discharge my gun once without killing. Henceforth I began to be treated with more consideration, and was allowed to hunt often, that I might become expert.

Great part of the summer and autumn passed before we returned to Shab-a-wy-wy-a-gun. When we arrived we found the Indians suffering very severely from the measles; and as Net-no-kwa was acquainted with the contagious nature of this disease, she was unwilling to expose her family, but passed immediately through the village, and encamped on the river above. But, notwithstanding her precaution, we soon began to fall sick. Of ten persons belonging to our family, including two young wives of Taw-ga-we-ninne, only Net-no-kwa and myself escaped an attack of this complaint. Several of them were very sick, and the old woman and myself found it as much as we could do to take care of them. In the village, numbers died, but all of our family escaped. As the winter approached, they began to get better, and went, at length, to our wintering ground, at the same place where we had spent the former winter. Here I was set to make martin traps, as the other hunters did. The first day I went out early, and spent the whole day, returning late at night, having made only three traps; whereas, in the same time, a good hunter would have made twenty-five or thirty. On the morning following, I visited my traps, and found but one martin. Thus I continued to do for some days, but my want of success, and my awkwardness, exposed me to the ridicule of the young men. At length, my father began to pity me, and he said, "My son, I must go and help you to make traps." So he went out and spent a day in making a large number of traps, which he gave me, and then I was able to take as many martins as the others. The young men, however, did not forget to tell me, on all occasions, of the assistance I had received from my father.

This winter was passed like the preceding; but as I became more and more expert and successful in hunting and trapping, I was no longer required to do the work of the women about the lodge.

In the following spring, Net-no-kwa, as usual, went to Mackinac. She always carried a flag in her canoe, and I was told, that whenever she came to Mackinac, she was saluted by a gun from the fort. I was now thirteen years old, or in my thirteenth year. Before we left the village, I heard Net-no-kwa talk of going to Red River, to the relations of her husband. Many of the Ottawwaws, when they heard this, determined to go with her. Among others, was Wah-ka-zee, a chief of the village at Wargun-uk-ke-zee,* or L'Arbre Croche, and others; in all, six canoes. Instead of leaving me, in this instance, at Point St. Ignace, they landed with me in the night, among the cedars, not far from the village of Mackinac; and the old woman then took me into the town, to the house of a French trader, [Shabboyer,] with whom she had sufficient influence to secure my confinement, for several days, in the cellar. Here I remained, not being allowed to go out at all, but was otherwise well treated. This confinement seemed to be unnecessary, as subsequently, when we were ready to go on our journey, we were detained by head winds, at the point now occupied by the missionaries, when I was suffered to run at large. While we remained here, the Indians began to be drunk. My father, who was drunk, but still able to walk about, spoke to two young men who were walking together, and taking hold of the shirt sleeve of one of them, he, without intending to do so, tore it. This young man, whose name was Sug-gut-taw-gun, [Spunk-wood,] was irritated, and giving my father a rough push, he fell on his back. Sug-gut-taw-gun then took up a large stone, and threw it at him, hitting him in the forehead. When I saw this, I became alarmed for my own safety; and, as I knew that Me-to-saw-gea, an Ojibbeway chief, was then on the island, with a party going against the whites; and, as I had understood they had sought opportu-

* *War-gun-uk-ke-zee* means, as Tanner says, the bent tree; and the pine, which gave name to the place called by the French *L'Arbre Croche*, was standing when he first visited that village. He spoke with great indignation of the Indian who, through mere wantonness, cut down this remarkable tree.

nities to kill me, I thought my situation unsafe. I accordingly made my escape to the woods, where I hid myself for the remainder of the day, and the night. On the following day, being pressed by hunger, I returned, and secreted myself, for some time, in the low cedars near our lodge, in order to observe what was passing, and to ascertain if I might return. At length, I discovered my mother calling me, and looking for me through the bushes. I went up to her, and she told me to go in and see my father, who was killed. When I went in, my father said to me, "I am killed." He made me sit down with the other children, and talked much to us. He said, "Now, my children, I have to leave you. I am sorry that I must leave you so poor." He said nothing to us about killing the Indian who had struck him with the stone, as some would have done. He was too good a man to wish to involve his family in the troubles which such a course would have brought upon them. The young man who had wounded him, remained with us, notwithstanding that Netno-kwa told him it would not be safe for him to go to Red River, where her husband's relatives were numerous and powerful, and disposed to take revenge.

When we came to the Saut of St. Marie, we put all our baggage on board the trader's vessel, which was about to sail to the upper end of Lake Superior, and went on ourselves in our canoes. The winds were light, which enabled us to run faster than the vessel, and we arrived ten days before it, at the Portage. When she at last came, and anchored out at a little distance from the shore, my father and his two sons, Wa-me-gon-a-biew, (he who puts on feathers,) the eldest, and Ke-wa-tin, (the north wind,) went out in a canoe to get the baggage. In jumping down into the hold of the vessel, the younger of these young men fell with his knee upon a knot of the rope tied around a bundle of goods, and received an injury from which he never recovered. The same night his knee was badly swollen, and on the next day he was not able to go out of the lodge. After about eight or ten days, we commenced crossing the Grand Portage: we carried him on our shoulders, by fastening a blanket to two poles; but he was so sick that we had to stop often, which made us long in passing. We left our canoes at the trading-house, and when we came to the other side of the Portage, were detained some days to make small canoes. When these were nearly finished, my father sent me, with one of his wives, back to the trading-house, to bring something which had been forgotten. On our return, we met the two boys at some distance, coming to tell me to hasten home, for my father was dying, and he wished to see me before he died. When I came into the lodge, I found that he was indeed dying, and though he could see, he was not able to speak to me. In a few minutes he ceased to breathe. Beside him lay the gun which he had taken in his hand a few minutes before, to shoot the young man who had wounded him at Mackinac. In the morning, when I left him to go to the Portage, he was apparently well; my mother told me it was not until afternoon, he began to complain; he then came into the lodge, saying, "I am now dying; but since I have to go, this young man, who has killed me, must go with me. I hoped to have lived till I had raised you all to be men; but now I must die, and leave you poor, and without any one to provide for you." So saying, he stepped out, with the gun in his hand, to shoot the young man, who was at that time sitting by the door of his own lodge. Ke-wa-tin, hearing this, began to cry, and, addressing his father, said, "My father, if I was well I could help you to kill this man, and could protect my young brothers from the vengeance of his friends, after he is dead; but you see my situation, and that I am about to die. My brothers are young and weak, and we shall all be murdered if you kill this man." My father replied, "My son, I love you too well to refuse you any thing you request." So saying, he returned, laid down his gun, and, after having said a very few words, inquired for me, and directed them to send for me, he expired. The old woman procured a coffin from the traders, and they brought my father's body, in a wagon, to the trading-house, on this side the Grand Portage, where they buried him, in the burying ground of the whites. His two sons, as well as the young man who killed him, accompanied his body to the Portage. This last was near being killed by one of my brothers; but the other prevented him, as he was about to strike.

It was but a very short time after my father died, that we started on our journey to Red River. My brother Ke-wa-tin we carried on a litter, as we had done before, whenever it was necessary to take him out of the canoe. We had passed two carrying places, and arrived at the third, called the Moose carrying place, when he said to us, "I must die here; I cannot go farther." So Net-no-kwa determined to stop here, and the remainder of the party went on. A part of our own family chose to continue on with those going to Red River. So that, after they had started, there remained only the old woman, and one of the younger wives of Tau-ga-we-ninne, Wa-me-gon-a-biew, the elder brother, Ke-wa-tin, the second, and myself, the youngest. It was about the middle of summer, for the small berries were ripe, when we stopped here on the borders of Moose Lake, which is of cool and clear water, like Lake Superior. It is small and round, and a canoe can be very plainly seen across the widest part of it. We were only two of us able to do any thing; and being myself very young, and without any experience as a hunter, we had apprehension that, being left thus alone, we might soon be in want. We had brought with us one of the nets used about Mackinac, and setting this, the first night, caught about eighty trout and white fish. After remaining here some time, we found beavers, of which we killed six; also, some otters and muskrats. We had brought with us some corn and grease, so that, with the fish we caught, and the game we killed, we lived comfortably. But, at the approach of winter, the old woman told us she could not venture to remain there by herself, as the winter would be long and cold, and no people, either whites or Indians, near us. Ke-wa-tin was now so sick and weak, that in going back to the Portage, we were compelled to move slowly; and when we arrived, the waters were beginning to freeze. He lived but a month or two after we arrived. It must have been in the early part, or before the middle of winter, that he died. The old woman buried him by the side of her husband, and hung up one of her flags at his grave.

We now, as the weather became severe, began to grow poor, Wa-me-gon-a-biew and myself being unable to kill as much game as we wanted. He was seventeen years of age, and I thirteen, and game was not plentiful. As the weather became more and more cold, we removed from the trading house, and set up our lodge in the woods, that we might get wood easier. Here my brother and myself had to exert ourselves to the utmost, to avoid starving. We used to hunt two or three days' distance from home, and often returned with but little meat. We had, on one of our hunting paths, a camp built of cedar boughs, in which we had kindled fire so often, that at length it became very dry, and at last caught fire as we were lying in it. The cedar had become so dry that it flashed up like powder, but fortunately we escaped with little injury. As we were returning, and still a great distance from home, we attempted to cross a river which was so rapid as never to freeze very sound. Though the weather was so cold that the trees were constantly cracking with the frost, we broke in, I first, and afterwards my brother; and he, in attempting to throw himself down upon the ice, wet himself nearly all over, while I had at first only my feet and legs wet. Owing to our hands being benumbed with the cold, it was long before we could extricate ourselves from our snow shoes, and we were no sooner out of the water, than our moccasins and leggins were frozen stiff. My brother was soon discouraged, and said he was willing to die. Our spunk wood had got wet when we fell in, and though we at length reached the shore, as we were unable to raise a fire, and our moccasins and cloathes were frozen so stiff that we could not travel, I began also to think that we must die. But I was not like my Indian brother, willing to sit down and wait patiently for death to come. I kept moving about to the best of my power, while he lay in a dry place by the side of the bank, where the wind had blown away the snow. I at length found some very dry rotten wood, which I used as a substitute for spunk, and was so happy as to raise a fire. We then applied ourselves to thaw and dry our moccasins, and when partly dry we put them on, and went to collect fuel for a larger fire than we had before been able to make. At length, when night came on, we had a comfortable fire and dry cloathes, and though we had nothing to eat, we did not regard this, after the more severe suffering from cold. At the earliest dawn we left our camp, and proceeded towards home; but at no great distance met our mother, bringing dry clothes and a little food. She knew that we ought to have been home on the preceding day by sun set, and was also aware of the difficult river we had to cross. Soon after dark, being convinced that we must have fallen through the ice, she started, and walking all night, met us not far from the place where the accident happened.

Thus we lived for some time, in a suffering and almost starving condition, when a Muskegoe, or Swamp Indian, called the Smoker,* came to the trading house, and learning that we were very poor, invited us home with him, to his own country, saying he could hunt for us, and would bring us back in the spring. We went two long days journey towards the west, and came to a place called We-sau-ko-ta See-bee, Burnt Wood River, where we found his lodge. He took us into his own lodge, and while we remained with him, we wanted for nothing. Such is still the custom of the Indians, remote from the whites; but the Ottawwaws, and those near the settlements, have learned to be like the whites, and to give only to those who can pay. If any one, who had at that time been of the family of Net-no-kwa, were now, after so many years, to meet one of the family of Pe-twaw-we-ninne, he would call him "brother," and treat him as such.

We had been but a few days at the Portage, when another man of the same band of Muskegoes, invited us to go with him to a large island in Lake Superior, where, he said, were plenty of Caribou and Sturgeon, and where, he had no doubt, he could provide all that would be necessary for our support. We went with him, accordingly; and starting at the earliest appearance of dawn, we reached the island somewhat before night, though there was a light wind ahead. In the low rocky points about this island, we found more gull's eggs than we were able to take away. We also took, with spears, two or three sturgeons, immediately on our arrival; so that our want of food was supplied. On the next day, Wa-ge-mah-wub, whom we called our brother-in-law, and who was, in some remote degree, related to Net-no-gua, went to hunt, and returned at evening, having killed two caribou. On this island, is a large lake, which it took us about a day to reach, from the shore; and into this lake runs a small river. Here we found beaver, otter, and other game; and as long as we remained in the island, we had an abundant supply

* *Pe-twaw-we-ninne.*—This, however, is a Cree word; the name among the Ojibbeways, is *Sug-guo-swaw-we-ninne.* Muskegoe is from *Mus-keek,* a swamp, and is applied to a band of the Ojibbeways, enjoying in general no very good name.

of provisions. We met here the relations of Wa-ge-mah-wub in eight canoes; with whom we at length started to return to the Portage. We were ten canoes in all, and we started, as we had done in coming, at the earliest dawn of the morning. The night had been calm, and the water, when we left the island, was perfectly smooth. We had proceeded about two hundred yards into the lake, when the canoes all stopped together, and the chief, in a very loud voice, addressed a prayer to the Great Spirit, entreating him to give us a good look to cross the lake. "You," said he, "have made this lake, and you have made us, your children; you can now cause that the water shall remain smooth, while we pass over in safety." In this manner, he continued praying for five or ten minutes; he then threw into the lake a small quantity of tobacco, in which each of the canoes followed his example. They then all started together, and the old chief commenced his song, which was a religious one; but I cannot remember exactly the meaning of what he sung. I had now forgotten my mother tongue, and retained few, if any, ideas of the religion of the whites. I can remember, that this address of the chief to the Great Spirit, appeared to me impressive and solemn, and the Indians seemed all somewhat impressed by it, or perhaps by their situation, being exposed, on the broad lake, in their frail bark canoes, they could not but feel their dependance upon that Power which controls the winds and the waves. They rowed and paddled, silently and diligently, and long before night, arrived in safety at the Grand Portage; the lake having remained perfectly calm. At this time, I was suffered to go entirely at large, being subjected to no manner of restraint, and might, at almost any time, have made my escape from the Indians; but I believed my father and all my friends had been murdered, and I remembered the laborious and confined manner in which I must live, if I returned among the whites; where, having no friends, and being destitute of money or property, I must, of necessity, be exposed to all the ills of extreme poverty. Among the Indians, I saw that those who were too young, or too weak to hunt for themselves, were sure to find some one to provide for them. I was also rising in the estimation of the Indians, and becoming as one of them. I therefore chose, for the present, to remain with them;

but always intended, at some future time, to return and live among the whites.

We were now again at the Portage, whence we had been twice removed by the friendly hospitality of the Muskegoes; and were left to consult about the course we would pursue. When our mother had at length made up her mind to continue on to Red River, according to her original plan, she heard, by one of the traders, that her son-in-law, the husband of one of her daughters, who had continued on from Moose Lake, at the time we had been compelled to stop with Ke-wa-tin, had been killed by an old man, in a drunken frolick. The traders had brought the widow as far as Rainy Lake, whence she had sent word to her mother, that she wished her to come and join her. This was an additional inducement to us to go to Red River, and we determined to proceed without delay.

Our canoe had been lent to the traders, and was sent on the route towards Red River to bring packs. As they were about to despatch more canoes, Net-no-gua requested they would distribute us about, one or two to each canoe, so that we might go on until we should meet our own canoe. After a day or two, we met the Frenchmen, with our canoe; but as they refused to give it up, the old woman took it from them without their consent, put it in the water, and put our baggage on board. The Frenchmen dared not make any resistance. I have never met with an Indian, either man or woman, who had so much authority as Net-no-kwa. She could accomplish whatever she pleased, either with the traders or the Indians; probably, in some measure, because she never attempted to do any thing which was not right and just.

At Rainy Lake, we found the old woman's daughter, in the care of some Indians, but very poor. Net-no-kwa conferred long with her, on our situation; she talked of all our misfortunes and losses, and the death of her husband and son. She knew, she said, that her two little sons who remained, were young, but they were now becoming able to do something; and that, since she had come so far, for the purpose of going to Red River to hunt beaver, she was not willing to turn back. My brother and myself, although deeply interested in these consultations, were not allowed to have any voice.

It being determined that we should go to Red River, we continued on to the Lake of the Woods. This lake is called by the Indians Pub-be-kwaw-waung-gaw Sau-gi-e-gun, "the Lake of the Sand Hills." Why it is called "Lake of the Woods" by the whites, I cannot tell, as there is not much wood about it. Here we were much endangered by high winds, the waves dashing into our canoe so fast, that I was scarcely able, with a large kettle, to throw out the water as fast as it came in.

In the fall of the year, we arrived at the Lake of Dirty Water, called by the whites Lake. Winnepeg.* Here old Net-no-gua, being much cast down with grief, in consequence of all the misfortunes and losses she had encountered since she left her own country, began to drink, which was unusual with her, and soon became drunk. We, being foolish, and unaccustomed to direct our own motions, seeing that the wind rose fair, determined to place the old woman in the canoe, and cross to the other side of the lake. The traders advised us not to attempt it in the present state of the wind, but we would not listen to them, and accordingly pushed off and raised our sail. As the wind blew directly off the shore, the waves did not there run high; but we had only been out a short time, when they began to dash with great violence into the canoe. We now found it would be more dangerous to attempt to turn about, and regain the shore we had left, than to continue on directly before the wind. At this time the sun went down, and the wind began to blow more violently. We looked upon ourselves as lost, and began to cry. At this time, the old woman began to wake from her drunken fit, and presently becoming conscious of our situation, she sprang up, and first addressing a loud and earnest prayer to the Great Spirit, she applied herself, with surprising activity, to the use of her paddle, at the same time encouraging us, and directing Wa-me-gon-a-biew how to steer the canoe. But at length, as we came near the shore, and she began to recognize the spot we were approaching, she also began to manifest much alarm; and said to us, "my children, it appears to me we must all perish, for this shore before us is full of large rocks lying in the water, and our canoe must be dashed in pieces: nevertheless, we can do nothing

---

* This word, Win-ne-peg, is derived from *win-ne-be-a*, "dirty water," or *ween-au-gum-ma*, which has nearly the same meaning. The lake is called by the Indians *Win-ne-be-a Sau-gie-gun*, "Dirty Water Lake."

but to run directly on, and though we cannot see where the rocks are, we may possibly pass between them." And it so happened, our canoe being thrown high upon a spot of smooth sand beach, where it first struck. We immediately sprang out, and soon dragged it up beyond the reach of the waves. We encamped, and had no sooner kindled a fire, than we began to laugh at the old woman for being drunk, and for the apprehension she had manifested after she waked. In the morning, we perceived that the shore was such as she had described, and that in utter darkness, we had landed, where, with such a wind, the boldest Indian would not venture by day light. We remained at this camp great part of the next day, which happened to be calm and fair, to dry our baggage, and towards evening, embarked, and ran for the mouth of Red River. We did not enter the mouth of the river until late at night, and perceiving a lodge, we landed, and laid down without kindling a fire, or making any noise to disturb the people, as we did not know who they were. In the morning they came and waked us, and we found them to be the family of one of the brothers of Taw-ga-we-ninne, and the very people we had come to seek.

CHAPTER III.

Friendly reception among the Indians on the Assinneboin—Prairie Portage—Net-no-kwa's dream, and its fulfilment—meet with Pe-shau-ba, a distinguished warrior of the Ottawwaws—journey to Kau-wau-koning, and residence there—return towards Lake Superior—war-party against the Minnetauks—mouth of Assinneboin river.

AFTER a few days, we started to go up the Red River, and in two days came to the mouth of the Assinneboin, where we found great numbers of Ojibbeways and Ottawwaws encamped. As soon as we arrived, the chiefs met, to take our case into consideration, and to agree on some method of providing for us. " These, our relations," said one of the chiefs, " have come to us from a distant country. These two little boys are not able to provide for them, and we must not suffer them to be in want among us." Then one man after another offered to hunt for us; and they agreed, also, since we had started to come for the purpose of hunting beaver, and as our hunters had died on the way, that each should give us some part of what they should kill. We then all started together to go up the Assinneboin river, and the first night we camped among the buffaloe. In the morning, I was allowed to go out with some Indians, who went to hunt buffaloes. We killed one of four bulls which we found. We continued to ascend the Assinneboin about ten days, killing many bears as we travelled along. The Assinneboin is broad, shallow, and crooked, and the water, like that of Red River, is turbid; but the bottom is sandy, while that of Red River is commonly muddy. The place to which we went on the Assinneboin, is seventy miles distant by land from the mouth; but the distance by water is greater. The banks of the river, on both sides, are covered with poplar and white oak, and some other trees, which grow to considerable size. The prairies, however, are not far distant, and sometimes come into the immediate bank of the river. We stopped at a place called Prairie Portage, where the Indians directed the trader who was with them, to build his house, and remain during the winter. We left all our canoes, and went up into the country to hunt for beaver, among the small streams. The Indians gave Wa-me-gon-a-biew and myself a little creek, where were plenty of beaver, and on which they said none but ourselves should hunt. My mother gave me three traps, and instructed me how to set them by the aid of a string tied around the spring, as I was not yet able to set them with my hands, as the Indians did. I set my three traps, and on the following morning found beavers in two of them. Being unable to take them out myself, I carried home the beavers and traps, one at a time, on my back, and had the old woman to assist me. She was, as usual, highly gratified and delighted at my success. She had always been kind to me, often taking my side, when the Indians would attempt to ridicule or annoy me. We remained in this place about three months, in which time we were as well provided for as any of the band; for if our own game was not sufficient, we were sure to be supplied by some of our friends, as long as any thing could be killed. The people that remained to spend the winter with us, were two lodges, our own making three; but we were at length joined by four lodges of Crees. These people are the relations of the Ojibbeways and Ottawwaws, but their language is somewhat different, so as not to be readily understood. Their country borders upon that of the Assinneboins, or Stone Roasters; and though they are not relations, or natural allies, they are sometimes at peace, and are more or less intermixed with each other.

After we had remained about three months in this place, game began to be scarce, and we all suffered from hunger. The chief man of our band was called As-sin-ne-boi-nainse, (the Little Assinneboin,) and he now proposed to us all to move, as the country where we were was exhausted. The day on which we were to commence our removal was fixed upon, but before it arrived our necessities became extreme. The evening before the day on which we intended to move, my mother talked much of all our misfortunes and losses, as well as of the urgent distress under which we were then labouring. At the usual hour I went to sleep, as did all the younger part of the family; but I was wakened again by the loud praying and singing of the old woman, who continued her devotions through great part of the night. Very early, on the following morning, she called us all to get up, and put on our moccasins, and be ready to move. She then called Wa-me-gon-a-biew to her, and said to him, in rather a low voice, "My son, last night I sung and prayed to the Great Spirit, and when I slept, there came to me one like a man, and said to me, 'Net-no-kwa, to-morrow you shall eat a bear. There is, at a distance from the path you are to travel to-morrow, and in such a direction, [which she described to him,] a small round meadow, with something like a path leading from it; in that path there is a bear.' Now, my son, I wish you to go to that place, without mentioning to any one what I have said, and you will certainly find the bear, as I have described to you." But the young man, who was not particularly dutiful, or apt to regard what his mother said, going out of the lodge, spoke sneeringly to the other Indians of the dream. "The old woman," said he, "tells me we are to eat a bear to-day; but I do not know who is to kill it." The old woman, hearing him, called him in, and reproved him; but she could not prevail upon him to go to hunt. The Indians, accordingly, all moved off towards the place where they were to encamp that night. The men went first by themselves, each carrying some article of baggage; and when they arrived where the camp was to be placed, they threw down their loads and went to hunt. Some of the boys, and I among them, who accompanied the men, remained with this baggage, until the women should come up. I had my gun with me, and I continued to think of the conversation I had heard between my mother and Wa-me-gon-a-biew, respecting her dream. At length, I resolved to go in search of the place she had spoken of, and without mentioning to any one my design, I loaded my gun as for a bear, and set off on our back track. I soon met a woman belonging to one of the brothers of Taw-ga-we-ninne, and of course my aunt. This woman had shown little friendship for us, considering us as a burthen upon her husband, who sometimes gave something for our support; she had also often ridiculed me. She asked me immediately what I was doing on the path, and whether I expected to kill Indians, that I came there with my gun. I made her no answer; and thinking I must be not far from the place where my mother had told Wa-me-gon-a-biew to leave the path, I turned off, continuing carefully to regard all the directions she had given. At length, I found what appeared at some former time to have been a pond. It was a small, round, open place in the woods, now grown up with grass and some small bushes. This I thought must be the meadow my mother had spoken of; and examining it around, I came to an open place in the bushes, where, it is probable, a small brook ran from the meadow; but the snow was now so deep that I could see nothing of it. My mother had mentioned, that when she saw the bear in her dream, she had, at the same time, seen a smoke rising from the ground. I was confident this was the place she had indicated, and I watched long, expecting to see the smoke; but wearied at length with waiting, I walked a few paces into the open place, resembling a path, when I unexpectedly fell up to my middle into the snow. I extricated myself without difficulty, and walked on; but remembering that I had heard the Indians speak of killing bears in their holes, it occurred to me that it might be a bear's hole into which I had fallen, and looking down into it, I saw the head of a bear lying close to the bottom of the hole. I placed the muzzle of my gun nearly between his eyes, and discharged it. As soon as the smoke cleared away, I took a piece of a stick and thrust it into the eyes and into the wound in the head of the bear, and being satisfied that he was dead, I endeavoured to lift him out of the hole; but being unable to do this, I returned home, following the track I had made in coming out. As I came near the camp, where the squaws had, by this time, set up the lodges, I met the same woman I had seen in going out, and she immediately began again to ridicule me. "Have you killed a bear, that you come back so soon, and walk so fast?" I thought to myself, "how does she know that I have killed a bear?" But I passed by her without saying any thing, and went into my mother's lodge. After a few minutes, the old woman said, "My son, look in that kettle, and you will find a mouthful of beaver meat, which a man gave me since you left us in the morning. You must leave half of it for Wa-me-gon-a-biew, who has not yet returned from hunting, and has eaten nothing to-day." I accordingly ate the beaver meat, and when I had finished it, observing an opportunity when she stood by herself, I stepped up to her, and whispered in her ear, "My mother, I have killed a bear." "What do you say, my son?"

said she. " I have killed a bear." " Are you sure you have killed him?" " Yes." " Is he quite dead?" " Yes." She watched my face for a moment, and then caught me in her arms, hugging and kissing me with great earnestness, and for a long time. I then told her what my aunt had said to me, both going and returning, and this being told to her husband when he returned, he not only reproved her for it, but gave her a severe flogging. The bear was sent for, and, as being the first I had killed, was cooked all together, and the hunters of the whole band invited to feast with us, according to the custom of the Indians. The same day, one of the Crees killed a bear and a moose, and gave a large share of the meat to my mother. For some time we had plenty of game in our new residence. Here Wa-me-gon-a-biew killed his first buffaloe, on which occasion my mother gave another feast to all the band. Soon afterwards, the Crees left us to go to their own country. They were friendly and hospitable people, and we were sorry to part with them; but we soon afterwards went down to the place where we had left the trader, and arrived there on the last day of December, as I remember the following was new year's day.

Near this trading-house we remained for sometime by ourselves; at length, we received a message from the trader, and on going up found there Pe-shau-ba, a celebrated war-chief of the Ottawwaws, who had come from Lake Huron several years before. He, it appeared, heard in his own country of an old Ottawwaw woman, who, with a family of two women, two boys, and three little children, having lost their men by death, were on the Assinneboin, and suffering from poverty. He had come, with his three companions, [which were what the Indians commonly call his young men, though one of them was, perhaps, older than himself.] These were, Waus-so, (the lightning,) Sag-git-to, (he that scares all men,) and Sa-ning-wub, (he that stretches his wings.) The old man, Waus-so, who was himself distinguished as a warrior, had fallen sick, and had been left at some distance behind. Pe-shau-ba had traced us from place to place, by the reports of the Indians, and at last found us at Prairie Portage. He was a large and very handsome old man, and when we were called in, he immediately recognised Net-no-kwa as a relative. But looking round upon us, he said, "Who are these?"

She answered, " They are my sons." He looked at me very closely, and said, " Come here, my brother." Then raising his blanket, he showed me the mark of a deep and dangerous wound on the chest. " Do you remember, my young brother, when we were playing together, with guns and spears, and you gave me this wound ?" Seeing my embarrassment, he continued to amuse himself for some time, by describing the circumstances attending the wound, at the time he received it. He at last relieved me from some suspense and anxiety, by saying, it was not myself who had wounded him, but one of my brothers, at a place which he mentioned. He spoke of Ke-wa-tin, who would have been of about my age, if he had lived, and inquired particularly to the time and the circumstances of my capture, which had happened after he left Lake Huron.

This was about new year's day, and soon after we started together for the country of Pe-shau-ba, which was at a great distance. The snow was deep, and our route lying, for the most part, through open prairies, we were not able to travel when the wind was high. When we commenced our journey, we were hungry, and in want of provisions; but soon found plenty of buffaloe, which were very fat and good. Notwithstanding the snow was deep, and the weather severe, the buffaloe could still feed, by pushing aside the snow with their heads, and thus coming at the grass below. We had thrown away our mats of Puk-kwi,* the journey being too long to admit of carrying them. In bad weather we used to make a little lodge, and cover it with three or four fresh buffaloe hides, and these being soon frozen, made a strong shelter from wind and snow. In calm weather, we commonly encamped with no other covering than our blankets. In all this journey, Pe-shau-ba and Sa-nin-kwub carried each one of our sister's little children on their backs. Thus we travelled on as diligently as the weather would permit, for about two months and a half. In the middle of our journey, we passed the trading-house and fort at Mouse River. The

* *Puk-kwi*, the cat-tail flag, (*Typha latifolia*,) of which we made the coarse mats called by the Menomonies *O-pah-keuk*, by the Ojibbeways of the Upper Mississippi, *O-pah-kwi-wuk*. There is a lake on the route from Green Bay to the Wisconsan, called on the maps *Puckaway*, but the word is, in the country, pronounced *Puk-kwi*.

general direction of our route was a little north of west, till we arrived, at last, at a place called Kau-wau-ko-mig Sah-kie-gun, Clear Water Lake, from which runs a small stream, called Saskaw-ja-wun, (Swift Water;) but this is not the source or a part of the great river Saskawjawun, [Saskutchawin,] which is farther towards the north. Clear Water Lake is not, however, the principal source of the Little Saskawjawun, the head of that river lying far to the north. On the bank of this lake was the small log hut of Pe-shau-ba, where he had lived, with the three men I have mentioned, for some years. He had left his wife at Lake Huron; and the other men, if they had ever been married, had no women with them. Immediately on his arrival, he opened his sun-je-gwun, and took out large quantities of beaver skins, dried meat, dressed skins, &c. &c. all of which he delivered to the women, saying, " We have long been our own squaws, but we must be so no longer. It must now be your business to dress our skins, dry our meat, make our moccasins, &c." The old woman herself took charge particularly of the property of Pe-shau-ba, whom she called her son, and treated as such. The daughter, and the daughter-in-law, made it their business to look after the other three men. Wa-me-gon-a-biew and myself were, as heretofore, under the particular care of our mother. In hunting, I was the companion of Pe-shau-ba, who was always kind to me, and seemed to take pleasure in teaching me how to become a great hunter. It must have been late in winter when we arrived at Clear Water Lake; but the weather was still so cold that water, when carried out of our lodge, would freeze immediately. When going to hunt, we started long before the sun rose, and returned long after it set. At noon, the sun would scarce rise to the tops of the trees, though they are very low there.

The country where we were was mostly prairie, with some low cedar and pine trees; but there are plenty of beavers and other game. It is not very far distant from the country of the Maudans, on the Missouri. From Mouse River a man may walk to the Mandan villages in four days. Just before the leaves began to appear in the spring, we started with all our peltries, and large quantities of dried meat, and dried beaver tails, to come down to the trading-house, on Mouse River. In that country there is no birch or cedar fit for making canoes, so that we were compelled to make one for our journey of green moose skins, which, being sewed together with great care, and stretched over a proper frame, then suffered to dry, make a very strong and good canoe; but in warm weather it will not last long. In a canoe of this kind, which would carry nearly half as much as a common Mackinac boat, [perhaps five tons,] we all embarked with whatever belonged to us, the intention of Net-no-kwa and Pe-shau-ba being to return to Lake Huron.

We descended the Little Saskawjawun for several days. On this river we found a village of Assinneboins, with whom we stopped a short time.. None of us could understand them except Waus-so, who had somewhere learned to speak their language. When we came from the Little Saskawjawun into the Assinneboin river, we came to the rapids, where was a village of one hundred and fifty lodges of Assinneboins, and some Crees. We now began to feel the want of fresh provisions, and determined to stop a day or two to kill sturgeons at this place, where we found a plenty of them. We went and stood near the Assinneboins, and saw an old man, when a sturgeon had just been drawn out of the water, cut off the pendant part of his mouth, and eat it without cooking, or any kind of condiment. These people generally appeared to us filthy and brutal. Something of our dislike may perhaps be attributed to the habitually unfriendly feeling which exists among the Ojibbeways for the Abbwoi-nug.* In two days from these rapids we came to Monk River, where both the Northwest and the Hudson's Bay Company have trading-houses. Here Pe-shau-ba and his friends began to drink, and in a short time expended all the peltries they had made in their long and successful hunt. We sold one hundred beaver skins in one day for liquor. The price was then six beaver skins for a quart of rum, but they put a great deal of water with it. After drinking here for some time, we began to make birch canoes, still intending to continue on our journey. But at this time the Assinneboins,† and Crees, and all the Indians of this part of the country, with whom the Mandans had made peace, were invited by the Mandans to come to their country,

---

* Or Spit Roasters, so called from their roasting their meats on wooden spits.
† Assinneboins, Stone Roasters, from using heated stones to boil their provisions.

and join in a war against the people called by the Ojibbeways A-gutch-a-ninne,* who live two days distant from the Mandans. Waus-so, hearing of this, determined to join the war-party, then assembling at Mouse River. " I will not," said he, " return to my country before I get scarred once more. I will see the people who have killed my brothers." Pe-shau-ba and Net-no-kwa endeavoured to dissuade him, but he would not listen, and Pe-shau-ba himself presently began to show evidence of excitement at witnessing the enthusiasm of his companion. After deliberating a day or two, he said to the old woman, " I cannot consent to return to the country of the Ottawwaws without Waus-so. Sa-ning-wub and Sag-git-to also wish to go with him to visit the neighbours of the Mandans. I will go also, and I wish you to wait for me at Lake Winnipeg, where I shall be in the fall, and you will not fail to have a keg of rum in readiness, as I shall be very thirsty when I return." They left the canoes unfinished, and all went off together with the war-party. Wa-me-gon-a-biew also accompanied them, leaving me only with the three women and three children. But this expedition, for which the Mandans had called assistance from such remote regions, failed for the want of concert and agreement between the different bands. Some of these being the hereditary enemies of the rest, quarrels were sure to arise, and the project was thus disconcerted, the A-gutch-a-ninne being left at peace in their own village.

After they had gone, I started with Net-no-kwa and the remainder of the family for Lake Winnipeg. We were compelled still to use the old moose-skin canoe, as none of the birch ones were finished, and we did not wish to remain any longer at Mouse River. We had left the trading-house but a short time, when we discovered a sturgeon, which, by some accident, had got into such shoal water, on a sand-bar, that considerable part of his back was to be seen above the surface. I jumped out of the canoe, and killed him with little difficulty; and as this was the first sturgeon I had ever taken, the old woman thought it necessary to celebrate the feast of Oskenetahgawin, or first fruits, though, as we were quite alone, we had no guests to assist us.

The mouth of the Assinneboin is a place much frequented by

* A-gutch-a-ninne-wug, the settled people, called by the whites Minnetarees.

the Sioux war-parties, where they lie concealed and fire upon such as are passing. We did not approach this place until dark, intending to pass through late at night; it was, accordingly, after midnight, when carefully avoiding either shore, we floated silently out into Red River. The night was dark, and we could not discern distinctly any object on shore; but we had scarce entered Red River, when the silence was broken by the hooting of an owl, on the left bank of the Assinneboin. This was quickly answered by another on the right bank, and presently by a third on the side of Red River, opposite the mouth. Net-no-kwa said, in a whisper scarce audible, " We are discovered," and directed to put the canoe about, with the utmost silence. In obedience to her direction, we ascended with the utmost caution, endeavouring to keep near the middle of Red River. I was in the bow of the canoe, and keeping my head as low as I could, I was carefully watching the surface of the water before us, hoping to be able to see and avoid any canoe, or other object, which might approach, when I saw a little ripple on the surface of the river, following a low, black object, which I took to be the head of a man, swimming cautiously across before us. I pointed this out to the women, and it was immediately agreed that we should pursue, and, if possible, kill the man in the water. For this purpose, a strong sturgeon-spear was put into my hand, and we commenced the pursuit; but the goose, (for it was one, with a brood of young ones,) soon became alarmed, and flew. When we perceived our mistake, we retraced our way up the river, with somewhat less of fear; but could by no means venture to turn about, and go on our way. I was, I remember, vexed at what I thought the groundless fears of the women; but I do not know, to this day, whether a war-party of Sioux, or three owls, frightened us back. We returned several miles, and expecting, in about ten days, that the traders would be on their way down, we determined to wait for them. Here we caught great numbers of young geese, swans, and ducks; and I killed an elk, which, as it was my first, must be celebrated by a feast, though there were none but our own family to partake of it.

With the traders who came, according to our expectation, we went down to the house at Lake Winnipeg, where we remained two months. When they were about to return to the Assinneboin, we purchased a bark canoe, and accompanied them. We had a good many beaver skins, and Net-no-kwa bought a keg of rum with some of them, for Pe-shau-ba. The keg held about five or six gallons, and we gave six beaver skins for a quart. Many of these beavers I had taken myself. I have killed as many as one hundred in the course of a month, but then I did not know the value of them.

CHAPTER IV.

Elk hunting—beaver and buffaloe hunting—endangered in killing a buffaloe cow—Fall Indians—return to Rainy Lake—Swamp River and Portage—the Begwionusko River and Lake—honesty and good faith in the intercourse of the Indians—hospitality—sufferings from hunger—Red River—loss of packs—supposed dishonesty of traders—rapacity of the traders of the N. W. company—disasters following the loss of our peltries.

In the Assinneboin river, at one or two days above the Prairie Portage, is a place called Ke-new-kau-neshe way-boant, (where they throw down the gray eagle,) at which the Indians frequently stop. Here we saw, as we were passing, some little stakes in the ground, with pieces of birch bark attached to them, and on two of these the figure of a bear, and on the others, those of other animals. Net-no-kwa immediately recognized the totems of Pe-shau-ba, Waus-so, and their companions. These had been left, to inform us that Pe-shau-ba had been at this place, and as directions to enable us to find them. We therefore left the traders, and taking the course indicated by the marks which Pe-shau-ba had caused to be made, we found him and his party at the distance of two days from the river. They had returned from the abortive war expedition, to the trading house on Mouse River, finished the canoes which they had left incomplete, and descended along to Kenewkauneshewayboant, where, knowing there were good hunting grounds, they had determined on remaining. We found at their camp plenty of game; they had killed, also, a great number of beavers. About this place elks were numerous, and it was now the rutting season. I remember one day, Pe-shau-ba sent me with the two young women, to bring some meat from an elk he had killed at some distance. The women, finding that the elk was large and fat, determined on remaining to dry the meat before they carried it home. I took a load of meat, and started for home by myself. I had my gun with me, and perceiving there were plenty of elk, I loaded it, and concealing myself in a small thicket of bushes, began to imitate the call of the female elk; presently a large buck came bounding so directly towards the spot where I was, and with such violence, that becoming alarmed for my own safety, I dropped my load and fled; he seeing me, turned and ran in an opposite direction. Remembering that the Indians would ridicule me for such conduct, I determined to make another attempt, and not suffer any apprehension for my own safety to be the cause of another failure. So hiding myself again, in a somewhat more carefully chosen place, I repeated my call from time to time, till at length another buck came up, and him I killed. In this manner, great part of the day had been consumed, and I now perceived it was time to hasten home with my load.

The old woman becoming uneasy at my long absence, sent Wa-me-gon-a-biew to look for me. He discovered me as I was coming out of a piece of woods into a large prairie. He had on a black capot, which, when he saw me, he turned over his head in such a manner as to make himself resemble a bear. At first I took it to be a common black bear, and sought a chance to shoot him; but it so happened that he was in such a situation as enabled him to see me, and I knew he would certainly have turned and fled from me had it been a black bear. As he continued to advance directly towards me, I concluded it must be a grizly bear, so I turned and began to run from him; the more swiftly I ran, the more closely he seemed to follow. Though much frightened, I remembered Pe-shau-ba's advice, never to fire upon one of these animals unless trees were near into which I could escape; also, in case of being pursued by one, never to fire until he came very close to me. Three times I turned, and raised my piece to fire, but thinking him still too far off, turned and run again. Fear must have blinded my eyes, or I should have seen that it was not a bear. At length, getting between him and the lodge, I ran with such speed as to outstrip him, when I heard a voice behind me, which I knew to be that of Wa-me-gon-a-biew. I looked in vain for the bear, and he soon convinced me that I owed all my terror to the disguise which he had effected, with the aid only of an old black coat. This affair being related to the old people when we came home, they reproved Wa-me-gon-a-biew; his mother telling him, that if I had shot him in that disguise, I should have done right, and according to the custom of the Indians she could have found no fault with me for so doing. We continued here hunting beaver, and killing great numbers, until the ice became too thick; we then went to the prairies in pursuit of buffaloes. When the snow began to have a crust upon it, the men said they must leave me with the women, as they were about to go to Clear Water Lake to make canoes, and to hunt beaver on their way down. But previous to their going, they said they would kill something for us to live on while they were gone. Waus-so, who was a great hunter, went out by himself, and killed one buffaloe; but in the night the weather became very cold and stormy, and the buffaloe came in to take shelter in the woods where we had our camp. Early in the morning, Net-no-kwa called us up, saying, there was a large herd close by the lodge. Pe-shau-ba and Waus-so, with Wa-me-gon-a-biew, Sa-ning-wub, and Sag-git-to, crept out, and took stations so as nearly to surround the herd. Me they would not suffer to go out, and they laughed at me when they saw me putting my gun in readiness; but old Net-no-gua, who was ever ready to befriend me, after they were gone, led me to a stand not far from the lodge, near which, her sagacity taught her, the herd would probably run. The Indians fired, but all failed to kill; the herd came past my stand, and I had the good fortune to kill a large cow, which was my first, much to the satisfaction of my mother. Shortly afterwards, having killed a considerable number of buffaloes, the Indians left us; myself, the old woman, one of the young women, and three children, six in all, with no one to provide for them but myself, and I was then very young. We dried considerable of the meat the Indians had killed, and this lasted us for some time; but I soon found that I was able to kill buffaloes, and for a long time we had no want of food. In one instance, an old cow which I had wounded, though she had no calf, ran at me, and I was barely able to escape from her by climbing into a tree. She was enraged, not so much by the wound I had given her, as by the dogs; and it is, I believe, very rare that a cow runs at a man, unless she has been worried by dogs. We made sugar this spring, ten miles above Mouse River Fort. About this time I was much endangered by the breaking of the ice. The weather had become mild, and the beavers began to come up through the holes on to the ice, and sometimes to go on shore. It was my practice to watch these holes, and shoot them as soon as they came up: once, having killed one, I ran hastily up on the ice to get him, and broke in; my snow shoes became entangled with some brush on the bottom, and had nearly dragged me under, but by great exertion I at length escaped. Buffaloes were so numerous about this place, that I often killed them with a bow and arrow, though I hunted them on foot, and with no other aid than that of dogs well trained and accustomed to hunt.

When the leaves began to appear upon the trees, Pe-shau-ba and the men returned in birch canoes, bringing many beaver skins and other valuable peltries. Old Net-no-gua was now anxious to return to Lake Huron, as was Pe-shau-ba; but Waus-so and Sa-ning-wub would not return, and Pe-shau-ba was unwilling to part with them. Sag-git-to had for some time been very sick, having a large ulcer or abscess near his navel. After having drank for some days, he had a violent pain in his belly, which at length swelled and broke. Pe-shau-ba said to the old woman, "it is not good that Sag-git-to should die here, at a distance from all his friends; and since we see he cannot live much longer, I think it best for you to take him and the little children, and return to Lake Huron. You may be able to reach the rapids, [Saut de St. Marie,] before Sag-git-to dies." Conformably to this advice, our family was divided. Pe-shau-ba, Waus-so, and Sa-ning-wub remained; Net-no-kwa, and the two other women, with Sag-git-to, Wa-me-gon-a-biew, and myself, with a little girl the old woman had bought, and three little children, started to return to Lake Huron. The little girl was brought from the country of the Bahwetego-weninnewug, the Fall Indians, by a war party of Ojibbeways, from whom Net-no-kwa had bought her. The Fall Indians live near the Rocky Mountains, and wander much with the Black Feet; their language being unlike that of both the Sioux and the Ojibbeways. These last, and the Crees, are more friendly with the Black Feet, than they are with the Fall Indians. The little Bahwetig girl that Net-no-kwa had bought, was now ten years of age, but having been some time among the Ojibbeways, had learned their language.

When we came to Rainy Lake, we had ten packs of beaver of forty skins each. Net-no-kwa sold some other peltries for rum, and was drunk for a day or two. We here met some of the trader's canoes, on their way to Red River; and Wa-me-gon-a-biew, who was now eighteen years old, being unwilling to return to Lake Huron, determined to go back to the north with the trader's people. The old woman said much to dissuade him, but he jumped into one of the canoes, as they were about to start off, and although, at the request of the old woman, they endeavoured to drive him out, he would not leave the canoe. Net-no-kwa was much distressed, but could not make up her mind to lose her only son; she determined on returning with him.

The packs of beaver she would not leave with the traders, not having sufficient confidence in their honesty. We therefore took them to a remote place in the woods, where we made a sunje-gwun, or deposite, in the usual manner. We then returned to the Lake of the Woods. From this lake the Indians have a road, to go to Red River, which the white men never follow; this is by the way of the Muskeek, or swamp carrying place. We went up a river which the Indians call Muskeego-ne-gum-me-we-see-bee, or Swamp River, for several days; we then dragged our canoes across a swamp for one day. This swamp is only of moss and some small bushes on the top of the water, so that it quakes to a great distance as people walk over it. Then we put our canoes into a small stream, which they called Begwionusk, from the begwionusk, or cow parsley, which grows upon it: this we descended into a small Sahkiegun,* called by the same name. This pond has no more than two or three feet of water, and great part of it is not one foot deep; but at this time its surface was

---

* Lakes of the largest class are called by the Ottawwaws, Kitchegawme; of these they reckon five; one which they commonly call Ojibbeway Kitchegawme, Lake Superior, two Ottawwaw Kitchegawme, Huron and Michigan, and Erie and Ontario. Lake Winnipeg, and the countless lakes in the north-west, they call Sah-kiegunnun.

covered with ducks, geese, swans, and other birds. Here we remained a long time, and made four packs of beaver skins. When the leaves began to fall, Sag-git-to died. We were now quite alone, no Indians or white men being within four or five days' journey from us. Here we had packs to deposite, as we were about to leave the country; and the ground being too swampy to admit of burying them in the usual manner, we made a sunje-gwun of logs, so tight that a mouse could not enter it; in which we left all our packs and other property, which we could not carry. If any of the Indians of this distant region, had found it in our absence, they would not have broken it up; and we did not fear that the traders would penetrate to so poor and solitary a place. Indians who live remote from the whites, have not learned to value their peltries so highly, that they will be guilty of stealing them from each other; and at the time of which I speak, and in the country where I was, I have often known a hunter leave his traps for many days, in the woods, without visiting them, or feeling any anxiety about their safety. It would often happen, that one man having finished his hunt, and left his traps behind him, another would say to him, "I am going to hunt in such a direction, where are your traps?" When he has used them, another, and sometimes four or five, take them in succession; but in the end, they are sure to return to the right owner.

When the snow had fallen, and the weather began to be cold, so that we could no longer kill beaver, we began to suffer from hunger. Wa-me-gon-a-biew was now our principal dependance, and he exerted himself greatly to supply our wants. In one of his remote excursions in pursuit of game, he met with a lodge of Ojibbeways, who, though they had plenty of meat, and knew that he and his friends were in distress, gave him nothing except what he wanted to eat at night. He remained with them all night, and in the morning started for home. On his way he killed a young Moose, which was extremely poor. When this small supply was exhausted, we were compelled to go and encamp with the inhospitable people whom Wa-me-gon-a-biew had seen. We found them well supplied with meat, but whatever we procured from them, was in exchange for our ornaments of silver, or other articles of value. I mention the niggardliness and inhospitality of these people, because I had not before met with such an instance among the Indians. They are commonly ready to divide what provisions they have, with any who come to them in need. We had been about three days with these Indians, when they killed two Moose. They called Wa-me-gon-a-biew and me to go after meat, but only gave us the poorest part of one leg. We bought some fat meat from them, giving them our silver ornaments. The patience of old Net-no-kwa was at length exhausted, and she forbade us all to purchase any thing more from them. During all the time we remained with these people, we were suffering almost the extremity of hunger. One morning Net-no-kwa rose very early, and tying on her blanket, took her hatchet and went out. She did not return that night; but the next day, towards evening, as we were all lying down inside the lodge, she came in, and shaking Wa-me-gon-a-biew by the shoulder, said to him, "get up, my son, you are a great runner, and now let us see with what speed you will go and bring the meat which the Great Spirit gave me last night. Nearly all night I prayed and sung, and when I fell asleep near morning, the Spirit came to me, and gave me a bear to feed my hungry children. You will find him in that little copse of bushes in the prairie. Go immediately, the bear will not run from you, even should he see you coming up."

"No, my mother," said Wa-me-gon-a-biew, "it is now near evening: the sun will soon set, and it will not be easy to find the track in the snow. In the morning Shaw-shaw-wa ne-ba-se shall take a blanket, and a small kettle, and in the course of the day I may overtake the bear and kill him, and my little brother will come up with my blanket, and we can spend the night where I shall kill him."

The old woman did not yield to the opinion of the hunter. Altercation and loud words followed; for Wa-me-gon-a-biew had little reverence for his mother, and as scarce any other Indian would have done, he ridiculed her pretensions to an intercourse with the Great Spirit, and particularly, for having said that the bear would not run if he saw hunters coming. The old woman was offended; and after reproaching her son, she went out of the lodge, and told the other Indians her dream, and directed them to the place where she said the bear would certainly be found. They agreed with Wa-me-gon-a-biew, that it was too late to go that night; but as they had confidence in the prayers of the old woman, they lost no time in following her direction at the earliest appearance of light in the morning. They found the bear at the place she had indicated, and killed it without difficulty. He was large and fat, but Wa-me-gon-a-biew, who accompanied them, received only a small piece for the portion of our family. The old woman was angry, and not without just cause; for although she pretended that the bear had been given her by the Great Spirit, and the place where he lay pointed out to her in a dream, the truth was, she had tracked him into the little thicket, and then circled it, to see that he had not gone out. Artifices of this kind, to make her people believe she had intercourse with the Great Spirit, were, I think, repeatedly assayed by her.

Our suffering from hunger now compelled us to move; and after we had eaten our small portion of the bear, we started on snow shoes to go to Red River; hoping either to meet some Indians, or to find some game on the way. I had now become acquainted with the method of taking rabbits in snares; and when we arrived at our first camp, I ran forward on the route I knew we should take on the following day, and placed several snares, intending to look at them, and take them up as we went on our journey. After we had supped, for when we were in want of provisions we commonly ate only at evening, all the food we had remaining, was a quart or more of bear's grease in a kettle. It was now frozen hard, and the kettle had a piece of skin tied over it as a cover. In the morning, this, among other articles, was put on my sled, and I went forward to look at my snares. Finding one rabbit, I thought I would surprise my mother, to make a laugh; so I took the rabbit, and put him alive under the cover of the kettle of bear's grease. At night, after we had encamped, I watched her when she went to open the kettle to get us something to eat, expecting the rabbit would jump out; but was much disappointed to find, that notwithstanding the extreme cold weather, the grease was dissolved, and the little animal nearly drowned. The old woman scolded me very severely at the time; but for many years afterwards, she used to talk and laugh of this rabbit, and his appearance when she opened the kettle. She continued also to talk, as long as she lived, of the niggardly conduct of the Indians we had then seen. After travelling some days, we discovered traces of hunters, and were at length so fortunate as to find the head of a buffaloe which they had left. This relieved us from the distress of hunger, and we followed on in their trail, until we came to the encampment of some of our friends on Red River.

This was a considerable band of Crees, under a chief called Assin-ne-boi-nainse, (the Little Assinneboin,) and his son-in-law, Sin-a-peg-a-gun. They received us in a very cordial and friendly manner, gave us plenty to eat, and supplied all our urgent wants. After we had remained with them about two months, buffaloe and other game became scarce, and the whole encampment was suffering from hunger. Wa-me-gon-a-biew and myself started to cross the prairie, one day's journey, to a stream called Pond River. We found an old bull, so poor and old that hair would not grow upon him; we could eat only the tongue. We had travelled very far, in the course of the day, and were much overcome with fatigue; the wind was high, and the snow driving violently. In a vast extent of the plain, which we overlooked, we could see no wood, but some small oak bushes, scarce as high as a man's shoulders; but in this poor cover we were compelled to encamp. The small and green stalks of the oaks were, with the utmost difficulty, kindled, and made but a poor fire. When the fire had remained some time in one place, and the ground under it become dry, we removed the brands and coals, and lay down upon the warm ashes. We spent the night without sleep, and the next morning, though the weather had become more severe, the wind having risen, we started to return home. It was a hard day's walk, and, as we were weak through hunger and cold, it was late when we reached the lodge. As we approached home, Wa-me-gon-a-biew was more able to walk fast than I was, and as he turned back to look at me, we perceived, at the same time, that each of our faces were frozen. When we came nearly in sight of home, as I was not able to walk much farther, he left me, and went to the lodge, and sent some of the women to help me to get home. Our hands and faces were much frozen; but as we had good moccasins, our feet were not at all injured. As hunger continued in the camp, we found it necessary to separate, and go in different directions. Net-no-kwa determined to go with her family to the trading-house of Mr. Henry, who was since drowned in the Columbia

River, by the upsetting of a boat. This place is near that where a settlement has since been made, called Pembina. With the people of the fur-traders, we hunted all the remainder of the winter. In the spring we returned, in company with these lodges of Indians, to the lake where we had left our canoes. We found all out property safe, and having got all together from our sunjegwuns, and all that we had brought from Red River, we had now eleven packs of beaver, of forty skins each, and ten packs of other skins. It was now our intention to return to Lake Huron, and to dispose of our peltries at Mackinac. We had still the large sunjegwun at Rainy Lake, the contents of which, added to all we now had, would have been sufficient to make us wealthy. It will be recollected, that in a former season, Net-no-kwa had made a deposit of valuable furs, near the trader's house, on Rainy Lake, not having confidence enough in the honesty of the trader, to leave them in his care. When we returned to this spot, we found the sunjegwun had been broken up, and not a pack, or a skin, left in it. We saw a pack in the trader's house, which we believed to be one of our own; but we could never ascertain whether they or some Indians, had taken them. The old woman was much irritated, and did not hesitate to ascribe the theft to the trader.

When we reached the small house, at the other side of the Grand Portage to Lake Superior, the people belonging to the traders urged us to put our packs in the wagons, and have them carried across. But the old woman, knowing if they were once in the hands of the traders, it would be difficult, if not impossible, for her to get them again, refused to comply with this request. It took us several days to carry all our packs across, as the old woman would not suffer them to be carried in the trader's road. Notwithstanding all this caution, when we came to this side the portage, Mr. M'Gilveray and Mr. Shabboyea, by treating her with much attention, and giving her some wine, induced her to place all her packs in a room, which they gave her to occupy. At first, they endeavoured, by friendly solicitation, to induce her to sell her furs; but finding she was determined not to part with them, they threatened her; and at length, a young man, the son of Mr. Shabboyea, attempted to take them by force; but the old man interfered, and ordering his son to desist, reproved him for his violence. Thus Net-no-kwa was enabled, for the present, to keep possession of her property, and might have done so, perhaps, until we should have reached Mackinac, had it not been for the obstinacy of one of her own family. We had not been many days at the Portage, before there arrived a man called Bit-te-gish-sho, (the crooked lightning,) who lived at Middle Lake,* accompanied by his small band. With these people Wa-me-gon-a-biew became intimate, and though none of us, at that time, knew it, he formed an attachment for one of the daughters of the Crooked Lightning. When we had made all our preparations to start for the Saut of St. Marie, and the baggage was in the canoe, Wa-me-gon-a-biew was not to be found. We sought, in every direction, for him, and it was not until after some days, that we heard by a Frenchman, that he was on the other side the Portage, with the family of Bit-te-gish-sho. I was sent for him; but could by no means induce him to return with me. Knowing his obstinacy, the old woman began to cry. "If I had but two children," said she, "I could be willing to lose this one; but as I have no other, I must go with him." She gave to the widow, her sister's daughter, but who had lived with her from a child, five packs of beaver, one of which was for her own use; the remaining four packs, together with sixty otter skins, she told her to take to Mackinac, and deliver them according to her direction. She came down in the trader's canoe, and delivered them to Mr. Lapomboise, of the North West Company, and took his due bill, as she was told it was, for the amount. But this paper was subsequently lost, by the burning of our lodge, and from that day to this, Net-no-kwa, or any of her family, have not received the value of a cent for those skins. The old woman, being much dissatisfied at the misconduct of her son, the disappointment of her hopes of returning to Lake Huron, and other misfortunes, began to drink. *In the course of a single day, she sold one hundred and twenty beaver skins, with a large quantity of buffaloe robes, dressed and smoked skins, and other articles, for rum.* It was her habit, whenever she drank, to make drunk all the Indians about her, at least as far as her means would extend.

* Naw-we-sah-ki-o-gun.

Of all our large load of peltries, the produce of so many days of toil, of so many long and difficult journeys, one blanket, and three kegs of rum, only remained, beside the poor and almost worn-out cloathing on our bodies. I did not, on this or any other occasion, witness the needless and wanton waste of our peltries, and other property, with that indifference which the Indians seemed always to feel.

Our return being determined on, we started, with Bit-te-gish-sho and some other Indians, for the Lake of the Woods. They assisted us in making a canoe, crossing portages, &c. At the Lake of the Woods we were overtaken by cold weather, and Net-no-kwa determined to remain, though most of the others went on. Here it was found that the attachment of Wa-me-gon-a-biew to the daughter of Bit-te-gish-sho, was not too strong to be broken; and, indeed, it is somewhat doubtful whether the anxiety of the traders at the Grand Portage, to possess themselves of our packs, had not as much to do in occasioning our return, as any thing on the part of this young man.

After these people had left us, we found our condition too desolate and hopeless to remain by ourselves, illy provided as we were for the coming winter. So we repaired to Rainy Lake trading-house, where we obtained a credit to the amount of one hundred and twenty beaver skins, and thus furnished ourselves with some blankets, clothing, and other things necessary for the winter. Here a man joined us, called Waw-be-be-nais-sa, who proposed to hunt for us, and assist us through the winter. We acceded cheerfully to his proposal; but soon found he was but a poor hunter, as I was always able to kill more than he did.

CHAPTER V.

Medicine hunting—indolence of an Indian hunter, and consequent suffering of his family—relief from humane traders—a hunter amputates his own arm—moose chase—hospitality of Sah-muk, and residence at Rainy Lake—carcase of a buffaloe-cow watched by a bull—severe suffering from cold—my lodge, and most of my property, destroyed by fire.

WITH the deep snow and thick ice, came poverty and hunger. We were no longer able to take beaver in traps, or by the ordinary methods, or kill moose, though there were some in the country. It was not until our sufferings from hunger began to be extreme, that the old woman had recourse to the expedient of spending a night in prayer and singing. In the morning she said to her son and Waw-be-be-nais-sa, "Go and hunt, for the Great Spirit has given me some meat." But Wa-me-gon-a-biew objected, as he said the weather was too cold and calm, and no moose could be approached so near as to shoot him. "I can make a wind," answered Net-no-kwa, "and though it is now still and cold, the warm wind shall come before night. Go, my sons, you cannot fail to kill something, for in my dream I saw Wa-me-gon-a-biew coming into the lodge with a beaver and a large load of meat on his back." At length they started, having suspended at their heads, and on their shot pouches, the little sacks of medicine, which the old woman had provided for them, with the assurance that, having them, they could not possibly fail of success. They had not been a long time absent, when the wind rose from the south, and soon blew high, the weather, at the same time, becoming warmer. At night, they returned, loaded with the flesh of a fat moose, and Wa-me-gon-a-biew with a beaver on his back, as the old woman had seen him in her dream. As the moose was very large and fat, we moved our lodge to it, and made preparations for drying the meat. This supply of our wants was, however, only temporary, though we found a few beaver, and succeeded in killing some. After about ten days we were again in want of food. As I was one day hunting for beavers, at some distance from our lodge, I found the tracks of four moose. I broke off the top of a bush, on which they had been browsing, and carried it home. On entering the lodge, I threw it down before Waw-be-be-nais-sa, who was lying by the fire, in his usual indolent manner, saying, " Look at this, good hunter, and go and kill us some moose." He took up the branch, and looking at it a moment, he said, " How many are there ?" I answered, " four." He replied, " I must kill them." Early in the morning he started on my road, and killed three of the moose. He was a good hunter, when he could rouse himself to exertion; but most of the time he was so lazy that he chose to starve rather than go far to find game, or to run after it, when it was found. We had now a short season of plenty, but soon became hungry again. It often happened, that for two or three days we had nothing to eat; then a rabbit or two, or a bird, would afford us a prospect of protracting the suffering of hunger for a few days longer. We said much to Waw-be-be-nais-sa, to try to rouse him to greater exertion, as we knew he could kill game where any thing was to be found; but he commonly replied, that he was too poor and sick. Wa-me-gon-a-biew and myself, thinking that something might be found in more distant excursions than we had been used to make, started very early one morning, and travelled hard all day; and when it was near night we killed a young beaver, and Wa-me-gon-a-biew said to me, " My brother, you must now make a camp, and cook a little of the beaver, while I go farther on and try to kill something." I did so, and about sunset he returned, bringing plenty of meat, having killed two caribou. Next day we started very early to drag the two caribous through all the long distance between us and our camp. I could not reach home with my load, but Wa-me-gon-a-biew having arrived, sent out the young woman to help me, so that I arrived before midnight. We now saw it would not be safe for us to remain longer by ourselves, and this small supply enabling us to move, we determined to go in quest of some people. The nearest trading-house was that at Clear Water Lake, distant about four or five days' journey. We left our lodge, and taking only our blankets, a kettle or two, and such articles as were necessary for our journey, started for the trading-house. The country we had to pass was full of lakes and islands, swamps and marshes; but they were all frozen, so that we endeavoured to take a direct route.

Early one morning, on this journey, Waw-be-be-nais-sa, roused perhaps by excessive hunger, or by the exercise he was compelled to take, to keep along with us, began to sing and pray for something to eat. At length he said, "to-day we shall see some caribou." The old woman, whose temper was somewhat sharpened by our long continued privations, and who did not consider Waw-be-be-nais-sa a very enterprising hunter, said, "And if you should see caribou you will not be able to kill them. Some men would not have said, ' we shall see game to-day,' but ' we shall eat it.' " After this conversation, we had gone but a little distance when we saw six caribous, coming directly towards us. We concealed ourselves in the bushes, on the point of a little island, and they came within shot. Wa-me-gon-a-biew flashed his piece, when he intended to fire, and the herd turned, at the sound of the lock, to run off. Waw-be-be-nais-sa fired as they ran, and broke the shoulder of one of them; but though they pursued all day, they returned to camp at night without any meat. Our prospect was now so discouraging, that we concluded to lighten ourselves, by leaving some baggage, in order to make the greater expedition. We also killed our last dog, who was getting too weak to keep up with us; but the flesh of this animal, for some reason, the old woman would not eat. After several days we were bewildered, not knowing what route to pursue, and too weak to travel. In this emergency, the old woman, who, in the last extremity, seemed always more capable of making great exertions than any of us, fixed our camp as usual, brought us a large pile of wood to keep a fire in her absence, then tying her blanket about her, took her tomahawk, and went off, as we very well knew, to seek for some method by which to relieve us from our present distress. She came to us again on the following day, and resorting to her often-tried expedient to rouse us to great exertion, she said, " My children, I slept last night in a distant and solitary place, after having continued long in prayer. Then I dreamed, and I saw the road in which I had come, and the end of it where I had stopped at night, and at no great distance from this I saw the beginning of another road, that led directly to the trader's house. In my dream I saw white men; let us, therefore, lose no time, for the Great Spirit is now willing to lead us to a good fire." Being somewhat animated by the confidence and hope the old woman was in this way able to inspire, we departed immediately; but having at length come to the end of her path, and passed a considerable distance beyond it, without discovering any traces of other human beings, we began to be incredulous, some reproaching and some ridiculing the old woman; but aftewards, to our great joy, we found a recent hunting path, which we knew must lead to the trader's house; then redoubling our efforts, we arrived on the next night but one, after that in which the old woman had slept by herself. Here we found the same trader from whom we had a credit of one hundred and twenty beaver skins, at Rainy Lake, and, as he was willing to send out and bring the packs, we paid him his credit, and had twenty beaver skins left. With these I bought four traps, for which I paid five skins each. They also gave the old woman three small kegs of rum. After remaining a few days, we started to return in the direction we came from; for some distance we followed the large hunting path of the people belonging to the trading-house; when we reached the point where we must leave this road, the old woman gave the three little kegs of rum to Waw-be-be-nais-sa, and told him to follow on the hunter's path until he should find them; then sell the rum for meat, and come back to us. One of the little kegs he immediately opened, and drank about half of it before he went to sleep. Next morning, however, he was sober, and started to go as the old woman had directed, being in the first place informed where to find us again. Wa-me-gon-a-biew accompanied him. After they had started, I went on with the women to Skut-tah-waw-wo-ne-gun, (the dry carrying place,) where we had appointed to wait for him. We had been here one day when Wa-me-gon-a-biew arrived with a load of meat; but Waw-be-be-nais-sa did not come, though his little children had that day been compelled to eat their moccasins. We fed the woman and her children, and then sent her to join her husband. The hunters with whom Waw-be-be-nais-sa had remained, sent us an invitation by Wa-me-gon-a-biew to come and live with them; but it was necessary, in the first place, to go and get our lodge, and the property we had left there. As we were on our return we were stopped at the dry carrying place with extreme hunger. Having subsisted for some time almost entirely on the inner bark of trees, and particularly of a climbing vine found there, our strength was much reduced. Wa-me-gon-a-biew could not walk at all, and every one of the family had failed more than the old woman. She would fast five or six days, and seem to be little affected by it. It was only because she feared the other members of the family would perish in her absence, that she now consented to let me go and try to get some assistance from the trading-house, which we believed to be nearer than the camp of the hunters. The former we knew was about two ordinary days' journey; but, in my weak condition, it was doubtful when I could reach it. I started very early in the morning; the weather was cold, and the wind high. I had a large lake to cross, and here, as the wind blew more violently, I suffered most. I gained the other side of it a little before sunset, and sat down to rest. As soon as I began to feel a little cold, I tried to get up, but found it so difficult that I judged it would not be prudent for me to rest again before I should reach the trading-house. The night was not dark, and as there was less wind than in the day time, I found the travelling more pleasant. I continued on all night, and arrived early next morning at the trader's house. As soon as I opened the door they knew by my face that I was starving, and immediately inquired after my people. As soon as I had given the necessary information, they despatched a swift Frenchman, with a load of provisions, to the family. I had been in the trader's house but a few hours, when I heard the voice of Net-no-kwa outside, asking, "is my son here?" And when I opened the door she expressed the utmost satisfaction at sight of me. She had not met the Frenchman, who had gone by a different route. The wind had become violent soon after I left our camp, and the old woman, thinking I could not cross the lake, started after me; and the drifting snow having obscured my track, she could not follow it, and came quite to the trading-house with the apprehension that I had perished by the way. After a day or two, Wa-me-gon-a-biew and the remainder of the family came in, having been relieved by the Frenchman. It appeared, also, that the Indians had sent

Waw-be-be-nais-sa, with a load of meat, to look for us at the dry carrying place, as they knew we could not reach their encampment without a supply, which it was not probable we could procure. He had been very near the camp of our family after I left, but either through wilfulness, or from stupidity, failed to find them. He had camped almost within call of them, and eaten a hearty meal, as they discovered by the traces he left. After remaining a few days at the trading house, we all went together to join the Indians. This party consisted of three lodges, the principal man being Wah-ge-kaut, (crooked legs.) Three of the best hunters were Ka-kaik, (the small hawk,) Meh-ke-nauk, (the turtle,) and Pa-ke-kun-ne-gah-bo, (he that stands in the smoke.) This last was, at the time I speak of, a very distinguished hunter. Some time afterwards he was accidentally wounded, receiving a whole charge of shot in his elbow, by which the joint and the bones of his arm were much shattered. As the wound did not show any tendency to heal, but, on the contrary, became worse and worse, he applied to many Indians, and to all the white men he saw, to cut it off for him. As all refused to do so, or to assist him in amputating it himself, he chose a time when he happened to be left alone in his lodge, and taking two knives, the edge of one of which he had hacked into a sort of saw, he with his right hand and arm cut off his left, and threw it from him as far as he could. Soon after, as he related the story himself, he fell asleep, in which situation he was found by his friends, having lost a very great quantity of blood; but he soon afterwards recovered, and notwithstanding the loss of one arm, he became again a great hunter. After this accident, he was commonly called Kosh-kin-ne-kait, (the cut off arm.) With this band we lived some time, having always plenty to eat, though Waw-be-be-nais-sa killed nothing.

When the weather began to be a little warm, we left the Indians, and went to hunt beaver near the trading house. Having lately suffered so much from hunger, we were afraid to go to any distant place, relying on large game for support. Here we found early one morning, a Moose track, not far from the trading house. There was now living with us, a man called Pa-bah-mew-in, (he that carries about,) who, together with Wa-me-gon-a-biew, started in pursuit. The dogs followed for an hour or two, and then returned; at this Pa-bah-mew-in was discouraged, and turned back; but Wa-me-gon-a-biew still kept on. This young man could run very swift, and for a long time he passed all the dogs, one or two of which continued on the track. It was after noon when he arrived at a lake which the moose had attempted to cross; but as in some parts the ice was quite smooth, which prevented him from running so fast as on land, Wa-me-gon-a-biew overtook him. When he came very near, the foremost dog, who had kept at no great distance from Wa-me-gon-a-biew, passed him, and got before the moose, which was now easily killed. We remained all this spring, about one day from the trading house, taking considerable game. I killed by myself twenty otters, besides a good many beavers and other animals. As I was one day going to look at my traps, I found some ducks in a pond; and taking the ball out of my gun, I put in some shot, and began to creep up to them. As I was crawling cautiously through the bushes, a bear started up near me, and ran into a white pine tree, almost over my head. I hastily threw a ball into my gun and fired; but the gun burst about midway of the barrel, and all the upper half of it was carried away. The bear was apparently untouched, but he ran up higher into the tree. I loaded what was left of my gun, and taking aim the second time, brought him to the ground.

While we lived here we made a number of packs; and as it was inconvenient to keep these in our small lodge, we left them, from time to time, with the traders, for safe keeping. When the time came for them to come down to the Grand Portage, they took our packs without our consent; but the old woman followed after them to Rainy Lake, and retook every thing that belonged to us. But she was prevailed upon to sell them. From Rainy Lake we went to the Lake of the Woods, where Pa-bah-mew-in left us. Here, also, Waw-be-be-nais-sa rejoined us, wishing to return with us to Rainy Lake; but Net-no-kwa had heard of a murder committed there by some of his relations, that would have been revenged on him; for which reason she would not suffer him to return there. At the invitation of a man called Sah-muk, an Ottawwaw chief, and a relative of Net-no-kwa, we returned to Rainy Lake, to live with him. Wa-me-gon-a-biew, with the two women, and the children, went on to Red River. Sah-muk treated us with much kindness. He built and gave us a large bark canoe, intended for the use of the fur traders, and which we sold to them for the value of one hundred dollars, which was at that time the common price of such canoes in that part of the country. He also built us a small canoe for our own use.

The river which falls into Rainy Lake, is called Kocheche-sc-bee, (Source River,) and in it is a considerable fall, not far distant from the lake. Here I used to take, with a hook and line, great numbers of the fish called by the French, dory. One day, as I was fishing here, a very large sturgeon came down the fall, and happening to get into shallow water, was unable to make his escape. I killed him with a stone; and as it was the first that had been killed here, Sah-muk made a feast on the occasion.

After some time we started from this place, with a considerable band of Ojibbeways, to cross Rainy Lake. At the point where we were to separate from them, and they were to disperse in various directions, all stopped to drink. In the course of this drunken frolick, they stole from us all our corn and grease, leaving us quite destitute of provisions. This was the first instance in which I had ever joined the Indians in drinking, and when I recovered from it, the old woman reproved me very sharply and sensibly, though she herself had drank much more than I had.

As soon as I recovered my wits, and perceived into what a condition we had brought ourselves, I put the old woman in the canoe, and went immediately to a place where I knew there was good fishing. The Ojibbeways had not left us a mouthful of food; but I soon caught three dories, so that we did not suffer from hunger. Next morning I stopped for breakfast at a carrying place where these fish were very abundant; and while the old woman was making a fire and cooking one that I had just caught, I took nearly an hundred. Before we were ready to re-embark, some trader's canoes came along, and the old woman, not having entirely recovered from her drunken frolick, sold my fish for rum. The traders continued to pass during the day, but I hid away from the old woman, so many fish as enabled me to purchase a large sack of corn and grease. When Net-no-kwa became sober, she was much pleased that I had taken this course with her.

In the middle of the Lake of the Woods, is a small, but high rocky island, almost without any trees or bushes. This was now covered with young gulls and cormorants, of which I killed great numbers; knocking them down with a stick. We selected one hundred and twenty of the fattest, and dried them in the smoke, packed them in sacks, and carried them along with us. Thence we went by way of the Muskeeg carrying place, to Red River. As we were passing down this river, I shot a large bear on shore, near the brink of the river. He screamed out in a very unusual manner, then ran down into the water, and sunk.

At this place, (since called Pembinah,) where the Nebeninnah-ne-sebee enters Red River, had formerly been a trading house. We found no people, whites or Indians; and as we had not plenty of provisions, we went on all night, hoping soon to meet with some people. After sunrise next morning, we landed, and the old woman, while collecting wood to make a fire, discovered some buffaloes in the woods. Giving me notice of this, I ran up and killed a bull; but perceiving that he was very poor, I crept a little farther and shot a large fat cow. She ran some distance, and fell in an open prairie. A bull that followed her, no sooner saw me enter the open prairie, at the distance of three or four hundred yards from her, than he ran at me with so much fury, that I thought it prudent to retire into the woods. We remained all day at this place, and I made several attempts to get at the cow; but she was so vigilantly watched by the same bull, that I was at last compelled to leave her. In the rutting season, it is not unusual to see the bulls behave in this way.

Next day, we met the traders coming up to Nebeninnah-ne-sebee,* and gave them a part of the meat we had taken from the bull. Without any other delay, we went on to the Prairie Portage of the Assinneboin River, where we found Wa-me-gon-a-biew and Waw-be-be-nais-sa, with the other members of our family, from whom we had been so long separated.

Waw-be-be-nais-sa, since they left us, had turned away his former wife, and married the daughter of Net-no-kwa's sister, who had been brought up in our family, and whom the old woman had always treated as her own child. Net-no-kwa no sooner un-

---

* Nebeninnah-ne-sebee—High Craneberry River; since called Pembinah. The Indian name is derived from that of the viburnum, with large red edible berries, somewhat resembling the craneberry; thence called v. oxycoccus. "Red River" is from the Indian Miskwawgumme-wesebee.

derstood what had taken place, than she took up what few articles she could see in the lodge, belonging to Waw-be-be-nais-sa, and throwing them out, said to him, "I have been starved by you already, and I wish to have nothing more to do with you. Go, and provide for your own wants; it is more than so miserable a hunter as you are, is able to do, you shall not have my daughter." So being turned out, he went off by himself for a few days; but as Net-no-kwa soon learned that his former wife was married to another man, and that he was destitute, she admitted him again into the lodge. It was probably from fear of the old woman, that he now became a better hunter than he had been before.

That winter I hunted for a trader, called by the Indians Aneeb, which means an elm tree. As the winter advanced, and the weather became more and more cold, I found it difficult to procure as much game as I had been in the habit of supplying, and as was wanted by the trader. Early one morning, about midwinter, I started an elk. I pursued until night, and had almost overtaken him; but hope and strength failed me at the same time. What clothing I had on me, notwithstanding the extreme coldness of the weather, was drenched with sweat. It was not long after I turned towards home, that I felt it stiffening about me. My leggins were of cloth, and were torn in pieces in running through the brush. I was conscious I was somewhat frozen, before I arrived at the place where I had left our lodge standing in the morning, and it was now midnight. I knew it had been the old woman's intention to move, and I knew where she would go; but I had not been informed she would go on that day. As I followed on their path, I soon ceased to suffer from cold, and felt that sleepy sensation which I knew preceded the last stage of weakness in such as die of cold. I redoubled my efforts, but with an entire consciousness of the danger of my situation, it was with no small difficulty that I could prevent myself from lying down. At length I lost all consciousness for some time, how long I cannot tell; and awaking as from a dream, I found I had been walking round and round in a small circle, not more than twenty or twenty-five yards over. After the return of my senses, I looked about to try to discover my path, as I had missed it; but while I was looking, I discovered a light at a distance, by which I directed my course. Once more, before I reached the lodge, I lost my senses; but I did not fall down; if I had, I should never have got up again: but I ran round and round in a circle as before. When I at last came into the lodge, I immediately fell down, but I did not lose myself as before. I can remember seeing the thick and sparkling coat of frost on the inside of the pukkwi lodge, and hearing my mother say that she had kept a large fire in expectation of my arrival; and that she had not thought I should have been so long gone in the morning, but that I should have known long before night of her having moved. It was a month before I was able to go out again, my face, hands, and legs, having been much frozen.

The weather was beginning to be a little warm, so that the snow sometimes melted, when I began to hunt again. Going one day with Waw-be-be-nais-sa, a good distance up the Assinneboin, we found a large herd of probably 200 elk, in a little prairie, which was almost surrounded by the river. In the gorge, which was no more than two hundred yards across, Waw-be-be-nais-sa and I stationed ourselves, and the frightened herd being unwilling to venture on the smooth ice in the river, began to run round and round the little prairie. It sometimes happened that one was pushed within the reach of our shot, and in this way we killed two. In our eagerness to get nearer, we advanced so far towards the centre of the prairie, that the herd was divided, a part being driven on the ice, and a part escaping to the high grounds. Waw-be-be-nais-sa followed the latter, and I ran on to the ice. The elks on the river, slipping on the smooth ice, and being much frightened, crowded so close together that their great weight broke the ice; and as they waded towards the opposite shore, and endeavoured in a body to rise upon the ice, it continued to break before them. I ran hastily and thoughtlessly along the brink of the open place, and as the water was not so deep as to swim the elks, I thought I might get those I killed, and therefore continued shooting them as fast as I could. When my balls were all expended, I drew my knife, and killed one or two with it; but all I killed in the water, were in a few minutes swept under the ice, and I got not one of them. One only, which I struck after he rose upon the ice on the shore, I saved. This, in addition to the others we had killed on the shore, made four; being all we were able to take out of a gang of not less than two hundred. Waw-be-be-nais-sa went immediately, under the pretence of notifying the traders, and sold the four elks as his own, though he killed but two of them.

At this time, Wa-me-gon-a-biew was unable to hunt, having, in a drunken frolick, been so severely burned, that he was not able to stand. In a few days, I went again with Waw-be-be-nais-sa to hunt elks. We discovered some in the prairie; but crawling up behind a little inequality of surface, which enabled us to conceal ourselves, we came within a short distance. There was a very large and fat buck which I wished to shoot, but Waw-be-be-nais-sa said, "not so, my brother, lest you should fail to kill him; as he is the best in the herd I will shoot him, and you may try to kill one of the smaller ones." So I told him that I would shoot at one that was lying down; we fired both together, but he missed and I killed. The herd then ran off, and I pursued without waiting to butcher, or even to examine the one I had killed. I continued the chase all day, and before night had killed two more, as the elks were so much fatigued that I came up to them pretty easily. As it was now night, I made the best of my way home, and when I arrived, found that Waw-be-be-nais-sa had brought home meat, and had been amusing the family by describing the manner in which he said he had killed the elk. I said to them, "I am very glad he has killed an elk, for I have killed three, and to-morrow we shall have plenty of meat." But as I had some suspicion of him, I took him outside, and asked him about the one he had killed, and easily made him acknowledge, that it was no other than the one I had shot, from which he brought in some of the meat. He was sent to the traders to call men to bring in the meat, and again sold all three as his own, when he had not helped to kill even one of them. The old woman, when she became acquainted with this conduct, persecuted him so much, that he was induced to leave us. Wa-me-gon-a-biew, also, who had married an Ojibbeway woman in the fall, now went to live with his father-in-law, and there remained in our family, only the old woman and myself, the Bowwetig girl, Ke-zhik-o-weninne, the son of Taw-ga-weninne, now something of a boy, and the two small children. I was now, for the first time, left to pass the winter by myself, with a family to provide for, and no one to assist me. Waw-be-be-nais-sa encamped about one day from us. I had, in the course of the fall, killed a good many beavers and other animals, and we had for some time enough to supply all our wants. We had also plenty of blankets and clothing. One very cold morning in the winter, as I was going out to hunt, I stripped off all my silver ornaments, and hung them up in the lodge. The old woman asked me why I did so; I told her that they were not comfortable in such extreme cold weather; moreover, that in pursuing game I was liable to lose them. She remonstrated for some time, but I persisted, and went to hunt without them. At the same time I started to hunt, the old woman started for Waw-be-be-nais-sa's lodge, intending to be absent two days. The lodge was left in the care of Skwah-shish, as the Bowwetig girl was called, and Ke-zhik-o-weninne. When I returned late at night, after a long and unsuccessful hunt, I found these two children standing shivering and crying by the side of the ashes of our lodge, which, owing to their carelessness, had been burned down, and every thing we had consumed in it. My silver ornaments, one of my guns, several blankets, and much clothing, were lost. We had been rather wealthy among the Indians of that country; now we had nothing left but a medicine bag and a keg of rum. When I saw the keg of rum, I felt angry that only what was useless and hurtful to us was left, while every thing valuable had been destroyed, and taking it up, threw it to a distance. I then stripped the blanket from the Bow-wetig girl, and sent her away to stay by herself in the snow; telling her that as her carelessness had stripped us of every thing, it was but right she should feel the cold more than I did. I then took the little boy, Ke-zhik-o-weninne, and we lay down together upon the warm ashes.

Very early the next morning I started out to hunt; and as I knew very well how the old woman would behave when she came to a knowledge of her misfortune, I did not wish to reach home until late at night. When approaching the place where our lodge had been, I heard the old woman scolding and beating the little girl. At length, when I went to the fire, she asked me why I had not killed her when I first came home and found the lodge burned down. "Since you did not," said she, "I must now kill her." "Oh my mother do not kill me, and I will pay you for all you have lost." "What have you to give? how can you pay me?" said the old woman. "I will give you the Manito," said the little girl, "the great Manito shall come down to reward you, if you do not kill me." We were now destitute of provisions, and almost naked; but we determined to go to Aneeb's trading-house, at Kenukauneshewayboant, where we obtained credit for the amount of one pack of beaver skins; and with the blankets and cloth which we purchased in this way, we returned to Wa-me-gon-a-biew's lodge, whence he and his wife accompanied us to our own place.

We commenced to repair our loss, by building a small grass lodge, in which to shelter ourselves while we should prepare the pukkwi for a new wigwam.* The women were very industrious in making these, and none more active than Skwah-shish, the Bowwetig girl. At night, also, when it was too dark to hunt, Wa-me-gon-a-biew and myself assisted at this labour. In a few days our lodge was completed, and Wa-me-gon-a-biew, having killed three elks, left us for his own home.

After a little time, plenty and good humour were restored. One evening the old woman called to her the little Bowwetig girl, and asked her if she remembered what promise she had made to her when she was whipped for burning the lodge. Skwah-shish could make no answer; but the old woman took the opportunity to admonish her of the impropriety of using the name of the Deity in a light and irreverent manner.

* Pronounced by the Indians, We-ge-wham.

CHAPTER VI.

Failure of an attempt to accompany a war-party to the Missouri—removal to Elk River—joined in my hunting grounds by some Naudoways, from Lower Canada—hospitality of the Crees—practice of medicine—dispute with a Naudoway—band of Tus-kwaw-go-nees—Brine Spring, on Elk River—I receive a severe injury by falling from my horse—involved in difficulty by my foster brother—habits of the moose-deer—range of the moose, the elk, and the reindeer.

AT this place we remained until spring, when, at the commencement of the sugar season, we went to Ke-nu-kau-ne-she-way-boant. We applied to the Indians there to give us some trees to make sugar. They gave us a place where were a few small trees; but the old woman was dissatisfied, and refused to remain. We therefore travelled two days by ourselves, until we found a good place to make sugar, and in the same district were plenty of beavers, as well as birch for troughs. When we had been here long enough to have finished making sugar, Wa-me-gon-a-biew came to us in distress, with his father-in-law, and all his large family. We were able to give them something, but old Net-no-kwa did not present him ten of my largest and best beaver skins without remarking, " these, and many more, have all been killed by my little son, who is much weaker and less experienced than either yourself or Wa-me-gon-a-biew." She was not very well pleased in giving, and the old man was a little ashamed to receive her present. After a few days, they left us for the trading-house, and Waw-be-be-nais-sa joined us when we started in company to go to the Mouse River trading-house. Leaves were out on the trees, the bark peeled, and we were killing sturgeons in the rivers, when there came a snow more than knee deep, and the frost was so severe that the trees cracked as in the middle of winter. The river was frozen over, and many trees were killed.

At the Mouse River trading-house, the Assinneboins, Crees, and Ojibbeways, were again assembling to go to join the Mandans, in making war upon the A-gutch-e-ninne-wug, the people I before mentioned. This time I wished to have accompanied them, and I said to the old woman, "I will go with my uncles, who are going to the Mandans." She tried to dissuade me, but finding me obstinate, took away my gun and moccasins. This opposition rather increased my ardour, and I followed the Indians, barefoot and unarmed, trusting that some among them would supply me; but in this I was mistaken, for they drove me back, and would by no means allow me to accompany them. I was irritated and dissatisfied, but I had no alternative but to return, and remain with the women and children. I did not ask the old woman for my gun again; but taking my traps, I went from home, and did not return until I had caught beavers enough to purchase one; but when I had done so, my anxiety to overtake and accompany the war-party had subsided. Many of the women they had left behind, now began to be hungry, and it was not without great exertion on my part, and that of the very few young boys and old men who were left, that their wants could be supplied.

The war-party at length returned, having accomplished little or nothing. We then left them, and in company with one man, a relative of Net-no-kwa, called Wau-zhe-gaw-maish-kum, (he that walks along the shore,) we started to go to Elk River. This man had two wives; the name of one was Me-sau-bis, (goslin's down.) He was also accompanied by another distinguished hunter, called Kau-wa-be-nit-to, (he that starts them all.) Our course from Mouse River was very near due north; and as we had six horses, we travelled with considerable rapidity; but it was many days before we reached the head of Elk River. Here Wau-zhe-gaw-maish-kum left us to go to the Missouri, on a war-party; but Kau-wa-be-nit-to remained, and gave us always the finest and best of the game he killed. He directed me also to a beaver dam and pond, at some distance, to which I went one day at evening, and having sat down I found a road which the beavers were then using to bring timber into the pond. By this road I sat down to watch, supposing I should soon see them pass one way or the other. I had scarce sat down, when I heard, at no great distance, a sound which I knew was that made by a woman in dressing skins. I was a little alarmed, as

I knew of no Indians in that quarter, and was apprehensive that some of an unfriendly tribe might have come to encamp there; but being determined not to return home ignorant who and what they were, I took my gun in my hands, in the position which would enable me to fire immediately, and proceded cautiously along the path, to examine. My eyes were commonly directed considerably ahead; but I had not walked far, when looking to one side, I saw in the bushes, close to my side, and not one step from the path, a naked and painted Indian, lying flat upon his belly, but, like myself, holding his gun in the attitude of firing. My eyes no sooner fell upon him, than simultaneously, and almost without knowing what I did, I sprang to the other side of the path, and pointed my gun directly at him. This movement he answered by a hearty laugh, which immediately removed my apprehensions, and he soon arose and addressed me in the Ojibbeway language. Like myself, he had supposed no other Indians than his own family were, at that time, in the country, and he had been walking from his own lodge, which stood very near to the beaver pond, when he was surprised to perceive a man approaching him through the bushes. He had first perceived me, and concealed himself, not knowing whether I was a friend or an enemy. After some conversation he returned home with me, and Net-no-kwa discovered that he was a relative of hers. The family of this man remained with us about ten days, and afterwards went to encamp by themselves, at a distance.

I was now left, for the second time, with the prospect of spending the winter alone, with the exception of those of our own family; but before the commencement of cold weather there came from Mo-ne-ong, (Montreal,) seven Naudoway hunters, one of them a nephew of Net-no-kwa. They remained with us, and in the fall and early part of winter, we killed great numbers of beaver. Five of the Naudoways I surpassed in hunting, and though they had ten traps each, and I only six, I caught more beavers than they did. Two of the seven men could beat me at almost any thing. In the course of the winter, two more Naudoways came to our camp, who were in the interest and employ of the company called by the Indians Ojibbeway Way-met-e-goosh-she-wug, (the Chippeway Frenchmen.) After these had been some time with us, the game was exhausted, and we began to be hungry. We agreed all to go one day in search of buffaloes. At night, all had returned except a tall young man, and a very small old man, of the Naudoways. Next day the tall man came home, bringing a new buffaloe robe, and having on a handsome pair of new moccasins. He said he had fallen in with seven lodges of Crees; that at first they had not known him, and it was with great difficulty he had made them understand him; but being received into one of the lodges, and fed, and treated with kindness, he had remained all night. In the morning, he folded up the buffaloe robe they had given him to sleep on, and would have left it, but they told him they had given it to him, and observing, at the same time, that his moccasins were not very good, one of the women had given him a pair of new ones. This kind of hospitality is much practised among Indians who have had but little intercourse with the whites, and it is among the foremost of the virtues which the old men inculcate upon the minds of children, in their evening conversations; but the Naudoway had been little accustomed to such treatment, in the country from which he came.

He had not been long at home, before the old man arrived, who pretended that he had seen fifty lodges of Assinneboins, and had been kindly received by them; and although he had nothing to show in proof of his assertions, that they had plenty of meat, and were disposed to be very hospitable, he persuaded us, that we had better go to join them. In the morning we were all ready to accompany him, but he said, "I cannot go yet, I have first to mend my moccasins." One of the young men, that there might be no unnecessary delay, gave him a pair of new moccasins; but in the next place, he said he must cut off a piece of his blanket, and make himself some mittens. One of them, who had some pieces of blanket, assisted him to make some mittens; but he still invented excuses for delaying his departure, most of which resulted in the supplying, by some one of the party, some of his little wants; but at length we began to suspect him of lying, and having sent some one to follow his trail, we ascertained that he had neither travelled far, seen Indians, or eaten a mouthful since he left home.

Knowing it would be in vain to search for the fifty lodges of Assinneboins, we went in pursuit of the Crees, whom our Naudoway had seen; but we unexpectedly met with another band of the same tribe. These were strangers to us, but inquiring for their chief, we went into his lodge and sat down. The women immediately hung the kettle over the fire, and then took out of a sack a substance which was then new and unknown to all of us, and which excited in our party considerable curiosity. When the food was placed before us, we found it consisted of little fishes, scarce an inch long, and all of the same size. When put into the kettle, they were in large masses, frozen together. These little fishes, with the taking and eating of which we afterwards became familiar, are found in small holes which remain open in the shallow ponds, crowded together in such numbers that one may scoop up hundreds of them at once, with the hands. After we had finished our meal, the woman who appeared to be the principal wife of the chief, examined our moccasins, and gave us each a new pair. These people were on a journey, and soon left us. We now determined to make a sun-jegwun, and deposite such of our property as would impede us in a long journey, and go to the plains in pursuit of buffaloe. We accordingly followed the path of the Crees, and overtook them in the Prairie.

It was about the middle of winter, when we arrived among them, and soon afterwards our tall Naudoway fell sick. His friends applied to an old medicine man of the Crees, called Mukkwah, (the bear,) requesting him to do something for his relief. "Give me," said the old man, "ten beaver skins, and I will use my art to relieve him." As we had left our peltries behind, and killed but few beaver since we started, we could raise only nine; but we gave him a piece of cloth, which was more than equal in value to one beaver, and he consented to begin. He prepared his lodge for the first days' practice before the patient was admitted; he then being brought in, was seated on a mat near the fire. Old Muk-kwah, who was a ventriloquist of but indifferent powers, and a medicine man of no great fame, imitated, as well as he could, various sounds, and endeavoured to make those standing by believe they proceeded from the breast of the sick man. At length he said, he heard the sound of bad fire in the breast of the Naudoway, and putting one hand to his breast, the other and his mouth to the back, he continued for some time blowing and rubbing, when he, as if by accident, dropped a little ball upon the ground. After again blowing and rubbing, alternately dropping the little ball, and rubbing it between his hands, he at length threw it into the fire, where it burned, with a little whizzing noise, like damp powder. This did not surprise me at all, as I saw he had taken the precaution to sprinkle a little powder on that part of the floor of the lodge where the ball fell. Perceiving, probably, that what he had now done was not likely to prove satisfactory to his employers, he pretended that there was a snake in the breast of the sick man, which he could not remove till the following day; when with similar preparations, and similar mummeries, he seemed to draw out of the body of the sick man, a small snake. One of his hands he kept for some time on the place from which he pretended to have drawn the snake, as he said the hole could not close immediately. The snake he refused to destroy; but laid it carefully aside for preservation, lest, as he said, it should get into somebody else. This ill-conducted imposition did not fail to excite the ridicule of the Naudoways, and had no perceptible effect upon the sick man. They soon learned to imitate his several noises, and made him a subject for sarcasm and ridicule. Some of the more sensible and respectable men among the Crees, advised us to have nothing more to say to Muk-kwah, as he was esteemed but a fool among them.

It was about this time that I had some difficulty with a Naudoway Indian, who was hunting for the Ojibbeway Way-me-ta-goo-she-wug. He had arrived since I had in the country, and his right to hunt in any part of it was certainly no better than mine. He had, in one or two instances, complained of me for hunting where he said I had no right to hunt. Having now found a gang of beavers, I set my traps for them, and, as usual, left them till the next day. On going next morning I found he had followed my trail, taken up all my traps, thrown them into the snow, and set his own in place of them. He had caught but one beaver, which I did not hesitate to carry home as my own, and throwing all his traps in the snow, I set mine again as before. The affair soon became public, but all the band, even his own friends, the Naudoways, sided against him, and assured me they would support me in the course I had taken. In affairs of this kind, the customs of the tribe are as a law to the Indians, and any one who ventures to depart from them, can expect neither support nor countenance. It is rare that oppression or injustice in affairs of private right, between man and man, take place among the Indians.

We staid about one month in the prairie, then returned to the lodge where we had left the old woman, thence to our trading-house on Elk River. Here a lodge of Tus-kwaw-go-mees, from Canada, came into our neighbourhood. I had now separated from the Naudoways, and was living by myself. When I first visited the Tus-kwaw-go-mees, and went into their lodge, I did not know who they were. The man presently went out, brought in my snow-shoes, and placed them by the fire to dry; finding they were a little out of repair, he directed an old man to mend them. He then proposed to go and hunt with me, until they should be repaired. He killed, in the course of the day, several beavers, all of which he gave me. The kindness of this family of Tus-kwaw-go-mees continued as long as we remained near them. Their language is like that of the Ojibbeways, differing from it only as the Cree differs from that of the Mus-ke-goes.

When the sugar season arrived, I went to Elk River, and made my camp about two miles below the fort. The sugar trees, called by the Indians she-she-ge-ma-winzh, are of the same kind as are commonly found in the bottom lands, on the Upper Mississippi, and are called by the whites "river maple." They are large, but scattered; for this reason we made two camps, one on each side of the river. I remained by myself in one, and in the other were the old woman and the little children. While I was making sugar, I killed plenty of birds, ducks, geese, and beaver. There was near my camp a large brine spring, at which the traders used to make salt. The spring is about thirty feet in diameter, the water is blue, and, with the longest poles, no bottom can be found. It is near the bank of the Elk River, between the Assinneboin and Sas-kow-ja-wun, about twenty days' journey from the trading-house at Lake Winnipeg. There are, in that part of the country, many brine springs and salt lakes, but I have seen no other as large as this.

At this trading post I met a gentleman who took much notice of me, and tried to persuade me to accompany him to England;

but I was apprehensive he might leave me there, and that I should not be able to reach my friends in the United States, even if any of them were living. I also felt attached to hunting, as a business and an amusement; therefore I declined his invitation. Among other Indians who assembled at this trading-house, in the spring, came our old companion and friend, Pe-shau-ba, and, as usual, they expended the products of their winter and spring hunts, their sugar, &c. for whiskey. After they had drank all they could purchase, old Net-no-kwa gave them an additional ten gallon keg, which she had hid the year before under the ashes back of the trader's house. Their long debauch was attended by mischievous quarrels, and followed by hunger and poverty. Some one proposed, as a method of relieving the pressure of hunger, now becoming severe, that a hunting match should be made, to see who, of all those that were assembled, could take, in one day, the greatest number of rabbits. In this strife I surpassed Pe-shau-ba, who had been one of my first instructors in hunting; but he was yet far my superior in taking large animals.

From this trading-house we returned by the way of Swan River, and the Me-nau-ko-nos-keeg, towards Red River. About the Me-nau-ko-nos-keeg and Ais-sug-se-bee, or Clam River, whose head waters interlock, we stopped for some time to trap beaver, being assisted by a young man called Nau-ba-shish, who had joined us some time before; but at length falling in with a trace on which Indians had passed only two days before, I determined to try to see them. Leaving the old woman and the family with Nau-ba-shish, I mounted my best horse, and followed the path through the prairie. After a few hours I passed a place where had been a lodge the day before, and my horse was stepping over a log which lay across the path, when a prairie hen flew from under it. The horse being frightened, threw me, and I fell upon the log, afterwards upon the ground; but as I still held the bridle rein, the horse stepped with his fore foot upon my breast. For some hours I was not able to get on my horse; when I at last succeeded, I determined still to follow on after the Indians, as I believed myself nearer to them than to my own lodge. When I arrived among them I could not speak; but they perceived that I had been hurt, and treated me with kindness. From this hurt, which was very severe, I have never since recovered entirely.

A part of my object in visiting this band, had been to try to hear something from Wa-me-gon-a-biew, but they had not met with him. I now determined to leave the old woman at Menaukonoskeeg, and go to Red River by myself. I had four horses, one of which was a very fleet and beautiful one, being considered the best out of one hundred and eighty, which a war-party of Crees, Assinneboins, and Ojibbeways, had recently brought from the Fall Indians. In this excursion they had been absent seven months; they had fallen upon and destroyed one village, and taken one hundred and fifty scalps, besides prisoners.

Ten days after I left Menaukonoskeeg on this horse, I arrived at the Mouse River trading-house. Here I learned that Wa-me-gon-a-biew was at Pembinah, on Red River. Mr. M'Kee sent a man to show me the road to the head of the Pembinah River, where I found Aneeb, a trader with whom I was well acquainted. One day's journey from this house, I found the lodge of the father-in-law of Wa-me-gon-a-biew, but I saw nothing of my brother, and the old man did not receive me kindly. He was living with a party of about one hundred lodges of Crees. Perceiving that something was not as I could have wished, I went to spend the night with an old Cree whom I had seen before. In the morning, the old man said to me, "I am afraid they will kill your horse, go and see how they are abusing him." I went as he directed, and found that a parcel of young men and boys had thrown my horse down upon the ground, and were beating him. When I came up, I found some were holding him by the head, while one man was standing on his body and beating him. To this man I said, "my friend,* you must come down;" he answered, "I wont." "I shall help you down," said I, and pushing him down, I took the bridle from those who held him, and led him home; but he had received an injury from which he could never recover.

I now enquired the cause of this unexpected and very unfriendly treatment, and learned that it was on account of Wa-me-

---

* Needjee—my friend, is commonly used in friendly conversation; but, as in our language, is often used with a peculiar tone and manner, when a threat is intended.

gon-a-biew, who had turned away his former wife, and quarrelled with his father-in-law. In this quarrel, the old man's horse and dog had been killed; which injury his young friends were visiting upon my horse. The origin of this quarrel seemed to me to be such as to leave some appearance of right on the part of Wa-me-gon-a-biew. He had treated his wife as well as is usual among them, and only parted with her because her father refused to part with her; insisting that Wa-me-gon-a-biew should accompany him in all his movements. Rather than do this, he chose to leave his wife altogether, and had done so in a peaceable manner, when her relatives showed a disposition to offer him some molestation. As I was alone, I feared they might follow me, and try to do me some injury at my next encampment; but they did not, and on the following day I arrived at the place where Wa-me-gon-a-biew was now living with his new wife. The old man, his father-in-law, whom I had seen before, met me outside of the lodge, and was surprised to hear that I had come from Menaukonoskego, the distance being greater than they usually go by themselves in that country.

Here I remained four days, hunting with my friends; then I started, accompanied by Wa-me-gon-a-biew and his wife, to return. We went to the village where they had tried to kill my horse; and though the old man had moved to some distance, he soon heard of us, and came in accompanied by his brothers. We slept at a lodge near the trader's tent. I intended to have watched, as I was apprehensive that they would attempt either to rob or otherwise injure us; but through fatigue, I fell asleep. Late at night I was waked by Wa-me-gon-a-biew, who said the old man had been in, and taken his gun from over his head. He admitted that he was awake when the old man entered, and had watched him from under his blanket until he went out with the gun. I reproached him for pusilanimity, telling him he deserved to lose his gun if he would suffer an old man to take it away while his eyes were open. Nevertheless, I made an attempt, though an unsuccessful one, to recover the gun.

Before we reached Mouse River, my horse had become so poor and feeble, that even the woman could not ride him. We rested two days, and then went on. We had suffered much from hunger, having for many days killed only one poor buffaloe, when we met with a small band of Crees, under a chief called O-ge-mah-wah-shish, a Cree word, meaning chief's son. Instead of relieving our wants, they treated us in an unfriendly manner, and I overheard them talking of killing us, on account of some old quarrel with a band of Ojibbeways. They would sell us nothing but a small badger, and we lost no time in escaping as far as we could from them. We were starved for two days more, when we met an Ojibbeway, called Wawb-uche-chawk, (the white crane,) who had very lately killed a fat moose.

With this man we lived about a month; during all which time we had plenty of food, and slept in his lodge. He was moving in the same direction that we were; he did not leave us until we arrived at Rush Lake River. The old woman had gone from the trading house where I left her, to live with Indians, at the distance of four days. My three horses, which, before starting, I had fettered and turned out, that they might become accustomed to the place, had been neglected, and were now dead; notwithstanding I had given very particular charge to Net-no-kwa to take off the fetters at the commencement of winter; but she had neglected it. My horse which I had rode to Red River, was also dead, and I had none left. Net-no-kwa having apparently relinquished her claim to me, and Wa-me-gon-a-biew now leaving me, I remained for some time entirely alone, about the trading house. The trader, whose name was M'Glees, at length took notice of me, and invited me to live with him. He said so much to induce me to leave the Indians, that I felt sometimes inclined to follow his advice; but whenever I thought of remaining long at the trading house, I found an intolerable irksomeness attending it. I felt an inclination to spend all my time in hunting, and a strong dislike to the less exciting employments of the men about a trading house.

At the head of the Menaukonoskego river, was a trading house, which I started to visit, in company with five Frenchmen and one Ojibbeway woman, sent by Mr. M'Glees. We were furnished only with enough meat for one meal; all of which we ate on the first night after we started. About the middle of the third day, we came to a small creek of salt water; and on the summit of a little hill by the side of it, we saw a man sitting. We went up to him, but he gave no answer to our questions; we then took hold and tried to rouse him by shaking, but we found him stiffened by the cold; and when we took our hands off him, he tumbled to the ground as if he had been frozen entirely stiff. His breath still came and went, but his limbs were no longer flexible, and he appeared in most respects like one dead. Beside him lay his small kettle, his bag, containing steel and flint, his moccasin awl, and one pair of moccasins. We tried all the means in our power to resuscitate him, but all in vain. Regarding him as one dead, I advised the Frenchmen to return with him to the trading house from which we came, that he might be properly buried. They did so, and I learned afterwards that he ceased breathing an hour or two after they started. It appeared that he had been sent away from the trading house at the head of the river, as too indolent to be suffered to remain. He had started almost destitute of provisions, and come some distance to Wa-me-gon-a-biew's lodge. Wa-me-gon-a-biew had fed him, and offered him plenty of provisions to take with him; but he declined, saying he should not have occasion for it. He was then very much enfeebled, and had been about two days in coming the short distance to the place where we had found him. After they started with him, I went on with the Ojibbeway woman, and soon arrived at Wa-me-gon-a-biew's.

I had remained here about a month, hunting with my brother, when Net-no-kwa arrived, having come in search of me. Wa-me-gon-a-biew went by my direction, to a place on Clam River, to hunt beaver, and I returned with Net-no-kwa to Menaukonoskeeg, where we made sugar. There were ten fires of us together; and after the sugar making was over, we all went to hunt beavers in concert. In hunts of this kind, the proceeds are sometimes equally divided; but in this instance every man retained what he had killed. In three days I collected as many skins as I could carry. But in these distant and hasty hunts, little meat could be brought in, and the whole band was soon suffering of hunger. Many of the hunters, and I, among others, for want of food, became extremely weak, and unable to hunt far from home. One day, when the ice in the ponds was covered midling deep with water, I reached a place about a mile distant from camp, and in a low swamp I discovered fresh moose signs. I followed up the animal, and killed it; and as it was the first, it was made a feast for the whole band, and all devoured in a single day.

Soon afterwards, all the Indians came down, in two days' journey, to the mouth of the river, where we were joined by Wa-me-gon-a-biew, who had made a very successful hunt on Clam River. We stopped at the trading house, one mile from the lake, and remained here drinking until our peltries were all sold. Then we started, accompanied only by Wa-me-gon-a-biew, to come down to the mouth of the river. The distance was so short, that we did not take the dogs on board the canoes; as they ran along the shore, they started an elk, and drove him into the water in the lake, whence we chased him on shore with the canoe, and killed him on the beach.

About this time, we met with an old Ottawwaw chief, called Wa-ge-to-tah-gun, (he that has a bell,) more commonly called Wa-ge-toat. He was a relative of Net-no-kwa; and had with him at that time, three lodges and two wives. One of his sons had also two wives. With him we remained two months; and almost every morning, as he was going out, he called me to accompany him to his hunt. Whenever he hunted with me, he gave me all, or the greater part of what he killed. He took much pains to teach me how to take moose and other animals which are difficult to kill. Wa-me-gon-a-biew, with his wife, left us here, and went to Red River.

There is an opinion prevalent among the Indians, that the moose, among the methods of self-preservation with which he seems better acquainted than almost any other animal, has the power of remaining for a long time under water. Two men of the band of Wa-ge-to-tah-gun, whom I knew perfectly well, and considered very good and credible Indians, after a long day's absence on a hunt, came in, and stated that they had chased a moose into a small pond, that they had seen him go to the middle of it, and disappear; and then choosing positions, from which they could see every part of the circumference of the pond, smoked, and waited until near evening; during all which time, they could see no motion of the water, or other indication of the position of the moose. At length, being discouraged, they had abandoned all hope of taking him, and returned home. Not long afterwards, came a solitary hunter loaded with meat, who related, that having followed the track of a moose for some distance, he had traced it to the pond before mentioned; but having also discovered the tracks of two men, made at the same time as those of the moose, he concluded they must have killed it. Nevertheless, approaching cautiously to the margin of the pond, he sat down to rest. Presently he saw the moose rise slowly in the centre of the pond, which was not very deep, and wade towards the shore where he was sitting. When he came sufficiently near, he shot him in the water. The Indians consider the moose shyer and more difficult to take than any other animal. He is more vigilant, and his senses more acute, than those of the buffaloe or caribou. He is fleeter than the elk, and more prudent and crafty than the antelope. In the most violent storm, when the wind, and the thunder, and the falling timber, are making the loudest and most incessant roar, if a man, either with his foot or his hand, breaks the smallest dry limb in the forest, the moose will hear it; and though he does not always run, he ceases eating, and rouses his attention to all sounds. If in the course of an hour, or thereabouts, the man neither moves, nor makes the least noise, the animal may begin to feed again, but does not forget what he has heard, and is for many hours more vigilant than before.

Wa-ge-to-tah-gun, the chief with whom we were living, took every opportunity to instruct me as to the habits of the moose and other animals, and showed great pleasure when my exertions in the chase were crowned with success. As we were now about to part from him, he called out all the young hunters to accompany him for one day; several young women went also. He killed a fat buck moose, which he gave to me.

The country between Lake Winnepeg and Hudson's Bay, is low and swampy; and is the region of the caribou. More to the west, towards the Assinneboin and Saskawjawun, is the prairie country, where are found elks and buffaloe. The caribou is not found among the elk, nor the latter among the former.

CHAPTER VII.

I receive a proposal from a chief to marry his daughter—theft and drunkenness—manner of pursuing the elk on foot—disease and great mortality among the beaver—second offer of marriage from an A-go-kwa—haunted encampment, called the " place of the two dead men"—Indian courtship—distressing sickness—insanity and attempt at suicide—gambling—several offers of young women in marriage—my courtship and marriage with Mis-kwa-bun-o-kwa, (the red sky of the morning.)

THE spring having now come, we returned by the way of our old sugar camp, towards Menaukonoskego; but as I disliked to be with the Indians in their seasons of drunkenness, I dissuaded the old woman from accompanying them to the trading-house. I talked to her of the foolishness of wasting all our peltries in purchasing what was not only useless, but hurtful and poisonous to us, and was happy to find that I had influence enough with her to take her immediately to the place I had selected for my hunting camp. She went to see Wa-ge-tote, to take leave of him; but when she returned, I readily perceived by her manner that something unusual had passed. Presently she took me to one side, and began to say to me, " My son, you see that I am now become old; I am scarce able to make you moccasins, to dress and preserve all your skins, and do all that is needful about your lodge. You are now about taking your place as a man and a hunter, and it is right you should have some one who is young and strong, to look after your property, and take care of your lodge. Wa-ge-tote, who is a good man, and one respected by all the Indians, will give you his daughter. You will thus gain a powerful friend and protector, who will be able to assist us in times of difficulty, and I shall be relieved from much anxiety and care for our family." Much more she said, in the same strain; but I told her, without-hesitation, that I would not comply with her request. I had as yet thought little of marriage among the Indians, still thinking I should return before I became old, to marry to the whites. At all events, I assured her I could not now marry the woman she proposed to me. She still insisted that I must take her, stating that the whole affair had been settled between Wa-ge-tote and herself, and that the young woman had said she was not disinclined to the match, and she pretended she could do no otherwise than bring her to the lodge. I told her if she did so I should not treat or consider her as my wife. The affair was in this situation the morning but one before we were to separate from Wa-ge-tote and all his band, and, without coming to any better understanding with the old woman, I took my gun early in the morning, and went to hunt elk. In the course of the day I killed a fat buck, and returning late in the evening, I hung up the meat I had brought before the lodge, and carefully reconnoitered the inside before I entered, intending, if the young woman was there, to go to some other lodge and sleep; but I could see nothing of her.

Next morning Wa-ge-tote came to my lodge to see me; he expressed all the interest in me which he had been in the habit of doing, and gave me much friendly advice, and many good wishes. After this Net-no-kwa returned again, urging me to marry the daughter, but I did not consent. These attempts were afterwards, from time to time, renewed, until the young woman found a husband in some other man.

After Wa-ge-tote and his band had left us, we went to the hunting ground I had chosen, where we spent great part of the summer by ourselves, having always plenty to eat, as I killed great numbers of elks, beavers, and other animals. Late in the fall we went to the trading-house at Me-nau-ko-nos-keeg, where we met with Waw-zhe-kwaw-maish-koon, who had left us the year before, and with him we remained.

As the trader was coming to his wintering ground, the Indians, having assembled in considerable numbers, met him at the lake, at the distance of a few miles from his house. He had brought a large quantity of rum, and, as was usual, he encamped for several days, that the Indians might buy and drink what they could before he went to his house, as they would give him less trouble at his camp. I had the presence of mind to purchase some of the most needful articles for the winter, such as blankets and ammunition, as soon as we met him. After we had completed our trade, the old woman took ten fine beaver skins, and presented them to the trader. In return for this accustomed present, she was in the habit of receiving every year a chief's dress and ornaments, and a ten gallon keg of spirits; but when the trader sent for her to deliver his present, she was too drunk to stand. In this emergency, it was necessary for me to go and receive the articles. I had been drinking something, and was not entirely sober. I put on the chief's coat and ornaments, and taking the keg on my shoulder, carried it home to our lodge, placed it on one end, and knocked out the head with an axe. "I am not," said I, " one of those chiefs who draw liquor out of a small hole in a cask, let all those who are thirsty come and drink;" but I took the precaution to hide away a small keg full, and some in a kettle, probably in all three gallons; the old woman then came in with three kettles, and in about five minutes the keg was emptied. This was the second time that I had joined the Indians in drinking, and now I was guilty of much greater excess than before. I visited my hidden keg frequently, and remained intoxicated two days. I took what I had in the kettle, and went into the lodge to drink with Waw-zhe-kwaw-maish-koon, whom I called my brother, he being the son of Net-no-kwa's sister. He was not yet drunk; but his wife, whose dress was profusely ornamented with silver, had been for some time drinking, and was now lying by the fire in a state of absolute insensibility. Waw-zhe-kwaw-maish-koon and myself took our little kettle and sat down to drink, and presently an Ojibbeway, of our acquaintance, staggered in and fell down by the fire near the woman. It was late at night, but the noise of drunkenness was heard in every part of the camp; and I and my companion started out to go and drink wherever we could find any to give us liquor. As, however, we were not excessively drunk, we were careful to hide away the kettle which contained our whiskey, in the back part of the lodge, covering it, as we thought, effectually from the view of any that might come in. After an excursion of some hours, we returned. The woman was still lying by the fire, insensible as before, but with her dress stripped of its profusion of silver ornaments; and when we went for our kettle of rum, it was not to be found. The Ojibbeway, who had been lying by the fire, had gone out, and some circumstances induced us to suspect him of the theft, and I soon understood that he had said I had given him something to drink. I went next morning to his lodge, and asked him for my little kettle, which he directed his squaw to bring to me. Having thus fixed the theft upon him, Waw-zhe-kwaw-maish-koon went and recovered the ornaments of his wife's dress. This Ojibbeway was a man of considerable pretensions, wishing to be reckoned a chief; but this unfortunate attempt at theft injured his standing in the estimation of the people. The affair was long remembered, and he was ever after mentioned with contempt.

About this time, old Net-no-kwa began to wake from her long continued drunkenness. She called me to her, and asked me whether I had received the chief's dress, and the keg of rum. She was unwilling to believe that I had suffered all the contents of the keg to be expended without reserving some for her; but when she came to be assured not only that this was the case, but that I had been drunk for two days, she reproached me severely, censuring me not only for ingratitude to her, but for being such a beast as to be drunk. The Indians hearing her, told her she had no right to complain of me for doing as she herself had taught me, and by way of pacifying her, they soon contributed rum enough to make her once more completely drunk.

As soon as their peltries were all disposed of, so that they were compelled to discontinue drinking, the Indians began to disperse to their hunting grounds. We went with the trader to his house, where we left our canoes, and thence to the woods with Waw-zhe-kwaw-maish-koon to hunt. We now constituted but one family, but his part of it was large, he having many young children. Cold weather had scarce commenced, and the snow was no more than a foot deep, when we began to be pinched with hunger. We found a herd of elks, and chasing them one day, overtook and killed four of them. When the Indians hunt elk in this manner, after starting the herd they follow them at such a gait as they think they can keep for many hours. The elks being frightened, outstrip them at first by many miles; but the Indians, following at a steady pace along the path, at length come in sight of them; they then make another effort, and are no more seen for an hour or two; but the intervals at which the Indians have them in sight, grow more and more frequent, and longer and longer, until they cease to lose sight of them at all. The elks are now so much fatigued that they can only move in a slow trot, at last they can but walk, by which time the strength of the Indians is nearly exhausted, but they are commonly able to come up and fire into the rear of the herd; but the discharge of a gun quickens the motions of the elks, and it is a very active and determined man that can in this way come near enough to do execution more than once or twice, unless when the snow is pretty deep. The elk, in running, does not lift his feet well from the ground, so that, in deep snow, he is easily taken. There are among the Indians some, but not many, men who can run down an elk on the smooth prairie, when there is neither snow or ice. The moose and the buffaloe surpass the elk in fleetness, and can rarely be taken by fair running, by a man on foot.

The flesh of the four elks was dried, but by no means equally divided between us, nor in proportion to the size and wants of our respective families; but I made no complaint, as I knew I was a poor hunter, and had aided but little in taking them. Afterwards, I directed my attention more to the hunting of beaver. I knew of more than twenty gangs of beaver in the country about my camp, and I now went and began to break up the lodges, but I was much surprised to find nearly all of them empty. At last I found that some kind of distemper was prevailing among these animals, which destroyed them in vast numbers. I found them dead and dying in the water, on the ice, and on the land; sometimes I found one that, having cut a tree half down, had died at its roots; sometimes one who had drawn a stick of timber half way to his lodge, was lying dead by his burthen. Many of them, which I opened, were red and bloody about the heart. Those in large rivers and running water suffered less; almost all of those that lived in ponds and stagnant water, died. Since that year the beaver have never been so plentiful in the country of Red River and Hudson's Bay, as they used formerly to be. Those animals which died of this sickness we were afraid to eat, but their skins were good.

It often happened while we lived with Waw-zhe-kwaw-maish-koon, that we were suffering from hunger. Once, after a day and night in which we had not tasted a mouthful, I went with him to hunt, and we found a herd of elks; we killed two and wounded a third, which we pursued until night, when we overtook it. We cut up the meat and covered it in the snow; but he took not a mouthful for our immediate use, though we were so far from home, and it was now so late that we did not think of moving towards home until the following day. I knew that he had fasted as long as I had, and though my suffering from hunger was extreme, I was ashamed to ask him for any thing to eat, thinking I could endure it as long as he could. In the morning he gave me a little meat, but without stopping to cook any thing, we started for home. It was afternoon when we arrived, and Net-no-kwa seeing we had brought meat, said, "well, my son, I suppose you have eaten very heartily last night, after your long fast." I told her I had as yet eaten nothing. She immediately cooked part of what he had given me, all of which lasted us no more than two days. I still knew of two gangs of beaver, that had escaped the prevailing sickness, and I took my traps and went in pursuit of them. In a day or two I had taken eight, two of which I gave to Waw-zhe-kwaw-maish-koon.

Some time in the course of this winter, there came to our lodge one of the sons of the celebrated Ojibbeway chief, called Wesh-ko-bug, (the sweet,) who lived at Leech Lake. This man was one of those who make themselves women, and are called women by the Indians. There are several of this sort among most, if not all the Indian tribes; they are commonly called A-go-kwa, a word which is expressive of their condition. This creature, called Ozaw-wen-dib, (the yellow head,) was now near fifty years old, and had lived with many husbands. I do not know whether she had seen me, or only heard of me, but she soon let me know she had come a long distance to see me, and with the hope of living with me. She often offered herself to me, but not being discouraged with one refusal, she repeated her disgusting advances until I was almost driven from the lodge. Old Net-no-kwa was perfectly well acquainted with her character, and only laughed at the embarrassment and shame which I evinced whenever she addressed me. She seemed rather to countenance and encourage the Yellow Head in remaining at our lodge. The latter was very expert in the various employments of the women, to which all her time was given. At length, despairing of success in her addresses to me, or being too much pinched by hunger, which was commonly felt in our lodge, she disappeared, and was absent three or four days. I began to hope I should be no more troubled with her, when she came back loaded with dry meat. She stated that she had found the band of Wa-ge-to-tah-gun, and that that chief had sent by her an invitation for us to join him. He had heard of the niggardly conduct of Waw-zhe-kwaw-maish-koon towards us, and had sent the A-go-kwa to say to me, "my nephew, I do not wish you to stay there to look at the meat that another kills, but is too mean to give you. Come to me, and neither you nor my sister shall want any thing it is in my power to give you." I was glad enough of this invitation, and started immediately. At the first encampment, as I was doing something by the fire, I heard the A-go-kwa at no great distance in the woods, whistling to call me. Approaching the place, I found she had her eyes on game of some kind, and presently I discovered a moose. I shot him twice in succession, and twice he fell at the report of the gun; but it is probable I shot too high, for at last he escaped. The old woman reproved me severely for this, telling me she feared I should never be a good hunter. But before night the next day, we arrived at Wa-ge-to-te's lodge, where we ate as much as we wished. Here, also, I found myself relieved from the persecutions of the A-go-kwa, which had become intolerable. Wa-ge-tote, who had two wives, married her. This introduction of a new inmate into the family of Wa-ge-tote, occasioned some laughter, and produced some ludicrous incidents, but was attended with less uneasiness and quarreling than would have been the bringing in of a new wife of the female sex.

This band consisted of a large number of Indians, and the country about them was hunted poor; so that few even of the best hunters were able to kill game often; but it so happened, that myself and another man, who, like me, was reputed a poor hunter, killed more frequently than others. The Indians now collected for the solemn ceremony of the meta or mediance dance, in which Net-no-kwa always bore a very conspicuous part. I began to be dissatisfied at remaining with large bands of Indians, as it was usual for them, after having remained a short time in a place, to suffer from hunger. I therefore made a road for myself, and set my traps in a gang of beavers. When I signified to Wa-ge-tote my intention of leaving him, he said he was much afraid I should perish of hunger, if I went far away by myself. I refused, however, to listen to his advice or persuasion to remain with him, and he then determined to accompany me to my traps, to see what place I had selected, and judge whether I should be able to support my family. When we arrived, he found I had caught one large beaver. He advised and encouraged me, and after telling me where I should find his camp, in case of being pressed by poverty, he returned.

My family had now been increased by the addition of a poor old Ojibbeway woman and two children, who being destitute of any men, had been taken up by Net-no-kwa. Notwithstanding this, I thought it was still best for us to live by ourselves. I hunted with considerable success, and remained by myself until the end of the season for making sugar, when Net-no-kwa determined to return to Menaukonoskeeg, while I should go to the trading house at Red River, to purchase some necessary articles. I made a pack of beaver, and started by myself, in a small buffaloe skin canoe, only large enough to carry me and my pack, and descended the Little Saskawjewun.

There is, on the bank of that river, a place which looks like one the Indians would always choose to encamp at. In a bend of the river is a beautiful landing place, behind it a little plain, a thick wood, and a small hill rising abruptly in the rear. But with that spot is connected a story of fratricide, a crime so uncommon, that the spot where it happened is held in detestation, and regarded with terror. No Indian will land his canoe, much less encamp, at "*the place of the two dead men.*"* They relate, that many years ago, the Indians were encamped here, when a quarrel arose between two brothers, having she-she-gwi for totems. One drew his knife and slew the other; but those of the band who were present, looked upon the crime as so horrid, that without hesitation or delay, they killed the murderer, and buried them together.

As I approached this spot, I thought much of the story of the two brothers, who bore the same totem with myself, and were, as

* Jebing-neezh-o-shin-naut—Two dead lie there.

I supposed, related to my Indian mother. I had heard it said, that if any man encamped near their graves, as some had done soon after they were buried, they would be seen to come out of the ground, and either react the quarrel and the murder, or in some other manner so annoy and disturb their visiters, that they could not sleep. Curiosity was in part my motive, and I wished to be able to tell the Indians, that *I* had not only stopped, but slept quietly at a place which they shunned with so much fear and caution. The sun was going down as I arrived; and I pushed my little canoe in to the shore, kindled a fire, and after eating my supper, lay down and slept. Very soon, I saw the two dead men come and sit down by my fire, opposite me. Their eyes were intently fixed upon me, but they neither smiled, nor said any thing. I got up and sat opposite them by the fire, and in this situation I awoke. The night was dark and gusty, but I saw no men, or heard any other sounds, than that of the wind in the trees. It is likely I fell asleep again, for I soon saw the same two men standing below the bank of the river, their heads just rising to the level of the ground I had made my fire on, and looking at me as before. After a few minutes, they rose one after the other, and sat down opposite me; but now they were laughing, and pushing at me with sticks, and using various methods of annoyance. I endeavoured to speak to them, but my voice failed me: I tried to fly, but my feet refused to do their office. Throughout the whole night I was in a state of agitation and alarm. Among other things which they said to me, one of them told me to look at the top of the little hill which stood near. I did so, and saw a horse fettered, and standing looking at me. "There, my brother," said the jebi, "is a horse which I give you to ride on your journey to-morrow; and as you pass here on your way home, you can call and leave the horse, and spend another night with us."

At last came the morning, and I was in no small degree pleased to find, that with the darkness of the night these terrifying visions vanished. But my long residence among the Indians, and the frequent instances in which I had known the intimations of dreams verified, occasioned me to think seriously of the horse the jebi had given me. Accordingly I went to the top of the hill, where I discovered tracks and other signs, and following a little distance, found a horse, which I knew belonged to the trader I was going to see. As several miles travel might be saved by crossing from this point on the Little Saskawjewun to the Assinneboin, I left the canoe, and having caught the horse, and put my load upon him, led him towards the trading house, where I arrived next day. In all subsequent journeys through this country, I carefully shunned "the place of the two dead;" and the account I gave of what I had seen and suffered there, confirmed the superstitious terrors of the Indians.

After I returned from trading at the Red River, I went to live at Naowawgunwudju, the hill of the buffaloe chase, near the Saskawjewun. This is a high rocky hill, where mines may probably be found, as there are in the rocks many singular looking masses. Here we found sugar trees in plenty, and a good place for passing the spring. Game was so abundant, and the situation so desirable, that I concluded to remain, instead of going with all the Indians to Clear Water Lake, where they assembled to have their usual drunken frolick. I had sent for Wa-me-gon-a-biew, and he now joined us here, with one horse, making our whole number three. All these, all our dogs, and ourselves, were loaded with the meat of one moose, which I killed at this time, the largest and the fattest one I had ever seen.

Wa-me-gon-a-biew, after remaining with me four days, went to look for Wa-ge-tote, but without telling me any thing of his business. In a few days he returned, and told me that he had been to see Wa-ge-tote on account of his daughter, that had been so often offered to me, and wished to know if I had any intention to marry her. I told him I had not, and that I was very willing to afford him any aid in my power in furtherance of his design. He wished me to return with him, probably that I might remove any impression the old people might have, that I would marry the girl, and accompany him in bringing her home. I assented, without reflection, to this proposal, and as we were about making our preparations to start, I perceived from Net-no-kwa's countenance, though she said nothing, that the course we were taking displeased her. I then recollected, that it was not the business of young men to bring home their wives, and I told Wa-me-gon-a-biew that we should be ridiculed by all the people, if we persisted in our design. "Here," said I, "is our mother, whose business it is to find wives for us when we want them, and she will bring them, and show them our places in the lodge, whenever it is right she should do so." The old woman was manifestly pleased with what I said, and expressed her willingness to go immediately and bring home the daughter of Wa-ge-tote. She went accordingly; and it so happened, that when she returned bringing the girl, Wa-me-gon-a-biew and myself were sitting inside the lodge. It appeared that neither Wa-me-gon-a-biew, nor the old woman, had been at the pains to give her any very particular information, for when she came in, she was evidently at a loss to know which of the young men before her had chosen her for a wife. Net-no-kwa perceiving her embarrassment, told her to sit down near Wa-me-gon-a-biew, for him it was whom she was to consider her husband. After a few days, he took her home to his other wife, with whom she lived in harmony.

In the ensuing fall, when I was something more than twenty-one years of age, I moved, with Wa-me-gon-a-biew, and many other families of Indians, to the Wild Rice. While we were engaged in collecting and preparing the grain, many among us were seized with a violent sickness. It commenced with cough and hoarseness, and sometimes bleeding from the mouth or nose. In a short time many died, and none were able to hunt. Although I did not escape entirely, my attack appeared at first less violent than that of most others. There had been for several days, no meat in the encampment; some of the children had not been sick, and some of those who had been sick, now began to recover, and needed some food. There was but one man beside myself, as capable of exertion as I was; and he, like myself, was recovering. We were wholly unable to walk, and could scarce mount our horses when they were brought to us by the children. Had we been able to walk, we coughed so loudly and so incessantly, that we could never have approached near enough to any game to kill it by still hunting. In this emergency, we rode into the plains, and were fortunate enough to overtake and kill a bear. Of the flesh of this animal, we could not eat a mouthful, but we took it home, and distributed to every lodge an equal portion. Still I continued to get better, and was among the first to regain my health, as I supposed. In a few days I went out to hunt elk; and in killing two of them in the space of two or three hours, I became somewhat excited and fatigued. I cut up the meat, and as is usual, took home a load on my back, when I returned. I ate heartily of some which they cooked for me, then lay down and slept; but before the middle of the night, I was waked by a dreadful pain in my ears. It appeared to me that something was eating into my ears, and I called Wa-me-gon-a-biew to look, but he could see nothing. The pain became more and more excruciating for two days; at the end of which time I became insensible. When my consciousness returned, which was, as I learned afterwards, at the end of two days, I found myself sitting outside the lodge. I saw the Indians on all sides of me, drinking, some trader having come among them. Some were quarrelling, particularly a groupe amongst which I distinguished Wa-me-gon-a-biew, and saw him stab a horse with his knife. Then I immediately became insensible, and remained so probably for some days, as I was unconscious of every thing that passed, until the band were nearly ready to move from the place where we had been living. My strength was not entirely gone, and when I came to my right mind, I could walk about. I reflected much on all that had passed since I had been among the Indians. I had in the main been contented since residing in the family of Net-no-kwa; but this sickness I looked upon as the commencement of misfortune, which was to follow me through life. My hearing was gone, for abscesses had formed and discharged in each ear, and I could now hear but very imperfectly. I sat down in the lodge, and could see the faces of men, and their lips moving, but knew not what they said. I took my gun and went to hunt; but the animals discovered me before I could see them, and if by accident I saw a moose or an elk, and endeavoured to get near him, I found that my cunning and my success had deserted me. I soon imagined that the very animals knew that I had become like an old and useless man.

Under the influence of these painful feelings, I resolved to destroy myself, as the only means of escaping the certain misery which I saw before me. When they were ready to move, Net-no-kwa had my horse brought to the door of the lodge, and asked me if I was able to get on and ride to the place where they intended to encamp. I told her I was, and requesting that my gun might be left with me, said I would follow the party at a little distance. I took the rein of my horse's bridle in my hand, and sitting down, watched the people, as group after group passed me and disappeared. When the last old woman, and her heavy load of pukkwi mats, sunk behind the little swell of the prairie that bounded my prospect, I felt much relieved. I cast loose the reins of the bridle, and suffered my horse to feed at large. I then cocked my gun, and resting the butt of it on the ground, I put the muzzle to my throat, and proceeded with the ramrod, which I had drawn for the purpose, to discharge it. I knew that the lock was in good order; also, that the piece had been well loaded but a day or two before; but I now found that the charge had been drawn. My powder horn and ball pouch always contained more or less ammunition; but on examination, I found them empty. My knife also, which I commonly carried appended to the strap of my shot pouch, was gone. Finding myself baffled in the attempt to take my own life, I seized my gun with both hands by the muzzle, and threw it from me with my utmost strength; then mounted my horse, who, contrary to his usual custom, and to what I had expected from him, had remained near me after being released. I soon overtook the party, for being probably aware of my intentions, Wa-me-gon-a-biew and Net-no-kwa had gone but far enough to conceal themselves from my view, and had then sat down to wait. It is probable, that in my insane ravings, I had talked of my intention to destroy myself, and on this account, they had been careful to deprive me of the most ordinary and direct means of effecting my purpose.

Suicide is not very unfrequent among the Indians, and is effected in various ways; shooting, hanging, drowning, poisoning, &c. The causes, also, which urge to the desperate act, are various. Some years previous to the time I now speak of, I was with Net-no-kwa, at Mackinac, when I knew a very promising and highly respected young man of the Ottawwaws, who shot himself in the Indian burying ground. He had, for the first time, drank to intoxication; and in the alienation of mind produced by the liquor, had torn off his own clothes, and behaved with so much violence, that his two sisters, to prevent him from injuring himself or others, tied his hands and feet, and laid him down in the lodge. Next morning, he awoke sober, and being untied, went to his sister's lodge, which was near the burying ground, borrowed a gun, under pretence of going to shoot pigeons, and went into the burying ground and shot himself. It is probable, that when he awoke and found himself tied, he thought he had done something very improper in his drunkenness, and to relieve himself from the pressure of shame and mortification, had ended his days by violence. Misfortunes and losses of various kinds, sometimes the death of friends, and possibly, in some instances, disappointment in affairs of love, may be considered the causes which produce suicide among the Indians.

I reproached Wa-me-gon-a-biew for his conduct towards me, in unloading my gun, and taking away my ammunition, though it was probably done by the old woman. After I recovered my health more perfectly, I began to feel ashamed of this attempt, but my friends were so considerate as never to mention it to me. Though my health soon became good, I did not recover my hearing, and it was several months before I could hunt as well as I had been able to do previous to my sickness; but I was not among those who suffered most severely by this terrible complaint. Of the Indians who survived, some were permanently deaf, others injured in their intellects, and some, in the fury occasioned by the disease, dashed themselves against trees and rocks, breaking their arms, or otherwise maiming themselves. Most of those who survived, had copious discharges from the ears, or in the earlier stages had bled profusely from the nose. This disease was entirely new to the Indians, and they attempted to use few or no remedies for it.

On going to Mouse River trading-house, I heard that some white people from the United States had been there, to purchase some articles for the use of their party, then living at the Mandan village. I regretted that I had missed the opportunity of seeing them; but as I had received the impression that they were to remain permanently there, I thought I would take some opportunity to visit them. I have since been informed, that these white men were some of the party of Governor Clark and Captain Lewis, then on their way to the Rocky Mountains and the Pacific Ocean.

Late in the fall, we went to Ke-nu-kau-ne-she-way-bo-ant, where game was then plenty, and where we determined to spend the winter. Here, for the first time, I joined deeply with Wa-me-gon-a-biew and other Indians, in gambling, a vice scarce less hurtful to them than drunkenness. One of the games we used was that of the moccasin, which is played by any number of persons, but usually in small parties. Four moccasins are used, and in one of them some small object, such as a little stick, or a small piece of cloth, is hid by one of the betting parties. The moccasins are laid down beside each other, and one of the adverse party is then to touch two of the moccasins with his finger, or a stick. If the one he first touches has the hidden thing in it, the player loses eight to the opposite party; if it is not in the second he touches, but in one of the two passed over, he loses two. If it is not in the one he touches first, and is in the last, he wins eight. The Crees play this game differently, putting the hand successively into all the moccasins, endeavouring to come last to that which contains the article; but if the hand is thrust first into the one containing it, he loses eight. They fix the value of articles staked by agreement; for instance, they sometimes call a beaver skin, or a blanket, ten; sometimes a horse is one hundred. With strangers, they are apt to play high; in such cases, a horse is sometimes valued at ten.

But it is the game called Bug-ga-sauk, or Beg-ga-sah, that they play with the most intense interest, and the most hurtful consequences. The beg-ga-sah-nuk are small pieces of wood, bone, or sometimes of brass, made by cutting up an old kettle. One side they stain or colour black, the other they aim to have bright. These may vary in number, but can never be fewer than nine; they are put together into a large wooden bowl, or tray, kept for the purpose. The two parties, sometimes twenty or thirty, sit down opposite each other, or in a circle. The play consists in striking the edge of the bowl in such a manner as to throw all the beg-ga-sah-nuk into the air, and on the manner in which they fall into the tray depends his gain or loss. If his stroke has been to a certain extent fortunate, the player strikes again, and again, as in the game of billiards, until he misses, when it passes to the next. The parties soon become much excited, and a frequent cause of quarrelling is, that one often snatches the tray from his neighbour, before the latter is satisfied that the throw has been against him.

Old and sensible people among them are much opposed to this game, and it was never until this winter that Net-no-kwa suffered me to join in it. In the beginning, our party had some success, but we returned to it again and again, until we were stripped of every thing. When we had nothing more to lose, the band which had played against us removed and camped at a distance, and, as is usual, boasted much of their success. When I heard of this, I called together the men of our party, and proposed to them, that by way of making an effort to regain our lost property, and put an end to their insolent boasting, we would go and shoot at a mark with them. We accordingly raised some property among our friends, and went, in a body, to visit them. Seeing that we had brought something, they consented to play with us. So we set down to Beg-ga-sah, and in the course of the evening re-took as much of our lost property as enabled us to offer, next morning, a very handsome bet, on the result of a trial of shooting the mark. We staked every thing we could command; they were loath to engage us, but could not decently decline. We fixed a mark at the distance of one hundred yards, and I shot first, placing my ball nearly in the centre. Not one of either party came near me; of course I won, and we thus regained the greater part of what we had lost during the winter.

Late in the spring, when we were nearly ready to leave Ke-nu-kau-ne-she-way-bo-ant, an old man, called O-zhusk-koo-koon, (the muskrat's liver,) a chief of the Me-tai, came to my lodge, bringing a young woman, his grand-daughter, together with the girl's parents. This was a handsome young girl, not more than fifteen years old; but Net-no-kwa did not think favourably of her. She said to me, "My son, these people will not cease to trouble you, if you remain here; and as the girl is by no means fit to become your wife; I advise you to take your gun and go away. Make a hunting camp at some distance, and do not return till they have time to see that you are decidedly disinclined to the match." I did so, and O-zhusk-koo-koon apparently relinquished the hope of marrying me to his grand-daughter.

Soon after I returned, I was standing by our lodge one evening, when I saw a good looking young woman walking about and smoking. She noticed me from time to time, and at last came up and asked me to smoke with her. I answered, that I never smoked. "You do not wish to touch my pipe; for that reason you will not smoke with me." I took her pipe and smoked a little, though I had not been in the habit of smoking before. She remained some time, and talked with me, and I began to be pleased with her. After this we saw each other often, and I became gradually attached to her.

I mention this because it was to this woman that I was afterwards married, and because the commencement of our acquaintance was not after the usual manner of the Indians. Among them, it most commonly happens, even when a young man marries a woman of his own band, he has previously had no personal acquaintance with her. They have seen each other in the village; he has perhaps looked at her in passing, but it is probable they have never spoken together. The match is agreed on by the old people, and when their intention is made known to the young couple, they commonly find, in themselves, no objection to the arrangement, as they know, should it prove disagreeable mutually, or to either party, it can at any time be broken off.

My conversations with Mis-kwa-bun-o-kwa, (the red sky of the morning,) for such was the name of the woman who offered me her pipe, was soon noised about the village. Hearing it, and inferring, probably, that like other young men of my age, I was thinking of taking a wife, old O-zhusk-koo-koon came one day to our lodge, leading by the hand another of his numerous grand-daughters. "This," said he, to Net-no-kwa, "is the handsomest and the best of all my descendants; I come to offer her to your son." So saying, he left her in the lodge and went away. This young woman was one Net-no-kwa had always treated with unusual kindness, and she was considered one of the most desirable in the band. The old woman was now somewhat embarrassed; but at length she found an opportunity to say to me, "My son, this girl which O-zhusk-koo-koon offers you, is handsome, and she is good; but you must not marry her, for she has that about her which will, in less than a year, bring her to her grave. It is necessary that you should have a woman who is strong and free of any disease. Let us, therefore, make this young woman a handsome present, for she deserves well at our hands, and send her back to her father." She accordingly gave her goods to a considerable amount, and she went home.

Less than a year afterwards, according to the old woman's prediction, she died.

In the mean time, Mis-kwa-bun-o-kwa and myself were becoming more and more intimate. It is probable Net-no-kwa did not disapprove of the course I was now about to take, as, though I said nothing to her on the subject, she could not have been ignorant of what I was doing. That she was not I found, when after spending, for the first time, a considerable part of the night with my mistress, I crept into the lodge at a late hour, and went to sleep. A smart rapping on my naked feet waked me at the first appearance of dawn, on the following morning. "Up," said the old woman, who stood by me, with a stick in her hand, " up, young man, you who are about to take for yourself a wife, up, and start after game. It will raise you more in the estimation of the woman you would marry, to see you bring home a load of meat early in the morning, than to see you dressed ever so gaily, standing about the village after the hunters are all gone out." I could make her no answer, but, putting on my moccasins, took my gun and went out. Returning before noon, with as heavy a load of fat moose meat as I could carry, I threw it down before Net-no-kwa, and with a harsh tone of voice said to her, " here, old woman, is what you called for in the morning." She was much pleased, and commended me for my exertion. I now became satisfied that she was not displeased on account of my affair with Mis-kwa-bun-o-kwa, and it gave me no small pleasure to think that my conduct met her approbation. There are many of the Indians who throw away and neglect their old people; but though Net-no-kwa was now decrepid and infirm, I felt the strongest regard for her, and continued to do so while she lived.

I now redoubled my diligence in hunting, and commonly came home with meat in the early part of the day, at least before night. I then dressed myself as handsomely as I could, and walked about the village, sometimes blowing the Pe-be-gwun, or flute. For some time Mis-kwa-bun-o-kwa pretended she was not willing to marry me, and it was not, perhaps, until she perceived some abatement of ardour on my part, that she laid this affected coyness entirely aside. For my own part, I found that my anxiety to take a wife home to my lodge, was rapidly becoming less and less. I made several efforts to break off the intercourse, and visit her no more; but a lingering inclination was too strong for me. When she perceived my growing indifference, she sometimes reproached me, and sometimes sought to move me by tears and entreaties; but I said nothing to the old woman about bringing her home, and became daily more and more unwilling to acknowledge her publicly as my wife.

About this time, I had occasion to go to the trading-house on Red River, and I started in company with a half breed, belonging to that establishment, who was mounted on a fleet horse. The distance we had to travel has since been called, by the English settlers, seventy miles. We rode and went on foot by turns, and the one who was on foot kept hold of the horse's tail, and ran. We passed over the whole distance in one day. In returning, I was by myself, and without a horse, and I made an effort, intending, if possible, to accomplish the same journey in one day; but darkness, and excessive fatigue, compelled me to stop when I was within about ten miles of home.

When I arrived at our lodge, on the following day, I saw Mis-kwa-bun-o-kwa sitting in my place. As I stopped at the door of the lodge, and hesitated to enter, she hung down her head; but Net-no-kwa greeted me in a tone somewhat harsher than was common for her to use to me. "Will you turn back from the door of the lodge, and put this young woman to shame, who is in all respects better than you are. This affair has been of your seeking, and not of mine or hers. You have followed her about the village heretofore; now you would turn from her, and make her appear like one who has attempted to thrust herself in your way." I was, in part, conscious of the justness of Net-no-kwa's reproaches, and in part prompted by inclination; I went in and sat down by the side of Mis-kwa-bun-o-kwa, and thus we became man and wife. Old Net-no-kwa had, while I was absent at Red River, without my knowledge or consent, made her bargain with the parents of the young woman, and brought her home, rightly supposing that it would be no difficult matter to reconcile me to the measure. In most of the marriages which happen between young persons, the parties most interested have less to do than in this case. The amount of presents which the parents of a woman expect to receive in exchange for her, diminishes in proportion to the number of husbands she may have had.

CHAPTER VIII.

Preparations for a war excursion—herds of buffaloe heard at a great distance—terrible conflicts among the bulls—observances of the young warriors—Ko-zau-bun-zich-e-gun, or divination to discover the situation of an enemy—Jeebi-ug, or memorials of deceased friends to be thrown away on the field of battle; and the design of the custom—war-party broken up by the interference of a rival chief—stupidity of the porcupine—I save the life of my foster brother—Albino bears—Waw-be-no—marriage of Pi-che-to and Skwa-shish—attack of a Sioux war-party, and pursuit to the village at Chief Mountain, and the head of the St. Peters, &c.

Four days after I returned from Red River, we moved to the woods; Wa-me-gon-a-biew, with his two wives, and his family; Waw-be-be-nais-sa, with one wife and several children; myself and wife, and the family of Net-no-kwa. We directed our course towards the Craneberry River, [Pembinah,] as we wished to select near that place a favourable spot where our women and children might remain encamped, it being our intention to join a war-party then preparing to go against the Sioux. When we had chosen a suitable place, we applied ourselves diligently to hunting, that we might leave dry meat enough to supply the wants of our families in our absence. It happened, one morning, that I went to hunt with only three balls in my pouch; and finding a large buck moose, I fired at him rather hastily, and missed him twice in succession. The third time I hit, but did not kill him, only wounding him in the shoulder. I pursued, and at length overtook him, but having no balls, I took the screws out of my gun, tying the lock on with a string, and it was not till after I had shot three of them into him, that he fell.

We had killed a considerable quantity of meat, and the women were engaged in drying it, when, feeling curious to know the state of forwardness of the war-party at Pembinah, and how soon they would start, we took our horses and rode down, leaving Waw-be-be-nais-sa with the women. When we arrived we found forty men of the Muskegoes, ready to depart on the following morning, and though we had come without our moccasins, or any of the usual preparations, we determined to accompany them. Great numbers of Ojibbeways and Crees had assembled, but they seemed, in general, unwilling to accompany the Muskegoes, as this band is not in very high repute among them. Wa-me-gon-a-biew was willing to dissuade me from going, urging, that we had better put it off, and go with the Ojibbeways in the fall. But I assured him I would by no means lose the present opportunity, inasmuch as we could both go now and in the fall also.

By the end of the second day after we left Pembinah, we had not a mouthful to eat, and were beginning to be hungry. When we laid down in our camp at night, and put our ears close to the ground, we could hear the tramp of buffaloes; but when we sat up we could hear nothing, and on the following morning nothing could be seen of them, though we could command a very extensive view of the prairie. As we knew they must not be far off, in the direction of the sounds we had heard, eight men, of whom I was one, were selected and despatched to kill some, and bring the meat to a point where it was agreed the party should stop next night. The noise we could still hear in the morning, by applying our ears to the ground, and it seemed about as far distant, and in the same direction, as before. We started early, and rode some hours before we could begin to see them, and when we first discovered the margin of the herd, it must have been at least ten miles distant. It was like a black line, drawn along the edge of the sky, or a low shore seen across a lake. The distance of the herd from the place where we first heard them, could not have been less than twenty miles. But it was now the rutting season, and various parts of the herd were all the time kept in rapid motion, by the severe fights of the bulls. To the noise produced by the knocking together of the two divisions of the hoof, when they raised their feet from the ground, and of their incessant tramping, was added the loud and furious roar of the bulls, engaged as they all were in their terrific and appalling conflicts. We were conscious that our approach to the herd would not occasion the alarm now, that it would have done at any other time, and we rode directly towards them. As we came near, we killed a wounded bull, which scarce made an effort to escape from us. He had wounds in his flanks, into which I could put my whole hand. As we knew that the flesh of the bulls was not now good to eat, we did not wish to kill them, though we might easily have shot any number. Dismounting, we put our horses in the care of some of our number, who were willing to stay back for that purpose, and then crept into the herd to try to kill some cows. I had separated from the others, and advancing, got entangled among the bulls. Before I found an opportunity to shoot a cow, the bulls began to fight very near me. In their fury they were totally unconscious of my presence, and came rushing towards me with such violence, that in some alarm for my safety, I took refuge in one of those holes which are so frequent where these animals abound, and which they themselves dig to wallow in. Here I found that they were pressing directly upon me, and I was compelled to fire to disperse them, in which I did not succeed until I had killed four of them. By this firing the cows were so frightened that I perceived I should not be able to kill any in this quarter; so regaining my horse, I rode to a distant part of the herd, where the Indians had succeeded in killing a fat cow. But from this cow, as is usual in similar cases, the herd had all moved off, except one bull, who, when I came up, still kept the Indians at bay. " You are warriors," said I, as I rode up, " going far from your own country, to seek an enemy; but you cannot take his wife from that old bull, who has nothing in his hands." So saying, I passed them directly, towards the bull, then standing something more than two hundred yards distant. He no sooner saw me approach, than he came plunging towards me with such impetuosity, that knowing the danger to my horse and myself, I turned and fled. The Indians laughed heartily at my repulse, but they did not give over their attempts to get at the cow. By dividing the attention of the bull, and creeping up to him on different sides, they at length shot him down. While we were cutting up the cow, the herd were at no great distance, and an old cow, which the Indians supposed to be the mother of the one we had killed, taking the scent of the blood, came running with great violence directly towards us. The Indians were alarmed and fled, many of them not having their guns in their hands;

but I had carefully re-loaded mine, and had it ready for use. Throwing myself down close to the body of the cow, and behind it, I waited till the other came up within a few yards of the carcase, when I fired upon her; she turned, gave one or two jumps, and fell dead. We had now the meat of two fat cows, which was as much as we wanted; accordingly, we repaired without delay to the appointed place, where we found our party, whose hunger was already somewhat allayed by a deer one of them had killed.

I now began to attend to some of the ceremonies of what may be called the initiation of warriors, this being the first time I had been on a war-party. For the three first times that a man accompanies a war-party, the customs of the Indians require some peculiar and painful observances, from which old warriors may, if they choose, be exempted. The young warrior must constantly paint his face black; must wear a cap, or head dress of some kind; must never precede the older warriors, but follow them, stepping in their tracks. He must never scratch his head, or any other part of his body, with his fingers, but if he is compelled to scratch, he must use a small stick; the vessel he eats or drinks out of, or the knife he uses, must be touched by no other person. In the two last mentioned particulars, the observances of the young warriors are like those the females, in some bands, use during their earliest periods of menstruation. The young warrior, however long and fatiguing the march, must neither eat, nor drink, nor sit down by day; if he halts for a moment, he must turn his face towards his own country, that the Great Spirit may see that it is his wish to return home again.

At night, they observe a certain order in their encampments. If there are bushes where they halt, the camp is enclosed by these stuck into the ground, so as to include a square, or oblong space, with a passage, or door, in one end, which is always that towards the enemy's country. If there are not bushes, they mark the ground in the same manner, with small sticks, or the stalks of the weeds which grow in the prairie. Near the gate, or entrance to this camp, is the principal chief and the old warriors; next follow in order, according to age and reputation, the younger men; and last of all, in the extreme end of the camp, those with blacked faces, who are making their first excursion. All the warriors, both old and young, sleep with their faces towards their own country, and, on no consideration, however uneasy their position, or however great their fatigue, must make any change of attitude, nor must any two lie upon, or be covered by the same blanket. In their marches, the warriors, if they ever sit down, must not sit upon the naked ground, but must at least have some grass or bushes under them. They must, if possible, avoid wetting their feet; but if they are ever compelled to wade through a swamp, or to cross a stream, they must keep their clothes dry, and whip their legs with bushes or grass, when they come out of the water. They must never walk in a beaten path if they can avoid it; but if they cannot at all times, then they must put medicine on their legs, which they carry for that purpose. Any article belonging to any of the party, such as his gun, his blanket, tomahawk, knife, or war club, must not be stepped over by any other person, neither must the legs, hands, or body of any one who is sitting or lying on the ground. Should this rule be inadvertently violated, it is the duty of the one to whom the article stepped over may belong, to seize the other and throw him on the ground, and the latter must suffer himself to be thrown down, even should he be much stronger than the other. The vessels which they carry to eat out of, are commonly small bowls of wood, or of birch bark; they are marked across the middle, and the Indians have some mark by which they distinguish the two sides; in going out from home they drink invariably out of one side, and in returning, from the other. When on their way home, and within one day of the village; they suspend all these bowls on trees, or throw them away in the prairie.

I should have mentioned, that in their encampments at night, the chief who conducts the party, sends some of his young men a little distance in advance, to prepare what is called Pushkwawgumme-genahgun, the piece of cleared ground where the kozaubun-zichegun, or divination by which the position of the enemy is to be discovered, is to be performed. This spot of cleared ground is prepared by removing the turf from a considerable surface, in form of a parallelogram, and with the hands breaking up the soil, to make it fine and soft, and which is so inclosed with poles that none can step on it. The chief, when he is informed that the place is ready, goes and sits down at the end opposite that of the enemy's country; then, after singing and praying, he places before him, on the margin of the piece of ground, which may be compared to a bed in a garden, two small roundish stones. After the chief has remained here by himself for some time, entreating the Great Spirit to show him the path in which he ought to lead his young men, a crier goes to him from the camp, and then returning part way, he calls by name some of the principal men, saying, "come smoke." Others also, if they wish it, who are not called, repair to the chief, and they then examine, by striking a light, the result of the kozau-bun-zichegun. The two stones which the chief placed on the margin of the bed, have moved across to the opposite end, and it is from the appearance of the path they have left in passing over the soft ground, that they infer the course they are to pursue.

At this place of divination, the offerings of cloth, beads, and whatever other articles the chief and each man may carry for sacrifice, are exposed during the night on a pole; also, their je-bi-ug, or memorials of their dead friends, which are to be thrown away on the field of battle, or, if possible, thrust into the ripped up bowels of their enemies, who may fall in the fight. If a warrior has lost, by death, a favourite child, he carries, if possible, some article of dress, or perhaps some toy, which belonged to the child, or more commonly a lock of his hair, which they seek to throw away on the field of battle. The scouts who precede a war party into an enemy's country, if they happen, in lurking about their lodges, or in their old encampments, to discover any of the toys that have been dropped by the children, such as little bows, or even a piece of a broken arrow, pick it up, and carefully preserve it until they return to the party; then, if they know of a man who has lost his child, they throw it to him, saying, "your little son is in that place, we saw him playing with the children of our enemies, will you go and see him?" The bereaved father commonly takes it up, and having looked upon it awhile, falls to crying, and is then ready and eager to go against the enemy. An Indian chief, when he leads out his war party, has no other means of control over the individuals composing it, than his personal influence gives him; it is therefore necessary they should have some method of rousing and stimulating themselves to exertion.

A-gus-ko-gaut, the Muskego chief, whom we accompanied on

this occasion, called himself a prophet of the Great Spirit, like the one who appeared some years since among the Shawanees. He had, some time before, lost his son, and on this party he carried the jebi, with the determination of leaving it in a bloody field; but this design was frustrated by the interference of Ta-bush-shah,* (he that dodges down,) who now overtook us with twenty men. This restless and ambitious Ojibbeway, was unwilling that any but himself should lead a party against the Sioux; more particularly, that any of his own daring actions should be eclipsed by the prowess of so despised a people as the Muskegoes. But on first joining us, his professions manifested nothing unfriendly to our undertaking; on the contrary, he pretended he had come to aid his brethren, the Muskegoes. A-gus-ko-gaut could scarce have been ignorant of the feelings and intentions of Ta-bush-shah; but nevertheless, he received him with the utmost apparent cordiality and pleasure.

We journeyed on in company for some days, when in crossing some of the wide prairies, our thirst became so excessive that we were compelled to violate some of the rules of the war party. The principal men were acquainted with the general features of the country we had to pass, and knew that water could be found within a few miles of us, but most of the older warriors being on foot, were exhausted with fatigue and thirst. In this emergency, it became necessary that such of the party as had horses, among whom were Wa-me-gon-a-biew and myself, should go forward and search for water; and when it was found, make such a signal as would inform the main body what course to pursue. I was among the first to discover a place where water could be had; but before all the men could come up to it, the suffering of some of them had become excessive. Those who had arrived at the spring, continued to discharge their guns during the night, and the stragglers dropped in from different directions, some vomiting blood, and some in a state of madness.

As we rested at this spring, an old man called Ah-tek-oons, (the Little Caribou,) made a Kozau-bun-zichegun, or divination, and announced afterwards, that in a particular direction which he pointed out, was a large band of Sioux warriors, coming directly

---

* From *tub-buz-zeen*, imperative, "Do thou dodge down."

towards us; that if we could turn to the right or to the left, and avoid meeting them, we might proceed unmolested to their country, and be able to do some mischief to the women in their villages; but that if we suffered them to come upon us, and attack us, we should be cut off, to a man. Ta-bush-shah affected to place the most implicit reliance on this prediction; but the Muskegoe chief, and the Muskegoes generally, would not listen to it.

There was now an incipient murmur of discontent, and some few openly talked of abandoning A-gus-ko-gaut, and returning to their own country; but for some days nothing occurred, except the discovery, by some of our spies, of a single Indian, at a distance, who fled immediately on being seen, and was from that circumstance supposed to be one of a Sioux war party. One morning we came to a herd of buffaloe, and being without any food, several of the young men were dispersed about to kill some. We had now, since the discovery of the Sioux, been travelling only by night, keeping ourselves concealed in the day time. But the unguarded manner in which the Muskegoes suffered their young men to pursue the buffaloe, riding about in open day, and discharging their guns, afforded Ta-bush-shah an opportunity to effect what was probably the sole design of his journey, a disunion of the party, and eventually the frustration of all the designs of A-gus-ko-gaut.

Our camp being profusely supplied with meat, we had something like a general feast; the party was regularly and compactly arranged, and after they had eaten, Ta-bush-shah arose and harangued them in a loud voice. "You, Muskegoes," said he, "are not warriors, though you have come very far from your own country, as you say, to find the Sioux; but though hundreds of your enemies may be, and probably are, immediately about us, you can never find one of them, unless they fall upon you to kill you." In the close of his address, he expressed his determination to abandon the cause of a party so badly conducted, and return to his own country with his twenty men.

When he had spoken, Pe-zhew-o-ste-gwon, (the wild cat's head,) the orator of A-gus-ko-gaut, replied to him. "Now," said he, "we see plainly why our brothers, the Ojibbeways and Crees, were not willing to come with us from Red River. You are near your own country, and it is of little importance to you, whether you see the Sioux now, or in the fall; but we have come a very great distance; we bear with us, as we have long borne, those that were our friends and children, but we cannot lay them down, except we come into the camp of our enemies. You know well that in a party like this, large as it even now is, if only one turns back, another and another will follow, until none are left. And it is for this reason that you have joined us; that you may draw off our young men, and thus compel us to return without having done any thing." After he had spoken, Ta-bush-shah, without making any answer, rose, and turning his face towards his own country, departed with his twenty men. A-gus-ko-gaut, and the principal men of the Muskegoes, sat silently together, and saw one after another of their own young men get up and follow the Ojibbeways. In the first moments, this defection of Ta-bush-shah seemed to arouse some indignation in the breasts of some of the young Muskegoes, for they imprudently fired upon the rear of the retiring Ojibbeways; but though some of the latter turned to resent this treatment, their prudent leader repressed their ardour, and by so doing, gained the good will of those who might so readily have been rendered dangerous enemies. For the greater part of the day did A-gus-ko-gaut, and the few that remained firm to him, continue sitting upon the ground, in the same spot where he had listened to the speech of Ta-bush-shah; and when at last he saw his band diminished from sixty to five, the old man could not refrain from tears.

Wa-me-gon-a-biew had joined the deserting party, and at that time I had removed to a place a few rods distant from the chief, where I remained during the whole time. I now rejoined the chief, and told him, if he was willing to go on himself, I would accompany him, if no other would. The other three men who remained, being his personal friends, were willing to have gone on if he had wished it; but he said he feared we could do very little, being so few in number, and if the Sioux should discover us; we could not fail to be cut off. So the excursion was abandoned, and every man sought to return home by the most convenient and expeditious way, no longer paying the least regard to any thing except his own safety and comfort. I soon overtook Wa-me-gon-a-biew, and with three other men, we formed a party to return together. We chose, in our return, a route different from that taken by most of the party. Game was plenty, and we did not suffer from hunger. Early one morning, I was lying wrapped in my blanket by a deep buffaloe path, which came down through a prairie to the little creek where we were encamped. It was now late in the fall, and the thick and heavy grasses of these prairies, having long before been killed by the frosts, had become perfectly dry. To avoid burning the grass, we had kindled our little fire in the bottom of the deep path, where it passed through the corner of the bank. Some of the Indians had got up, and were sitting part on one and part on the other side of the path, preparing something for breakfast, when our attention was called to some unusual sound, and we saw a porcupine come walking slowly and slouchingly down the path. I had heard much of the stupidity of this animal, but never had an opportunity to witness it till now. On he came, without giving any attention to surrounding objects, until his nose was actually in the fire; then bracing stiffly back with his fore feet, he stood so near that the flame, when driven towards him by the wind, still singed the hairs on his face, for some minutes, stupidly opening and shutting his eyes. At length one of the Indians, tired of looking at him, hit him a blow in the face with a piece of moose meat he had on a little stick to roast. One of them then killed him with a tomahawk, and we ate some of the meat, which was very good. The Indians then, in conversation respecting the habits of this animal, related to me what I have since seen, namely: that as a porcupine is feeding in the night, along the bank of a river, a man may sometimes take up some of his food on the blade of a paddle, and holding it to his nose, he will eat it without ever perceiving the presence of the man. When taken, they can neither bite nor scratch, having no protection or defence except what is yielded them by their barbed and dangerous spines. Dogs can rarely, if ever, be urged to attack them; when they do, severe injury and suffering, if not death, is the certain consequence.

In four days after we started to return, we reached Large Wood River, which heads in a mountain, and running a long distance through the prairie, and ten miles under ground, empties into Red River. Below the place where it disappears under the prairie, it is called by another name, but it is no doubt the same river.

Here we killed one of the common red deer, like those of Kentucky, though this kind is not often seen in the north.

When I returned to my family, I had but seven balls left, but as there was no trader near, I could not at present get any more. With those seven I killed twenty moose and elk. Often times, in shooting an elk or a moose, the ball does not pass quite through, and may be used again.

Late in the fall, I went to the Mouse River trading house, to get some goods, and there Wa-me-gon-a-biew determined to go and live by himself, but Net-no-kwa preferred to live with me. Before Wa-me-gon-a-biew left me, we met at the Mouse River trading house some of the members of a family that in times long past, had quarrelled with the predecessors of Wa-me-gon-a-biew. They were part of a considerable band, strangers to us, and in themselves were far too powerful for us. We heard of their intention to kill Wa-me-gon-a-biew, and as we could not avoid being thrown more or less into their power, we thought best to conciliate their good will, or at least purchase their forbearance by a present. We had two kegs of whiskey, which we gave to the band, presenting one particularly to the head of the family who had threatened us. When they began to drink, I noticed one man, who, with great show of cordiality, invited Wa-me-gon-a-biew to drink, and pretended to drink with him. The more effectually to throw my brother off his guard; this man, in due time, began to act like a drunken man, though I could perceive he was perfectly sober, and knew that he had drank very little, if any thing, since we had been together. I had no difficulty to comprehend his intentions, and determined, if possible, to protect Wa-me-gon-a-biew from the mischief intended him. We had, with the hope of securing the friendship of the family of Crees, made our fire very near theirs, and as I found Wa-me-gon-a-biew becoming too drunk to have much discretion, I withdrew him to our camp. Here I had scarce laid him down, and thrown his blanket over him, when I found myself surrounded by the hostile family, with their guns and knives in their hands, and I heard them speak openly of killing my brother. Fortunately our present of spirits had nearly overcome the senses of all except the man I have before mentioned, and I regarded him as the most formidable among them. As two of them approached, apparently intending to stab Wa-me-gon-a-biew, I stepped between and prevented them; they then seized me by the arms, which I allowed them to hold without any resistance on my part, knowing that when about to stab me, they must let go at least with one hand each, and intending then to make an effort to escape from them. I grasped firmly in my right hand, and at the same time kept hid in the corner of my blanket, a large and strong knife, on which I placed great reliance. Very soon after they had seized me, the Indian on my left, still holding my left hand by his, raised his knife in his right to strike me in the ribs. His companion, who was somewhat drunk, having felt his belt for his own knife, found he had dropped it, and calling out to his companion to wait until he could find his knife, that he might help to kill me, quitted my right hand and went towards the fire, searching for it. This was my opportunity, and with a sudden spring I disengaged myself from the one who still held my left hand, and at the same time showing him a glimpse of my knife. I was now free, and might have secured my own safety by flight; but was determined not to abandon Wa-me-gon-a-biew, in a situation where I knew, for me to leave him, would be certain death. The Indians seemed for a moment astonished at my sudden resistance and escape, and not less so, when they saw me catch up the body of my drunken companion, and at two or three leaps, place him in a canoe on the beach. I lost no time in passing over the small distance between their camp and the trading house. Why they did not fire upon me, before I was out of the light of their camp fire, I cannot tell; perhaps they were somewhat intimidated at seeing me so well armed, so active, and so entirely sober; which last circumstance, gave me an evident advantage over most of them.

Shortly after this, Wa-me-gon-a-biew left me, acccording to his previous determination, and I went to live by myself, at a place on the Assinneboin River. I had been here but a few days, when A-ke-wah-zains, a brother of Net-no-kwa, came to stay at our lodge. He had not been long with us, when we one day discovered a very old man, in a small wooden canoe, coming up the river. A-ke-wah-zains immediately knew him to be the father of the men from whom I had so lately rescued Wa-me-gon-a-biew. The old man came promptly to the shore when called.

but it soon appeared that he was ignorant of what had passed between his children and us. A-ke-wah-zains, as he related these affairs to him, became excessively enraged, and it was not without difficulty I prevented him from murdering the helpless old man on the spot. I was content to suffer him to take part of the rum the old man had brought, and I assisted the latter to escape immediately, as I knew it would be unsafe for him to remain among us, after his liquor had begun to have its effect.

The same evening, A-ke-wah-zains asked me for my gun, which was a long, heavy, and very excellent one, in exchange for his, which was short and light. I was unwilling to exchange, though I did not as yet know how great was the disparity between the two pieces; and though Net-no-kwa was unwilling I should exchange, I did not know how to refuse the man's request, such a thing being almost unknown among the Indians of this country.

Shortly after this, I killed an old she bear, which was perfectly white. She had four cubs, one white, with red eyes, and red nails, like herself; one red, [brown?] and two black. In size, and other respects, she was the same as the common black bear, but she had nothing black about her except the skin of the lips. The fur of this kind is very fine, but not so highly valued by the traders as the red. The old one was very tame, and I killed her without difficulty; two of the young I shot in the hole, and two escaped into a tree. I had but just shot them, when there came along three men, attracted, probably, by the sound of my gun. As these men were very hungry, I took them home with me, fed them, and gave each of them a piece of meat to carry home. Next day, I chased another bear into a low poplar tree, when I became convinced of the worthlessness of the gun I had from A-ke-wah-zains, for I shot fifteen times without killing the bear, and was compelled, at last, to climb into the tree and put the muzzle of my gun close to his head, before I could kill him. A few days afterwards, as I was hunting, I started, at the same moment, an elk and three young bears, the latter running into a tree. I shot at the young bears, and two of them fell; as I thought one or both of them must be only wounded, I sprang immediately towards the root of the tree, but had scarce reached it, when I saw the old she bear come jumping in an opposite direction. She caught up the cub which had fallen nearest her, and raising it with her paws, while she stood on her hind feet, holding it as a woman holds her child; she looked at it for a moment, smelled the ball hole which was in its belly, and perceiving it was dead, dashed it down, and came directly towards me, gnashing her teeth, and walking so erect that her head stood as high as mine. All this was so sudden that I had scarce re-loaded my gun, having only time to raise it when she came within reach of the muzzle. I was now made to feel the necessity of a lesson the Indians had taught me, and which I very rarely neglected, namely, after discharging my gun, to think of nothing else before loading it again.

In about a month that I remained here, I killed, notwithstanding the poorness of my gun, twenty-four bears, and about ten moose. Having now a great deal of bear's fat, which we could not eat, I visited the sunjegwun I had made, where I killed the twenty moose, with seven balls, and put the fat into it. At length, when provisions became very scarce, I returned with my family to this place, expecting to live until spring on the meat I had saved; but I found that Wa-me-gon-a-biew, with his own family, and several others, had been there, broken it open, and taken away every pound of meat. Being thus reduced to the apprehension of immediate starvation, I was compelled to go in pursuit of buffaloe. Fortunately, the severity of the winter now drove these animals in towards the woods, and in a very few days I killed plenty of them. I was now joined by Wa-me-gon-a-biew and other Indians. We were encamped at a little grove of trees in the prairie. It happened one night, that the old woman, as well as several others of our family, dreamed of a bear close to our lodge. Next morning I searched for him, and found him in his hole. I shot him, and waiting a moment for the smoke to clear away, as I saw him lying at the bottom, I went down head foremost to draw him out. As my body partly filled the hole, and excluded the light, I did not perceive that he was alive until I laid my hand on him. He then turned and sprang upon me. I retreated as fast as I could, but all the way he was snapping his teeth so near me that I felt his breath warm on my face. He might have seized me at any moment, but did not. I caught my gun as I leaped from the mouth of the den, the bear pursuing me very closely. As soon as I thought I had gained a little distance, I fired behind me, and broke his jaw, and soon killed him. Afterwards I became more cautious about going down into bear's holes, before I had ascertained that the animals were dead. Late in winter, the buffaloe were so plenty about us, that we killed them with bows, and caught some of the younger ones with nooses of leather.

As the sugar season came on, we went to Pe-kau-kau-ne Sah-ki-e-gun, (Buffaloe Hump Lake,) two days' journey from the head of Pembinah River, to hunt beavers. We took our wives to the hunting grounds, but left old Net-no-kwa, with the children, to make sugar. It was now our object to kill beaver enough to enable us to purchase each a good horse, intending to accompany the war-party against the Sioux, the ensuing summer. In ten days I killed forty-two large and fine beavers, and Wa-me-gon-a-biew about as many. With these we repaired to the Mouse River trading-house, to buy horses. Mr. M'Kie had promised to sell me a very large and beautiful horse of his, which I had before seen, and I was much-dissatisfied when I found the horse had been sold to the North West Company. I told him, since the horse had gone to the north west, the beavers might go there also. So crossing to the other side, I bought a large gray mare for thirty beaver skins. This was, in some respects, as good a horse as the other, but it did not please me as well. Wa-me-gon-a-biew also bought a horse from the Indians, and then we returned to Great Wood River, to look for old Net-no-kwa; but she had gone to Red River, whither we followed her.

As we remained for some time at the mouth of the Assinneboin, many Indians gathered around us, and among others, several of my wife's relatives, whom I had not before seen. Among these was an uncle, who was a cripple, and had not for years been able to walk. As he had only heard that I was a white man, he supposed that I could not hunt. When he saw my wife, he said to her, " Well, my daughter, I hear you are married ; does your husband ever kill any game ?" " Yes," said she, " if a moose or an elk has lost his road, or wants to die, and comes and stands in his path, he will sometimes kill him." " He has gone to hunt to-day, has he not ? If he kills any thing I shall go and bring it in, and you will give me the skin to make some moccasins." This he said in derision, but I gave him the skin of the elk I killed that day, to make his moccasins, and continuing to be successful, I gave game to all my wife's relatives, and soon heard no more of their ridicule. After some time, the game was exhausted, and we found it necessary to disperse in various directions. I went about ten miles up the Assinneboin, where we found two lodges, under a man called Po-ko-taw-ga-maw, (the little pond.) These people were relatives of my wife. When we first arrived, the wife of Po-ko-taw-ga-maw happened to be cooking a moose's tongue for her husband, who had not yet returned from hunting. This she gave us immediately, and would, perhaps, have farther relieved our distress, had not the man then arrived. After this, they gave us nothing, though our little children were crying for hunger, and they had plenty of meat about their lodge. It was now too late, and I too much fatigued to go a hunting that evening; nevertheless, I would not suffer the women to buy meat from them, as they wished to do. At the earliest appearance of dawn, on the ensuing morning, I took my gun, and standing at the door of my lodge, I said purposely in a loud voice, " Can none but Po-ko-taw-ga-maw kill elks ?" My wife came out of my lodge, and handed me a piece of dried meat, about as large as my hand, which she said her sister had stolen to give to her. By this time, many of the people had come out of the lodges, and I threw the piece of meat from me, among the dogs, saying, "Shall such food as this be offered to my children, when there are plenty of elks in the woods ?" Before noon I had killed two fat elks, and returned to my lodge with a heavy load of meat. I soon killed great numbers of buffaloes, and we dispersed ourselves about to make dry meat, prepatory to leaving our families to go on the proposed war-party. We then returned to the woods, to select some good elk and moose skins, for moccasins. The skins of animals living in the open prairies are tender, and do not make good leather.

As we were one day travelling through the prairie, we looked back, and saw at a distance a man loaded with baggage, and having two of the large Ta-wa-e-gun-num, or drums used in the ceremonies of the Waw-be-no. We looked to our young women for an explanation, as we soon recognised the approaching traveller to be no other than Pich-e-to, one of the band of inhospitable relatives we had lately left. The face of Skwaw-shish, the Bow-we-tig girl, betrayed the consciousness of some knowledge respecting the motives of Pich-e-to.

At this time, the Waw-be-no was fashionable among the Ojibbeways, but it has ever been considered by the older and more respectable men, as a false and dangerous religion. The ceremonies of the Waw-be-no differ very essentially from those of the Metai, and are usually accompanied by much licentiousness and irregularity. The Ta-wa-e-gun used for a drum in this dance, differs from the Woin Ah-keek, or Me-ti-kwaw-keek, used in the Me-tai, it being made of a hoop of bent wood, like a soldier's drum, while the latter is a portion of the trunk of a tree, hollowed by fire, and having the skin tied over it. The Shezhe-gwun, or rattle, differs, also, in its construction from that used in the Metai. In the Waw-be-no, men and women dance and sing together, and there is much juggling and playing with fire. The initiated take coals of fire, and red hot stones, in their hands, and sometimes in their mouths. Sometimes they put powder on the insides of their hands, first moistening them, to make it stick; then by rubbing them on coals, or a red hot stone, they make the powder burn. Sometimes one of the principal performers at a Waw-be-no, has a kettle brought and set down before him, which is taken boiling from the fire, and before it has time to cool, he plunges his hands to the bottom, and brings up the head of the dog, or whatever other animal it may be which had been purposely put there. He then, while it remains hot, tears off the flesh with his teeth, at the same time singing and dancing madly about. After devouring the meat, he dashes down the bone, still dancing and capering as before. They are able to withstand the effects of fire and of heated substances, by what they would persuade the ignorant to be a supernatural power; but this is nothing else than a certain preparation, effected by the application of herbs, which make the parts to which they are applied, insensible to fire. The plants they use are the Wa-be-no-wusk, and Pe-zhe-ke-wusk; the former grows in abundance on the island of Mackinac, and is called yarrow by the people of the United States; the other grows only in the prairies. These they mix and bruise, or chew together, and rub over their hands and arms. The Waw-be-no-wusk, or yarrow, in the form of a poultice, is an excellent remedy for burns, and is much used by the Indians; but the two, when mixed together, seem to give to the skin, even of the lips and tongue, an astonishing power of resisting the effects of fire.

Pich-e-to, with his two Ta-wa-e-guns, at length came up, and stopped with us.. Old Net-no-kwa was not backward about inquiring his business, and when she found that his designs extended no farther than to the Bow-we-tig girl, she gave her consent to the match, and married them immediately. Next morning, Waw-be-be-nais-sa, who, as well as Wa-me-gon-a-biew, had come with me from the mouth of the Assinneboin, killed a buck elk, and I a moose. I now made a change in my manner of hunting, which contributed much towards the skill I finally acquired. I resolved that I would, whenever it was possible, even at the expense of the greatest exertions, get every animal I should shoot at. When I came to look upon it as necessary that I should kill every animal I shot at, I became more cautious in my approaches, and more careful never to fire until my prospect of being able to kill was good. I made this resolution in the spring, and hunted much, and killed many animals during the summer; I missed only two that I fired at. It requires much skill, and great caution, to be able to kill moose at all, particularly in summer. As I began to be considered a good hunter, Waw-be-be-nais-sa became envious of my success, and often, when I was absent, he went slily into my lodge, and bent my gun, or borrowed it under pretence of his own being out of repair, and returned it to me bent, or otherwise injured.

Very early in the spring, we had much severe thunder and lightning. One night, Pich-e-to becoming much alarmed at the violence of the storm, got up and offered some tobacco to the thunder, intreating it to stop. The Ojibbeways and Ottawwaws believe that thunder is the voice of living beings, which they call An-nim-me-keeg.* Some considering them to be like men, while others say they have more resemblance to birds. It is doubtful whether they are aware of any necessary connexion between the thunder and the lightning which precedes it. They

---

* *An-nim-me-keeg wus-re-tah goos-e-wuk,* (Ottawwaw,) it thunders.—*Na-mah-kc-wuk kau-ke-to-wuk,* (Menomine,) it thunders.—They are both, however, plural nominations, and have verbs in the plural.

think the lightning is fire, and many of them will assert, that by searching in the ground, at the root of the tree that has been struck, immediately after the flash, a ball of fire may be found. I have myself many times sought for this ball, but could never find it. I have traced the path of the lightning along the wood, almost to the end of some large root, but where it disappeared I was never able to find any thing more in the soil than what belonged there. After the storm which I first mentioned, we found in the morning an elm tree still burning, which had been set on fire by the lightning. The Indians have a superstitious dread of this fire, and none of them would go to bring some of it, to replace ours, which had been extinguished by the rain. I at last went and brought some of it, though not without apprehension. I had fewer fears than the Indians, but I was not entirely free from the same unfounded apprehensions which so constantly pursue them.

After we had killed and dried large quantities of meat, we erected a sunjegwun, or a scaffold, where we deposited as much as we thought would supply the wants of our women in our absence. Before we had entirely finished the preparations for our journey, we were fallen upon by a war-party of about two hundred Sioux, and some of our people killed. A small party of Assinneboins and Crees had already gone out towards the Sioux country, and falling, by accident, on the trace of this war-party of two hundred, had dogged them for some time, coming repeatedly near enough to see the crane's head, used by their chief instead of stones, in the Ko-sau-bun-zitch-e-gun, or nightly divination, to discover the position of the enemy. This little band of Crees and Assinneboins, had not courage enough to fall upon the Sioux, but they sent messengers to the Ojibbeways, by a circuitous route. These came to the lodge of the principal chief of the Ojibbeways, who was hunting in advance of his people; but this man scorned to betray fear. By retreating immediately to the trader's fort, he might have escaped the threatening danger. He made his preparations to move, but his old wife, being jealous of the younger one, which was now in higher favour than herself, reproached him, and complained that he had given more to the young woman than to her. He said to her, "You have for a long time annoyed me with your jealousy, and your complaints; but I shall hear no more of it. The Sioux are near, and I shall wait for them." He accordingly remained, and continued hunting. Early one morning, he went up into an oak tree that stood near his lodge, to look out over the prairie for buffaloe, and in descending he was shot from below by two young men of the Sioux, that had been concealed there great part of the night. It is probable they would have fallen upon him sooner, but for fear. Now the trampling of horses was heard, and the men who were with the chief had scarce time to run out of the lodge, when the two hundred Sioux, on their horses, were at the door. One of the two runners who had come forward, and had been concealed in the hazle bushes, was an uncle of Wah-ne-taw,* at present a well known chief of the Yanktongs, and the party was led by his father. Wah-ne-taw himself was of the party, but was then less distinguished than he has since become. The fight continued during the day; all the Ojibbeways, about twenty in number, being killed, except Aisainse, (the little clam,) a brother of the chief, two women, and one child.

Mr. H., the trader at Pembinah, gave the Ojibbeways a ten gallon keg of powder, and one hundred pounds of balls, to pursue after the party that had killed the chief, his father-in-law. Of the four hundred men that started, one hundred were Assinneboins, the remaining three hundred Crees and Ojibbeways, with some Muskegoes. In the course of the first day after we left Pembinah, about one hundred Ojibbeways deserted and went back. In the following night, the Assinneboins left in considerable numbers, having stolen many horses, and, among others, four belonging to me and Wa-me-gon-a-biew. I had taken but seven pairs of moccasins, having intended to make the whole journey on horse back, and it was now a great misfortune for me to lose my horses. I went to Pe-shau-ba, who was chief of the band of Ottowwaws, to which I belonged, and told him that I wished to make reprisals from the few Assinneboins still belonging to our party; but he would not consent, saying, very

* The name of this distinguished chief is spelt in "Major Long's Second Expedition," *Wa-no-tan.* To an English reader, this orthography conveys as incorrect an idea of the sound of his name, as the engraved portrait in that work, does of his handsome face and person.

justly, that the dissension growing out of such a measure, on my part, might lead to quarrels, which would entirely interrupt and frustrate the designs of the whole party. His advice, though I knew it to be good, as far as the interest of the whole was concerned, did nothing to remove my private grievances, and I went from one to another of the Ottawwaws, and those whom I considered my friends among the Ojibbeways, and endeavoured to persuade them to join me in taking horses from the Assinneboins. None would consent, but a young man called Gish-kau-ko, a relative of him by whom I was taken prisoner. He agreed to watch with me the thirteen Assinneboins remaining with our party, and, if an opportunity offered, to assist in taking horses from them. Soon after, I saw eight of these men lingering in the encampment one morning, and I believed it was their intention to turn back. I called Gish-kau-ko to watch them with me, and when most of the Ojibbeways had left the camp, we saw them get on their horses, and turn their faces towards home. We followed after them, though they were well armed. As we knew we could not take their horses by violence, we threw down our arms in our camp, and followed them with nothing in our hands. One of them stopped some distance in the rear of the retiring party, and dismounted, to hold a parley with us; but they were too wary and cautious to give us any opportunity of taking their horses. We tried entreaties, and at last, as I saw there was no hope, I told them their five companions that were left in our camp, would not be safe among us; but this, instead of having any good effect, only induced them to send a messenger on their swiftest horse, to warn those men to beware of me.

We returned to the main party on foot, and took the first opportunity to visit the camp of the five remaining Assinneboins; but they were notified of our approach, and fled with their horses. At a lake near Red River, we found hanging on a tree in the woods, the body of a young Sioux, called the Red Thunder. We were now on the path of the retiring war-party, which had killed our chief, and to which this young man had belonged. The Ojibbeways threw down the body, beat, kicked, and scalped it. Pe-shau-ba forbade me and the other young men of his party, to join the Ojibbeways in these unmanly outrages. Not far from this place we found a prisoner's pole, where they had danced some prisoners, which first convinced us that some of our friends had been taken alive. The trail of the party was still recent, and we thought ourselves but two or three days behind them.

At Lake Traverse, our number had diminished to one hundred and twenty; of these, three men were half breed Assinneboins, about twenty Crees, and as many Ottawwaws, the rest Ojibbeways. Many of the party had been discouraged by unfavourable divinations; among others, one by Pe-shau-ba, the Ottawwaw chief, made on the first night after we left Pembinah. He told us, that in his dream he saw the eyes of the Sioux, like the sun; they saw every where, and always discovered the Ojibbeways before the latter came near enough to strike them; also, that he had seen all our party returning, unharmed, and without scalps; but he said, that on the left hand side of Lake Traverse, opposite our road, he saw two lodges of Sioux by themselves, which he intended to visit on his return.

Due west from Lake Traverse, and at the distance of two days' travel, is a mountain, called O-ge-mah-wud-ju, (chief mountain,) and near this is the village to which the party we were pursuing belonged. As we approached this mountain, we moved in a more cautious and guarded manner, most commonly lying hid in the woods during the day, and travelling at night. When at last we were within a few miles, we halted in the middle of the night, and waited for the approach of the earliest dawn, the time the Indians commonly choose for an attack. Late in the night, a warrior of high reputation, called the Black Duck, took the reins of his horse's bridle in his hand, and walked on towards the village, allowing me to accompany him. We arrived at early dawn, at the little hill which sheltered our approach from the village. Raising his head cautiously, the Black Duck saw two men walking at some distance before him. He then descended the hill a little, and tossing his blanket in a peculiar manner, made a signal to the Ojibbeways to rush on. Then followed tearing off of leggins, stripping off of blankets, and in an instant the whole band leaped naked to the feet of the Black Duck; and now they moved silently, but swiftly, over the crest of the hill, and stood upon the site of the village. The two men, when they discovered the war-party, instead of flying, came deliberately towards them, and presently stood before the leaders—two of the young men of their own band. They had left the party when they halted, and, without giving notice of their intention, gone forward to reconnoitre what they supposed to be the position of the enemy; but they found the camp had been deserted many hours before, and when the party came up they were walking about, and scaring away the wolves from among the rubbish. The Sas-sah-kwi, or war whoop, was raised by the whole band, as they rushed up. This loud and piercing shout intimidates and overcomes the weak, or those who are surprised without arms in their hands, while it rouses the spirit of such as are prepared for battle. It has also, as I have seen in many instances, a surprising effect upon animals. I have seen a buffaloe so frightened by it as to fall down in his steps, being able neither to run, nor to make resistance; and a bear, at hearing it, is sometimes so terror-stricken, as to quit his hold, and fall from the tree in utter helplessness. The chiefs whom we followed, were not willing to relinquish the objects of the journey, and we still followed, from day to day, along the recent trail of the Sioux. We found, at each of their encampments, the place of their ko-sau-bun-zitch-e-gun, from the appearance of which we were able to infer, that they knew accurately our position, from day to day. There was now manifest among the young men of our party, a prevailing disposition to desert. This the chiefs laboured to prevent, by appointing certain persons, whom they could trust, to act as sentinels, both in the encampments and during the marches; but this measure, though often tried, is always so far from being effectual, that it seems greatly to increase the number of desertions, perhaps because the young men despise the idea of restraint of any kind. They, on this occasion, became more and more restless and troublesome, after we had crossed over to the head of the river St. Peters, in pursuit of the Sioux. The traders have a fort somewhere on the upper part of this river, to which the Sioux had fled. When we arrived within a day's march of this place, fear and hesitancy became manifest nearly throughout the band. The chiefs talked of sending young men forward to examine the position of the enemy; but no young men offered themselves for the undertaking.

We remained some time stationary, and the opportunity was taken to supply the wants of some who were deficient in moccasins, or other important articles. Any man who is on a war party, and whose supply of moccasins, or of powder and ball, or any other common and necessary article, has failed, takes a little of what he stands in need, and if it be moccasins, he takes a single moccasin in his hand, and walks about the encampment, pausing a moment before such of his companions as he hopes will supply his demand. He has no occasion to say any thing, as those who happen to have plenty of the article he wants, are commonly ready to furnish him. Should this method fail, the chief of the party goes from one man to another, and from those who have the greatest quantity, he takes as much as may be necessary, of the article required. He is, on these occasions, dressed as for battle, and accompanied by two or three young warriors.

After a delay of two days, on that part of our path nearest the Sioux trader's fort, we all turned back: but not entirely relinquishing the object of our journey, we returned to the vicinity of the village at the Chief Mountain, hoping we might find some of our enemies there. We had many horses, and the young men rode so recklessly and noisily about, that there was no chance of coming near them. After leaving Chief Mountain, and proceeding some distance into the plain, in our way towards home, we found we were followed by a party of about one hundred Sioux.

At the Gaunenoway, a considerable river which heads in the Chief Mountain, and runs into Red River, several days' journey from Lake Traverse, Pe-shau-ba quarrelled with an Ojibbeway called Ma-men-o-guaw-sink, on account of a horse I had taken from some Crees who were the friends of the Assinneboins, by whom I had long before been robbed of mine. This man having killed a Cree, was now anxious to do something to gain friends among that people. It happened that Pe-shau-ba and myself were travelling together, at a little distance from the main body, and I was leading the horse I had taken, when Ma-me-no-guaw-sink came up to us, accompanied by a few friends, and demanded the horse. Pe-shau-ba, cocking his gun, placed the muzzle of it to his heart, and so intimidated him by threats and reproaches, that he desisted. The Ottawwaws, to the number of ten, now stopped, Pe-shau-ba remaining at their head, and fell in the rear of the main body, in order to avoid farther trouble on account of this horse, all of them being apparently unwilling that I should relinquish it.

There were four men of this war party, who walked, in six days, from the Chief Mountain to Pembinah; but our band, though many of us had horses, took ten days to travel the same distance. One of the four was an old man, an Ottawwaw, of Wau-gun-uk-kezze, or L'Arbre Croche. When I arrived at Pembinah, I found my family had gone down to the mouth of the Assinneboin. After the separation of our party, most of my particular friends having left my route at Pembinah, my horse was stolen from me at night. I knew who had taken him, and as the man was encamped at no great distance, I took my arms in my hands, and went in the morning to retake him; but on my way I met Pe-shau-ba, who, without a word of enquiry, comprehended my purpose, and peremptorily forbade me to proceed. Pe-shau-ba was a good man, and had great influence with the people of his band. I might have gone on to take my horse, contrary to his positive injunction, but I did not choose to do so, and therefore returned with him on my way. I had now no moccasins, and felt so much irritated on account of the loss of my horse, that I could not eat. When I arrived at home, in two day's walk from Pembinah, I found I was worn out with fatigue, my feet swollen and raw, and I found my family starving. Three months I had been absent, my time having been occupied in long and toilsome marches, all resulting in nothing.

It was necessary for me to go to hunt immediately, although the condition of my feet was such, that I could not stand without great pain, and I had the good fortune to kill a moose the first time I went out, on the morning after my return. The same day snow fell about two feet deep, which enabled me to kill game in great plenty.

CHAPTER IX.

Visit to several Assinneboin villages, in pursuit of stolen horses—peculiar customs—I seize a horse belonging to an Assinneboin—war excursion to Turtle Mountain—battle at a village of the Mandans—doctrines of the Shawnese prophet—drunkenness, and its effects.

I HAD been at home but a short time, when I heard that the Assinneboins had boasted of taking my horse. As I was preparing to go in pursuit of them, an Ojibbeway, who had often tried to dissuade me from any attempt to recover him, gave me a horse, on condition that I would not attempt to retake my own; accordingly, for some time, I said no more about it.

Having spent the winter at the mouth of the Assinneboin, I went to make sugar at Great Wood River; but here it was told me that the Assinneboins were still boasting of having taken my horse from me; and I, with some persuasion, prevailed upon Wa-me-gon-a-biew to accompany me in an attempt to recover him. At the end of four day's journey, we came to the first Assinneboin village, ten miles from the Mouse River trading house. This village consisted of about thirty leather lodges. We were discovered before we came to the village, as the Assinneboins, being a revolted band of the Sioux, and in alliance with the Ojibbeways, are in constant apprehension of attacks from the former, and therefore always station some persons to watch for the approach of strangers. The quarrel which resulted in the separation of this band of the Bwoif-nug, or "roasters," as the Ojibbeways call the Sioux, originated in a dispute concerning a woman, and happened, as we are informed, not many years ago. So many Ojibbeways and Crees now live among them, that they are most commonly able to understand something of the Ojibbeway language, though their own dialect is very unlike it, resembling closely that of the Sioux.

One of the men who came out to meet us, was Ma-me-nokwaw-sink, with whom Pe-shau-ba had quarrelled, some time before, on my account. When he came up to us, he asked whither we were going. I told him, "I am come for our horses, which the Assinneboins stole." "You had better," said he, "return as you came, for if you go to the village, they will take your life." To these threats I paid no attention, but enquired for Ba-gis-kun-nung, the men of whose family had taken our horses. They replied they could not tell; that Ba-gis-kun-nung and his sons had, soon after the return of the war party, gone to the Mandans, and had not yet come back; that when they came among the Mandans, the former owner of my mare, recognizing the animal, had taken her from the son of Ba-gis-kun-nung; but that the latter contrived to remunerate himself, by stealing a fine black horse, with which he escaped, and had not been heard of since. Wa-me-gon-a-biew being discouraged, and perhaps intimidated by the reception we met in this village, endeavoured to dissuade me from going farther; and when he found he could not prevail, he left me to pursue my horse by myself, and returned home. I would not be discouraged, but determined to visit every village and camp of the Assinneboins, rather than return without my horse. I went to the Mouse River trading house, and having explained the object of my journey, they gave me two pounds of powder and thirty balls, with some knives and small articles, and directions to enable me to find the next village. As I was pursuing my journey by myself, I had occasion to cross a very wide prairie, in which I discovered at a distance, something lying on the ground, resembling a log of wood. As I knew there could be no wood in such a place, unless it were dropped by some person, I thought it was most probably some article of dress, or perhaps the body of a man, who might have perished on a journey, or when out hunting. I made my approach cautiously, and at length discovered it was a man, lying on his belly, with his gun in his hands, and waiting for wild geese to fly over. His attention was fixed in the direction opposite that on which I approached, and I came very near him without being discovered, when he rose and discharged his gun at a flock of geese. I now sprang upon him; the noise of hawk bells, and the silver ornaments of my dress, notified him of my approach, but I caught him in my arms before he had time to make any resistance, his gun being unloaded. When he saw himself captured, he cried out "Assinneboin," and I answered, "Ojibbeway." We were both glad to find that we could treat each other as friends; and though we could not converse, on account of the dissimilarity of our dialects, I motioned to him to sit down upon the ground beside me, with which request he immediately complied. I gave him a goose I had killed not long before, and after resting for a few moments, signified to him that I would accompany him to his lodge. A walk of about two hours, brought us in sight of his village, and when we entered it, I followed him immediately to his lodge. As I entered after him, I saw the old man and woman cover their heads with their blankets, and my companion immediately entered a small lodge, merely large enough to admit one, and to conceal him from the remainder of the family. Here he remained, his food being handed to him by his wife; but though secluded from sight, he maintained, by conversation, some intercourse with those without. When he wished to pass out of the lodge, his wife gave notice to her parents, and they concealed their heads, and again, in the same manner, when he came in.

This formality is strictly observed by the married men among the Assinneboins, and I believe among all the Bwoi-nug, or Dah-ko-tah, as they call themselves. It is known to exist among the Omowhows of the Missouri. It affects not only the intercourse between men and the parents of their wives, but that with their aunts and uncles; and it is the business of all parties alike, to avoid seeing each other. If a man enters a dwelling in which his son-in-law is seated, the latter conceals his face until he departs. While the young men remain with the parents of their wives, they have a little separate lodge within, or a part divided off by suspending mats or skins; and into this little apartment the wife retires at night; by day she is the organ of communication with those without. A man rarely, if ever, mentions the name of his father-in-law, and it is considered highly indecorous and disrespectful for him to do so. This custom does not exist in any shape among the Ojibbeways, and they look upon it as a very foolish and troublesome one.

The people of this lodge treated me with much kindness. Notwithstanding the great scarcity of corn in the country, they had a little reserved, which they cooked and gave me. The young man told them how much he had been frightened by me in the prairie, at which they all laughed heartily. This village consisted of twenty-five lodges; but although I inquired of many of them, none knew where Ba-gis-kun-nung was to be found. There was another village at the distance of about one day's journey: he might be there. I remained a little while at the lodge of the young man I had found in the prairie, and then went out to start for the next village. Geese were flying over, and I raised my gun and shot one. It fell in the midst of a number of Assinneboins. Seeing there a very old and miserable looking man, I motioned to him to go and get it. But he must first come up to me to express his gratitude, by a method I had not before seen used. He came up, and placing both hands on the top of my head, passed them several times down the long hair that hung over my shoulders, at the same time saying something in his own language, which I could not understand. He then went and took up the goose, and returning, communicated to me by signs which I had no difficulty to understand, that I must go to his lodge and eat with him, before I could leave the village. While he was cooking the goose, I went about from lodge to lodge, to look at their horses, thinking I might see mine among them, but I did not. Some of the young men of the village accompanied me, but without any arms, and all seemed friendly; but when I was ready to start for the next village, I noticed that one of them, mounted on a fleet horse, started to precede me.

When I arrived at this village, no one took the slightest notice of me, or even seemed to see me. They were a band with which I had previously had no acquaintance, and I could perceive that they had been prejudiced against me. Their chief, whom we used to call Kah-oge-maw-weet Assinneboin, (the chief Assinneboin,) was a distinguished hunter, but he was soon afterwards killed. He had been unusually long absent from home, and by following his track, they found he had been attacked by a grizzly bear in the prairie, and killed.

Finding the people of this band decidedly unfriendly, I went into none of their lodges, but stood about, watching their horses, to see if I could discover mine among them. I had heard much of the fleetness and beauty of a young horse belonging to the chief, and I soon recognized this animal, known to me only by description. I had a halter under my blanket, and watching a favourable opportunity, I slipped it on the head of this horse, mounted him, and flew rather than fled. I was excited to this action, principally by a feeling of irritation at the unfriendly conduct of the people of the village, as it had not been my intention to take any horse but the one which belonged to me. When the horse and myself were out of breath, I stopped to look back, and the Assinneboin lodges were scarce visible, like little specks on the distant prairie. I now reflected that I was doing wrong, to steal away the favourite horse of a man who had never absolutely injured me, though he had refused the customary dues of hospitality towards a stranger. I got down and left the horse, but had scarce done so, when I saw thirty or forty men on horseback, who had before been concealed in a depression in the prairie: they were in pursuit, and very near me. I had scarce time to fly to a thicket of low hazel bushes, when they were upon me. They rode about for some time on horseback searching, and this delay gave me some little time to choose a place of concealment. At length they dismounted, and dispersed themselves in various directions, seeking for me. Some came near me, and then turned off to search in other directions. My position was such that I could watch their motions without the risk of exposing myself. One young man stripped himself as for battle, sung his war song, laid aside his gun, and came with only his war club directly towards the spot where I lay. He was within about twenty steps of me, my gun was cocked and aimed at his heart, when he turned and went back. It is not probable he saw me; but the idea of being watched by an unseen enemy armed with a gun, and whose position he could not hope to ascertain until he was almost over him, probably overcame his resolution. They continued their unavailing search until near night, and then returned, taking the chief's horse to their village.

I travelled towards home, rejoicing in my escape, and without stopping for the night, either on that or the succeeding one, and the third night arrived at the Mouse River trading house. The traders told me I was a fool that I had not brought the chief's horse; they had heard much of his qualities, and would, as they said, have paid me a high price for him.

In the Assinneboin village, ten miles from this trading house,

I had a friend called Be-na, (pheasant,) and when I had passed through I requested him, while I should be absent, to endeavour to discover my horse, or at least to ascertain, and be able to tell me, where I could find Ba-gis-kun-nung. When I returned thither, after visiting Mouse River trading house, Be-na took me immediately into a lodge where a couple of old women lived, and looking through the crevices, he pointed out to me the lodge of Ba-gis-kun-nung, and those of his four sons. Their horses were feeding about, and among them we distinguished the fine black one they had brought from the Mandans in place of mine.

Wa-me-gon-a-biew had been to the trading house, but returned thence to the village before I arrived, and was now waiting for me at the lodge of some of the sons of a brother of Taw-ga-we-ninne, who were of course his cousins, and were very friendly to him. He had sent messengers to Ba-gis-kun-nung, offering him a good gun, a chief's coat, and all the property he had about him, for a horse to ride home on. But when I heard this, I reproved him severely, and told him that if Ba-gis-kun-nung had accepted his presents, it would only have occasioned additional trouble to me, as I should have been compelled to take not only a horse, but those presents also.

Soon after my arrival in the village, I went to Ba-gis-kun-nung, and said to him, "I want a horse." "I shall not give you one," he answered. "I will take one from you." "If you do I will shoot you." With this I returned to the lodge of Be-na, and made my preparations for starting at an early hour in the morning. Be-na gave me a new buffaloe robe to ride home on, and I got from an old woman, a piece of leather thong for a halter, having left mine on the chief's horse. I did not sleep in Be-na's lodge, but with our cousins, and very early in the morning, as I was ready to start, I went to Be-na's lodge, but he was not awake. I had a very good new blanket, which I spread over him without making any noise; then, together with Wa-me-gon-a-biew, I started. When we came in sight of the lodge of Ba-gis-kun-nung, we saw the eldest of his sons sitting on the outside, and watching the horses. Wa-me-gon-a-biew endeavoured to dissuade me from the design of attempting to take one, since we could not do it without being seen, and had every reason to believe they were prepared to use violent measures to prevent us from succeeding in the attempt. I told him I would not listen to his advice, but consented to go with him two hundred yards on our road, and lay down our baggage; then we were to return together, and take the horse. When we had proceeded as far as I thought necessary, I laid down my load; but Wa-me-gon-a-biew, seeing me resolute in my determination, began to run. At the same time that he started to run from the village, I ran towards it, and the son of Ba-gis-kun-nung, when he saw me coming, began to call out as loud as he could in his own language. I could only distinguish the words "Wah-kah-towah," and "Shoonk-ton-gah," (Ojibbeway—horse.) I supposed he said, "an Ojibbeway is taking a horse." I answered, "Kah-ween-gwautch Ojibbeway," (not altogether an Ojibbeway.) The village was instantly in motion. In the faces of most of those who gathered round, I could see no settled determination to act in any way; but there was encouragement in the countenances of my friend Be-na and a number of Crees who were about him. There was manifest hostility only in the Ba-gis-kun-nungs. I was so agitated that I could not feel my feet touch the ground, but I think I was not afraid. When I had got my halter on the head of the black horse, I stood for a moment hesitating to get on him; as in the act of doing so, I must for the moment, deprive myself of the power of using my arms, and could not avoid exposing myself to an attack behind. But recollecting that any thing like indecision, would at this time have a most unfavourable effect, I gave a jump to mount the horse, but jumped so much higher and farther than was necessary, that I fell sprawling on the ground on the other side of the horse, my gun in one hand, my bow and arrows in the other. I regained my feet as soon as I could, and looked round to watch the motions of my enemies; but presently an universal shout of laughter, in which all joined but the Ba-gis-kun-nungs, gave me some confidence, and I proceeded more deliberately to mount. I knew if they could have ventured to make any open attack on me, it would have been at the time I was lying on the ground, and not in a situation to make any dangerous resistance. The loud and hearty laughter of the Indians, convinced me also, that what I was doing was not generally offensive to them.

When I turned to ride off, I saw Wa-me-gon-a-biew still running like a frightened turkey; he was almost out of sight. When

I overtook him, I said, "My brother, you must be tired, I will lend you my horse," and we went on together. At length, we saw two men coming on horseback from the village, to pursue us. Wa-me-gon-a-biew was alarmed, and would have rode off, leaving me to settle the difficulty with them as I could; but perceiving his intention, I called to him to leave the horse, which he did, and resumed his race on foot. When the two men had approached within about half a mile of me, I got down from the horse, and taking the halter in my hand, stood with my face towards them. They stopped in the path, at a distance from me, and looking around in the other direction, I perceived that Wa-me-gon-a-biew had concealed himself in the bushes. The two men stood in the road, and I remained holding my horse nearly in the same place until near noon. The people of the village stood, in great numbers, on a little elevation close by the lodges, and watched to see what would be done. The two Ba-gis-kun-nungs, after they were tired of standing, separated, and one came round on one side, the other on the other, and came up opposite to me; and it was then I thought they would approach me, one on one side, the other on the other, and thus get an opportunity to shoot me down; but after coming near me once or twice, they went on, and got together in the road, between me and Wa-me-gon-a-biew. I now began to tire of their pusilanimous behaviour, and getting on my horse, I rode toward them; but they turned out of my way, and went around to the village. In this affair, I found Wa-me-gon-a-biew more cowardly than it was usual even for him to be; but it happened that the chiefs, and the considerate men of the band to whom Ba-gis-kun-nung belonged, were glad I had come to take a horse. Ba-gis-kun-nung and his sons were considered troublesome and bad men; hence it was, that I was able to carry through this enterprise without any assistance from Wa-me-gon-a-biew.

After the two men turned back, I rode along, and Wa-me-gon-a-biew joined me from the bushes, where he had been concealed. We found that night the lodge of our old friend, Waw-so, who used formerly to live with Pe-shau-ba. The horse I had taken I concealed in the woods, and did not wish to tell Waw-so of what I had done. But in the middle of the night, after I fell asleep, Wa-me-gon-a-biew began to relate to him all that had happened the preceding day, and when he came to hear of my jumping over the horse, of which I had told Wa-me-gon-a-biew, the old man waked me with his loud and hearty laughter.

We spent the night with Waw-so, and next morning continued on our journey, towards Ko-te-kwaw-wi-ah-we-se-be, where I lived. I had now two horses, and a friend of mine coming along, who had none, I promised to give him one; but as he was not then going home, he deferred taking it until he should pass again. In the mean time, the horse I had intended for him, died of a broken blood vessel, so that I had none remaining but the black horse, which I called Mandan, and to which I had become much attached; but when the man returned, I could do no otherwise than give him this one. My wife cried, and I felt much regret at parting with this valuable horse.

Three months after this, the Crees sent tobacco to the Ojibbeways, to accompany them to the Mandans, and join in an attack on some of the Bwoi-nug, in the country of the Missouri. As these messages were going about, I received word from Ba-gis-kun-nung, that he did not wish to have me join in the war-party. This amounted to a threat to take my life if I went, but I paid no attention to it.

In six days I could go from my place to Turtle Mountain, where the Crees were assembling, in considerable numbers. I had been waiting about one month, when Wa-ge-tote arrived with sixty men, on his way to the rendezvous. Here eight of us joined him, and gave what assistance we could in provisions, to his party, who had been starving for some time. Soon we were all suffering alike; we had travelled on two or three days, when twenty young men were selected to go and hunt buffaloe. Wa-ge-tote insisted that I must go with them, but I declined. He urged it upon me repeatedly, and, at last, taking my load on his own shoulders, he said, "Now, my nephew, you must go, and I will carry your load for you, till you join us again." I went forward a short distance, and had the good fortune to kill an elk. The Indians fell on it like hungry dogs, and soon not a particle of it was left, though I believe not more than half of those that were in a starving condition tasted of it. The twenty men that had been sent out, returned without having killed any thing. They now became so weak from hunger, that numbers were left, being unable to walk. For many days we had no other food than the roots of the Me-tush-koo-she-min,* (grass berry,) an esculent root, called Pommeblanch by the Frenchmen. I was myself about to fail, when late one night, as all were asleep, an old man, a relative of my wife, waked me, and put carefully into my hand a small quantity of pemmican, which he had carried concealed about him. This enabled me to reach the Turtle Mountain, to which place, probably, about half of Wa-ge-tote's band arrived at the same time. Of those that had parted from us, some afterwards joined, some returned to their own country, and others were no more heard of.

The Assinneboins and Crees whom we had expected to meet at Turtle Mountain, had left it some time before, and we had followed on their trail but a few days, when we met them returning. They related to us, that they had arrived at the Mandan village just as a war-party of the Sioux had reached the same place, with a design to attack the town. The Mandan chief said to them, as soon as they came, "My friends, these Sioux have come hither to put out my fire. They know not that you are here. As they have not come against you, why should your blood flow in our quarrel? Remain, therefore, in my village, and you shall see that we are men, and need no help when they come to fight us at our own doors." The Mandan village was surrounded by a wall of pickets, and close to these the Sioux fought all day. At length, an intermission took place, and the Mandan chief, calling to the Sioux from the inside, said to them, "Depart from about our village, or we will let out upon you our friends, the Ojibbeways, who have been sitting here all day, and are now fresh and unwearied." The Sioux answered, "This is a vain boast, made with a design to conceal your weakness. You have no Ojibbeways in your house, and if you had hundreds, we neither fear nor regard them. The Ojibbeways are women, and if your village were full of them, we would, for that reason, the sooner come among you." The Crees and Assinneboins, hearing these taunts, became irritated, and ran out to at-

---

* This is one of the species of Psoralea, so abundant in the open countries of the Missouri. When boiled or roasted, the roots are exceedingly palatable and nutritious; but the exclusive use of them commonly occasions derangement of the bowels.

tack the Sioux, which the latter perceiving, fled in all directions. The Ojibbeways, though they had little share in the fight, were allowed to have some of the scalps taken during the day, and one of these fell into the hands of our chief, Wa-ge-tote, though he had not been within several days' march of the scene of action, and with this trophy he returned towards his own country. When we reached Turtle Mountain, on our return, we were all suffering the extremity of hunger, and many were quite unable to travel farther. We were, therefore, compelled to stop, and of the whole party, there were found only four who had strength and resolution enough remaining, to undertake to hunt. These were an old man, called Gitch-e-weesh, (big beaver lodge,) two young men, and myself. Gitch-e-weesh, the old man, was in high spirits, and expressed the utmost confidence that he should kill something. " When I was yet a little boy," said he, " the Great Spirit came to me, after I had been fasting for three days, and told me he had heard my crying, and had come to tell me that he did not wish to hear me cry and complain so often, but that if ever I was reduced to the danger of immediately perishing of hunger, then I should call upon him, and he would hear and give me something. I have never called before, but last night I spent in prayer and singing, and I have assurance that I shall this day be fed by the bounty of the Great God. I have never asked before, and I know that he will not forget his promise." We all started at the same time in the morning, but went to hunt in different directions. I hunted all day without finding any thing, and so weak was I, that I could traverse but a very small extent of ground. It was late when I came in; the two young men were in before me; all began to despair; but old Gitch-e-weesh was still absent. At a very late hour he arrived, bending under a heavy load of meat. I was selected to cook and make an equal division of what he had brought. Next day we went to the place where the moose had been killed, all the remainder of which we soon devoured.

Near this place, Wa-me-gon-a-biew discovered a large quantity of property, which had been left by a band of Assinneboins, as a medicine sacrifice. Property left in this way is called metai sas-sah-ge-witch-e-gun, or puk-ketch-e-gun-nun, and may be taken by any friendly party. But the offerings made to ensure success in war, commonly called sah-sah-ge-witch-e-gun, may not be taken from the place where they are left. Wa-me-gon-a-biew having been in the top of a tree, at the time he made this discovery, and having pointed out the place to the Indians immediately, was so late in coming down, that every blanket, every piece of cloth, and, indeed, every thing of value, was seized and appropriated before he came up. He said little of his dissatisfaction at this, though it was evident enough. He went aside and sat down by himself on a log. Disturbing with his foot a pile of dry leaves, he found buried under it a brass kettle, inverted, and covering a quantity of valuable offerings to the earth. These he of course seized upon for himself, and his portion was more valuable than that of any other. The blankets, robes, strouding, &c. &c. were suspended in trees; but the quantity was larger than is usually seen in places where such sacrifices have been made. The Assinneboins had worshipped here, when on their way to the country of the Sioux. In travelling from this place to my home, I killed no more game, and was of course nearly famished. When I arrived, my family were in the same situation; but next day I had good luck, and killed an elk; afterwards I was able, by my own exertions, to procure a plentiful supply.

It was while I was living here at Great Wood River, that news came of a great man among the Shawneese, who had been favoured by a revelation of the mind and will of the Great Spirit. I was hunting in the prairie, at a great distance from my lodge, when I saw a stranger approaching; at first, I was apprehensive of an enemy, but, as he drew nearer, his dress showed him to be an Ojibbeway; but when he came up, there was something very strange and peculiar in his manner. He signified to me, that I must go home, but gave no explanation of the cause. He refused to look at me, or enter into any kind of conversation. I thought he must be crazy, but nevertheless accompanied him to my lodge. When we had smoked, he remained a long time silent, but, at last, began to tell me he had come with a message from the prophet of the Shawneese. "Henceforth," said he, "the fire must never be suffered to go out in your lodge. Summer and winter, day and night, in the storm, or when it is calm, you must remember that the life in your body, and the fire in your lodge, are the same, and of the same date. If you suffer your fire to be extinguished, at that moment your life will be at its end. You must not suffer a dog to live; you must never strike either a man, a woman, a child, or a dog. The prophet himself is coming to shake hands with you; but I have come before, that you may know what is the will of the Great Spirit, communicated to us by him, and to inform you that the preservation of your life, for a single moment, depends on your entire obedience. From this time forward, we are neither to be drunk, to steal, to lie, or to go against our enemies. While we yield an entire obedience to these commands of the Great Spirit, the Sioux, even if they come to our country, will not be able to see us: we shall be protected and made happy." I listened to all he had to say, but told him, in answer, that I could not believe we should all die, in case our fire went out; in many instances, also, it would be difficult to avoid punishing our children; our dogs were useful in aiding us to hunt and take animals, so that I could not believe the Great Spirit had any wish to take them from us. He continued talking to us until late at night; then he lay down to sleep in my lodge. I happened to wake first in the morning, and perceiving the fire had gone out, I called him to get up, and see how many of us were living, and how many dead. He was prepared for the ridicule I attempted to throw upon his doctrine, and told me that I had not yet shaken hands with the prophet. His visit had been to prepare me for this important event, and to make me aware of the obligations and risks I should incur, by entering into the engagement implied in taking in my hand the message of the prophet. I did not rest entirely easy in my unbelief. The Indians, generally, received the doctrine of this man with great humility and fear. Distress and anxiety was visible in every countenance. Many killed their dogs, and endeavoured to practice obedience to all the commands of this new preacher, who still remained among us. But, as was usual with me, in any emergency of this kind, I went to the traders, firmly believing, that if the Deity had any communications to make to men, they would be given, in the first instance, to white men. The traders ridiculed and despised the idea of a new revelation of the Divine will, and the thought that it should be given to a poor Shawnee. Thus was I confirmed in my infidelity. Nevertheless, I did not openly avow my unbelief to the Indians, only I refused to kill my dogs, and showed no great degree of anxiety to comply with his other requirements. As long as I remained among the Indians, I made it my business to conform, as far as appeared consistent with my immediate convenience and comfort, with all their customs. Many of their ideas I have adopted; but I always found among them opinions which I could not hold. The Ojibbeway whom I have mentioned, remained some time among the Indians, in my neighbourhood, and gained the attention of the principal men so effectually, that a time was appointed, and a lodge prepared, for the solemn and public espousing of the doctrines of the prophet. When the people, and I among them, were brought into the long lodge, prepared for this solemnity, we saw something carefully concealed under a blanket, in figure and dimensions bearing some resemblance to the form of a man. This was accompanied by two young men, who, it was understood, attended constantly upon it, made its bed at night, as for a man, and slept near it. But while we remained, no one went near it, or raised the blanket which was spread over its unknown contents. Four strings of mouldy and discoloured beans, were all the remaining visible insignia of this important mission. After a long harangue, in which the prominent features of the new revelation were stated and urged upon the attention of all, the four strings of beans, which we were told were made of the flesh itself of the prophet, were carried, with much solemnity, to each man in the lodge, and he was expected to take hold of each string at the top, and draw them gently through his hand. This was called shaking hands with the prophet, and was considered as solemnly engaging to obey his injunctions, and accept his mission as from the Supreme. All the Indians who touched the beans, had previously killed their dogs; they gave up their medicine bags, and showed a disposition to comply with all that should be required of them.

We had now been for some time assembled in considerable numbers; much agitation and terror had prevailed among us, and now famine began to be felt. The faces of men wore an aspect of unusual gloominess; the active became indolent, and the spirits of the bravest seemed to be subdued. I started to hunt with my dogs, which I had constantly refused to kill, or suffer to be killed. By their assistance, I found and killed a bear. On returning home, I said to some of the Indians, "Has not the Great Spirit given us our dogs to aid us in procuring what is needful for the support of our life, and can you believe he wishes now to deprive us of their services? The prophet, we are told, has forbid us to suffer our fire to be extinguished in our lodges, and when we travel or hunt, he will not allow us to use a flint and steel, and we are told he requires that no man should give fire to another. Can it please the Great Spirit that we should lie in our hunting camps without fire; or is it more agreeable to him that we should make fire by rubbing together two sticks, than with a flint and a piece of steel?" But they would not listen to me, and the serious enthusiasm which prevailed among them so far affected me, that I threw away my flint and steel, laid aside my medicine bag, and, in many particulars, complied with the new doctrines; but I would not kill my dogs. I soon learned to kindle a fire by rubbing some dry cedar, which I was careful to carry always about me; but the discontinuance of the use of flint and steel subjected many of the Indians to much inconvenience and suffering. The influence of the Shawnee prophet was very sensibly and painfully felt by the remotest Ojibbeways of whom I had any knowledge; but it was not the common impression among them, that his doctrines had any tendency to unite them in the accomplishment of any human purpose. For two or three years drunkenness was much less frequent than formerly; war was less thought of, and the entire aspect of affairs among them, was somewhat changed by the influence of one man. But gradually the impression was obliterated, medicine bags, flints, and steels, were resumed; dogs were raised, women and children were beaten as before, and the Shawnee prophet was despised. At this day he is looked upon by the Indians as an impostor and a bad man.

After the excitement of this affair had somewhat subsided, and the messengers had left us to visit remoter bands, I went with a large party of Indians to some of the upper branches of Red River, to hunt beaver. I know not whether it was that we were emboldened by the promise of the prophet, that we should be invisible to the Sioux, but we went much nearer than we had formerly ventured to their country. It was here, in a border region, where both they and ourselves had been afraid to hunt, that we now found beaver in the greatest abundance; here, without the aid of my gun, I took one hundred large beavers in a single month, by trapping merely. My family was now ten in number, six of whom were orphan children, and although there was no one but myself to hunt or trap, I was able, for some time, to supply all their wants. At length, beaver began to grow scarce, and I was compelled to shoot an elk. My family had been so long unaccustomed to hear guns, that at the sound of mine they left the lodge and fled to the woods, believing the Sioux had fired upon me. I was compelled to carry my traps to a greater distance, and to visit them only in the middle of the day. My gun was constantly in my hand; if I had occasion to do any thing, I held my gun in one hand and laboured with the other. I slept a little by day, but during the night, and every night, I watched around my lodge. Being again out of meat, I went to the woods to hunt moose, and in one day killed four. I butchered and cut them open without laying down my gun. As I was cleaning the last, I heard a gun not more than two hundred yards from me. I knew that I had advanced nearer to the frontier of the Sioux than any Ojibbeway, and I did not believe there were any of the latter tribe living near me. I therefore believed this must be the gun of a Sioux, and immediately called out to him, as I supposed he must have heard my firing; but no answer was returned. I watched about me more anxiously than before, and at the approach of night stole toward home as silently and as cautiously as I could. On the following day, I ventured to examine in the direction of the place where I had heard the gun, and found the tracks, which proved to be those of an Ojibbeway, who had fired upon a bear which he was pursuing, probably with too much eagerness to hear me call. Soon after this, I found many tracks, and ascertained that I was not far distant from a place where the Ojibbeways had built and fortified a camp. Three times I received messages from the chiefs of the band living in this camp, stating that my situation was too exposed and dangerous, and urging me to come in. I disliked to live in a crowded place, and it was not until I discovered the tracks of some Sioux, that had been reconnoitering my camp, that I determined to fly into this work. The night before my departure, was one, at my lodge, of terror and alarm, greater even than is commonly felt among the Indians. I had mentioned the tracks that I had seen, and I did not doubt that a party of the Sioux were in my immediate neighbourhood, and would fall upon me before morning. More than half the night had passed, and not one of us had slept, when we heard a sudden rushing without, and our dogs came running in in evident alarm. I told my children that the time was come for us all to die together. I placed myself in the front part of my lodge, and raising the door a little, put out the muzzle of my gun, and sat in momentary expectation of the approach of the enemy. Footsteps were distinctly audible; but the night being dark, I could as yet see nothing. At length a little black object, not larger in appearance than a man's head, came slowly and directly towards my lodge. Here again I experienced how much fear influences the power of sight; for this little object, as it came near, seemed at one instant to shoot up to the height of a man, and at the next, to be no larger than it really was. When I was entirely convinced that it was nothing but a small animal, I stepped out, and finding it to be a porcupine, killed it with a tomahawk; the remainder of the night was spent in the same manner as the beginning. Early next morning, I fled to the fortified camp. On my arrival, the chiefs councilled, and sent two young men to look after the property left in my lodge; but as I knew the Sioux were lurking in that direction, and that, should the young men be killed, or injured, their friends would consider me the cause of their misfortune, I went before them, but by a circuitous route, determining that if any thing happened, I would be present, and have a part in it. I found my lodge safe, and we experienced no molestation in removing my baggage to the fort.

The Sioux, from time to time, came near and looked at our work, but never ventured to attack it. When the spring arrived, all the Ojibbeways left it in one day; but I was compelled to remain, having taken charge of some packs for a trader who was then absent, and which I could not remove. The chiefs remonstrated, telling me it was little better than throwing myself away, to remain, as the Sioux would immediately know when the main body left, and would not lose the opportunity of falling on me when I should be left alone. The saddening and alarming effect of these admonitions was somewhat increased by the many instances they related of men, women, and children, that had been killed on this very spot by the Sioux, but I was compelled to remain. At night I closed the entrances to the camp as effectually as I could, and cautioning my family to remain entirely silent, I stationed myself by the wall to watch. The night was but little advanced, when by the light of the moon, which then shone brightly, I discovered two men, who came directly towards the usual entrance, and finding it closed, began to walk around and look at the wall. Fear strongly prompted me to shoot them without hailing; but recollecting that they might not be Sioux, I took an opportunity, when I could aim my gun directly at them without being much exposed, and called out. They proved to be the trader on whose account I had stayed back, and a Frenchman. I gladly opened my fort to let them in, and with this addition of strength, spent a pretty quiet night. Next morning we moved, taking the trader's packs, and following the path of the Ojibbeways.

I did not wish to rejoin this band, but went to live for some time, by myself, in the woods; afterwards I joined some Red River Ojibbeways, under a chief called Be-gwa-is, (he that cuts up the beaver lodge.) All the hunters of this band had been for some days trying to kill an old buck moose, who had become notorious among them for his shyness and cunning. The first day that I went to hunt, I saw this moose, but could not kill him; I however killed another, and next day returned to the pursuit, with the full determination to kill him if possible. It so happened, that the weather and wind were favourable, and I killed the buck moose. My success was attributable, in a great measure, to accident, or to circumstances beyond my control; but the Indians gave me credit for superior skill, and I was thenceforth reckoned the best hunter in that band.

We now started, twelve men in number, under Be-gwa-is, to go to the Sioux country, to hunt beaver, leaving our women behind. On this hunt all the Indians became snow-blind, and I being the only one able to hunt, fed and took care of them for several days. As soon as the snow went off in the spring, they began to get better. We then separated into three parties; one of which being four in number, went to Buffaloe River, where they were attacked by the Sioux, had one man killed, and another wounded and made prisoner.

I had wounded myself by accident, in my ancle bone, with a tomahawk, and became, in consequence, unable to travel fast. About this time my companions became panic struck, supposing the Sioux to be near us, and on our trail. They paid not the least regard to my situation, but fled with all the speed they could make. It was now early in the spring; rain and snow had been falling throughout the day, and at night the wind began to blow from the north-west, and the water to freeze. I followed my companions, though at a distance, and came up with them late at night, when I found them perishing in their comfortless camp; they being the disciples of the prophet, and not having ventured to strike a fire. Wa-me-gon-a-biew was one of these men, and he, as well as the rest of them, was willing to desert me, whenever there was any apprehension of danger. Next morning ice was strong enough in the river to walk upon, and as this cold had been preceded by warm weather, we suffered severely. We spent four days at the sugar camp of our women, and then started to return to the Sioux country. On our way we met the two who had escaped, of the party on which the Sioux had fallen. Their appearance was that of extreme misery and starvation.

We met also, in this journey, an American trader, whose name I do not now recollect, but who treated me with much attention, and urged me to leave the Indians and return with him to the States. But I was poor, having few peltries of any value; I had also a wife and one child. He told me the government, and the people of the United States, would be generous to me, and he himself promised to render me all the aid in his power; but I declined accepting his offer, preferring for the present to remain among the Indians, though it was still my wish and intention, ultimately to leave them. I heard from this man, that some of my relations had been as far as Mackinac in search of me, and I dictated a letter to them, which this gentleman undertook to have conveyed to its destination. When about to part from us, he gave to Wa-me-gon-a-biew and myself, each a bark canoe, and some other valuable presents.

As we were travelling towards Red River, our principal man,

Wy-ong-je-cheween, to whom we had committed the direction of our party, became alarmed. We were following a long river which discharges into Red River; I saw him anxiously looking about, on one side and the other, and attentively watching for all those indications of the proximity of men, which could be afforded by the tracks of animals, the flight of birds, and other marks, which they so well know how to understand. He said nothing of fear; an Indian in such circumstances, rarely, if ever, does. But when he saw me, at night, trying to kindle a fire for our encampment, he rose up, wrapped his blanket about him, and without saying a word, walked away. I watched him until I saw him select a place, combining the requisites for the entire concealment of his person, and affording him the power of overlooking a considerable extent of country. Knowing the motive which had occasioned this, I followed his example, as did the remaining men of our party. Next morning we met, and ventured to kindle a fire to prepare a little breakfast. Our kettle was but just hung over the fire and filled, when we discovered the Sioux, on a point not half a mile behind us. We dashed the contents of the kettle on the fire, and fled. At some distance below, we built a strong camp, and I set my traps.

Among the presents I had received from the American trader, was a small keg containing sixteen quarts of strong rum, which I had brought thus far on my back. Wa-me-gon-a-biew and the other Indians had often begged me for a taste of it, which I had constantly refused; telling them the old men, and the chiefs, and all, should taste it together, when we reached home. But now they took an opportunity when I was absent to look at my traps, to open it; and when I returned, I found them all drunk, and quarrelling with each other. I was aware of our dangerous and exposed situation, and felt somewhat alarmed, when I found so many of us totally disabled by intoxication. I tried, however, to quiet their noise; but in so doing, I endangered my own safety. As I held two of them apart, one in one hand, the other in the other, the third, an old man, came behind and made a thrust at my back with a knife, which I very narrowly avoided. They were all affronted, as I had reproached them with cowardice; telling them they preferred remaining, like rabbits, in their hole, and dared neither venture out to go against their enemies, or even to hunt for something to eat. In fact, I had for some time fed and supported them, and I was not a little vexed at their foolishness. We had, however, no more alarms immediately, and the Indians at length venturing to hunt, we met with so much success as nearly to load one canoe with skins. The remainder of my little cask of rum, which I had used great care to keep out of their way, caused them one more drunken frolick, they having stolen it in my absence.

After we had completed our hunt, we started down together. Approaching Red River, we heard great numbers of guns before us, and my companions, supposing them to be those of the Sioux, left me and fled across land, in which way they could reach home in less than a day. As I was determined not to abandon our property in the canoe, I continued on by myself, and in about four days, arrived safely at home.

The Indians were now about assembling at Pembinah, to dispose of their peltries, and have their usual drunken frolick. I had but just arrived at the encampment of our band, when they began to start; some going forward by land, and leaving the women to bring on their loads in the canoes. I tried to persuade Wa-me-gon-a-biew and others, which were particularly my friends, not to join in this foolish and destructive indulgence, but I could not prevail upon them; they all went on in advance of me. I moved slowly along, hunting and making dry meat, and did not reach Pembinah, until most of the men of the band had passed several days there in drinking. As soon as I arrived, some Indians came to tell me that Wa-me-gon-a-biew had lost his nose; another had a large piece bitten out of his cheek; one was injured in one way, another in another.

I learned that my brother, as I always called Wa-me-gon-a-biew, had but just arrived, when he happened to go into a lodge, where a young man, a son of Ta-bush-shish, was beating an old woman. Wa-me-gon-a-biew held his arms; but presently old Ta-bush-shish coming in, and in his drunkenness, probably misapprehending the nature of my brother's interference, seized him by the hair, and bit his nose off. At this stage of the affair, Be-gwa-is, an old chief who had always been very friendly to us, came in, and seeing that a scuffle was going on, thought it necessary to join in it. Wa-me-gon-a-biew perceiving the loss of his nose, suddenly raised his hands, though still stooping his head, and seizing by the hair the head that was nearest him, bit the nose off. It happened to be that of our friend Be-gwa-is. After his rage had a little abated, he recognized his friend, and exclaimed, "wah! my cousin!" Be-gwa-is was a kind and good man, and being perfectly aware of the erroneous impression under which Wa-me-gon-a-biew had acted, never for one moment betrayed any thing like anger or resentment, towards the man who had thus been the unwilling cause of his mutilation. "I am an old man," said he, "and it is but a short time that they will laugh at me for the loss of my nose."

For my own part, I felt much irritated against Ta-bush-shish, inasmuch as I doubted whether he had not taken the present opportunity to wreak an old grudge upon Wa-me-gon-a-biew. I went into my brother's lodge, and sat by him; his face, and all his clothes, were covered with blood. For some time he said nothing; and when he spoke, I found that he was perfectly sober. "To-morrow," said he, "I will cry with my children, and the next day I will go and see Ta-bush-shish. We must die together, as I am not willing to live, when I must always expect to be ridiculed." I told him I would join him in any attempt to kill Ta-bush-shish, and held myself in readiness accordingly. But a little sober reflection, and the day's time he had given himself to cry with his children, diverted Wa-me-gon-a-biew from his bloody intention, and like Be-gwa-is, he resolved to bear his loss as well as he could.

CHAPTER X.

Presence of mind and self-devotedness in an Indian mother—Indian warfare—conversation of a chief—winter hunt on the Begwionusko River—medicine hunting—customs, in cases of manslaughter—symbolic, or picture writing—death of Pe-shau-ba—disaster at Spirit Lake, and death of the Little Clam.

WITHIN a few days after this drunken quarrel, Ta-bush-shish was seized with a violent sickness. He had for many days a burning fever, his flesh wasted, and he was apparently near dying, when he sent to Wa-me-gon-a-biew two kettles, and other presents, of considerable value, with a message, " My friend, I have made you look ugly, and you have made me sick. I have suffered much, and if I die now my children must suffer much more. I have sent you this present, that you may let me live." Wa-me-gon-a-biew instructed his messenger to say to Ta-bush-shish, " I have not made you sick. I cannot restore you to health, and will not accept your presents." He lingered for a month or more in a state of such severe illness, that his hair all fell from his head. After this, he began to amend, and when he was nearly well, we all removed to the prairie; but were scattered about in different directions, and at considerable distances from each other.

After our spring hunting, we began to think of going against the Sioux, and an inconsiderable party assembled, among those who lived immediately about me. Wa-me-gon-a-biew and I accompanied them, and in four days we arrived at the little village where Ta-bush-shish then lived. Before our arrival here we had been joined by Wa-ge-tote, with sixty men. After we had rested and eaten at our encampment near Ta-bush-shish's lodge, and were about to start, we saw him come out naked, but painted and ornamented as for a war, and having his arms in his hands. He came stalking up to us with a very angry face, but none of us fully comprehended his design, until we saw him go up and present the muzzle of his gun to Wa-me-gon-a-biew's back. "My friend," said he, "we have lived long enough, and have given trouble and distress enough to each other. I sent to you my request that you would be satisfied with the sickness and pain you had made me suffer, but you refused to listen to me; and the evils you continue to inflict on me, render my life wearisome; let us therefore die together." A son of Wa-ge-tote, and another young man, seeing the intention of Ta-bush-shish, presented the point of their spears, one to one of his sides, the other to the other; but he took no notice of them. Wa-me-gon-a-biew was intimidated, and dared not raise his head. Ta-bush-shish wished to have fought, and to have given Wa-me-gon-a-biew an equal chance for his life, but the latter had not courage enough to accept his offer. Henceforth I esteemed Wa-me-gon-a-biew less even than I had formerly done. He had less of bravery and generosity in his disposition than is common among the Indians. Neither Ta-bush-shish nor any of his band joined in our war-party.

We went on, wandering about from place to place, and instead of going against our enemies, spent the greater part of the summer among the buffaloe. In the fall, I returned to Pembinah, my intention being to go thence to the wintering ground of the trader above mentioned, who had proposed to assist me in getting to the states. I now heard of the war between the United States and Great Britain, and of the capture of Mackinac, and this intelligence deterred me from any attempt to pass through the frontier of the United States territory, which were then the scenes of warlike operations.

In the ensuing spring, there was a very general movement among the Ojibbeways of the Red River, toward the Sioux country; but the design was not, at least avowedly, to fall upon or molest the Sioux, but to hunt. I travelled in company with a large band, under the direction of Ais-ainse, (the little clam.) His brother, called Wa-ge-tone, was a man of considerable consequence. We had ascended Red River about one hundred miles, when we met Mr. Hanie, a trader, who gave us a little rum. I lived, at this time, in a long lodge, having two or three fires, and I occupied it in common with several other men, with their families, mostly the relatives of my wife. It was midnight, or after, and I was sleeping in my lodge, when I was waked by some man seizing me roughly by the hand, and raising me up. There was still a little fire burning in the lodge, and by the light it gave I recognised, in the angry and threatening countenance which hung over me, the face of Wa-ge-tone, the brother of the Little Clam, our principal chief. "I have solemnly promised," said he, "that if you should come with us to this country, you should not live; up, therefore, and be ready to answer me." He then went on to Wah-zhe-gwun, the man who slept next me, and used to him similar insolent and threatening language; but, by this time, an old man, a relative of mine, called Mah-nuge, who slept beyond, had comprehended the purport of his visit, and raised himself up, with his knife in his hand. When Wa-ge-tone came to him, he received a sharp answer. He then returned to me, drew his knife, and threatened me with instant death. "You are a stranger," said he, "and one of many who have come from a distant country, to feed yourself and your children with that which does not belong to you. You are driven out from your own country, and you come among us because you are too feeble and worthless to have a home or a country of your own. You have visited our best hunting grounds, and wherever you have been you have destroyed all the animals which the Great Spirit gave us for our sustenance. Go back, therefore, from this place, and be no longer a burthen to us, or I will certainly take your life." I answered him, that I was not going to the country we were now about to visit, particularly to hunt beaver, but that even if I were to do so, I had an equal right with him, and was as strong to maintain that right. This dispute was becoming somewhat noisy, when old Mah-nuge came up, with his knife in his hand, and drove the noisy and half drunken Wa-ge-tone out of the lodge. We saw this man no more for a long time, but his brother, the Little Clam, told us to think nothing of what he said.

Here a messenger overtook us to bring to the Ottawwaws the information that Muk-kud-da-be-na-sa, (the black bird,) an Ottawwaw of Waw-gun-uk-ke-zie, or L'Arbre Croche, had arrived from Lake Huron, to call us all home to that country. So we turned back, and one after another fell back, till Wa-ge-tone only was left, and he went on and joined a war-party of Ojibbeways then starting from Leech Lake. A part of this band stopped at the Wild Rice River,* and went into the fort, or fortified camp before mentioned. Here they began to hunt and trap, and were heedlessly dispersed about, when a large party of Sioux came into their neighbourhood.

Ais-ainse, the Ojibbeway chief, returned one evening from a successful hunt, having killed two elks; and on the following morning, his wife, with her young son, started out to dry the meat. They had proceeded a great distance from the lodge, when the lad first discovered the Sioux party, at no great distance, and called out to his mother, " the Sioux are coming." The old woman drew her knife, and cutting the belt which bound the boy's blanket to his body, told him to run for home with all his strength. She then, with her knife in her hand, ran to meet the approaching war-party. The boy heard many guns, and the old woman was no more heard of. The boy ran long, when, perceiving that his pursuers were near, he lost consciousness; and when he arrived at the fortified camp, still in a state of mental alienation, the Sioux were about one hundred and fifty yards behind him. He vomited blood for some days, and never recovered his health and strength, though he lived about one year afterwards.

Several of the Ojibbeways were hunting in a different direction from that in which the wife of the Little Clam had met the war-party. As soon as the Sioux disappeared from about the fort, young men were sent out, who discovered that they had taken the path of the hunters, and one or two, taking a circuitous direction, reached the Little Clam just as the Sioux were creeping up to fire upon him. A fight ensued, which lasted a long time, without loss on either side. At length, one of the Ojibbeways being wounded in the leg, his companions retired a little, in order to give him an opportunity of escaping under cover of some bushes; but this movement did not escape the notice of the Sioux. One of their number followed the young man, continuing to elude the notice of the Ojibbeways while he did so, killed

* *Gah Menomonie gah-wun-zhe-gaw-wie see-bee,* (the river of the wild rice straw.) *Gaw-wun-je,* or *gaw-wunzk,* is applicable to the stalks or trunks of many plants, shrubs, &c. as *Mee-na-gaw-wunge,* (whortleberry bush,) or, in the plural, *Meena-gaw-wa-cheen,* (whortleberry bushes.)

him, and took his scalp and medal, he being a favourite son of Ais-ainse, the Ojibbeway chief; then returning, he shook these trophies at the Ojibbeways, with some exulting and vaunting words. The enraged father, at sight of the scalp and medal, rushed from his cover, shot down one of the Sioux, cut off his head, and shook it exultingly at the survivors. The other Ojibbeways, being emboldened at this conduct of the Little Clam, rushed forward together, and the Sioux fled.

Another considerable man of the Ojibbeways, who was also named Ta-bush-shish, had been hunting in a different direction, accompanied by one man, and had heard the firing, either where the old woman had been killed, or where Ais-ainse was fighting, and had returned home. The Indians said of him, as, indeed, they often say of a man after his death, that he had some presentiments or forewarnings of what was about to happen. On the preceding evening, he had come home, as the Indian hunter often comes, to be annoyed by the tongue of an old wife, jealous of the attentions bestowed on a younger and more attractive one. On this occasion, he said to her, " Scold away, old woman, for now I hear you the last time." He was in the fort when some one arrived, who had skulked and fled with the news of the fight the Little Clam was engaged in. Ta-bush-shish had two fine horses, and he said to one of his friends, " Be-na, I believe you are a man; will you take one of my horses, and go with me to see what Ais-ainse has been doing all day? Shall we not be ashamed to let him fight so long, within hearing, and never attempt to give him assistance? Here are more than one hundred of us, who have stood trembling within this camp, while our brother has been fighting like a man, with only four or five young men to assist him." They started, and following a trail of the Sioux, it brought them to a place where a party had kindled a fire, and were, for a moment, resting themselves around it. They crept up near, but not thinking this a favourable opportunity to fire, Ta-bush-shish and Be-na went forward on the route they knew the party would pursue, and laid themselves down in the snow. It was now night, but not very dark. When the Sioux began to move, and a number of them came near the place where they had concealed themselves, Ta-bush-shish and Be-na rose up together, and fired upon them, and the latter, as he had been instructed to do, instantly fled. When at a considerable distance, and finding he was not pursued, he stopped to listen, and for great part of the night heard now and then a gun, and sometimes the shrill and solitary sah-sah-kwi of Ta-bush-shish, shifting from place to place; at last, many guns discharged at the same moment; then the shouts and whoops of the Sioux at the fall of their enemy; then all was silent, and he returned home. These were all that were killed at that time, the old woman, Ta-bush-shish, and the son of Ais-ainse.

It was on the same day, as we afterwards heard, that the war-party from Leech Lake, which Wa-ge-tone had joined, fell upon forty Sioux lodges, at the long prairie. They had fought for two days, and many were killed on each side. Wa-ge-tone was the first man to strike a Sioux lodge. Wah-ka-zhe, the brother of Muk-kud-da-be-na-sa, met those Ottawwaws who returned from the Wild Rice River, at Lake Winnipeg. He had been ten years in the Rocky Mountains, and the country near them, but now wished to return to his own people. He had, in the course of his long life, been much among the whites, and was well acquainted with the different methods of gaining a subsistence among them. He told me that I would be much better situated among the whites, but that I could not become a trader, as I was unable to write; I should not like to submit to constant labour, therefore I could not be a farmer. There was but one situation exactly adapted to my habits and qualifications, that of an interpreter.

He gave us, among other information, some account of a missionary who had come among the Ottawwaws of Waw-gun-uk-kezie, or some of the Indian settlements about the lakes, and urged them to renounce their own religion, and adopt that of the whites. In connexion with this subject, he told us the anecdote of the baptized Indian, who, after death, went to the gate of the white man's heaven, and demanded admittance; but the man who kept watch at the gate told him no redskins could be allowed to enter there. "Go," said he, "for to the west there are the villages and the hunting grounds of those of your own people, who have been on the earth before you." So he departed thence; but when he came to the villages where the dead of his own people resided, the chief refused him admittance. "You have been ashamed of us while you lived; you have chosen to worship the white man's God. Go now to his village, and let him provide for you." Thus he was rejected by both parties.

Wah-ka-zhe being the most considerable man among us, it devolved on him to direct our movements; but through indolence, or perhaps out of regard to me, he determined that not only himself, but his band, should, for the winter, be guided by me. As we had in view no object beyond bare subsistence, and as I was reckoned a very good hunter, and knew this part of the country better than any other man of the band, his course was not an impolitic one.

It was in conformity to my advice that we went to spend the winter at the Be-gwi-o-nush-ko River. The Be-gwi-o-nush-ko enters Red River, about ten miles below Pembinah, and at the time I speak of, the country on it was well stocked with game. We lived here in great plenty and comfort, and Wah-ka-zhe often boasted of his sagacity in choosing me to direct the motions of his party. But a part of the winter had passed, when Wa-me-gon-a-biew began to talk of sacrificing Wah-ka-zhe, the latter being in some manner connected with the man who, many years before, had killed Taw-ga-we-ninne, Wa-me-gon-a-biew's father. I refused to join, or in any manner countenance him in this undertaking; but notwithstanding my remonstrances, he went one day to the lodge of Wah-ka-zhe, with his knife in his hand, intending to kill him; but as he was entering, Muk-kud-da-be-na-sa, a son of Wah-ka-zhe, perceived his intention, and prevented him. He immediately tried to provoke Wa-me-gon-a-biew to engage him in single combat, but he retreated in his accustomed manner. I not only reproved Wa-me-gon-a-biew for this unmanly conduct, but proposed to Wah-ka-zhe to have him driven from the band, and no longer considered him my brother; but Wah-ka-zhe was a considerate and friendly man, and unwilling that trouble or disturbance should be made, and therefore forgave his offence.

One of the young men, the son of Wah-ka-zhe, was accounted the best hunter among the Indians of this band, and there was, between us, while we resided at Be-gwi-o-nush-ko, a friendly rivalry in hunting. O-ke-mah-we-nin-ne, as he was called, killed nineteen moose, one beaver, and one bear; I killed seventeen moose, one hundred beavers, and seven bears; but he was considered the better hunter, moose being the most difficult of all animals to kill. There are many Indians who hunt through the winter in that country, and kill no more than two or three moose, and some never are able to kill one.

We had plenty of game at the Be-gwi-o-nush-ko, until another band of Ojibbeways came upon us, in great numbers, and in a starving condition. While we were in this situation, and many of those who had recently joined us on the point of perishing with hunger, a man called Gish-kaw-ko, the nephew of him by whom I was taken prisoner, went a hunting, and in one day killed two moose. He called me to go with him and get some meat, at the same time signifying his intention to keep his success concealed from the remainder of the band; but I refused to have any part with him in such a transaction. I immediately started on a hunt with Muk-kud-da-be-na-sa, and one or two others, and we having good luck, killed four bears, which we distributed among the hungry.

We now found it necessary for our large party to disperse in various directions. With Muk-kud-da-be-na-sa, Black Bird, and Wah-ka-zhe, and one other man, I went and encamped at the distance of two days' journey from the place where we had been living. While here, we all started together one morning, to hunt, but in the course of the day scattered from each other. Late at night I returned, and was surprised to find, in place of our lodge, nothing remaining but a little pile of the dried grass we had used for a bed. Under this I found Black Bird, who, having come in but a little before me, and after the removal of the lodge, had laid down to sleep, supposing himself the only one left behind. As we followed the trail of our companions on the succeeding day, we met messengers coming to inform us that the son of Nah-gitch-e-gum-me, the man who, with Wah-ka-zhe, had left us so unexpectedly, had killed himself by an accidental discharge of his gun. The young man had been resting carelessly on the muzzle of his gun, when the butt slipping from the snow-shoe on which he had placed it, it had fired, and the contents passing through the arm-pit, had entered his head; but though so shockingly wounded, the young man lived twenty days in a state of stupor and insensibility, and then died. The

Indians attributed to a presentiment of evil on the part of Nah-gitch-e-gum-me and Wah-ka-zhe, their abrupt abandonment of Black Bird and myself.

Shortly after this, we were so reduced by hunger, that it was thought necessary to have recourse to a medicine hunt. Nah-gitch-e-gum-me sent to me and O-ge-mah-we-ninne, the two best hunters of the band, each a little leather sack of medicine, consisting of certain roots, pounded fine and mixed with red paint, to be applied to the little images or figures of the animals we wished to kill. Precisely the same method is practised in this kind of hunting, at least as far as the use of medicine is concerned, as in those instances where one Indian attempts to inflict disease or suffering on another. A drawing, or a little image, is made to represent the man, the woman, or the animal, on which the power of the medicine is to be tried; then the part representing the heart is punctured with a sharp instrument, if the design be to cause death, and a little of the medicine is applied. The drawing or image of an animal used in this case is called muzzi-ne-neen, muzzi-ne-neen-ug, (pl.) and the same name is applicable to the little figures of a man or woman, and is sometimes rudely traced on birch bark, in other instances more carefully carved of wood. We started with much confidence of success, but Wah-ka-zhe followed, and overtaking us at some distance, cautioned us against using the medicine Nah-gitch-e-gum-me had given us, as he said it would be the means of mischief and misery to us, not at present, but when we came to die. We therefore did not make use of it, but, nevertheless, happening to kill some game, Nah-gitch-e-gum-me thought himself, on account of the supposed efficacy of his medicine, entitled to a handsome share of it. Finding that hunger was like to press severely upon us, I separated from the band, and went to live by myself, feeling always confident that by so doing I could ensure a plentiful supply for the wants of my family. Wah-ka-zhe and Black Bird came to Lake Winnipeg, from whence they did not return, as I had expected they would.

After I had finished my hunt, and at about the usual time for assembling in the spring, I began to descend the Be-gwi-o-nush-ko to go to the traders on Red River. Most of the Indians had left their camps, and gone on before me; as I was one morning passing one of our usual encamping places, I saw on shore a little stick standing in the bank, and attached to the top of it a piece of birch bark. On examination, I found the mark of a rattle snake with a knife, the handle touching the snake, and the point sticking into a bear, the head of the latter being down. Near the rattlesnake was the mark of a beaver, one of its dugs, it being a female, touching the snake. This was left for my information, and I learned from it, that Wa-me-gon-a-biew, whose totem was She-she-gwah, the rattlesnake, had killed a man whose totem was Muk-kwah, the bear. The murderer could be no other than Wa-me-gon-a-biew, as it was specified that he was the son of a woman whose totem was the beaver, and this I knew could be no other than Net-no-kwa. As there were but few of the bear totem in our band, I was confident the man killed was a young man called Ke-zha-zhoons; that he was dead, and not wounded merely, was indicated by the drooping down of the head of the bear. I was not deterred by this information from continuing my journey; on the contrary, I hastened on, and arrived in time to witness the interment of the young man my brother had killed. Wa-me-gon-a-biew went by himself, and dug a grave wide enough for two men; then the friends of Ke-zha-zhoons brought his body, and when it was let down into the grave, Wa-me-gon-a-biew took off all his clothes, except his breech cloth, and sitting down naked at the head of the grave, drew his knife, and offered the handle to the nearest male relative of the deceased. "My friend," said he, "I have killed your brother. You see I have made a grave wide enough for both of us, and I am now ready and willing to sleep with him." The first and second, and eventually all the friends of the murdered young man, refused the knife which Wa-me-gon-a-biew offered them in succession. The relations of Wa-me-gon-a-biew were powerful, and it was fear of them which now saved his life. The offence of the young man whom he killed, had been the calling him "cut nose." Finding that none of the male relations of the deceased were willing to undertake publicly the punishment of his murderer, Wa-me-gon-a-biew said to them, " trouble me no more, now or hereafter, about this business; I shall do again as I have now done, if any of you venture to give me similar provocation."

The method by which information of this affair was communicated to me at a distance, is one in common use among the Indians, and, in most cases, it is perfectly explicit and satisfactory. The men of the same tribe are extensively acquainted with the totems which belong to each; and if on any record of this kind, the figure of a man appears without any designatory mark, it is immediately understood that he is a Sioux, or at least a stranger. Indeed, in most instances, as in that above mentioned, the figures of men are not used at all, merely the totem, or sirname, being given. In cases where the information to be communicated is that the party mentioned is starving, the figure of a man is sometimes drawn, and his mouth is painted white, or white paint may be smeared about the mouth of the animal, if it happens to be one, which is his totem.

After visiting the trader on Red River, I started with the intention of coming to the States; but at Lake Winnipeg I heard that the war between Great Britain and the United States still continued, with such disturbances on the frontier as would render it difficult for me to pass with safety. I was therefore compelled to stop by myself at that place, where I was after some time joined by Pe-shau-ba, Waw-zhe-kah-maish-koon, and others, to the number of three lodges. The old companion and associate of Pe-shau-ba, Waw-so, had been accidentally killed by an Assinneboin in hunting. Here we lived in plenty and contentment, but Pe-shau-ba, upon whom the death of his friend Waw-so had made some impression, was soon taken violently ill. He was conscious that his end was approaching, and very frequently told us he should not live long. One day he said to me, "I remember before I came to live in this world, I was with the Great Spirit above. And I often looked down, and saw men upon the earth. I saw many good and desirable things, and among others, a beautiful woman, and as I looked day after day at the woman, he said to me, 'Pe-shau-ba, do you love the woman you are so often looking at?' I told him I did: then he said to me, 'Go down and spend a few winters on the earth. You cannot stay long, and you must remember to be always kind and good to my children whom you see below.' So I came down, but I have never forgotten what was said to me. I have always stood in the smoke between the two bands, when my people have fought with their enemies. I have not struck my friends in their lodges. I have disregarded the foolishness of young men who would have offended me, but have always been ready and willing to lead our brave men against the Sioux. I have always gone into battle painted black, as I now am, and I now hear the same voice that talked to me before I came to this world: it tells me I can remain here no longer. To you, my brother, I have been a protector, and you will be sorry when I leave you; but be not like a woman, you will soon follow in my path." He then put on the new clothes I had given him to wear below, walked out of the lodge, looked at the sun, the sky, the lake, and the distant hills; then came in, and lay down composedly in his place in the lodge, and in a few minutes ceased to breathe.

After the death of Pe-shau-ba, I wished to have made another attempt to come to the States; but Waw-zhe-kah-maish-koon prevented me. I lived with him the remainder of the winter, and in the spring went to Ne-bo-wese-be, (Dead River,) where we planted corn, and spent the summer. In the fall, after the corn was gathered, we went to our hunting grounds.

An old Ojibbeway, called Crooked Finger, had been living in my lodge about a year; in all that time, having never killed any thing. When I started to hunt buffaloe, he followed me, and we came at the same time in view of a large herd, when the old man endeavoured to raise a quarrel about my right to use those hunting grounds. "You Ottawwaws," said he, "have no right in this part of the country; and though I cannot control all of you, I have you, at last, now in my power, and I am determined, that if you do not go back to your own country from this very spot, I will kill you." I had no apprehension on account of his threat, and I defied him to injure or molest me. After an hour or more of altercation, he crept up, and at length began to shoot at the herd of buffaloe. Soon after he had left me, two Ottawwaws, who had overheard the quarrel as they were coming up, and had concealed themselves in the bushes near, joined me. The old man, after three or four unsuccessful shots at the buffaloe, turned and went home, ashamed alike of his insolence to me, and of his want of success. Then I went forward with the two young Ottawwaws who had joined me, and we killed a considerable number of fat cows.

Shortly after this, when I had been hunting all day, on returning home late at night, I found a very unusual gloominess in the countenances of all the inmates of my lodge. I saw there a man named Chik-ah-to, who was almost a stranger to me. He, and all the rest of them, seemed as if cast down by some sudden and unexpected bad news; and when I asked my wife the cause of this apparent distress, she returned me no answer. At length, Waw-zhe-kah-maish-koon, in reply to my earnest inquiries, told me, with the utmost seriousness, and a voice of solemn concern, that the Great Spirit had come down again. "What, has he come again so soon?" said I; "He comes often of late; but I suppose we must hear what he has to say." The light and irreverent manner in which I treated the subject, was very offensive to many of the Indians, and they apparently all determined to withhold from me all communications respecting it. This was to me a matter of little consequence, and I went, as usual, to my hunting, on the following morning. My own indifference and contempt for these pretended revelations of the Divine will, kept me in ignorance, for some time, of the purport of the present one. But at a subsequent period of my life, I found, that though my skepticism might not be offensive to the Great God, in whose name these revelations were made to us, still it was highly so to those who were pleased to stile themselves his messengers; and that, by incurring their ill will, I exposed myself to much inconvenience and danger.

In the spring of the year, after we had assembled at the trading house at Pembinah, the chiefs built a great lodge, and called all the men together to receive some information concerning the newly revealed will of the Great Spirit. The messenger of this revelation, was Manito-o-geezhik, a man of no great fame, but well known to most of the Ojibbeways of that country. He had disappeared for about one year, and in that time, he pretended to have visited the abode of the Great Spirit, and to have listened to his instructions: but some of the traders informed me, he had only been to St. Louis, on the Mississippi.

The Little Clam took it upon him to explain the object of the meeting. He then sung and prayed, and proceeded to detail the principal features of the revelation to Manito-o-geezhik. The Indians were no more to go against their enemies; they must no longer steal, defraud, or lie; they must neither be drunk, nor eat their food, nor drink their broth when it was hot. Few of the injunctions of Manito-o-geezhik were troublesome or difficult of observance, like those of the Shawnee prophet. Many of the maxims and instructions communicated to the Indians, at this time, were of a kind to be permanently and valuably useful to them; and the effect of their influence was manifest for two or three years, in the more orderly conduct, and somewhat amended condition of the Indians.

When we were ready to separate from the trading-house, Aisainse, (the little clam,) invited several of us, myself in particular, to accompany him to his residence at Man-e-to Sah-gi-e-gun, or Spirit Lake,* but I would not join him, as I wished to remain in a woody country, for the purpose of hunting the fur-bearing animals. Ten men, among whom were Wa-ge-tone and Gi-ah-gegit, together with great numbers of women, accepted his invitation, and went with him. A young man, a friend of the Little Clam, named Se-gwun-oons, (spring deer,) before they separated from us at Pembinah, predicted that he would be killed at Spirit Lake. Many other predictions he made, which were verified from day to day, until the Indians came to have such confidence in him, that his admonitions of impending danger to those who should go to Spirit Lake, began to be so much regarded, that Wa-me-gon-a-biew, and many others, became alarmed, and returned. Last of all came Match-e-toons, a foolish and lying young man, who reported that the indications of danger thickening around the Little Clam and his band, he had stolen away in the night, and the next morning, though he had fled a considerable distance, he heard the guns of the Sioux at the camp he had left. We did not immediately credit the account of this man, but waited anxiously, from day to day, till at last the chiefs determined to send twenty men, to ascertain whether there was any foundation for his statement. This party, when they arrived at the place where the Little Clam had been encamped, found that the whole band had been cut off. First, and in advance of all the camp, lay the body of Se-gwun-oons, the young man who had predicted the attack before he left Pembinah. Near him lay some young men of his own age, and farther back

* *Devil Lake*, and on the North West Company's map, *God's Lake*.

the stout body of the Little Clam, stuck full of arrows. In the camp the ground was strewed with the bodies of the women and children. At a distance was the body of one of the Sioux, in a sitting posture, and covered with the puk-kwi, or mats, which had belonged to the Ojibbeway lodges. Not one escaped except Match-e-toons, but some afterwards doubted whether he had not fled in the time of the fight, instead of the evening before, as he had stated. Thus died the Little Clam, the last of the considerable men of his age, belonging to the Ojibbeways of Red River. Our village seemed desolate after the recent loss of so many men.

We then went down to Dead River, planted corn, and spent the summer there. Sha-gwaw-koo-sink, an Ottawwaw, a friend of mine, and an old man, first introduced the cultivation of corn among the Ojibbeways of the Red River country.

In the ensuing fall, when we went to our hunting grounds, the wolves were unusually numerous and troublesome. They attacked and killed my horse, and several of my dogs. One day, when I had killed a moose, and gone with all my family to bring in the meat, I found, on my return, the wolves had pulled down my lodge, carried off many skins, carrying-straps, and, in fine, whatever articles of skin, or leather, they could come at. I killed great numbers, but they still continued to trouble me, particularly an old dog wolf, who had been so often at my door that I knew his appearance, and was perfectly acquainted with his habits. He used, whenever he came, to advance boldly upon my dogs, and drive them in; he would then prowl about, to seize whatever he could find of food. At last, I loaded my gun, and went out, when he sprang directly at me; but I shot him before he had time to fasten upon me. Half his hair had fallen off.

CHAPTER XI.

Rapacity of the traders—revelation of Manito-o-geezhik—pretensions of As-kaw-ba-wis—credulity of the Indians—colony at Red River, planted by the Hudson's Bay traders—large war-party assembled at Turtle Mountain—want of discipline.

MR. HENRY had traded ten years at Pembinah; he was succeeded by a Mr. M'Kenzie, who remained but a short time, and after him came Mr. Wells, called by the Indians Gah-se-moan, (a sail,) from the roundness and fulness of his person. He built a strong fort on Red River, near the mouth of the Assinneboin. The Hudson's Bay Company had now no post in that part of the country, and the Indians were soon made conscious of the advantage which had formerly resulted to them from the competition between rival trading companies. Mr. Wells, at the commencement of winter, called us all together, gave the Indians a ten gallon keg of rum, and some tobacco, telling them, at the same time, he would not credit one of them the value of a single needle. When they brought skins, he would buy them, and give in exchange such articles as were necessary for their comfort and subsistence during the winter. I was not with the Indians when this talk was held. When it was reported to me, and a share of the presents offered me, I not only refused to accept any thing, but reproached the Indians for their pusillanimity in submitting to such terms. They had been accustomed, for many years, to receive credits in the fall; they were now entirely destitute not of clothing merely, but of ammunition, and many of them of guns and traps. How were they, without the accustomed aid from the traders, to subsist themselves and their families during the ensuing winter? A few days afterwards, I went to Mr. Wells, and told him that I was poor, with a large family to support by my own exertions, and that I must unavoidably suffer, and perhaps perish, unless he would give me such a credit as I had always, in the fall, been accustomed to receive. He would not listen to my representation, and told me, roughly, to be gone from his house. I then took eight silver beavers, such as are worn by the women, as ornaments on their dress, and which I had purchased the year before at just twice the price that was commonly given for a capote; I laid them before him, on the table, and asked him to give me a capote for them, or retain them as a pledge for the payment of the price of the garment, as soon as I could procure the peltries. He took up the ornaments, threw them in my face, and told me never to come inside of his house again. The cold weather of the winter had not yet set in, and I went immediately to my hunting ground, killed a number of moose, and set my wife to make the skins into such garments as were best adapted to the winter season, and which I now saw we should be compelled to substitute for the blankets and woollen clothes we had been accustomed to receive from the traders.

I continued my hunting with good success, but the winter had not half passed, when I heard that Mr. Hanie, a trader for the Hudson's Bay people, had arrived at Pembinah. I went immediately to him, and he gave me all the credit I asked, which was to the amount of seventy skins. Then I went to Muskrat River, where I hunted the remainder of the winter, killing great numbers of martens, beavers, otters, &c.

Early in the spring, I sent word by some Indians to Mr. Hanie, that I would go down to the mouth of the Assinneboin, and meet him there, to pay my credit, as I had skins more than enough for this purpose.

When I arrived at the Assinneboin, Mr. Hanie had not yet passed, and I stopped to wait for him opposite Mr. Well's trading house. An old Frenchman offered me a lodging in his house, and I went in and deposited my peltries under the place he gave me to sleep in. Mr. Wells, having heard of my arrival, sent three times, urging me to come and see him. At last, I yielded to the solicitations of my brother-in-law, and crossed over with him. Mr. Wells was glad to see me, and treated me with much politeness; he offered me wine and provisions, and whatever his house afforded. I had taken nothing except a little tobacco, when I saw his Frenchman come in with my packs. They carried them past me into Mr. Well's bed room; he then locked the door, and took out the key. Immediately his kindness and attentions to me relaxed. I said nothing, but felt not the less anxious and uneasy, as I was very unwilling to be deprived of the means of paying Mr. Hanie his credit, still more so to have my property taken from me by violence, or without my own consent. I watched about the house, and at length found an opportunity to slip into the bed room, while Mr. Wells was then taking something from a trunk. He tried to drive me, and afterwards to push me out, but I was too strong for him. After he had proceeded to this violence, I did not hesitate to take up my packs, but he snatched them from me. Again I seized them, and in the struggle that ensued, the thongs that bound them were broken, and the skins strewed about the floor. As I went to gather them up, he drew a pistol, cocked it, and presented it to my breast. For a moment I stood motionless, thinking he would certainly kill me, as I saw he was much enraged; then I seized his hand, and turned it aside, at the same moment drawing from my belt a large knife, which I grasped firmly in my right hand, still holding him by my left. Seeing himself thus suddenly and entirely in my power, he called first for his wife, then for his interpreter, and told them to put me out of the house. To this, the interpreter answered, "You are as able to put him out as I am." Some of the Frenchmen were also in the house, but they refused to give him any assistance. Finding he was not likely to intimidate or overcome me by violence, he had recourse once more to milder measures. He offered to divide with me, and to allow me to retain half my peltries for the Hudson's Bay people. "You have always," said he, "belonged to the north west; why should you now desert us for the Hudson's Bay?" He then proceeded to count the skins, dividing them into two parcels; but I told him it was unnecessary, as I was determined he should not have one of them. "I went to you," said I, "last fall, when I was hungry and destitute, and you drove me, like a dog, from your door. The ammunition with which I killed these animals, was credited to me by Mr. Hanie, and the skins belong to him; but if this was not the case, you should not have one of them. You are a coward; you have not so much courage as a child. If you had the heart of a squaw, you would not have pointed your pistol at my breast, and have failed to shoot me. My life was in your power, and there was nothing to prevent your taking it, not even the fear of my friends, for you know that I am a stranger here, and not one among the Indians would raise his hand to avenge my death. You might have thrown my body into the river, as you would a dog, and no one would have asked you what you had done; but you wanted the spirit to do even this." He asked me if I had not a knife in my hand. I then showed him two, a large and a small one, and told him to beware how he provoked me to use them. At last, wearied with this altercation, he went and sat down opposite me in the large room; though he was at considerable distance, so great was his agitation, that I could distinctly hear his heart beat. He sat awhile, then went and began to walk back and forth in the yard. I collected my skins together, and the interpreter helped me to tie them up; then taking them on my back, I walked out, passed close by him, put them in my canoe, and returned to the old Frenchman's house, on the other side.

Next morning, it appeared that Mr. Wells had thought better of the subject, than to wish to take my property from me by violence, for he sent his interpreter to offer me his horse, which was a very valuable one, if I would think no more of what he had done. "Tell him," said I, to the interpreter, "he is a child, and wishes to quarrel and forget his quarrel in one day; but he shall not find I am like him; I have a horse of my own; I will keep my packs; nor will I forget that he pointed his pistol at my breast, when he had not the courage to shoot me."

On the following morning, one of the clerks of the North West Company arrived from the trading-house at Mouse River, and he, it appeared, told Mr. Wells, when he heard what had passed, that he would take my packs from me; and though Mr. Wells cautioned him against it, he determined on making the attempt. It was near noon, when the old Frenchman, after looking out of his house, said to me, "My friend, I believe you will lose your packs now; four men are coming this way, all well armed; their visit, I am sure, is for no good or friendly purpose." Hearing this, I placed my packs in the middle of the floor, and taking a beaver trap in my hand, sat down on them. When the clerk came in, accompanied by three young men, he asked me for my packs. "What right have you," said I, "to demand them?" "You are indebted to me," said he. "When did I owe the North West any thing, that was not paid at the time agreed on?" "Ten years ago," said he, "your brother, Wa-me-gon-a-biew, had a credit from me, which he paid all but ten skins; those are still due, and I wish you to pay them." "Very well," said I, "I will pay your demand, but you must, at the same time, pay me for those four packs of beaver we sent to you from the Grand Portage. Your due bill was, as you know, burned with my lodge, at Ke-nu-kaw-ne-she-wa-bo-ant, and you have never paid me, or any member of our family, the value of a single needle for those one hundred and sixty beaver skins." Finding this method would not succeed, and knowing, though he disregarded it, the justice of my reply, he tried the effect of violent measures, like those used on the preceding day by Mr. Wells; but when he perceived these were and would be equally unavailing, he returned to the fort, without having taken a single marten skin from me.

When I ascertained that it would be some time before Mr. Hanie would arrive, I went down to Dead River, and while I was waiting there, killed four hundred muskrats. At last, Mr. Hanie arrived at the place where I, with another man, had been waiting for him. He told me that he had passed Mr. Wells' trading-house, at the mouth of the Assinneboin, in the middle of the day, with his crew singing. Mr. Wells, on seeing him, had immediately started after him, with a canoe strongly manned and armed. On perceiving this pursuit, Mr. Hanie went on shore, and leaving his men in his canoe, went up about twenty yards into a smooth prairie. Hither Mr. Wells followed him, attended by several armed men; but Mr. Hanie made him stop at the distance of ten yards, and a long dispute followed, which ended in his permitting Mr. Hanie to pass down. I related to him my story of the treatment I had received, and paid him his credit. I traded with him for the remainder of my peltries, and after we had finished, he gave me some handsome presents, among which was a valuable gun, and then went on his way. As I was re-ascending Red River, I met Mr. Wells. He was destitute of fresh game, and asked me for some, which I should have given, had it been in my power; but he attributed my refusal to ill will. Afterwards, though I was living at a distance from him, he sent his horse to me, and again subsequently to Pembinah, but I constantly refused to accept it. Notwithstanding my steady and repeated refusal, I was informed he always said the horse belonged to me, and after his death, which happened three years later, the other traders told me I ought to take the horse; but I would not, and it fell into the hands of an old Frenchman. After the death of Mr. Wells, I returned to the North West Company, and traded with them, as before; but never while he lived. If he had shot me, and wounded me ever so severely, I should have been less offended with him, than to have him present his pistol, as he did, to my breast, and take it away without firing.

Esh-ke-buk-ke-koo-sa, a chief of Leech Lake, came after this to Pembinah, with about forty young men, and I went, by invitation, from the Be-gwi-o-nus-ko, with others, to hear him give some account of the recent revelation from the Great Spirit to Manito-o-geezhik. We were all assembled one night in a long lodge, erected for the purpose, to dance and feast, and listen to the discourse of the chief, when suddenly we heard two guns, in quick succession, in the direction of the North West Company's trading-house, now unoccupied, except by two Frenchmen, who had that day arrived. The old men looked at each other in doubt and dismay. Some said the Frenchmen are killing wolves, but Esh-ke-buk-ke-koo-sa said, " I know the sound of the guns of the Sioux." The night was very dark, but all the young men took their arms and started immediately, and I among the foremost. Many getting entangled among logs and stumps, made but little progress. I kept the path, and was still foremost, when a dark figure shot past me, and, at the same moment, I heard the voice of the Black Duck, saying, neen-dow-in-nin-ne, (I am a man.) I had often heard of the prowess of this man, and in one instance had seen him at the Sioux village, at Chief Mountain, lead in what we all supposed would be an attack. Now I determined to keep near him. We had advanced within about gun shot of the fort, when he began to leap, first to one side, and then to the other, thus moving in a zigzag line, though rapidly, towards the gate of the fort. I followed his example, and when he leapt into the open gate of the fort, it was with a surprising effort of activity, which carried his feet near two yards from the ground. We saw within the fort a house, at the window and door of which we perceived a bright light. The Black Duck had a buffaloe robe over his shoulders, the dark colour of which enabled him to pass the window undiscovered by the man who was watching within; but my white blanket betraying me, the muzzle of a gun was instantly presented to my head, but not discharged, for the Black Duck at that instant caught in his arms the affrighted Frenchman, who had mistaken me for one of the Sioux, and was in the act of firing upon me. The second Frenchman was with the women and children, who were all lying in a heap in the corner of the room, crying through fear. It appeared that the one who was watching by the window, who was the most manly of the two, had, a few minutes before, been driving his horse out of the fort, to give him water, when the animal had been shot dead in the gate by some men concealed near at hand. He at first thought we were the people who had shot his horse; but he was soon convinced of his error, as we did not even know that the body of the horse was lying at the gate, having jumped entirely over it when we entered. This Frenchman would not leave the fort; but the Black Duck, who was a relative of one of the women, insisted that they should be taken to the Indian camp. Others of our young men had by this time come up, and we determined to watch in the fort all night. Next morning we found the trail of the two men who had crossed the Pembinah river, a considerable war party having been concealed on the other side. The two men were the celebrated Yauktong chief, Wah-ne-tow, and his uncle. They had concealed themselves near the gate of the fort, with the determination to shoot down whatever came out or went in. The first that passed, happening to be the Frenchman's horse, he was shot down; and the two men, probably without knowing whether they had killed man or beast, fled across the river.

When it was ascertained that the Sioux war party was not a very large one, many were disposed to pursue after it, but Eshke-buk-ke-koo-sha said, "not so, my brethren; Manito-o-geezhik, whose messenger I am to you, tells us we must no more go against our enemies. And is it not manifest, that in this instance the Great Spirit has protected us. Had the Sioux come about our lodge when we were feasting in security, without our arms in our hands, how easily might they have killed all of us; but they were misled, and made to mistake a Frenchman's horse for an Ojibbeway. So will it continue to be, if we are obedient to the injunctions we have received." I began to be apprehensive for my family, having left them at home, and fearing that the Sioux might visit them, on their way to their own country. "Go," said Esh-ke-buk-ke-koo-sha, when I told him of my anxiety, "but do not fear that the Sioux can do any injury to your wife or children; but I wish you to go, that on your return you may bring me your medicine bag, and I shall show you what to do with the contents." I did accordingly, and he ordered the contents of my medicine bag, except the medicines for war and hunting, to be thrown into the fire. "This," said he, "is what we must henceforth do; if any one is sick, let them take a bowl of birch bark, and a little tobacco; the sick person himself, if he is able to walk, otherwise his nearest relative, and let them go to the nearest running water. Let the tobacco be offered to the stream, then dipping the bowl in the same direction in which the water runs, let them take a little, and carry it home, for the sick person to drink. But if the sickness be very severe, then let the person that dips up the water, plunge the bowl so deep that the edge of it shall touch the mud in the bottom of the stream." He then gave me a small hoop of wood to wear on my head like a cap. On one half of this hoop, was marked the figure of a snake, whose office, as the chief told me, was to take care of the water; on the other half, the figure of a man, to represent the Great Spirit. This band, or fillet, was not to be worn on ordinary occasions—only when I should go to bring water for some of my family or friends who should be sick. I was much dissatisfied at the destruction of the contents of my medicine bag, many of them being such roots and other substances, as I had found useful, in the disorders incident to my situation; and I was still more displeased, that we were not, henceforth, to be allowed to use these remedies, some of which I knew to be of great value. But all the Indians of the band were in the same situation with myself, and I was compelled to submit.

When the spring came on, I went to fulfil an appointment I had made the preceding fall, with Sha-gwaw-ko-sink, to meet him at a certain place. I arrived on the spot at the time appointed, and shortly afterwards, the old man came, on foot and alone, to search for me. He had encamped about two miles distant, where he had been for two days, and they had plenty of fresh meat, which was particularly grateful to me, as for some time past I had killed but little.

I lived with him during the summer. Sha-gwaw-ko-sink was now too old and feeble to hunt; but he had some young men with him, who kept him supplied, while game was to be had; but late in the fall, the hunting grounds about us became poor. The weather was very cold, and the ground hard frozen, but no snow fell; so that it was difficult to follow the tracks of the moose, and the noise of our walking on hard ground and dry leaves, gave the animals timely warning of our approach. This state of things continuing for some time, we were all reduced nearly to starvation, and had recourse, as a last resort, to medicine hunting. Half the night I sung and prayed, and then lay down to sleep. I saw, in my dream, a beautiful young man come down through the hole in the top of my lodge, and he stood directly before me. "What," said he, "is this noise and crying that I hear? Do I not know when you are hungry and in distress? I look down upon you at all times, and it is not necessary you should call me with such loud cries." Then pointing directly towards the sun's setting, he said, " do you see those tracks?" "Yes," I answered, "they are the tracks of two moose." "I give you those two moose to eat." Then pointing in an opposite direction, towards the place of the sun's rising, he showed me a bear's track, and said, "that also I give you." He then went out at the door of my lodge, and as he raised the blanket. I saw that snow was falling rapidly.

I very soon awoke, and feeling too much excited to sleep, I called old Sha-gwaw-ko-sink to smoke with me, and then prepared my Muz-zin-ne-neen-suk,* as in the subjoined sketch, to re-

* *Muz-zin-ne-neen, muz-zin-ne-neen-sug*—singular and plural. *Meshe-nin-ne-shah, Meshe-nin-ne-shuk*—Menomonie dialect. These little images, or drawings, for they are called by the same names, whether of carved wood, or rags, or only rudely sketched on birch bark, or even traced in sand, are much in use among several, and probably all the Algonkin tribes. Their use is not confined to hunting, but extends to the making of love, and the gratification of hatred, revenge, and all malignant passions.

It is a prevailing belief, to which the influence of established superstition has given an astonishing power, that the necromancers, men and women of medicine,

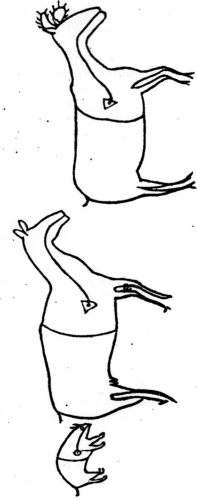

MUZZINNENEENSUK,

Used in Medicine Hunting.

present the animals whose tracks had been shown me in my dream. At the earliest dawn, I started from the lodge in a heavy fall of snow, and taking the course pointed out to me, long before noon I fell on the track of two moose, and killed them both, a male and a female, and extremely fat.

or those who are acquainted with the hidden powers of their *wusks*, can, by practising upon the Muz-zin-ne-neence, exercise an unlimited control over the body and mind of the person represented. As it may have been, in former times, among the people of our race, many a simple Indian girl gives to some crafty old squaw her most valued ornaments, or whatever property she may possess, to purchase from her the love of the man she is most anxious to please. The old woman, in a case of this kind, commonly makes up a little image of stained wood and rags, to which she gives the name of the person whose inclinations she is expected to control; and to the heart, the eyes, or to some other part of this, she, from time to time, applies her medicines, or professes to have done so, as she may find necessary to dupe and encourage her credulous employer.

But the influence of these images and conjurations, is more frequently tested in cases of an opposite character; where the inciting cause is not love, but hatred, and the object to be attained, the gratification of a deadly revenge. In cases of this kind, the practices are similar to those above mentioned, only different medicines are used. Sometimes the Muz-zin-ne-neence is pricked with a pin, or needle, in various parts, and pain or disease is supposed to be produced in the corresponding part of the person practised upon. Sometimes they blacken the hands and mouth of the image, and the effect expected, is the change which marks the near approach of death.

In the sanguinary chapter of the Calica Puran, we find reference to a similar superstition among the Asiatics.

"Let a figure be made, either of barley meal or earth, representing the person with whom the sacrificer is at variance, and the head of the figure struck off. After the usual texts have been used, the following is to be used in invoking the axe on the occasion: *Effuse, effuse blood! be terrific, be terrific! seize, seize! destroy, for the love of Ambica, the head of this enemy.* Having struck off the head, let him present it, using the texts laid down hereafter for the occasion, concluding with the word *phat.* Water must be sprinkled on the meal or earthen victim, which represents the sacrificer's enemy, using the text commencing with *Racta draibaih,* (i. e. by streams of blood,) and marks must be made on the forehead with red sanders; garlands of red flowers must be put round the neck of the image, and it must be dressed in red garments, tied with red cords, and girt with a red girdle. Then placing the head towards the north, let it be struck off with an axe, using the *Scanda* text."

So general and prevalent, among the Indians, is the confidence in the efficacy of these charms, and of those practised by means of a hair from the head of the intended victim, that the belief in them, has extended to many of the more ignorant of the Canadians who reside with the Indians, and even to some of the traders. Instances in which a hair is used in place of the image, or muz-zin-ne-neence,

The songs used on occasion of these medicine hunts, have relation to the religious opinions of the Indians. They are often addressed to Na-na-boo-shoo, or Na-na-bush, whom they intreat to

are frequently those of young women; and various, and sometimes dreadful, are the consequences supposed to result. So confident are the representations of whites, and those even of some shrewdness, and so strong the belief of the Indians, in the power of these drawings, as to enforce the conviction, that effects have been produced, in connexion with these mummeries, either by the influence of imagination, or the still more powerful and certain operation of poison, administered secretly. Poisoning is a crime of perhaps greater frequency among the Indians, than could have been expected from their situation; and they attribute equal guilt to the poisoner, whether he actually and craftily administers some powerful drug, or whether, at the distance of one or two hundred miles, or at any place, however remote, he so applies medicine to the Muz-zin-ne-neence, or to a hair, as to produce pain, sickness, death, or other suffering, in his enemy. The influence of these superstitious and absurd fears, is boundless, and would, perhaps, surpass comprehension and belief, if we could not look back to the time, when the minds of our own race were similarly enthralled; and when the dread of supernatural powers, in the hands of the malicious or the envious, formed one among the most serious and real evils, in the life even of the most enlightened and independent. Many cases of sudden sickness occur among them, and many deaths happen entirely in the way of nature, which they, being ignorant of the true cause, attribute to poison, or more frequently to bad medicine; but enough of well authenticated instances exist to prove that they, in some cases, practice upon each other by poison; sometimes using such noxious plants, or other substances, as their own country affords, and in other instances procuring arsenic, or other drugs, from the whites. To destroy life in this way, is perfectly in accordance with their ideas of bravery, or toughness of heart, (Soug-ge-da-win;) he being often esteemed the bravest man, who destroys his enemy with least risk to his own life.

The Chippewyans, whose bleak and inhospitable country, affords neither birch bark or other similar article, indeed nothing from the vegetable kingdom to serve as a substitute for the birch bark, and whose extreme rudeness has left them ignorant of any method of preparing from stones or earth, any thing suitable to write or delineate figures upon, use, in their preparations for the medicine hunt, the scapular bone of the rein deer, or such other animals as are found in their country. With an apparent poverty of language, corresponding to the meagerness of their soil, and the bluntness of their intellects, they denominate the drawing used in this kind of hunting, *El-kul-lah ki-eet-ze*, (the shoulder blade bone.) It would appear, also, that the accompanying ceremonies of this superstition are proportionably rude and inartificial. After awkwardly sketching the rein deer, or whatever animal they may happen to consider as indicated to them by their dream, they cast the bone on which the drawing is made into the fire, if, by chance, they happen to have one; and this fulfils all those important ends, which, in the imagination of the Ojibbeway hunter, are dependant upon the proper application of his medicines, and the patient chanting of his prayers.

be their interpreter, and communicate their requests to the Supreme; oftentimes, also, to Me-suk-kum-mik O-kwi, or the earth, the great-grand-mother of all. In these songs, they relate how Na-na-bush created the ground, in obedience to the commands of the Great Spirit, and how all things for the use, and to supply the wants of the uncles and aunts of Na-na-bush, (by which are meant men and women,) were committed to the care and keeping of the great mother. Na-na-bush, ever the benevolent intercessor between the Supreme Being and mankind, procured to be created for their benefit, the animals whose flesh should be for their food, and whose skins were for their clothing. He sent down roots and medicines, of sovereign power, to heal their sicknesses, and in times of hunger, to enable them to kill the animals of the chase. All these things were committed to the care of Me-suk-kum-mik O-kwi; and that his uncles and aunts might never call on her in vain, the old woman was directed to remain constantly at home in her lodge. Hence it is, that good Indians never dig up the roots of which their medicines are made, without at the same time depositing in the earth something as an offering to Me-suk-kum-mik O-kwi. They sing also, how, in former times, the Great Spirit having killed the brother of Na-na-bush, the latter was angry, and strengthened himself against the Supreme. Na-na-bush waxed stronger and stronger, and was likely to prevail against Gitch-e-manito, when the latter, to appease him, gave him the Me-tai. With this, Na-na-bush was so pleased, that he brought it down to his uncles and aunts on the earth.

Many of these songs are noted down, by a method probably peculiar to the Indians, on birch bark, or small flat pieces of wood; the ideas being conveyed by emblematic figures, somewhat like those before mentioned, as used in communicating ordinary information.

Two years previous to this time, a man of our band, called Ais-kaw-ba-wis, a quiet and rather insignificant person, and a poor hunter, lost his wife by death; and his children began, even more than formerly, to suffer of hunger. The death of his wife was attended with peculiar circumstances, and Ais-kaw-ba-wis became melancholy and despondent, which we attributed to the sluggishness of his disposition; but he at length called the chiefs together, and with much solemnity, announced to them that he had been favoured by a new revelation from the Great Spirit. He showed them a round ball of earth, about four or five inches in diameter, or more than half as large as a man's head, rolled round and smooth, and smeared with red paint. "The Great Spirit," said he, "as I sat, from day to day, crying, and praying, and singing in my lodge, at last called to me, and said, 'Ais-kaw-ba-wis, I have heard your prayers, I have seen the mats in your lodge wet with your tears, and have listened to your request. I give you this ball, and as you see it is clean and new, I give it to you for your business to make the whole earth like it, even as it was when Na-na-bush first made it. All old things must be destroyed and done away; every thing must be made anew, and to your hands, Ais-kaw-ba-wis, I commit this great work.'"

I was among those whom he called in to listen to this first annunciation of his mission. It was not until after he dismissed us that I said any thing; but then, in conversation with my companions, I soon betrayed my want of credulity. "It is well," said I, "that we may be made acquainted with the whole mind and will of the Great Spirit, at so cheap a rate. We have now these divinely taught instructors springing up among ourselves, and, fortunately, such men as are worth nothing for any other purpose. The Shawnee prophet was far off. Ke-zhi-ko-we-ninne and Manito-o-geezhik, though of our own tribe, were not with us; they were also men; but here we have one too poor, and indolent, and spiritless, to feed his own family, yet he is made the instrument, in the hand of the Great Spirit, as he would have us believe, to renovate the whole earth." I had always entertained an unfavourable opinion of this man, as I knew him to be one of the most worthless among the Indians, and I now felt indignant at his attempt to pass himself upon us as a chosen and favoured messenger of the Supreme Spirit. I hesitated not to ridicule his pretensions wherever I went; but notwithstanding that bad luck constantly attended him, he gained a powerful ascendancy over the minds of the Indians. His incessant beating of his drum at night, scared away the game from our neighbourhood, and his insolent hypocrisy made him offensive to me, at all times; but he had found the way to control the minds of many of the people, and all my efforts in opposition to him were in vain.

On one occasion, while we remained at this place, and had been suffering some days from hunger, I went out to hunt, and wounded a moose. On my return, I related this, and said I believed the moose was so badly wounded that he must die. Early next morning, Ais-kaw-ba-wis came to my lodge, and, with the utmost seriousness in his manner, said to me, that the Great Spirit had been down, and told him of the moose I had wounded. "He is now dead," said he, "and you will find him in such a place. It is the will of the Great Spirit that he should be brought here and cooked for a sacrifice." I thought it not improbable that the moose was killed, and went in search of him accordingly, but I found he was not dead. This afforded me another opportunity to ridicule the pretensions of Ais-kaw-ba-wis; but all seemed in no degree to impair the confidence of the Indians. Very shortly afterwards, it happened that I again wounded a moose, and went home without getting it. "This," said Ais-kaw-ba-wis, "is the moose which the Great Spirit showed me." So I went out and brought him in, and as I knew many of the Indians were hungry, I was willing to make a feast, though not out of deference to Ais-kaw-ba-wis. As we were too few in number to consume all the meat, we cut it off the bones, and these were heaped up before Ais-kaw-ba-wis, care being taken that not one of them should be broken. They were afterwards carried to a safe place, and hung up out of the reach of the dogs or wolves, as no bone of an animal offered in this way must, by any means, be broken. On the following day, I killed another fat moose, on which occasion Ais-kaw-ba-wis made a long address to the Great Spirit, and afterwards said to me, " You see, my son, how your goodness is rewarded; you gave the first you killed to the Spirit; he will take care you shall not want." Next day I went with my brother-in-law, and we killed each one, and now Ais-kaw-ba-wis exulted much in the efficacy of the sacrifice he had caused me to make, and his ascendancy over the superstitious minds of the Indians was confirmed. Notwithstanding this high degree of favour he had obtained by his cunning, he was a man who, once in his life, had eaten his own wife for hunger, and whom the Indians would then have killed as one unworthy to live.

When the snow began to harden on the top, at the approach

of the spring, the men of our band, Sha-gwaw-koo-sink, Wau-zhe-gaw-maish-koon, Ba-po-wash, Gish-kau-ko, myself, and some others, went to make a hunting camp at some distance, for the purpose of making dry meat, and left only Ais-kaw-ba-wis at home with the women. We killed much game, as it is very easy to take moose and elk at that season; the crust on the snow, while it will bear a man, almost deprives them of the power of motion. At length, Gish-kan-ko went home to see his family, and on his return he brought me a little tobacco from Ais-kaw-ba-wis, with this message, " Your life is in danger." " My life," said I, " belongs neither to Ais-kaw-ba-wis nor myself; it is in the hands of the Great Spirit, and when he sees fit to place it in danger, or bring it to an end, I shall have no cause to complain; but I cannot believe that he has revealed any part of his intentions to so worthless a man as Ais-kaw-ba-wis." But this intimation alarmed all the Indians who were with me, and they made the best of their way to the place where Ais-kaw-ba-wis was encamped with the women. I took a circuitous route by myself, to visit some of my traps, and having caught an otter, I took him on my back, and arrived at home some time after them. Here I found all our lodges converted into one large one; the women and children, together with the men who had arrived long before me, were shivering with cold by a fire in the open air. When I inquired the meaning of all this, they told me that Ais-kaw-ba-wis was preparing for some important communication to be given through him from the Great Spirit. He had been a long time in preparing the lodge, during which every one was excluded, and he had arranged that at a certain signal Ba-po-wash, who was to lead the dance, should enter, and the others were to follow him, and after having danced four times around the lodge, to sit down, each in his place. Hearing this, I immediately entered the long lodge, and throwing down my otter, seated myself by the fire. Ais-kaw-ba-wis gave me one angry and malicious look, then closed his eyes, and affected to go on with a prayer that I had interrupted. After some time, he began to drum and sing aloud, and at the third interval of silence, which was the signal agreed upon with Ba-po-wash, the latter came dancing in, followed by men, women, and children, and after circling the lodge four times, they all sat down in their places. ⁕ For a few moments all was silence, while Ais-kaw-ba-wis continued sitting with his eyes closed, in the middle of the lodge, by a spot of smooth and soft ground, which he had prepared, like that used by the war chiefs in their Ko-zau-bun-zitch-e-kun; then he began to call the men, one by one, to come and sit down by him. Last of all, he called me, and I went and sat down as he directed. Then addressing himself to me, he said, " Shaw-shaw-wa ne-ba-se, my son, it is probable you will now be frightened, as I have very unpleasant information to give you. The Great Spirit has, as you, my friends, all know, in former times, favoured me with the free communication of his mind ar will; lately he has been pleased to show me what is to happe to each of us in future. For you, my friends, [to Sha-gwaw-gc nuck and the other Indians,] who have been careful to regard and obey the injunctions of the Great Spirit, as communicated by me, to each of you he has given to live to the full age of man; this long and straight line is the image of your several lives. For you, Shaw-shaw-wa ne-ba-se, who have turned aside from the right path, and despised the admonitions you have received, this short and crooked line represents your life. You are to attain only to half of the full age of man. This line, turning off on the other side, is that which shows what is determined in relation to the young wife of Ba-po-wash." As he said this, he showed us the marks he had made on the ground, as below. The long, straight line, *a*, representing, as he said, the life of the Indians, Sha-gwaw-koo-sink, Wau-zhe-gaw-maish-koon, &c. The short crooked one, *b*, showing the irregular course and short con-

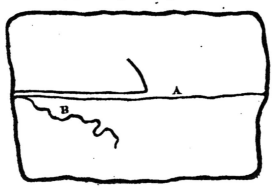

tinuance of mine; and the abruptly terminating one on the other side, showing the life of the favourite wife of Ba-po-wash. It happened that Ba-po-wash had dried the choice parts of a fat bear, intending, in the spring, to make a feast to his medicine; and a few days previous to this time, while we were absent at our hunting camp, Ais-kaw-ba-wis had said to the old woman, the mother of Ba-po-wash's wife, "The Great Spirit has signified to me, that all things are not as they should be; send out and see, therefore, if the fat bear which your son has hung up for a feast to his medicine, is all where it was left." She went out accordingly, and found that the feet of the bear were gone, Ais-kaw-ba-wis himself, who was a great glutton, having stolen them. This was now made known to Ba-po-wash, who was much alarmed at the threatened evil, and to avert it he not only gave Ais-kaw-ba-wis the remainder of the bear, but a large quantity of marrow he had saved for his feast, and other valuable presents.

After this, we started to come to an island called Me-nau-zhe-taw-naun, in the Lake of the Woods, where we had concluded to plant corn, instead of our old fields, at Dead River. On our way we stopped at a place to make sugar; then we went to visit the traders, leaving Ais-kaw-ba-wis with our women. It happened that the wife of Gish-kau-ko had left her kettle at the sugar camp, some distance from the place where they were to wait for our return. Some time after the men had gone, Ais-kaw-ba-wis, who lived by himself, in a little lodge, pretending to be too holy to go into a common house, or to mingle with men in their ordinary pursuits, sent for the wife of Gish-kau-ko, and when she came to him, he said, "The Great Spirit is not pleased that you should abandon and lose your property. Go, therefore, and get the kettle that you have left at the sugar camp." The woman obeyed; and he, soon after she had left the camp, took his gun, and under the pretence of going to hunt, went out in a different direction; but he had no sooner got out of sight of the lodges, than he turned, and by a circuitous route came upon the track of the wife of Gish-kau-ko. She, who had been before annoyed by his particular attentions, and surmised the real object he had in view, in sending her for the kettle, kept a look out behind her, and when she saw him come running after her, she began to run also. Just at this time I was returning from the trading-house with the other Indians, when we descried this chase at a distance. It occasioned us much alarm, when we saw first a woman, then a man, running with so much apparent earnestness; we thought nothing less than that the Sioux had come to the country, and were murdering our women and children. But when we came a little nearer, the pretended prophet gave over his pursuit of the woman, and came and sat down with us, to drink of the rum which the Indians had brought from the trading-house, and which they gave him very liberally. The woman was, however, after her arrival at home, compelled to give some account of the race, and she acknowledged that Ais-kaw-ba-wis had often sought similar opportunities to be alone with her, though such was her fear of him that she never dared make any disclosure, or offer any other resistance than an attempt to escape by flight. This discovery occasioned no disturbance, and seemed, in no degree, to diminish the influence of Ais-kaw-ba-wis. A large proportion of the rum we had brought from the trading-house was set apart for him, but when the principal man among us sent for him to come and receive it, he returned for answer, that he could not come. "Tell the chief," said he, "that if he has any business with me, he can come to my lodge." The liquor was accordingly carried to him; but its effect seemed to render his disposition somewhat more social and condescending, for about the middle of the night he came staggering into the lodge where I was, without the least covering on any part of his body. To me his appearance was ludicrous in the extreme, and I did not refrain from a good deal of irreverent merriment on the occasion.

After this, we came to the Lake of the Woods, where I hunted for about a month, then went back into the country I had left, all the Indians remaining behind to clear the ground where they intended planting corn at Me-nau-zhe-tau-naung. I now began to experience the inconveniences resulting from having incurred the ill will of Ais-kaw-ba-wis. He it was who prejudiced the Indians so much against me, and particularly the relatives of my wife, that my situation at Me-nau-zhe-tau-naung was uncomfortable, and I was compelled to return to Red River.

It was about this time that the Scots people, to the number of one hundred or more, arrived to settle at Red River, under the protection of the Hudson's Bay Company, and among these I saw, for the first time in many years, since I had become a man, a white woman. Soon after my arrival, I was taken into the employment of the Hudson's Bay Company, and Mr. Hanie, the agent, sent me, accompanied by Mr. Hess, an interpreter, and some men, to kill buffaloe. The buffaloe were, at that time, at a great distance, and the Scots people in great distress for want of provisions. I happened to find and kill two bulls near home, and after sending back the meat, I went on to the herds.

I had hunted here a few days, when our number was increased to four clerks and about twenty men, the latter employed in bringing in the meat I killed to my lodge, whence it was carried in carts to the settlement. All of these lived in my lodge; but one of the clerks, named M'Donald, was very abusive to my wife and children. Mr. Hess repeatedly checked him for this conduct, but as he continued it, he complained to Mr. Hanie, who sent M'Donald to a place several miles distant, where the Indians had killed about twenty buffaloes, which it was not convenient, at present, to bring out, and there he remained by himself for two months, having no other occupation or amusement than to scare the wolves away from the meat. Mr. M'Kenzie was one of the three remaining clerks who lived in my lodge, and he was so different from M'Donald, that at the end of four months, when the greater part of the people were called in to the settlement, he solicited and obtained from Mr. Hanie permission to remain longer with me, to improve himself in the Ojibbeway language, and he did not leave me until after the sugar season.

I killed, in the four months that I hunted for the Hudson's Bay Company, about one hundred buffaloes; but as part, or all of many of these were eaten in my own lodge, I delivered only forty entire and fat ones to the company's people, for which Mr. Hanie paid me, in the spring, three hundred and ten dollars. Those Scots labourers who were with me, were much more rough and brutal in their manners than any people I had before seen. Even when they had plenty, they ate like starved dogs, and never failed to quarrel over their meat. The clerks frequently beat and punished them, but they would still quarrel.

Mr. Hanie, and the governor for the Hudson's Bay's Company, proposed to me to build me a house, and engage me permanently in their employment; but I delayed accepting their offer, as I thought it doubtful whether their attempt at settling the country would finally succeed. Some of the Indians whom I had left at the Lake of the Woods, had followed me out, spent the winter with me, and returned long ago. I was still by myself at Red River, when Wa-ge-tote came from Me-nau-zhe-tau-naung, with a message from my father and mother-in-law. They had lost several of their children by death, and feeling lonely, they sent for me to come to them. This message Wa-ge-tote delivered to me in the presence of the traders, and some other persons; but afterwards he called me out by myself, and said to me, "Do not believe that your father-in-law calls you to Me-nau-zhe-tau-naung, to be at peace, or with any kind intention. When the children were sick, they called Ais-kaw-ba-wis to do something for them, and he having made a chees-suk-kon, said he had called you into his enclosure, and made you confess that you had shot bad medicine at the children, though you was at that time at Red River. He made your father-in-law believe that you had the power of life and death over his children, and he continues to believe, as do most of the Indians of the band, that it was your medicine which killed them. Be assured, therefore, that they call you thither with the design of killing you." Notwithstanding this admonition, I started immediately, as I knew if I did not they would be but the more confirmed in their unfounded opinion of my culpability.

I had bought a shirt from some of the Scots people at Red River, which I put on as I was about to start on this journey. Probably it was from this I contracted a disease of the skin, which became so troublesome and violent that I was compelled to stop at the Be-gwi-o-nus-ko River. Here I remained for a month, being for a long time unable to move. When I first stopped I set up my lodge on the brink of the river, and after I was unable to walk, I subsisted myself and family by lying in my canoe and fishing. After being placed in my canoe, sometimes I lay there for three or four days without being moved, covering myself with a mat at night. My wife was not so severely affected, being, though very sick, still able to walk. When I began to get a little better, I tried all sorts of medicines

I could procure, but none seemed to do me so much good as gun powder, moistened a little, and rubbed upon the sores, which were very large. This disorder, caught originally from the Scotch people, spread among the Indians, and killed numbers of them.

After I had recovered, I went up the Be-gwi-o-nus-ko, to the small lake of the same name, where I stopped to hunt, and killed plenty of meat. While I remained here, there came one day to my lodge, four young men from our village at Me-nau-zhe-tau-naung. In one of them, who was painted black, I recognized my brother-in-law. The three other children being dead, grief, and a feeling of loneliness, influenced him to leave his father, and start in search of some war party, that he might accompany them against their enemies, and thus have an opportunity of sacrificing, honourably, a life that had become irksome to him. The three young men his companions, being unwilling to see him depart alone, had voluntarily accompanied him. I gave him my horse, and then went up to the Lake of the Woods to my father-in-law, where I remained a few days. As it was then the time when the wild geese, having cast their quills, are unable to fly, we caught great numbers of them.

After four days, I said to the old people, "I cannot remain here, while my little brother has gone crying about, with none to protect him. I know there is danger in the path he will walk, and I ought to follow, to show him where it lies. He wishes to join a war party, that he may walk in a dangerous road; but there is often danger where we least expect it." I knew that Wa-me-gon-a-biew would fall upon this boy, and insult, or perhaps kill him, on account of his remote relationship to the man who wounded Taw-ga-we-ninne, at Mackinac, or at least with this pretence. Sha-gwaw-koo-sink, hearing my determination, and the reasons I gave for it, said he would accompany me; so we started together, and on our arrival at Red River, we heard that Wa-me-gon-a-biew had taken from the boy the horse I gave him, and had already threatened to kill him. I went immediately to Wa me-gon-a-biew, and a quarrel would probably have taken place at once, on account of the young man, had not old Net-no-kwa come between and separated us, as we were about to come to blows. We were all now about to join the Crees and Assinneboins, to go against the Sioux, and I cautioned my young brother-in-law to be, on this journey, always watchful of the movements of Wa-me-gon-a-biew. We were about forty men in number when we started from Red River. As we passed along through the Cree and Assinneboin encampments and villages on our route, our party was augmented to the number of two hundred men, long before we arrived at Turtle Mountain. While we were encamped near one of the Cree villages, Wa-ge-tote and the principal chiefs being called away to a feast, Wa-me-gon-a-biew began to talk of my brother-in-law; and as I did not like to hear him, I went out and walked about at a distance from the camp. When I thought the chiefs had returned from the feast, I re-entered the camp; but from the expression of concern and interest visible in the faces of those about me, I immediately comprehended that something had happened. I went to search for the young man, on whose account particularly I felt anxious; and finding him safe, was returning to my own place, when I discovered in the hands of an old man, who was trying to replace them in their original shape, the splinters and fragments of my new gun. I was at no loss to comprehend the nature of the accident which had deprived me of the use of my gun, at a time when it was likely to prove so important to me; and in the first moment of irritation, I seized the barrel, and was walking towards Wa-me-gon-a-biew, to beat him with it, when I met Wa ge-tote, who interfered to prevent me from striking him; though Wa-ge-tote himself, as well as the other chiefs, expressed the greatest dissatisfaction at what he had done.

But notwithstanding the loss of my gun, I did not turn back. Arming myself with my gun barrel in place of war club and spear, I went on. In two days from this camp, we arrived at the head of Turtle Mountain, being now about four hundred men. This was the place agreed upon for the assembling of all who should join in the party; and we had supposed that those we should meet here, would be few in number in comparison with ourselves. We were therefore somewhat surprised, when we found already on the ground, one thousand Assinneboins, Crees, and Ojibbeways.

We stopped at a little distance, and some communication took place between the chiefs, respecting the ceremony of salutation to be used. It is customary for war parties, engaged in the same cause, or friendly to each other, when they meet, to exchange a few shots by way of a sham battle, in which they use all the jumping, the whooping, and yelling of a real fight. But on this occasion both bands were so large, and one so much larger than the other, that the chiefs thought it more prudent to use a different method of exchanging compliments on meeting. It was agreed, on the part of Match-a-to-ge-wub,* the principal chief, that his young men should all remain in their lodges, and that twenty warriors of our band should salute their encampment, by practising the manoeuvres of attacking a village. A large lodge was set up for them to cut in pieces by their firing. I was one of the twenty selected for this performance, having supplied myself with a gun, which I procured from a man who turned back. It was not without the utmost exertion of all my strength, that I kept even pace with my companions, in running, leaping, loading, and yelling; and though we rested four times, when we arrived at the chief's lodge, and had blown it to fragments, I was entirely exhausted with fatigue. A man of our own party, imprudently, and without any authority, exposed himself in the village, while this salute was in progress; but his clothes were blown and scorched off his back, his lodge shot down, and himself much hurt. But as the exposure had been altogether voluntary on his part, and the notice taken of him rather honourable than otherwise, he had no cause of complaint.

On the first night after we came together, three men of the Ojibbeways were killed; on the next, two horses belonging to the Assinneboins, and on the third, three more. When such numbers of men assemble from different and remote parts of the country, some must be brought into contact, between whom old grudges and enmities exist; and it is not surprising, that the unstable power and influence of the chiefs, should be insufficient to prevent disturbances and bloodshed. On this occasion, men were assembled from a vast extent of country, of dissimilar feelings and dialects, and of the whole fourteen hundred, not one who would acknowledge any authority superior to his own will. It is true, that ordinarily they yield a certain deference, and a degree of

* *Match-a-to-ge-wub*, (in the Cree, *Mait-cha-to-ke-wub*,) in the Ojibbeway, means nearly "Many Eagles sitting."

obedience to the chief each may have undertaken to follow ; but this obedience, in most instances, continues no longer than the will of the chief corresponds entirely with the inclination of those he leads. In this party, were some who had been a year on their journey to reach this place. Two hundred lodges had their women with them.

Soon after we joined the main body at Turtle Mountain, a Cree, of Prairie Fort, adopted me into his family, taking my baggage, and inviting me into his lodge. He called me constantly Ne-je,* (my friend,) and treated me with great kindness. Many other men who were without lodges, were in like manner taken into the families of those that had.

But a few days had passed, when the little boys commenced, in the first instance a very small number, by kicking at each other in playfulness merely ; but it happened that on one side were Assinneboin children only, and on the other Crees and Ojibbeways ; by degrees larger and larger boys, and at last men, joined in on either side, and what had commenced in play, was like to terminate in a serious and bloody brawl. Match-a-to-ge-wub ran between the combatants, exerted his voice and his hands; afterwards Wa-ge-tote and all the other principal chiefs, but the young men paid little or no regard to them. The excitement which had kindled among them, was maddening to rage, and the chiefs were running about in the utmost distress and fear, when an old man, whose head was white as snow, and who was so bent down with age that he walked on two sticks, and looking more like a dog than a man, came out ; and though his voice was too feeble to be heard at any distance, he no sooner appeared, than all the Assinneboins desisted entirely from their violence, and the quarrel ended. Of those that were wounded and injured in this affair, only two died immediately ; but many were so much injured, that they were sent back to their own country. Had not the greater number entered into the affray without their arms, more extensive mischief would have resulted. Though I inquired much, I could neither learn the name, or hear any thing satisfactory of the history of the old man, by whose interference this affair was brought so timely to an end. Vague, and probably very extravagant reports, circulated among us respecting him.

* *Ne-je*, my friend, used to males; and *nin-dong-gwa*, used by females to one another.

CHAPTER XII.

Superstitions of the Indians—violent and unjust prejudice—family misfortunes—remarkable tenacity of life in the otter, and some other small animals—disturbances between the Hudson's Bay and North West Fur Companies.

In the evening after this affair, the chiefs walked through the village, and addressed all the people. The amount of what they said, was to direct, that instead of remaining longer to quarrel with and destroy each other, we should all move on the following morning towards the Sioux country. Accordingly, the camp was broken up, about half the number returning towards home, the remainder continuing on. It was now late in the fall, and we had travelled only two days from Turtle Mountain, when there came on a cold and violent storm of rain and snow. Two horses perished, and many men were near sharing the same fate; but most or all of the Ojibbeways, carrying each man on his back a puk-kwi of birch bark, large enough to afford a partial covering for three men, and all being disposed to extend to the destitute all possible assistance and relief, many of them were sheltered.

It was immediately after this storm that some one told me Ba-gis-kun-nung was coming to see me about the horse I had taken away from him. "Very well," said I, "I believe Ba-gis-kun-nung has one or two more horses, and if he gives me any trouble about the one I have taken, I will take another." At noon he came, but Wa-ge-tote, Ke-me-wun-nis-kung, and other men of my friends, had prepared themselves to resist any violence he might attempt to practise on me. He walked up to me as I was roasting some meat, and stood a very long time, I should say two hours, regarding me sternly, without saying a single word, and then walked off.

Two days afterwards, two hundred of the Assinneboins turned back. They were reviled and insulted at parting, by those who still continued on; but this seemed not in the least to shake their determination. Desertions, in small bodies, were now very numerous, and the remaining chiefs, with the hope of checking it, appointed fifty of the best of the young men to act as sentinels over the others; but this measure was productive of no benefit. When at last we arrived within two days' march of the village it was our intention to attack, four hundred men were all that remained, and the next day very few of these were found willing to follow Match-a-to-ge-wub. He started at the usual time, and walked on by himself, but when at the distance of about a mile, he saw that none followed him, he sat down in the prairie. From time to time, one or two men would start forward to join him; but for one who went forward, twenty or more would commonly start to go back. With my young brother-in-law I stood at the camp to see what would be the result, and when, at last, I saw that of the four hundred, only about twenty were willing to follow the chief farther, we determined to join them. We had proceeded but a little distance, when one of the Assinneboins, who had turned back, purposely set fire to the prairie, and we now all turned back except the chief and one or two men. He went on to the Sioux village, and was lurking about it for one or two days, when, finding himself discovered, he fled without attempting any thing. The Sioux pursued on our trail, and came in sight of us, but offered no molestation, and, in due time, we all arrived at home in safety. Thus ended this war excursion, for which such extensive preparations had been made, and from which so much had been expected. On the way home, Ke-me-wun-nis-kung took away the horse of the Assinneboin who had set the prairie on fire, and beat him, he daring to make no resistance.

When we returned to Pembinah, there was, as is usual on a return from a war-party, a drunken frolick, in which I joined, though not to very great excess. After I had drank a little, I heard some one speak sneeringly about my gun, which Wa-me-gon-a-biew had broken. I had lent my knife to some one to cut tobacco, but there was lying by the fire a pointed stick, on which meat had been roasted. This I seized, ran out, and finding his horse standing by the door of his own lodge, I stabbed him with it, using, at the same time, in a loud voice, the same words I had been told he had spoken when he broke my gun. The horse fell immediately, but did not die until next morning.

There were six of us to return together to the Lake of the Woods, and our principal man, She-gwaw-koo-sink, being alarmed, took a little canoe and set off in the night. I would not start then, nor even early in the morning, lest Wa-me-gon-a-biew should think I was afraid of him. I remained near his lodge until I had seen him and Net-no-kwa, and shaken hands with all my friends, and at about noon I was ready to follow She-gwaw-koo-sink, whom I found waiting for me in the woods. Wa-me-gon-a-biew made no complaints of my having killed his horse; probably he was perfectly satisfied that I had done so, as an Indian always expects any outrage he commits shall be retaliated, according to their customs, and a man who omits to take proper revenge is but lightly esteemed among them.

Heavy snow and severe cold came upon us at the Muskeeg* carrying place; the trees cracked with the cold, but the water in the swamp was not yet frozen hard enough to bear; our canoes, however, could not be pushed through. The utmost exertion of our strength would no longer avail to move them. We were hungry and much fatigued, and sat deliberating what was best to be done, when we discovered our women coming from the Lake of the Woods, and dragging their light canoes through water, ice, and snow above their knees. When they came up, we found they were my wife, the wives of She-gwaw-koo-sink and Ba-po-wash, and my mother-in-law. Three of our party, whose women had not come, had to continue on to the Lake of the Woods. Our wives laughed at us, telling us it was more like old women, than like warriors returning to their village, to sit shivering in a canoe which could move neither way, through fear of a little water and ice. They had brought us a supply of corn, sturgeon, and other food, and with them we returned to our last encampment, where we rested a few days, then went down to Red River, with the intention of spending the winter there.

There was now no snow on the ground at Red River, though the weather was very cold, and the ground so hard frozen that it was nearly impossible to kill any game. I hunted day after

* Mus-keeg, a marsh or swamp.

day without the least success, and we were reduced to extreme hunger, when one day I found a moose, and after I had, with the greatest difficulty, crept near, I was about to shoot him, when my best dog, which I had confined at home, came running past me, and scared the moose away. I returned home, and calling my dog to me, outside the lodge, I told him that it was his fault that there was now no food for my children. I then killed and gave him to my family to eat.

Other families beside my own being in distress for the want of food, the Indians called on me to make a medicine hunt. I accordingly told Me-zhick-ko-naum to go for my drum, and as preparatory to the commencement of my prayers and songs, I directed all my family to take such positions as they could keep for at least half the night, as, after I began, no one must move until I had finished. I have always been conscious of my entire dependence on a superior and invisible Power, but I have felt this conviction most powerfully in times of distress and danger. I now prayed earnestly, and with the consciousness that I addressed myself to a Being willing to hear and able to assist, and I called upon him to see and to pity the sufferings of my family. The next day I killed a moose, and soon after, a heavy snow having fallen, we were relieved from the apprehension of immediate starvation.

But though we were temporarily relieved, plenty did not return to us. I was about this time hunting one day, and fell on the track of a bear. My dogs followed for three days, and most of the time I kept nearly even pace with them; but at the end of that time they had not overtaken him. My moccasins and leggings were worn out, and I was almost in a state of starvation. I was compelled to return home, having killed nothing but eight pheasants. Me-zhick-ko-naum, Ba-po-wash, and the other Indians, now left me by myself, and I was soon able to kill enough to supply the wants of my family. I spent the winter here, and in the spring my friends rejoined me, and we returned together to our village at the Lake of the Woods.

At Me-nau-zhe-tau-naung great misfortunes awaited me. I omitted to mention an event of some importance, which happened long before the time I have now arrived at, being a very short time after the death of my friend Pe-shau-ba. I was then at

Dead River, at our corn fields, where an Ojibbeway of Red Lake, called Gi-ah-ge-wa-go-mo, came to my lodge in my absence, and took away one of my sons, a boy six years old. On my return, my wife told me what had happened, and I immediately pursued, and overtaking Gi-ah-ge-wa-go-mo at the distance of one day's journey, without his consent took one of his horses to bring my son back. I threatened him, that if he should make any similar attempt in future, he should not escape unpunished. But about four months after, when the snow was on the ground, I returned home from my days' hunt to hear the same account of my son being taken away by Gi-ah-ge-wa-go-mo. I now felt much irritated, and having inquired from the men in my lodge what horse he rode, I mounted my best, and pursued after him. They had lately moved from the place where I found them before, but following on, I overtook them on their journey. As I was coming near their party, I discovered Gi-ah-ge-wa-go-mo and another man, called Na-na-bush, watching for me in the bushes, a little behind their party. Before I came within gunshot, I called out to let them know I had discovered them, and holding my gun in my hand, cocked, and in a position for immediate use, I passed them, overtook the party, and discovering my little boy, without dismounting I stooped down and lifted him into my lap; then turning back, went to meet Gi-ah-ge-wa-go-mo and Na-na-bush. They had now left the thicket, and were standing in the path, the former holding his favourite horse by the halter. When I rode up to them, I left my son on the horse, with the reins in his hand, got down, and stabbed Gi-ah-ge-wa-go-mo's horse twice, with a large knife I had carried for the purpose. He clubbed his gun, and was about to strike me, but I caught it in descending, and wrested it out of his hands. He threatened he would shoot my horse whenever he could get a gun. I handed his own to him, and told him to shoot the horse now; but he dared not. "It seems," said I, "you have forgotten what I told you four months since, when you took away my son before; but I have not forgotten it, as you see. I am disposed to kill you now, but as you are so much frightened, I will let you live, to see if you will steal away any of my children hereafter." With this I left him. My friends could scarce believe I had killed his horse, but they did not blame me, neither did Gi-ah-ge-wa-go-mo ; at least I never heard that he complained of it, and at the time he molested me no more.

It was on my return to Me-nau-zhe-tau-naung, and when I was about clearing for myself a field there, that I found the ill will of the Indians, influenced, as I thought, principally by the unfriendly offices of Ais-kaw-ba-wis, becoming so strong against me that I determined to leave them. But at this time an accident happened to me, which disabled me for many months. I had ascended a large tree, to cut off the limbs, and having trimmed off the greatest part, I went up to cut the top off. Some of the upper branches struck the top of another tree, and threw the trunk, which I had cut off, against my breast, by which blow I was thrown off, and fell from a great height to the ground, where I lay for some time insensible, and when consciousness returned I could not use my voice, so that it was some time before I could make the Indians understand that I wished them to bring me water. I fainted three times in attempting to reach the lodge where I then lived.

Several of my ribs being broken, it was long before I recovered so as to walk about without assistance. Dr. M'Laughlin, a trader at Rainy Lake, hearing of my situation, sent Mr. Tace, with instructions to take me to his house, at White Fish Lake. For a long time I vomited blood, and felt, if moved, the sensation of a hot liquid in the cavity of my body. At Rainy Lake I experienced much attention and kindness from Mr. Tace, and other gentlemen belonging to the North West Company. In the latter part of the ensuing winter, I was better, but when the warm weather of the spring came on, I again relapsed, and became unable to hunt.

In ascending the long rapids of Rainy Lake River, in the spring, our canoes sunk, and I carried my children ashore on my back. Mr. Tace's canoe sunk also, but all the men were saved. A few days after this, we reached the trading-house of Dr. M'Laughlin, at Rainy Lake. This gentleman gave me a room in his house, where my children took care of me for some time. Every thing necessary was furnished me, and the Doctor would have had me remain with him a year; but I felt lonely and dissatisfied, and determined on going back to the Lake of the Woods, where my wife was, hoping that the trouble Ais-kaw-ba-wis had caused me, might now be at an end.

My reception was not such as I could have wished; but nevertheless, I remained in the village until the corn was planted; then we went to collect and dry the blue berries which grow in great quantities in that country. Afterwards to the rice swamps; then we returned to gather our corn. Thus we were busy during all the summer.

Late in the fall I became sick again, not having yet recovered from the hurt I had received in falling from the tree; and at about the same time some kind of sickness became frequent among the Indians. I was one day lying in my lodge, unable to sit up or walk about, and the women were at work in the field, when my mother-in-law unexpectedly came in with a hoe in her hands, and began to beat me on the head with it. I was unable to make much resistance, and as I did not attempt it, I endeavoured to reconcile myself to die, as I believed she would certainly kill me. While at work in the field, she had begun to cry for her children; and probably thinking that the man who had caused their death was now in her power, she ran in with the determination of killing me; but for some reason unknown to me, she desisted after she had beaten me for some time, and as I covered my head with my blanket, and with my hands and arms warded off the blows after the first, I was less severely injured, than I had cause to apprehend. So entire was the confidence my mother-in-law reposed upon the representations of Ais-kaw-ba-wis, that she did not doubt but I was in reality guilty of the death of her children; and as I well knew that this was the case, I blamed her less for her conduct, than I should otherwise have done. But notwithstanding she forbore to take my life, the unfriendly feeling on her part, and that of my wife, was becoming every day more and more manifest. This might have been in some measure owing to those misfortunes which had now impaired my health, and disqualified me for making so comfortable provision for my family as I formerly had done. But notwithstanding all the discouraging and distressing circumstances attendant on my present situation, I gradually recovered health and strength, and late in the fall, when the Indians were about to move to visit a trader, I was able to accompany them.

I had a small canoe of my own, in which I embarked myself and my children, but my wife and my mother-in-law were in the large canoe, with the provisions, and the baggage. During the first day of our journey, I went forward, with others of the Indians, leaving the women to come up to the encamping place, after we had stopped. I cut and put up the poles for my lodge, but no pukkwi, no provisions, and no women came. Next day I was ashamed to tell the Indians I had nothing to eat, though my children began to cry of hunger; and for the same reason, I would not encamp with them. I knew that my wife had deserted, and I had no reason to suppose she would immediately rejoin me. I therefore kept ahead of the Indians, and went, before I stopped, beyond the place where I knew they would encamp. Here I killed a fat swan, and was able to give my children some food. The weather was now becoming very cold, and I had about this time a wide traverse to cross. The weather was somewhat rough, but as I did not wish to remain to be overtaken by the Indians, I made my children lie down in the canoe, and covered the whole, as well as I could, with a buffaloe skin. The wind blew more and more violently, and the waves broke over my little canoe. The water froze upon the sides, and the children getting wet, suffered severely. I, also, was so much overpowered by the cold, that I could not manage the canoe properly, and it struck and was dashed in pieces on a rocky shoal, not far from the shore where I wished to land. Fortunately the water was not deep about the rock, nor between it and the land, and though a thin ice had formed, I was able to break it, and carry my children on shore. But here we had nearly perished from cold, as my spunk wood was wet, and I had no means of kindling a fire, until I thought to split open my powder horn, when I found in the middle of the mass of powder, a little which the water had not reached. This enabled me to kindle a fire, and was the means of saving all our lives. Next day, Mr. Sayre, at the trading house near by, heard of my situation; or at least the Indians having come up, and reported that I was lost, he sent out some men, who found me, and assisted me to reach the house. Here I took a credit for my whole family, not knowing but my wife would join me at some future time.

The chief of that country, from whom I had previously obtained permission to hunt in a little piece of ground which I had selected, and a promise that none of his people should interfere with me there, now endeavoured to dissuade me from going to spend the winter by myself. I ought, he said, either to remain near the Indians, or to take some other woman for a wife; as my children were young and unable to assist me, and my own health somewhat uncertain, he thought it would be very imprudent for me to attempt wintering alone. But I would not listen to his advice. At present, I had no inclination, either to remain with the Indians, or to take another wife. I therefore began to make a road immediately to my wintering ground. First I took the goods I had purchased, and carried them forward, then returned and brought up my children. My daughter Martha was then three years old, and the other children were yet small. In two or three days I reached my hunting ground, but was soon after reduced to great distress, from which I was relieved by a medicine hunt.

I had no pukkwi, or mats, for a lodge, and therefore had to build one of poles and long grass. I dressed moose skins, made my own moccasins and leggins, and those for my children; cut wood and cooked for myself and my family, made my snow shoes, &c. &c. All the attention and labour I had to bestow about home, sometimes kept me from hunting, and I was occasionally distressed for want of provisions. I busied myself about my lodge in the night time. When it was sufficiently light, I would bring wood, and attend to other things without; at other times I was repairing my snow shoes, or my own or my children's clothes. For nearly all the winter, I slept but a very small part of each night.

I was still living in this way in the spring, when a young man called Se-bis-kuk-gu-un-na, (tough legs,) a son of Wau-zhe-gaw-maish-koon, who was now dead, came to me. He was in a starving condition, as were his friends, who were encamped at no great distance from me. My dogs were now so well trained, that they could draw half a moose. I put on a full load of meat, and told him to go with the team, meet his people, and bring them to live with me. In three days they arrived; but though their hunger had been relieved by the supply I sent them, their appearance was extremely miserable, and it is probable they must have perished if they had not found me.

As the spring was approaching, we returned to the Lake of the Woods. Ice was still in the lake when we arrived on the shore of it; and as I, with my companions, was standing on the shore, I saw an otter coming on the ice at a distance. I had often heard the Indians say that the strongest man, without arms of some kind, cannot kill an otter. Pe-shau-ba, and other strong men and good hunters, had told me this, but I still doubted it. I now, therefore, proposed to test the truth of this common opinion. I caught the otter, and for the space of an hour or more, exerted myself, to the extent of my power, to kill him. I beat him, and kicked him, and jumped upon him, but all to no purpose. I tried to strangle him with my hands; but after lying still for a time, he would shorten his neck, and draw his head down between my hands, so that the breath would pass through, and I was at last compelled to acknowledge, that I was not able to kill him without arms. There are other small, and apparently not very strong animals, which an unarmed man cannot kill. Once while on a war party, in a sort of bravado, I had tried to kill a pole cat with my naked hands, but I had nearly lost my eyes by the means. The liquid which he threw upon my face, caused a painful inflammation, and the skin came off. The white crane, also, is dangerous, if approached too near; they can, and sometimes do, inflict mortal wounds with their sharp beaks.

After I had killed this otter, I went in pursuit of a bear. I had now three dogs, one of which was not yet fully grown. This dog, which was of a valuable breed, and had been given me by Mr. Tace, escaped from his halter at home, and came after me. When he came up, he passed me and the other dogs, and immediately assailed the bear's head; but the enraged animal almost instantly killed him, caught him up in his mouth, and carried him more than a mile, until he himself was overcome and killed.

It is usually very late in the spring, before the ice is gone from the Lake of the Woods. When I arrived at our village with the son of Wau-zhe-gaw-maish-koon, the Indians who were there had been for a long time suffering from hunger; but I had my canoe loaded with provisions, which I immediately distributed for their relief. On the day after my arrival, came my wife and her mother. She laughed when she saw me, and came to live with me, as heretofore. She-gwaw-koo-sink and Ais-kaw-ba-wis were both there, and both unfriendly to me; but I made it my business to seem wholly ignorant of the many attempts they made to injure me. About planting time, the traders of the North West Company sent messengers and presents to all the Indians, to call them to join in an attack on the Hudson's Bay establishment at Red River. For my own part, I thought these quarrels between relatives unnatural, and I wished to take no share in them, though I had long traded with the people of the North West Company, and considered myself as in some measure belonging to them. Many of the Indians obeyed the call, and many cruelties and murders were committed. On the part of the North West were many half-breeds, among whom, one called Grant, distinguished himself as a leader. Some of the Hudson's Bay people were killed in open fight, others were murdered after being taken prisoners.

A Mr. M'Donald, or M'Dolland,* who was called a governor for the Hudson's Bay, was waylaid, and fell into the hands of a Mr. Herschel, or Harshield, a clerk of the North West. This man sent him in a canoe with some Frenchmen and a half-breed, with directions to kill him and throw him into the water. When they had gone some distance, the half-breed, whose name was Maveen, wished to have killed him, but the Frenchmen would not consent. They left him on a small rocky island, from which he had no means of escape, and where they thought he must perish; but he was discovered and taken up by some Muskegoe Indians, who set him at liberty. Mr. Harshield beat and abused the Frenchmen for having neglected to kill the governor when he was in their power, and despatched other men in pursuit of him. When again taken, he entrusted him to the half-breed Maveen, and one

* Some of the circumstances of this murder, seem to identify it with that of Keveny, for which Charles De Reinhard and Archibald M'Lellan were tried at Quebec, in 1818, and the former condemned to death. De Reinhard, Mainville, and Jose, or Joseph, an Indian, otherwise called the Son of the White Partridge, seem to have been the immediate actors in this affair. It is not surprising that Tanner, who was then, as far as opportunities for particular information on this subject were concerned, on a par with the wildest Indian, should have mistaken foreign names, as well as the comparative rank and importance of foreigners in the country.

white man, who had been a soldier, but whose well known cruelty of disposition made him fit to be chosen for such business. These two murdered him, in a manner too cruel and shameful to be particularly narrated, and then returned with the account of what they had done to Mr. Harshield.

After the settlement at Red River was reduced to ashes, and the Hudson's Bay people driven out of the country, the Indians and half-breeds in the employ of the North West, stationed themselves at a place called Sah-gi-uk, at the outlet of Lake Winnipeg, to watch for, and destroy, any of the Hudson's Bay people who should attempt to enter the country in that direction. Ba-po-wash, my brother-in-law, was at length tired of starving there, and started by himself to come to our village, where I remained, refusing to take part with either side. On his way up, he met a Mr. M'Dolland, of the Hudson's Bay Company, who, with Mr. Bruce for his interpreter, was going into the country. This gentleman was slow to listen to the advice of Mr. Bruce, who being better acquainted with the state of affairs in the country, had many fears on his account. On meeting Ba-po-wash, whom he well knew, Mr. Bruce, by pretending to be still in the interest of the North West, was able to gain full intelligence of all that had passed. Being convinced of the truth of this information, Mr. M'Dolland was persuaded to turn back, and probably saved his life by so doing.

He came to me at Me-nau-zhe-tau-naung, and I confirming the statement of Ba-po-wash; he hastened back to the Saut De St. Marie, where he met Lord Selkirk, then coming into the country to settle the affairs of the two rival companies.

For my own part, I spent the summer in the usual quiet manner, being occupied with hunting, and the employments about our cornfields; in gathering wild rice, and fishing. When we were returning from the rice swamps, I stopped on one of the small islands in the route towards Rainy Lake, to hunt a bear with whose haunt I had long been acquainted. Late at night, after I had killed my bear, and as I was lying quietly in my lodge, I was surprised to hear at the door, a voice, which I knew immediately to be that of the Mr. Harshield I have already mentioned. I soon learned that he was on the look out for some one he had not found. Having discovered my light at a distance, he had supposed it to be that in the camp of Lord Selkirk, and had crept up with the stealth of an Indian warrior, or he could not have approached my lodge without my being aware of it. He did not immediately mention his intention of killing Selkirk; but I knew him and his companions, and was not at a loss to comprehend his purpose. Nor was I ignorant of the design with which he, with much art, endeavoured to get me to accompany him to Rainy Lake. But when he found that insinuations and dubious hints would not effect what he had in view, he openly avowed that it was his intention to kill Lord Selkirk, whenever he should meet him, and he then called up his two canoes, and showed them to me, each with ten strong and resolute men, well armed. He tried many methods to induce me to join him, but I would not.

After leaving me, he went on to Rainy Lake, to the trading house of Mr. Tace; but that gentleman being less inclined to violent measures, advised him to return immediately to his own country. What arguments Mr. Tace made use of I know not, but after two days Mr. Harshield returned towards Red River, leaving concealed in the woods near the trading house, the soldier who had taken part with Maveen, in the murder of the governor the year before. It was not certainly known among us what this man's instructions were, but it appeared he did not like his solitary residence in the woods, for after four days he returned to the fort.

In the mean time, Lord Selkirk had taken Fort William, which was then held by Mr. M'Gillivray, for the North West. From Fort William, he sent on an officer, with some troops, to take possession of Mr. Tace's trading house, in which the soldier who had killed governor M'Dolland was found. He was sent, with others who had attempted to rise after they had surrendered at Fort William, to Montreal, and I have heard that he was hung.

About this time, I made up my mind to leave the Indian country, and return to the States. I had many difficulties to encounter, originating in the ill will which had been raised against me among the Indians, particularly in the family of my father-in-law, by Ais-kaw-ba-wis. Mr. Bruce, with whom I now met, gave me much information and advice; he had travelled more, and seen more of white men than I had, and his statements encouraged me. The war of 1812 was now over, and there was, I thought, no insurmountable obstacle in the way of my return to my own country.

I had a fine crop of corn, and plenty of wild rice; and as I wished to move to Rainy Lake, where I could spend the winter, Mr. Bruce, who was going the same way, agreed to take twenty sacks of my corn, and at length I followed with my family. When I arrived near the trading-house at Rainy Lake, and where I expected to have found Mr. Tace, being as yet ignorant of the changes that had taken place, I found the captain I have before mentioned. He treated me with much attention, and would have given me some goods; but all those left in the house by the North West, had already been disposed of to the Indians. After several days' conversation with me, he succeeded in convincing me that the Hudson's Bay Company was that which, in the present quarrel, had the right on its side, or rather, was that which was acting with the sanction of the British government; and by promising to aid me in my return to the states, by liberal presents, good treatment, and fair promises, he induced me to consent to guide him and his party to the North West Company's house, at the mouth of the Assinneboin. The winter was now coming on, and had already commenced, but Capt. Tussenon, for that was his name, as nearly as I can recollect, said his party could not live at Rainy Lake, and it was necessary for him to go immediately on to Red River.

I started with twenty men in advance, and went to Be-gwi-o-nus-ko Sah-gie-gun, or Rush Lake, whence the horses were sent back, and the captain, with the remaining fifty men, came up. At Rush Lake we had snow shoes made, and engaged Shegwaw-koo-sink, Me-zhuk-ko-nong, and other Indians, to accompany us, as hunters, and as we had great quantities of wild rice, we were pretty well supplied with food. We had, however, a long distance to travel over the prairie, and the snow was deep. When we were out of meat, there was occasionally something of a mutinous disposition manifest among the soldiers, but little serious difficulty occurred. In forty days after we left Rainy Lake, we arrived at Red River, and took the fort at the mouth of the Pembinah, without any difficulty, there being few or no persons there, except squaws and children, and a few old Frenchmen.

From Pembinah, where I left my children, we went, in four days, to the Assinneboin, ten miles above the mouth, having crossed Red River a short time before. Here Be-gwais, a principal man of the Ojibbeways, met us, with twelve young men. Our captain and governor, who was with us, though they understood there were no more than twelve men in the North West Company's fort, at the mouth of the Assinneboin, seemed at a loss to know in what manner to attempt its reduction.

They counselled with Be-gwais, and he advised them to march immediately up to the fort, and show their force before it, which he thought would be sufficient to insure immediate surrender. When Capt. Tussenon had engaged me at Rainy Lake, I had told him I could make a road from that place to the door of Mr. Harshield's bed room, and considering myself able to do so, I was dissatisfied that they took no notice of me in these consultations; and at night, we at that time having approached very near, I communicated my dissatisfaction to Loueson Nowlan, an interpreter, who was well acquainted with the country, and who had a half brother in the fort, a clerk for Mr. Harshield. We talked together, as we left the place where they had been counselling, and after we had lain down by our own fire, and Nowlan agreed with me that it would be in the power of us two to go forward, and surprise, and take the fort, and we determined to attempt it; but we communicated our intention to some soldiers, who followed us. There were no hills, bushes, or other objects, to cover our approach; but the night was dark, and so extremely cold, that we did not suppose the people within could be very vigilant. We made a ladder in the way the Indians make them, by cutting the trunk of a tree, with the limbs trimmed long enough to serve to step on, and placing it against the wall, we went over and got down on the inside, on the top of the blacksmith's shop, whence we descended silently, one after another, to the ground. When a sufficient number of the men had got in, we went to find the people, first cautiously placing two or three armed men at the doors of the occupied rooms, to prevent them from getting together, or concerting any means of resistance.

We did not discover the bed room of Harshield until day light. When he found we were in the fort, he came out, strongly armed, and attempted to make resistance, but we easily overpowered him. He was at first bound, and as he was loud and abusive, the governor, who, with the captain, had now arrived, directed us to throw him out into the snow; but the weather being too cold for him to remain there without much danger of being frozen, they allowed him to come in, and he was placed by the fire. When he recognised me among his captors, he knew at once that I must have guided the party, and he reproached me loudly with my ingratitude, as he pretended formerly to have done me many favours. I told him, in reply, of the murders he had committed on his own friends, and the people of his own colour, and that it was on account of them, and his numerous crimes, that I had joined against him. "When you came to my lodge last fall, and I treated you with kindness, it was because I did not then see that your hands were red with the blood of your own relatives. I did not see the ashes of the houses of your brothers, which you had caused to be burned down at Red River." But he continued to curse and abuse not only me, but the soldiers, and every one that came near him.

Only three persons were kept in confinement, of those that had been captured in this trading-house. These were Mr. Harshield, the half breed boy, Maveen, who had been concerned in the murder of the Hudson's Bay governor above mentioned, and one clerk. The rest were suffered to go at large. Joseph Cadotte, the half brother of Nowlan, made a very humble and submissive apology for his conduct, and promised, if they would release him, he would go to his hunting, and be henceforth no more concerned with traders. He was accordingly liberated, but instead of doing as he had promised, he went immediately to Mouse River trading-house, and having collected forty or fifty half breeds, he returned to retake the place; but they approached no nearer than about a mile distant, where they remained for some time in camp.

After twenty days, I returned to Pembinah to my family, and then went, with Wa-ge-tote, to hunt buffaloe in the prairie. I now heard that many of the half breed people in the country were enraged against me, for the part I had taken against the

North West Company, and from some of the principal men I heard that they intended to take my life. I sent them back for answer, that they must fall on me as I had done on the people of the North West, when I was sleeping, or they would not be able to injure me. They came near, and were several times lurking about, with intention to kill me, but they were never able to effect their object. I spent what remained of the winter among the Indians, and in the spring returned to the Assinneboin. Lord Selkirk arrived from Fort William in the spring, and a few days afterwards Mr. Cumberland, and another clerk, belonging to the North West, came up in a canoe. As they did not stop at the fort, Lord Selkirk sent a canoe after them, and they were brought back and placed in confinement.

The people of the Mouse River trading-house, belonging to the North West Company, came down about this time; but being afraid to pass by the fort, they stopped and encamped at no great distance above. The Indians from distant parts of the country, not having heard of the disturbances and changes that had taken place, now began to assemble; but they manifested great astonishment when they found that their old traders were no longer in possession of the fort.

A letter was this spring, or in the early part of summer, received from Judge Codman, offering two hundred dollars reward for the apprehension and delivery of three half breeds, who had been very active in the preceding disturbances, namely, Grant, the principal leader of the half breeds for the North West, Joseph Cadotte, and one called Assinneboin. These were all taken by a party from our fort, aided by the interpreter, Nowlan, but they were released upon their promise to appear again when Judge Codman should arrive. This party had scarce returned home, when Assinneboin came and surrendered himself, at the same time giving information that Grant and Cadotte had fled the moment Nowlan and his party turned their backs. They went to the country of the Assinneboins, from whence they did not return until they were sent for, and brought to attend the court; but the man who had given himself up was pardoned.

Lord Selkirk had, for a long time, expected the arrival of the judge appointed to try those accused of capital crimes, and to adjust the dispute between the two rival companies; and becoming very impatient, he despatched a messenger to Sah-gi-uk, with provisions and other presents, who was instructed to proceed on until he should meet the judge. At one of the North West Company's houses, beyond Sah-gi-uk, this man was taken prisoner, and severely beaten by the company's agent, Mr. Black; but about this time the judge arrived, and Mr. Black, with a Mr. M'Cloud, fled, and secreted themselves among the Indians, so that when Judge Codman sent for them from Red River, they were not to be found.

The trial continued a long time, and many prisoners were, from day to day, released; but Mr. Harshield, and the half breed Maveen, were loaded with irons, and put in more rigorous confinement. The judge had his camp in the middle, between our fort and the camp of the North West Company's people, probably that he might not seem partial to either.

One morning, as I was standing in the gate of the fort, I saw the judge, who was a large, fat man, come towards me, attended by Mr. M'Kenzie, and a half breed, called Cambell, and an old Naudoway Indian. They came into the house, looked from room to room, and at last entered the one in which Selkirk then was. Cambell followed the judge in, and having a paper in one hand, he laid the other on Selkirk's shoulder, and said something I did not understand. Much discussion followed, all of which was incomprehensible to me; but I observed that Mr. M'Kenzie and Cambell were standing near the whole day. It was nearly night when Nowlan told me that the judge had fined the North West a considerable sum, I think either three hundred or three thousand dollars, and that Lord Selkirk was released from arrest. After this, Mr. M'Kenzie and Cambell went out, and were much insulted on the way to their camp, by the people belonging to the Hudson's Bay; but the judge remained to dine with Lord Selkirk.

Col. Dickson, who was now at Red River, sent a man for the Sioux, as it was thought desirable that they should be called in, and made acquainted with the state of affairs. In the preceding winter, after I had returned to Pembinah, two Ojibbeway women had arrived there, with pipes from the Sioux country, to invite the Ojibbeways to make peace. These women had been prisoners among the Sioux, and their release, as well as the message they bore, was considered as indicative of a disposition on the part of the Sioux to bring about a peace with the Ojibbeways.

One of these women had been married to a Sioux, and her husband had become attached to her. When the common voice of his people made it necessary she should be sent back to her own country, he sent a message to her husband, among the Ojibbeways, offering to give him, in exchange for her, whichever of his own wives the Ojibbeway might choose to take. But this man was not disposed to accept the offer of the Sioux, and there was no one to return to answer the messages the women had brought, until Mr. Bruce, the interpreter before mentioned, offered his services. These negotiations, though they had produced little apparent effect, had prepared the minds of the Sioux, in some measure, for the message from Mr. Dickson, and they sent, according to his request, twenty-two men, and two Ojibbeway prisoners, that were to be given up. One of these prisoners was a young woman, the daughter of Gitche-ope-zhe-ke, (the big buffaloe,) and she also had been married among the Sioux. Her husband, who was one of the twenty two who now arrived, was a young man, and was extremely fond of his Ojibbeway wife. The chiefs of the party, when they were about to return, tried to persuade him to leave her; but this he obstinately refused to do, and they were at last compelled to abandon him, though it was evidently at the imminent peril of his life, that he ventured to remain by himself among the Ojibbeways. After his companions had left him, he went out, and wandered about, crying like a child. Seeing his distress, I called him into my lodge, and though, on account of difference of language, I could not say much to him, I endeavoured to console him, and make him believe that he would find some friends even among the Ojibbeways. On the following day, he determined to follow his companions, and to return to his own country. He started out, and followed along their path two or three hundred yards, then he threw himself down upon the ground, cried, and rolled about like a mad man; but his affection for his wife getting the better of his wish to return, and his fears for his own life, he came back, and would have remained among us. But about this time we heard of other Ojibbeways, who had threatened to come and kill him, and we well knew that it would be scarce possible for him to remain long among us, without attempts being made against his life. Wage-tote and Be-gwais, our chiefs, interfered to send him away, and having selected eight trusty men, of whom I was one, directed that he should be taken one day's journey towards the Sioux country. We were compelled to drag him away by violence, nor could we urge him forward in any other manner, until we arrived at the crossing place of the Assinneboin River, where we met a party of two hundred Assinneboins. The young Sioux had taken the precaution to dress himself like an Ojibbeway, and when the chief of the Assinneboins asked us where we were going, we told him our chiefs had sent us to hunt buffaloe. This man, Ne-zho-ta-we-nau-ba, was a good and discreet chief, and although the terror of the young Sioux immediately made him acquainted with the deception we tried to practice upon him, he appeared to take no notice of it; he even placed himself in such a situation as to divert the attention of his own people from the young man, until the band had passed. He then addressed the Sioux in his own language: "Fly, young man," said he, "and remember if you are overtaken before you reach your own country, there are few among the Assinneboins, or Ojibbeways, who would not gladly take your life." The young man started to run accordingly. At the distance of one hundred yards we heard him burst out crying; but afterwards, we understood that he overtook his party at Pembinah, and returned in safety to his own country.

Much was said of this peace between the Sioux and Ojibbeways, and Col. Dickson often boasted that the Sioux would not be the first to violate the treaty, as he said they would venture to do nothing without his consent. He was even boasting in this way, when a chief of the Ojibbeways, with forty men, arrived, having in their hands the still bloody arrows they had taken from the bodies of those the Sioux had recently killed at a trading-house belonging to Mr. Dickson himself. This, for some time, checked his boasting. Lord Selkirk, also, about the same time, called all the Indians together, and presenting them a quantity of tobacco, spirits, &c. &c. made one of those long and fatherly speeches so common in Indian councils. "My children," said he, "the sky which has long been dark and cloudy over your heads, is now once more clear and bright. Your great father beyond the waters, who has ever, as you know, nearest his heart the interests of his red children, has sent me to remove the briars out of your path, that your feet may no more bleed. We have taken care to remove from you those evil minded white men who sought, for the sake of their own profit, to make you forget your duty to your great father; they will no more return to trouble you. We have also called to us the Sioux, who, though their skins are red, like your own, have long been your enemies. They are henceforth to remain in their own country. This peace now places you in safety. Long before your fathers were born, this war began, and instead of quietly pursuing the game for the support of your women and children, you have been murdering one another; but that time has passed away, and you can now hunt where you please. Your young men must observe this peace; and your great father will consider as his enemy any one who takes up the tomahawk."

The Indians answered with the usual promises and professions, and being about to leave the fort that evening, they stole every horse belonging to Lord Selkirk and his party. In the morning, not a single horse was left, and the Indians had most of them disappeared also.

It was now so late that I could not come that fall to the states. Lord Selkirk having, perhaps, heard something of my history, began to be attentive to me. He inquired about the events of my past life, and I related many things to him, particularly the part I had borne in capturing the fort. Judge Codman,* also,

---

* Many of the names of white men, in the north west, and in other parts of the country, which are mentioned in this narrative, are grossly misspelt; the same principle having been followed in writing both foreign and Indian names, in all instances where the name the narrator intended to mention did not immediately recur to the recollection of the writer. Thus Codman is here written for *Coltman*; in other places, Maveen for *Mainville*; Tussenon for *D'Orsonnens*, &c. It is also not improbable that names may have become confounded in the mind of our hunter himself, who appears to have been more conversant with Indians than white men. Thus, in his account of the murder of a governor of the Hudson's Bay Company, of the name of M'Donald, or M'Dolland, he may possibly have used one of these names in place of that of Mr. Semple, who was one of the victims to that spirit of bloody rivalry which occasioned these troubles between the trading companies. This want of precision, particularly in the spelling of names, will not, with the candid, impair the credibility of this humble narrative.

who remained there, often spoke to Lork Selkirk respecting me. " This man," said he, " conducted your party from the Lake of the Woods hither, in the winter season, and performed a very important part in the taking of this fort, at the expense of great labour, and at the hazard of his life, and all for the sum of forty dollars. The least you ought to do is to make his forty dollars eighty, and give him an annuity of twenty dollars per year for life." Lord Selkirk did acordingly. The annuity for the five first years has been paid me. The second five have not yet expired.

Lord Selkirk was not able to leave the mouth of the Assinneboin so early as he had intended, for fear of the North West. They had sent men, disguised as Indians, among whom was one they called Sacksayre; they had also sent Indians, with instructions to waylay and murder him. Hearing of this, he thought it best to despatch Col. Dickson to the Sioux country for a guard of one hundred Sioux, and it was not until these arrived, that he dared venture out. Then he escaped from the fort at night, and joined Dickson at Pembinah.

He took with him a letter, which he had himself written for me, and in my name, to my friends in the states, giving some of the most prominent of the particulars of my early history. He had used much persuasion to induce me to accompany him, and I had inclination enough to do so; but I then believed that most of my near relatives had been murdered by the Indians; and if any remained, I knew that so great a lapse of time must have made us, in all respects, like strangers to each other. He also proposed to take me to England with him; but my attachments were among the Indians, and my home was in the Indian country. I had spent great part of my life there, and I knew it was too late for me to form new associations. He however sent six men to take me to the Lake of the Woods, where I arrived late in the fall, after the corn was gathered. In the beginning of winter, I went to the Be-gwi-o-nus-ko Lake, thence, when the snow had fallen, to the prairie, to hunt buffaloe.

The Indians gathered around, one after another, until we became a considerable band, and then we began to suffer of hunger. The weather was very severe, and our suffering increased. A young woman was the first to die of hunger. Soon after this, a young man, her brother, was taken with that kind of delirium, or madness, which precedes death in such as die of starvation. In this condition, he had left the lodge of his debilitated and desponding parents; and when, at a late hour in the evening, I returned from my hunt, they could not tell what had become of him. I left the camp about the middle of the night, and following his track, I found him at some distance lying dead in the snow.

CHAPTER XIII.

Sufferings of the Ojibbeways from hunger—persecutions of Waw-be-be-nai-sa, and unkindness of my Indian relatives—journey to Detroit—Governor Cass—council at St. Mary, on the Miami.

ALL the men who were still able to walk, now determined to start after buffaloe, which we knew could not then be very near us. For my own part, I chose to remain, as did one good hunter besides, who knew that the prospect of getting buffaloes was not good. We remained behind, and in a short time killed five moose; all the flesh of which being immediately distributed among the suffering women and children, afforded some relief, and checked the progress of death, which was making extensive havoc among us. The men returned one after another, more worn out and reduced than when they had left us. Only a single buffaloe had been killed. As the most incessant, and the most laborious exertions alone, could save us from perishing, I went immediately out to hunt again, and having started a bear, I pursued him for three days, without being able to come up with him. At the end of this time I found myself so far exhausted, that I knew I could never overtake the bear, and I should not have reached home, had not some Indians, little less miserable and hungry than myself, happened to meet with me. I had stopped at night, and being unable to make a camp, or kindle a fire, I was endeavouring to reconcile myself to the immediate approach of death, which I thought inevitable, when these people unexpectedly found me, and helped me to return to camp. This is but a fair specimen of the life which many of the Ojibbeways of the north lead during the winter. Their barren and inhospitable country affords them so scantily the means of subsistence, that it is only with the utmost exertion and activity, that life can be sustained; and it not unfrequently happens that the strongest men, and the best hunters, perish of absolute hunger.

Now the Indians again determined to move all together, towards the buffaloes, and endeavour to reach them with their families. Only Oon-di-no, the man who had remained with me before, wished to stay, that his women might dry the skin of the last moose he had killed, so that they might carry it with them, to be eaten in case of the failure of all other supplies. I concluded to remain with him; but in the middle of the first night after the Indians left, the distress of my children became so great, that I could no longer remain in my lodge. I got up and started, and told him that if I could kill or procure any game, I would return to his relief. I pursued, rapidly as my strength would permit, the path of the Indians, and about morning came up with their camp. I had no sooner arrived, than I heard the sounds of a feast, and going up to the lodge, I heard the voice of an old man, thanking the Great Spirit for the supply that had been bestowed in the time of their necessity. He did not mention the animal by name that had been killed, only calling it Manito-wais-se, which means nearly "Spirit beast." From this I could not ascertain what had been killed, but from another source, I learned it was an old and poor buffaloe. From this I inferred that herds must be near, and two young men being willing to join me, we went immediately in the direction in which we believed the herd would be found, and after having walked about three hours, ascended a little hill, and saw before us the ground black with buffaloes. We crawled up, and I killed immediately two fat cows. As I was cutting these up, I began to hear the guns of the men of our party, they having followed me on, and being now arrived among the buffaloes. It was somewhat late when I was ready to go to our camp, most of the men were in before me. I had expected to have heard the sounds of feasting and rejoicing; but when I entered the camp, not a voice was to be heard. No women and children were running about, all was silent and sad. Can it be, thought I, that this relief has come too late, and that our women and children are all dead. I looked into one lodge after another; in all, the people were alive, but none had any thing to eat. The men having most of them come from a forest country, and having never hunted buffaloe before, all failed to kill except myself. The supply I had brought, I having loaded the two young men that were with me, somewhat allayed the hunger that was prevailing.

There was at this time with us, a man called Waw-bebe-nai-sa, (White Bird,) with whom I had formerly been somewhat acquainted, and whose jealousy and ill will against me, seemed to be excited and irritated by my success in hunting. It was on account of this man, and because I wished to avoid all ostentation, that I now forbore to make a feast in my own lodge, as would have been proper for me to have done on this occasion. Nevertheless, one of the young men who had been with me, made a feast, and I, after reserving sufficient food to allay the pressing hunger of my own children, sent the remainder to the families about me. The young man who made the feast, called, among others, Waw-bebe-nais-sa, the man I have mentioned. In the course of the evening, he said, as I understood, much to prejudice me in the opinion of the Indians; accusing me of pride, insolence, and of having in various ways done mischief among them. But I remained in my own lodge, and at present took no notice of this, farther than to contradict his unfair statements.

Next morning, long before the dawn, the women started for the remains of the two buffaloe I had killed; and several of the men, most of them having obtained from me some instruction about the part to be aimed at, again went in pursuit of the herds, and this day several of them killed. We soon had plenty of meat, and all that were sick and near death recovered, except one woman, who having gone mad with hunger, remained in a state of derangement for more than a month.

The principal man of this band was called O-poih-gun,* (the pipe.) He, with three lodges, remained with me, the others scattered here and there in pursuit of the buffaloe. One of the men who remained back with me, was Waw-bebe-nais-sa, and another his son-in-law. I killed great numbers of fat buffaloe, and the choice parts of forty of them I had dried. We had suf-

---

* O-poih-gun—pipe; O-poih-gun-nun—pipes.

fered so much from hunger, that I wished to secure my family against a return of it. I also still had it in contemplation to make my way to the States, when I knew it would be necessary for me to leave them for some time, without any one to hunt for them. I made twenty large sacks of pemmican; ten kegs of ten gallons each, which I procured from the Indians, I filled with tallow, and preserved, besides, a considerable number of tongues, &c.

It was not immediately that I discovered Waw-bebe-nais-sa's design in remaining near my camp, which was solely to annoy and molest me. I had such large quantities of meat to carry, when we came finally to move, that I was compelled to return with my dogs four times, to carry forward to my camping place, one load after another. One day he contrived to meet me alone, at the place where I deposited my loads, and I had no sooner stopped, than he thrust both his hands into my long hair, which then hung down on both sides of my head. "This," said he, "is the head of your road, look down and see the place where the wolves and the carrion birds shall pick your bones." I asked him why he offered me this violence. "You are a stranger," said he, "and have no right among us; but you set youself up for the best hunter, and would make us treat you as a great man. For my own part, I have long been weary of your insolence, and I am determined you shall not live another day." Finding that remonstrance was likely to have no effect upon him, but that he was proceeding to beat my head against a poplar tree that stood there, by a sudden exertion of strength, I threw him upon the ground, and disengaged my head at the expense of part of my hair. But in the struggle, he caught three of the fingers of my right hand between his teeth. Having sunk his strong teeth quite to the bones of my fingers, I could not draw them out of his mouth, but with my left hand aimed a blow at one of his eyes; his jaws flew open, and he leapt instantly to his feet. My tomahawk was lying near me, and his eye happening to fall upon it, he caught it in his hand, and aimed so hearty a blow at my head, that as I eluded it, his own violence brought him to the ground. I jumped upon him, wrenched the tomahawk from his hand, and threw it as far as I could, while I continued to hold him fast to the ground. I was much enraged at his unprovoked and violent attack upon me; nevertheless I would not kill him, but seeing there a piece of a stout lodge pole, I caught it in my hands, and told him to get up. When he did so, I commenced beating him; and as he fled immediately, I followed, and continued to beat him while he ran two or three hundred yards.

When I returned to my load, his son-in-law and two other young men belonging to him, having heard his cries, had come up. One of them said angrily to me, "what is this you have done?" and immediately the three rushed upon me, and I being already overcome with fatigue, they threw me upon the ground. At this time Waw-bebe-nais-sa had returned, and he caught me by a black silk handkerchief that I wore about my neck, strangled, kicked, and beat me, and thrust me down in the snow. I remember hearing one of them say, "he is dead," and as I knew I could not hope, while I was down, to make resistance against four, I endeavoured to encourage this opinion. When they took their hands off me, and stood at a little distance, I sprang upon my feet, and seized a lodge pole, probably very contrary to their expectations. Whether through surprise or fear I know not, they all fled, and seeing this, I pursued Waw-bebe-nais-sa, and gave him another severe beating with my pole. For this time they left me, and I returned once more to hang up the meat I had brought. But Waw-bebe-nais-sa and his people returned to the lodges, where my dogs, which my wife had taken back, were lying, much fatigued, before the door. He drew his knife, and stabbed one of them. My wife hearing the noise, ran out, but he threatened to kill her also.

Next day, as Waw-bebe-nais-sa was much bruised and sore, and his face in particular very badly swollen, I thought probable he would remain in his lodge; and apprehending danger to my wife, if she should be left alone in the lodge, I sent her to carry forward meat, and remained myself at home. But I was much fatigued, and being alone in my lodge, about the middle of the day I fell asleep. Suspecting, or perhaps knowing this, Waw-bebe-nais-sa crept slyly in with his knife in his hand, and was almost near enough to strike me, when I awoke and sprang up. As I was not unarmed, he started back and fled, but I did not pursue him. He still continued to threaten and molest me. Whenever he met me in the path, he would not turn aside, though he was unloaded, and I might have a heavy burthen on my back.

His eye was for many days so swollen that he could not see out of it, and his whole appearance very ludicrous, he being at best but an awkward and homely man. Once, after an unsuccessful attempt to stab me, he went home, and in the impatience of his baffled rage, made the squaw's gesture of contempt towards my lodge,* which exposed him to the ridicule, even of his own friends among the Indians.

His persecutions were, however, troublesome to me, and I endeavoured to avoid him. One day I had preceded the party, and as we were travelling in a beaten path, which I knew they would follow, I turned a little out of it, to place my camp where I should not necessarily be in the way of seeing him. But when he came to the fork of my road, with his little son twelve years old, I heard him say to the lad, "stop here while I go and kill this white man." He then threw down his load, and though his son entreated him not to do any thing, he came up within about fifty yards of me, drew his gun from its case, cocked it, and pointed it at me. Having held it in this position some time, and seeing he did not excite my fears, he began to approach me, jumping from side to side, and yelling in the manner of warriors when they approach each other in battle. He continued pointing his gun at me, and threatening me so loudly, that I was at last irritated, and caught up my own gun. The little boy ran up, and throwing his arms about me, entreated me to spare his father, though he was a fool. I then threw down my gun, seized the old man, and took his from him. I reproached him for his obstinate perseverance in such foolish practices. "I have," said I, "put myself so often in your power, that you ought by this time to know you have not courage to kill me. You are not a man; you have not the heart even of a squaw, nor the courage of a dog. Now for the first time I speak to you. I wish you to know that I am tired of your foolishness, and that if you trouble me any more hereafter, it will be at the hazard of your own life."

He then left me, and with all the others, except my own family, went on in advance. Next day I followed, drawing a loaded sled myself, and driving my dogs, with their loads, before me. As we

* *Nin-us-kun-je-ga kwi-uk we-ke-wah-mik.* See note at the end of the volume, on the menomonie word *Ke-kish-kosh-kaw-po-nin.*

approached a thicket of bushes, I cautioned my daughter Martha, that Waw-bebe-nais-sa might probably be lying in ambush somewhere among them. Presently I saw her leap several feet from the ground, then she came running towards me, with her hands raised, and crying, "*my father! my father!*" I seized my gun and sprang forward, examined every place for concealment, passed the lodge poles, and the almost extinguished fires of their last encampment, and returned without having discovered any thing. When I inquired of my daughter what had occasioned her alarm, she said she had "smelt fire." So great was the terror and apprehension with which her mind was agitated, on account of the annoyances Waw-bebe-nais-sa had given us.

I was so glad to be released from the persecutions of this troublesome man, that I now resolved to stop at Rush Lake, and remain there by myself, as I thought it was the intention of Waw-bebe-nais-sa and the other Indians, to proceed immediately to the Lake of the Woods. So I selected a place where I intended to establish my camp for the remainder of the winter. Here I left my children to take care of the lodge, and my wife and myself returned to bring up loads of meat. On coming home at night, the children told us, their grandmother had in our absence been to see them, and had left word, that her daughter must come on the following day to see her; and that there were, in that place, three or four lodges of our friends encamped together. I readily gave my consent to this arrangement, and as my mother-in-law had left a message particularly for me, I consented to accompany her, saying that we could bring up the remainder of the meat after we should return. But that night I dreamed, and the same young man whom I had repeatedly seen in the preparations for my medicine hunts, came down as usual through the hole in the top of my lodge, and stood directly before me. "You must not go," said he, "to the place you propose to visit to-morrow; but if you persist, and will disregard my admonition, you shall see what will happen to you there. Look there," said he, pointing in the opposite direction, and I saw She-gwaw-koo-sink, Me-zhuk-ko-naun, and others of my friends coming. Then pointing upwards, he told me to look, and I saw a small hawk with a banded tail, flying about over my head. He said no more, but turned and went out at the door of my lodge. I awoke much troubled in my mind, and could sleep no more. In the morning, I told my wife I could not go with her. "What is the reason," said she, "you cannot accompany me, as you promised yesterday?" I told her my dream, but she accused me of fear, and as she continued her solicitations, I finally consented to go.

In the morning, I told my children that their uncle and other Indians would come to the lodge that day. That they must tell them, if I returned at all, it would be by noon : if I did not come then, they might conclude I was dead. I then started with my wife, but I had not gone two hundred yards, when I looked up and saw the same small hawk that had appeared to me in my dream. I knew that this was sent to forewarn me of evil, and again I told my wife I could not go. But though I turned back to go towards my own lodge, she again reproached me with fear, and pretended to ridicule my apprehensions. I knew, also, the strong prejudice that existed against me in the family of my mother-in-law, and the tendency of my refusing, in this case, to visit her, would be to confirm, and make them stronger. I therefore, though contrary to my better judgment, consented to go on.

When I arrived at the lodge of my mother-in-law, I left my gun at the door, went in, and took a seat between two of the sisters of my wife, who were the wives of one man. They had young children, and I was playing with two of these, with my head down, when I heard a loud and sudden noise, and immediately lost my senses. I saw no one, and I remembered nothing, till I began to revive; then I found several women holding my hands and arms, and I saw the expression of terror and alarm in the faces of all about me. I could not comprehend my situation, and knew nothing of what had happened, until I heard on the outside of the lodge, a loud and insulting voice, which I knew to be that of Waw-bebe-nais-sa. I now began to feel something like warm water on my face, and putting my hand to my head, I laid my fingers on my naked skull. I at length broke away from the women who held me, and pursued after Waw-bebe-nais-sa; but I could not overtake him, as the Indians assisted him in keeping out of my way. Towards night I returned to my lodge, though very severely wounded, and, as I believed, with the bones of my skull broken. A very little blood had run down upon my face when I was first wounded, but for a considerable time afterwards none flowed, and though I heard strange noises in my head, I did not faint or fall down until I reached my own lodge. My gun Waw-bebe-nais-sa had taken from the door of the lodge of my mother-in-law, and I had to return without it.

At my lodge, I found She-gwaw-koo-sink, Me-zhuk-ko-naun, and Nah-gaun-esh-kaw-waw, a son-in-law of Wa-ge-tote, more commonly called Oto-pun-ne-be. The moment I took She-gwaw-koo-sink by the hand, the blood spouted in a stream from my head. "What is the matter my son?" said he. "I have been at play with another man, and the water of the Be-gwi-o-mus-ko having made us drunk, we have played rather roughly." I wished to treat the matter lightly, but as I immediately fainted away, they saw the extent of the wound I had received. Oto-pun-ne-be had formerly been an acquaintance of mine, and had always shown a friendly disposition towards me. He now seemed much affected at my misfortune, and of his own accord, undertook to punish Waw-bebe-nais-sa for his unjust violence. This man, to whom I was often under obligation for the kindnesses he bestowed upon me, has since experienced the fate which overtakes so many of all characters and descriptions of people among the Ojibbeways of that country: he has perished of hunger.

When I had entered the lodge of my mother-in-law, I had omitted to pull off the hood of my thick moose-skin capote, and it was this which prevented me from noticing the entrance of Waw-bebe-nais-sa into the lodge, or seeing, or hearing his approach towards me. It is probable also, that had not my head been thus covered, the blow, had it been made, would have proved instantly fatal to me, as the force of it must have been somewhat broken by this thick covering of leather. But as it was, the skull was fractured, and there is still a large ridge upon that part of it where the edge of the tomahawk fell. It was very long before I recovered from this wound, though the immediate confinement which followed it, did not last so long as I had feared it must.

Waw-bebe-nais-sa fled immediately to our village at Me-naw-zhe-tau-naung; and the remainder of the people, having never hunted in the prairie before, now became panic struck, at the idea that the Sioux would fall upon their trail and pursue them. I was too weak to travel, and moreover I knew well we were in no danger from the Sioux; but my mother-in-law found much fault because I was not willing to start with the Indians. I knew that my mother-in-law, and I had reason to suppose that my wife, had been willing to aid Waw-bebe-nais-sa in his attempt on my life, and I therefore told them both to leave me if they wished. They went accordingly, and took all my children with them. The only person who did not desert me at this time, was Oto-pun-ne-be, as he was called from his bear totem, with his cousin, a lad of fourteen years old. These two remained and performed for me those offices of attention and kindness which my situation required, while those who should have been my friends abandoned me to my fate. After the fourth day, I became much worse, and was unable to sit up, and almost to move, until the tenth day, when I began to recover.

After I had gained a little strength, we left the lodges as they had been abandoned by the Indians in their fright, all standing, some of them filled with meat, and other valuable property, and started together for the village. Our trader lived at some distance from the village, and when we arrived at the place where the roads forked, I agreed with Oto-pun-ne-be that I would meet him at an appointed place, on the day which he named, as that on which he would return from the village. I went accordingly to the trader's, and he to the Indian's camp. We met again at the time and place agreed on, when he related to me, that he went to the village, entered the lodge of one of the principal chiefs, and sat down. He had not been long there, when Waw-bebe-nais-sa came in and sat down opposite him. After regarding each other for some time, Waw-bebe-nais-sa said to him, "You, Oto-pun-ne-be, have never been in our village before, and I am not ignorant of the occasion which has brought you so far to see us. You have no brothers of your own, the Long Knives having killed all of them; and you are now so foolish as to call the man whom I beat the other day your brother." "It is not true," said Oto-pun-ne-be, "that the Long Knives have killed any brother of mine; but if they had, I would not suffer you to fall upon my friend, who is as one of us, and abuse and injure him, as you have done, without cause or provocation. It is true, I call him my brother, and I will avenge his cause as if he were such; but I will not spill blood in the lodge of this chief, who has received me as a friend." So saying, he took Waw-bebe-nais-sa by the hand, dragged him out of the lodge, and was about to plunge the knife to his heart, when the chief, who was a strong man, caught his hand, took away the knife, and broke it. In the scuffle which ensued, three or four men were at once upon Oto-pun-ne-be; but he being a powerful man, and not forgetting the object of his journey, kept fast his gripe upon Waw-bebe-nais-sa, and did not quit him until two of his ribs were broken, and he was otherwise severely injured. Oto-pun-ne-be was a quiet man, even when drunk, and if he ever entered into a quarrel, it was more commonly, as in this case, in the cause of his friend, rather than his own.

I was content with the punishment that had been thus bestowed upon Waw-bebe-nais-sa, as I thought two broken ribs about equal to the broken head he had given me. We feasted together on game I had killed, so rapid had been my recovery, and then returned to the deserted camp, where we found the lodges all standing as we had left them. After about ten days more, the people began to come back to look after their property. Oto-pun-ne-be took my canoe and returned to Red River, where he lived.

All our people returned, and removed their lodges and their property to Me-naw-zhe-tau-naung. I had now a great store of meat, sufficient, as I knew, to supply the wants of my family for a year or more. After making the best disposition I could of all my affairs, I took a small canoe, and started by myself, with the intention of coming to Mackinac, intending to go thence to the states, and endeavour to find some of my relatives, if any remained.

At Rainy Lake, I fell in with Mr. Giasson and others, in the employ of the Hudson's Bay Company, who told me it would not be safe for me to suffer myself to be seen by any of the North West Company's people, as they were all much enraged against me, on account of the course I had taken. Nevertheless, I knew well that the Hudson's Bay people, having no occasion to go to the lower end of Lake Superior, could not conveniently aid me themselves, and that if I attempted to go alone, I must unavoidably fall in with some of the North West; I went, therefore, directly to the trading-house at Rainy Lake, where I found my old trader, Mr. Tace. He was standing on the bank when I came up with my little canoe. He told me to come into the house, and I followed him in accordingly; he then asked me, rather sternly, what I had come to him for. "Why do you not go," said he, "to your own people of the Hudson's Bay Company?" I told him I was now wishing to go to the states. "It would have been well," he replied, "had you gone long ago." I waited there twenty days, receiving all the time the kindest treatment from Mr. Tace. He then brought me in his own canoe to Fort William, whence Dr. M'Laughlin sent me in one of his boats to the Saut De St. Marie, and thence Mr. Ermatinger brought me to Mackinac. All the people of the North West Company, whom I saw on this journey, treated me kindly, and no one mentioned a word of my connexion with the Hudson's Bay.

Major Puthuff, the United States Indian Agent, at Mackinac, gave me a birch bark canoe, some provisions, and a letter to Gov. Cass, at Detroit. My canoe was lashed to the side of the schooner, on board which I sailed for Detroit, under the care of a gentleman, whose name I do not recollect, but who, as I thought, was sent by Major Puthuff expressly to take care of me on the way. In five days we arrived, and the gentleman telling me to wait until he could go on shore and return, he left me, and I heard no more of him. Next day I went on shore by myself, and walking up into the street, I stood for some time gazing around me. At length, I saw an Indian, and going up to him, asked who he was, and where he belonged. He answered me, "An Ottawwaw, of Saw-ge-nong." "Do you know Gish-kaw-ko?" said I. "He is my father." "And where," said I, "is Manito-o-geezhik, his father, and your grand-father?" "He died last fall." I told him to go and call his father to come and see me. He called him, but the old man would not come.

Next day, as I was again standing in the street, and looking one way and the other, I saw an old Indian, and ran after him. When he heard me coming, he turned about, and after looking anxiously at me for a few moments, caught me in his arms. It was Gish-kaw-ko; but he looked very unlike the young man who had taken me prisoner so many years before. He asked me, in a hurried manner, many questions; inquired what had happened to me, and where I had been since I left him, and many such questions. I tried to induce him to take me to the house of Gov. Cass, but he appeared afraid to go. Finding I could not prevail upon him, I took Major Puthuff's letter in my hand, and having learned from the Indians in which house the governor lived, I went toward the gate, till a soldier, who was walking up and down before it, stopped me. I could not speak English so as to be at all understood; but seeing the governor sitting in his porch, I held up the letter towards him. He then told the soldier to let me pass in. As soon as he had opened the letter, he gave me his hand, and having sent for an interpreter, he talked a long time with me. Gish-kaw-ko having been sent for, confirmed my statement respecting the circumstances of my capture, and my two years residence with the Ottawwaws of Saw-ge-nong.

The governor gave me clothing to the amount of sixty or seventy dollars value, and sent me to remain, for the present, at the house of his interpreter, more than a mile distant, where he told me I must wait till he should assemble many Indians and white men, to hold a council at St. Mary's, on the Miami, whence he would send me to my relatives on the Ohio.

I waited two months or more, and becoming extremely impatient to go on my way, I started with Be-nais-sa, the brother of Gish-kaw-ko, and eight other men, who were going to the council. I went without the knowledge of Gov. Cass, and was therefore destitute of any supply of provisions. We suffered much from fatigue, and still more from hunger, particularly after we passed the rapids of the Miami, where we left our canoe. The Indians among whom we passed, oftentimes refused to give us any thing, though they had plenty. Sometimes we stopped to sleep near a white man's corn field, and though the corn was now fit to roast, and we almost perishing with hunger, we dared not take any thing. One night, we stopped near a good looking house, where was a large and fine corn field. The Indians, being very hungry, said to me, " Shaw-shaw-wa ne-ba-se, you have come very far to see your relations, now go in and see whether they will give you any thing to eat.". I went and stood in the door, but the people within, who were then eating, drove me away, and on my return the Indians laughed at me.

Some time after this, as we were sleeping one night in the road, some one came up on horseback, and asked us, in the Ottawwaw dialect, who we were. One of the Indians answered, "We are Ottawwaws and Ojibbeways, and have with us one Long Knife, from Red River, who was taken prisoner many years ago by Gish-kaw-ko." He told us, after he understood who we were, and where we were going, that his name was Ah-koo-nah-goo-zik. "If you are brisk travellers," said he, "you may reach my house next day after to-morrow, at noon, and then you will find plenty to eat. It is necessary that I should travel on all night, that I may reach home to-morrow;" and thus he left us. Next day, my strength failed so much that I was only able to keep up by being released from my load. One took my gun, another my blanket, and we reached that night the forks of the Miami, where was a settlement of Indians, and a trading-house, as well as several families of whites. I applied to the trader, and stated my situation, and that of the Indians with me, but we could obtain no relief, and on the next day I was totally unable to travel. We were indebted to the Indians for what relief we obtained, which was sufficient to enable us the day after to reach the hospitable dwelling of Ah-koo-nah-goo-zik.

This man had two large kettles of corn and venison ready cooked, and awaiting our arrival. One he placed before me, with some wooden dishes, and spoons; the other before Be-nais-sa. After we had eaten, he told us we had better remain with him ten or fifteen days, and refresh ourselves. from our long journey, as he had plenty of corn, and fat venison was abundant about him. I told him, that for my own part I had for many years been wishing to make the journey I had now so nearly accomplished, and that I was extremely impatient to see whether or not any of my own relatives were still alive; but that I should be glad to rest with him two or three days, and afterwards to borrow one of his horses to ride as far as Kau-wis-se-no-ki-ug, or St. Mary's. "I will tell you," said he. After two or three days, as we were, early one morning, making up our loads to start, he came to me, leading a fine horse, and putting the halter in my hand, he said, "I give you this for your journey." I did not again tell him I would leave it at Kau-wis-se-no-ki-ug, as I had already told him this, and I knew that in such cases the Indians do not wish to hear much said. In two days I arrived at the place appointed for the council. As yet, no Indians had assembled, but a man was stationed there to issue provisions to such as should come. I had been but a short time at this place, when I was seized with fever and ague, which, though it did not confine me all the time, was yet extremely painful and distressing.

After about ten days, a young man, of the Ottawwaws, whom Be-nais-sa had given me to cook for me, and assist about me in my sickness, went across the creek, to a camp of the Po-ta-wa-to-mies, who had recently arrived, and were drinking. At midnight, he was brought into the lodge drunk, and one of the men who came with him, said to me, as he pushed him in, "take care of your young man, he has been doing mischief." I immediately called Be-nais-sa to kindle a fire, when we saw, by the light of it, the young man standing with his knife in his hand, and that, together with his arm, and great part of his body, covered with blood. The Indians could not make him lie down, but when I told him to, he obeyed immediately, and I forbade them to make any inquiries about what he had done, or take any notice of his bloody knife. In the morning, having slept soundly, he was perfectly unconscious of all that had passed. He said he believed that he had been very drunk, and as he was now hungry, he must hurry and get ready something to eat. He was astonished and confounded when I told him he had killed a man. He remembered only, that in his drunkenness, he had began to cry for his father, who had been killed on that spot, several years before, by white men. He expressed much concern, and went immediately to see the man he had stabbed, who was not yet dead. We learned from the Po-ta-wato-mies that he had found the young man sleeping, or lying in a state of insensibility from intoxication, and had stabbed him, without any words having been exchanged, and apparently without knowing who he was. The relations of the wounded man said nothing to him, but the interpreter of Gov. Cass reproved him very sharply.

It was evident to all, that the young man he had wounded could not recover; indeed, he was now manifestly near his end. When our companion returned, we had made up a considerable present, one giving a blanket, one a piece of strouding, some one thing, and some another. With these he immediately returned, and placing them on the ground beside the wounded man, he said to the relatives, who were standing about, "My friends, I have, as you see, killed this, your brother; but I knew not what I did. I had no ill will against him, and when, a few days since, he came to our camp, I was glad to see him. But drunkenness made me a fool, and my life is justly forfeited to you. I am poor, and among strangers; but some of those who came from my own country with me, would gladly bring me back to my parents; they have, therefore, sent me with this small present. My life is in your hands, and my present is before you, take which ever you choose, my friends will have no cause to complain." He then sat down beside the wounded man, and stooping his head, hid his eyes with his hands, and waited for them to strike. But the mother of the man he had wounded, an old woman, came a little forward, and said, "For myself and my children, I can answer, that we wish not to take your life; but I cannot promise to protect you from the resentment of my husband, who is now absent; nevertheless, I will accept your present, and whatever influence I may have with him, I shall not fail to use it in your behalf. I know that it was not from design, or on account of any previous hatred, that you have done this, and why should your mother be made to cry as well as myself?" She took the presents, and the whole affair being reported to Gov. Cass, he was satisfied with the course that had been taken.

On the following day, the wounded man died, and some of our party assisted the young man who had killed him, in making his grave. When this was completed, the governor gave the dead man a valuable present of blankets, cloth, &c. to be buried with him, according to the Indian custom, and these were brought and heaped up on the brink of the grave. But the old woman, instead of having them buried, proposed to the young men to play for them. As the articles were somewhat numerous, various games were used, as shooting at the mark, leaping, wrestling, &c. but the handsomest piece of cloth was reserved as the prize for the swiftest in the foot race, and was won by the young man himself who had killed the other. The old woman immediately afterwards called him to her, and said, "Young man, he who was my son, was very dear to me, and I fear I shall cry much and often for him. I would be glad if you would consent to be my son in his stead, to love me and take care of me as he did, only I fear my husband." The young man, who was grateful to her for the anxiety she showed to save his life, immediately consented to this arrangement, and entered heartily upon it. But the governor had heard that some of the friends of the deceased were still determined to avenge his death, and he sent his interpreter to the young man, to direct him, without loss of time, to make his escape, and fly to his own country. He was unwilling to go, but as Be-nais-sa and myself concurred with the governor in his advice, and assisted him in his preparations, he went off in the night; but instead of going immediately home, as he had been directed to do, he lay concealed in the woods, only a few hundred yards from our lodge.

Very early next morning, I saw two of the friends of the young man that was killed, coming towards our lodge. At first I was somewhat alarmed, as I supposed they came with the intention of doing violence; but I soon perceived they were without arms. They came in, and sat a long time silent. At last one of them said, "Where is our brother? We are sometimes lonely at home, and we wish to talk with him." I told them, he had but lately gone out, and would soon return. As they remained a long time, and insisted on seeing him, I went out, with the pretence of seeking for him, but without the remotest expectation that he would be found. He, however, had observed, from his hiding place, the visit of the two young men to our lodge, and not believing it to have been made with any unfriendly design, discovered himself to me, and we returned together. They shook hands with him, and treated him with great kindness, and we soon afterwards ascertained that all the reports of their wishing to kill him were false.

CHAPTER XIV.

Journey to Kentucky—hospitalities of the whites—return to Detroit—Jackson—St. Louis—General Clark—return to the Lake of the Woods—Col. Dickson—second journey to St. Louis, by Chikago and Fort Clark—kindness of the Potawattomies.

ABOUT the time of the conclusion of the council, Gov. Cass called me to dine with him; and as many gentlemen asked me to drink wine with them, I was, after dinner, scarce able to walk home. A few days afterwards, the interpreter told me the governor had a curiosity to know whether I had acquired the same fondness the Indians usually have for intoxicating liquors, and whether, when drunk, I would behave as they did. But I had not felt the influence of the wine so much as to forget myself, or become unconscious of my situation, and I went immediately to my lodge, and lay there until I was entirely sober.

Some of the Potawattomies had stolen the horse that was lent me on the road by the friendly old man, called Ah-koo-nah-goo-zik; but he was recovered by the young men who followed my friend Be-nais-sa, and I restored him to the owner, who was at the council. Governor Cass, understanding how kind this man had been to me, directed that a very handsome and valuable saddle should be given him. The old man for some time persisted in declining this present; but at last, when prevailed upon to receive it, he expressed much gratitude. "This," said he, "is that which was told me by the old men who gave me instruction many years ago, when I was a child. They told me to be kind, and to do good to all men, particularly to the stranger who should come from a distant country, and to all who were destitute and afflicted; saying, if I did so, the Great Spirit would also remember me, to do good to me, and reward me for what I had done. Now, though I have done so little for this man, how amply and honourably am I rewarded!" He would have persuaded me to take his horse, as he said he had more, and the saddle was more valuable than the horse he had lent me; and though I declined his offer, still he insisted upon it, until I consented that he should consider it as belonging to me, and should take care of it until I returned and called for it. Here the governor gave me goods to the amount of one hundred and twenty dollars value, and as I had still a considerable journey to make, I purchased a horse for eighty dollars, for which I gave a part of the goods I had received. There were at the council, among others, two men from Kentucky, who knew something of my relations, one of them having lived from a child in the family of one of my sisters.

With these two men I started, though my health was still very poor. In a few days I had become so much worse, that I could not sit on my horse, and they concluded to purchase a skiff, and one of them to take me down by water, while the other went with the horses, by the usual route. In that part of the Big Miami, are many mill-dams, and other obstructions, which rendered even this method, not only slow and laborious, but extremely distressing to me, on account of my ill health. At last I was reduced to such a state of weakness, as to be quite unable to move, and I stopped at the house of a poor man, who lived on the bank of the river, and as he seemed greatly to pity me, and was disposed to do all in his power for my relief, I determined to remain with him, the man with whom I had travelled thus far, making me understand that he would go to the Ohio, and either come back himself, or send some one after me.

This man with whom I stopped, could speak a few words of Ottawwaw, and he did every thing in his power to render my situation comfortable, until my nephew, who was the person sent by my friends in Kentucky, came for me. By him I heard of the death of my father, and also some particulars of my surviving relatives. Before I saw Gish-kau-ko, at Detroit, I had always supposed that the greater part, if not all of my father's family, had been murdered by Manito-o-geezhik and his party, the year subsequent to my capture.

Our journey was very tedious and difficult to Cincinnati, where we rested a little. Thence we descended the Ohio in a skiff. My fever continued to return daily, and when the chill commenced, we were compelled to stop for some time, so that our progress was not rapid. We were accompanied by one man, who assisted my nephew to put me in and take me out of the skiff, for I was now reduced to a mere skeleton, and had not strength enough to walk or stand by myself.

As the night was coming on, after a very dark and cloudy day, we arrived at a handsome farm, where was a large and rather good looking house. It was quite dark when we were ready to leave the skiff; they then raised me by the arms, and led, or rather carried me to the house. My nephew told the man our situation, and stated that I was so unwell, it would be extremely difficult, and must even endanger my life, if we attempted to go farther; but he told us we could not stay at his house all night; and when my nephew persisted in his request, he drove us roughly and violently out of the house. The night had now considerably advanced, and the distance to the next house was a mile and an half; but as it stood back from the river, we could not go to it in our skiff. They accordingly supported me between them, and we went on. It was probably after midnight when we arrived at a large brick house; the people within were all in bed, and all the windows were dark, but my nephew knocked at the door, and after a little time a man came out. When he saw me he took hold of me, and assisted me to go in; then he called up his wife and daughters, and gave some supper to my companions. For me he prepared some medicine, and then made me go to bed, where I slept very quietly until late in the morning. At this house I remained nearly all the next day, and was treated with the utmost kindness. From this time I began to get a little better, and without much more difficulty, I reached the place where my sister's children were living. I staid one night at the house of one of my nephews, whose name was John; then I went to the house of another brother, where I lay sick about a month.

A letter was now received, which they made me understand was for me, but though they read it to me repeatedly, I could not comprehend a single word of the contents. All the time since my arrival here, I had lain sick, and no one being for any considerable part of the time with me, I had not learned either to understand, or make myself understood; but as I was now some better, and able often to walk about, when a second letter came, I could understand from it, that my brother Edward, whose name

I had never forgotten, had gone to Red River to search for me. Also, that one of my uncles, who lived one hundred miles distant, had sent for me to come to him.

My greatest anxiety was now on account of my brother Edward, and I immediately called for my horse, intending to return towards Red River and search for him. Twenty or thirty of the neighbours assembled around me when they heard that I wished to go back, and I could comprehend that they wished to dissuade me from going. But when they found I was obstinate, they gave me each a little money: some one shilling, some two shillings, and others larger sums, and I got upon my horse and started. I had rode about ten miles, when fatigue and sickness overcame me, and I was compelled to stop at the house of a man, whose name, as I afterwards learned, was Morgan. Here I staid four days, and when I again called for my horse, the neighbours, as before, began to gather round me, and each to give me something. One gave me some bread in a bag, another tied a young pig behind my saddle, and among them all, they furnished me with a good outfit of provisions, and some money. I wished to return to Detroit; but as I was still very weak, Mr. Morgan accompanied me to Cincinnati. I had found that it made me sick to sleep in a house, and on this journey I constantly refused to do so. Mr. Morgan would sleep in the houses where we stopped at night, but I chose a good place outside, where I lay down and slept, and I found the advantage of doing so, by the partial recovery of my health. After Mr. Morgan returned from Cincinnati, I travelled on alone, and was before long destitute of provisions. About this time, an old man who was standing by the door of his house, when he saw me, called out stop! come! I could understand no more than these two words, but I knew from the expression of his countenance, and his manner, that his design was friendly, and accordingly went into his yard. He took my horse and gave him plenty of corn, and I accompanied him into the house, where, though they placed food before me, I could not eat. Seeing this, he gave me some nuts, a few of which I ate. When he saw that my horse had eaten, and I was impatient to start, he put on the saddle, and brought the horse. I offered him money, but he would not take it.

A day or two afterwards, I stopped at a house where I saw a

great quantity of corn lying in the yard. My horse was very hungry, therefore I got down, and taking a dollar out of my pocket, I handed it to the man who stood there, and then I counted ten ears of corn, and took them and laid them before my horse. I could not make the people comprehend that I was hungry; at least they seemed determined not to understand me. I went into the house, and the woman looked displeased; but seeing there part of a loaf of corn bread, I pointed first to it, next to my mouth; but as she appeared not to understand my meaning, I took it in my hand and raised it to my mouth, as if I would eat it. Seeing this, she called to the man outside, and he coming in, took the bread from me, pushed me violently out of the house, then went and took the corn from my horse, and motioned to me to be gone. I came next to a large brick house, and hoping I might meet gentler treatment, I determined to try here. But as I was riding up, a very fat man came out and spoke to me in a loud and harsh tone of voice. Though I could not understand his words, his meaning, which I thought was very evident, was, as I supposed, to forbid my entering the yard. I was willing to pass on, and was about to do so, when he ran out and caught my horse by the bridle. He said much to me, of which I understood little or nothing. I thought I could comprehend that he was cursing me for an Indian. He took hold of my gun, and tried to wrench it out of my hand. I have since understood that he kept a tavern, and was a magistrate; but at that time I was sick, and hungry, and irritable, and when I found that he wanted to take my gun from me, I became angry; and having in my hand a hickory stick, about as large as my thumb, and three or four feet long, I struck him over the head with it, so hearty a blow, that he immediately quitted his hold on my gun, and I rode off. Two young men, whose horses were standing by this house, and who appeared to me to be travellers, soon overtook me, and we rode on together.

This journey was a painful and unpleasant one to me. I travelled on, from day to day, weak, dispirited, and alone, meeting with little sympathy or attention from the people among whom I passed, often suffering from hunger and from sickness. I was willing to sleep in the woods, as I constantly did; but it was not easy to kill any game, nor did the state of my health allow me to go far from the road to hunt. I had ascended nearly to the head of the Big Miami, when one night, after having offered a dollar to a farmer, and been driven away without refreshment for myself or my horse, I lay down in the woods near by, and after I supposed them to be asleep, I took as much corn as was sufficient to feed my horse. I had, some time in the course of the preceding day, bought a chicken for twenty-five cents, a part of which I now ate, and the next day I began to feel a little stronger. I had now arrived where the intervals between the settlements were very wide, and seeing a gang of hogs in the woods, I shot one, skinned him, and hung the meat on my saddle, so that I was, for some time, well supplied with provisions. At the forks of the Miami of Lake Erie, was a trader with whom I was well acquainted, and who spoke Ottawwaw as well as I did; but when I asked him for something for my horse, he told me to begone, as he would give me nothing, though he offered to sell me some corn for my bear meat, as he called the pork I had hanging at my saddle; but I disliked him, and therefore went across the river to sleep in the woods.

This night I was again taken very sick, and when in the morning I found that my horse had escaped and gone back, I was scarce able to follow him. When I arrived at the river opposite the trader's house, I saw the horse standing on the other side, and calling to the trader, I asked him to send or bring the horse over to me, as I was sick. When he replied that he would not, I asked him to bring me a canoe, as being sick myself, I did not wish to go into the water; but this he refused to do, and I was compelled to swim across. I took my horse and returned to my camp, but was too sick to travel farther that day.

On the day after I resumed my journey, and had the good fortune to come to a house where the woman treated me kindly. She fed my horse, and then offered me some salt pork; but as I could not eat this, I returned it to her. Then she brought me some fresh venison, and I took a shoulder of it. She made signs to me to sit down in the house; but as I preferred the woods, I declined her offer, and selected near by a pleasant place to encamp, and there cooked the meat she had given me. Before my supper was cooked, she sent a little boy to bring me some bread, and some fresh and sweet butter.

Next day my route was principally out of settlements. At the village of Ah-koo-nah-goo-zik, I would not stop, as I was already under sufficient obligation to him, and I thought he would again urge me to take his horse. I had arrived within about one hundred miles of Detroit, when I was again taken very sick. Feeling wholly unable to travel, I determined to take some emetic tartar, which I had carried for a long time about me, having received it from Dr. M'Laughlin, at Rainy Lake. Soon after I had taken it, rain began to fall, and as the weather was now somewhat cold, and I was unable to avoid getting wet, the cramp affected me very violently. After the rain had ceased, the creek near which I was encamped froze over, but as I was suffering under a most violent fever, I broke the ice, and plunged myself all over into the water. In this situation I remained for some time, totally unable to travel, and almost without a hope of recovering. Two men passed me with the mail, one of whom could speak a little Indian; but they said they could do nothing for me, as they were compelled to proceed on their journey without loss of time.

But at length, I was again able to travel, and resumed my journey. I was two days' journey from Detroit, when I met a man in the road, with a Sioux pipe in his hand, whose strong resemblace to my father immediately arrested my attention. I endeavoured to make him stop and take notice of me, but he gave me a hasty look, and passed on. When I arrived, two days afterwards, at Detroit, I learned that this man was, as I supposed, my brother; but the governor would not allow me to return after him, as he knew that my having passed towards Detroit would be known at the Indian traders' houses on the way, and that my brother, who would inquire at all of them, would very soon hear of me, and return. His opinion appeared to have been well founded, for about three days afterwards my brother arrived. He held me a long time in his arms; but on account of my ignorance of the English language, we were unable to speak to each other, except through an interpreter. He next cut off my long hair, on which, till this time, I had worn strings of broaches, in the manner of the Indians. We visited Gov. Cass together, and he expressed much satisfaction at my having laid aside the Indian costume. But the dress of a white man was extremely uncomfortable to me, so that I was, from time to time, compelled to resume my old dress for the sake of convenience.

I endeavoured to persuade my brother, with whom I still conversed through an interpreter, to accompany me to my residence at the Lake of the Woods; but to this he would by no means consent, insisting that I must go with him to his house, beyond the Mississippi, and we set off together accordingly. From the military commandant at Fort Wayne, we received much friendly attention, and our journey was, in the main, a pleasant one. Forty days brought us to the Mississippi, fifteen miles above New Madrid, where my brother resided. Another of my brother's lived near by, and they both accompanied me to Jackson, fifteen miles from Cape Girardeau, where two of my sisters were living. From this place we started, six or seven in number, to go to Kentucky; and crossing the Mississippi, a little above Cape Girardeau, we went by the way of Golconda, on the Ohio, to Kentucky, where many of my relatives lived, not far from the small villages called Salem and Princeton.

My sister Lucy had, the night before my arrival, dreamed that she saw me coming through the corn field that surrounded her house. She had ten children. Relatives, friends, and neighbours, crowded around to witness my meeting with my sisters, and though we could converse together but little, they, and most of those who assembled about us, shed many tears. On the Sabbath day after my arrival, greater numbers than usual came to my sister's house, and divine worship was performed there. My brother-in-law, Jeremiah Rukker, endeavoured to find in my father's will some provision for me. He took me to the court at Princeton, and showed me to the people there; but nothing could be accomplished. My step-mother, who lived near by, gave me one hundred and thirty-seven dollars.

I went, accompanied by seven of my relatives, some men, some women, to Scottsville, where I had an uncle, who had sent for me. Here the people collected and gave me one hundred dollars, and on my return, Col. Ewing, of Hopkinsville, raised, in about one hour that I remained with him, one hundred dollars more, which he gave me. This gentleman showed me very distinguished attention and kindness, and remains, to this day, a cordial and active friend to me.

From Hopkinsville I returned to the house of my step-mother, where I made my preparations to go to the Lake of the Woods. Part of my relatives, who had accompanied me from beyond the Mississippi, had returned to their own homes; but my brother and his wife stayed to travel with me. From my brother Edward's house, near New Madrid, I went again to Jackson, where I was taken sick. My stock of money had now increased, through the voluntary donations of those friendly and charitable people among whom I had passed, to five hundred dollars, and, this being all in silver, would, my brother thought, be the means of exposing me to danger, and bringing me into difficulty, should I travel by myself; he, therefore, refused to leave me.

From Jackson we went together to St. Louis, where we saw Gov. Clark, who had already given much assistance to my brother in his journeys in search of me. He received us with great kindness, and offered us whatever assistance we might think necessary in accomplishing the object I now had in view, which was, to bring my family from the Indian country. My brother wished to accompany me, and to take a considerable number of men, to aid, if it should be necessary, in taking my children from the Indians; but I went one day to Gov. Clark, by myself, and told him he must not listen to my brother, who knew little of the country I was going to visit, or of what was needful to my success in the attempt to bring out my family. In truth, I did not wish my brother, or any other white man, to accompany me, as I knew he could not submit to all the hardships of the journey, and live as I should be compelled to live, in an Indian lodge, all winter. Furthermore, I was aware that he would be rather an incumbrance than any help to me. Gov. Clark wished to send me to the Lake of the Woods by way of the Upper Mississippi; but I was not willing to go that way, on account of the Sioux, through whose country I must pass. He gave me a Mackinac boat, large enough to carry sixty men, with a sufficient crew, three barrels of flour, two of hard bread, guns, tents, axes, &c. &c. Having prevailed on my brother to return, I set off. The current of the Mississippi, below the Missouri, soon convinced me that my large and heavy boat was not well adapted to the nature of my undertaking, and at Portage De Sioux I left it.

From this place I proceeded in a small canoe, with two men, to the head of the Illinois River, thence to Chikago.

I had a letter from Gov. Clark to Mr. M'Kenzie, the Indian agent at that place, and as there was no vessel about to sail for Mackinac, he fitted out a bark canoe, with a crew of Indians, to take me on my journey; but the Indians stopped to drink several days, and, in the mean time, a vessel arrived, in which I sailed on her return. I had waited ten days at Mackinac, when Capt. Knapp, of the revenue cutter, offered me a passage to Drummond's Island. Here Dr. Mitchell, and the Indian agent, Col. Anderson, treated me in a very friendly manner, until the latter had an opportunity to send me to the Saut De St. Marie.

At the Saut I remained two or three months, as Col. Dickson, who was there, would not allow me to go up Lake Superior in the North West Company's vessel, which went and returned three times while I was detained waiting for him. At last, he was ready to start, and I went on board his boat. We were no sooner out from shore, than he handed me an oar, and though my health was very poor, he compelled me to row as long as I was able to set up. Being at last quite disabled, he left me on shore, at a spot twenty miles above Fort William, where we found Mr. Giarson, who was there to take care of some property for the Hudson's Bay people. I was much dissatisfied with the treatment I received from Col. Dickson, and at parting I told him, that notwithstanding he left me so far from the end of my journey, I would still reach Me-naw-zhe-tau-naung before him. All my baggage I left in the care of Mr. Giarson, and went on in a small canoe, with one old Frenchman, whom I hired, and having good luck to cross the lake, I arrived before him.

My family were all well. Next day, some one told me that the red headed Englishman, as they called Col. Dickson, was coming up to my lodge. I told him, without going out, that he need not come in. "You find me here in my lodge," said I, "though you abandoned me on the lake shore, when very far from my home, or from any place where I could have expected to find help; but my lodge is not fit for such as you, therefore I hope you will not come in." I knew he wished to ask me for something to eat, but I was determined not to see him, or give him any thing. He left our village, and went by the Indians' road to Red River, though, as the water was unusually low, we heard he had a journey of extreme difficulty, and had nearly perished of hunger. There was, on the way, an enclosed burying ground, where one of my brother's-in-law, a daughter of Oto-pun-ne-be, and others of my friends and acquaintances, had been buried. Many of these graves were well covered, but Col. Dickson broke down the pailings, and destroyed the little houses that had been raised over the graves; at which conduct the Indians were much offended. They threatened to take his life, and might have done so had an opportunity offered; he went to Pembinah, thence to Lake Traverse, and returned no more into the country of the Ojibbeways.

A few days after my arrival at Me-naw-zhe-tau-naung, one of my children sickened and died of the measles, a complaint at that time very fatal among the Indians. The others were subsequently attacked, but I now knew better how to take care of them, and no more died. Soon after this, provisions became scarce, and I was, with Me-zhuk-ko-naum, making preparations for a medicine hunt. In my dream I saw the same young man I had before seen on similar occasions, come down in the usual manner, and stand before me. He reproved me with more than usual harshness for my complaints, and because I cried for the child I had recently lost. "Henceforth," said he, "you shall see me no more, and that which remains before you, of your path, shall be full of briers and thorns. It is on account of the many crimes, and the bad conduct of your wife, that all your coming days are to be filled with trouble. Nevertheless, as you have called me this time, I give you something to eat." When he said this, I looked and saw before me many ducks covering the surface of the water, and in another place a sturgeon, in a third a raindeer. This dream was fulfilled, as usual, at least as much of it as related to my hunting and fishing.

As the winter came on, I went to Red River to hunt buffaloe, and make dry meat, and early in the spring I started to come to the states. From my first wife I had parted ten years before the time I now speak of; but the urgency of the Indians, and, in part, the necessity of my situation, had compelled me to take another.* By this woman I had three children; those by my former wife were not at present in the village. My wife refusing to accompany me, I took the three children and started without her. At Rainy Lake she overtook me, and agreed to accompany me to Mackinac.

On my way down, I was assisted by the North West Company. At Drummond's Island I was disappointed of large presents given me when on my way to the Lake of the Woods, but which, as I did not then wish to take, were promised me on my return. The commanding officer who had shown me so much kindness, had been relieved by another, of a very different character, one who seemed to find no satisfaction in doing any thing for any person connected with the Indians. This man refused to see me, or afford me any assistance. By the kindness, however, of Mr. Ermatinger, of the Saut De St. Marie, I was enabled to reach Mackinac.

Col. Boyd, the Indian agent at that time at Mackinac, called me to him, and wished to hire me as a striker in his smith's shop; but not liking the employment, I did not wish to remain. He gave me one hundred pounds of flour, the same quantity of pork, some whiskey, tobacco, &c. There were two vessels about to sail for Chikago, but neither of them would take me as a passenger, though I had money enough, and was willing to pay them. As I had no other alternative, I was compelled to purchase from the Indians a poor and old bark canoe, for which I gave sixty dollars, and I engaged three Frenchmen to accompany me; but Col. B—— would not permit them to go. He gave me, however, a letter to Dr. Wolcott, who was now Indian agent at Chikago, and I started with only one man to assist me.

At the Ottawwaw settlement of Waw-gun-nuk-kiz-ze I stopped for a short time, and finding that my canoe was too frail and leaky to perform the voyage, I purchased another, a new one, for which I gave eighty dollars. Several of my acquaint-

---

* The painful topic of domestic troubles, and the misconduct of persons nearly allied to him, seems to be the only one on which the narrator has not spoken with clearness. There is, in relation to this subject, some want of distinctness; but it is believed this will not be thought to affect the credibility of the narrative, inasmuch as we discover no departure from truth, unless the suppression of some facts can be considered such.

ances among the Otawwaws, determined to accompany me, and started accordingly, eight men in one canoe, and six in another, with some women. They went on with me until we arrived within one or two days' journey of Chikago, when meeting other Indians, with discouraging accounts of the state of the water in the Illinois, they left me and went back. My wife returned with them.

When I arrived at Chikago, I was sick of a fever, and my provisions being exhausted, I was in great distress. I went to Dr. Wolcott to present him the letter from Col. Boyd, the Indian agent at Mackinac, but he would not receive it, nor take any notice of me. He knew well who I was, as he had seen me when I passed Chikago before, and I could not tell why he refused me assistance. I had my tent set up at a little distance from his house, near a wild rice swamp, and for several days, though I was so much more unwell that I was scarce able to sit up five minutes at a time, I subsisted my children by shooting the black birds as they came and settled on the rice. When I was again able, with the aid of two sticks, to crawl to the house of Dr. Wolcott, I went to represent to him that my children were in danger of perishing of hunger; but he drove me harshly away. When I left his door, I shed some tears, which it was not common for me to do; but I was rendered womanish by my sickness. Three or four times I fainted, and lay long by the road side, on the way from his house to my tent. But my sufferings, and those of my children, were shortly afterwards relieved by a Frenchman, who had been to carry some boats across the Portage. His wife was an Ojibbeway woman, and commonly accompanied him when he went to take any boats across. Though his horses were now much worn out with the long journey from which he had returned, he agreed to take me and my canoe sixty miles, and if his horses could hold out, the whole one hundred and twenty, which was, at the present stage of water, the length of the Portage, for which I agreed to pay him agreeable to his demand, which I thought very moderate. He lent me, also, a young horse to ride, as I was far too weak to think of walking, and he thought I could ride on horseback much more comfortably than in the cart with the canoe. Before we arrived at the end of the sixty miles, he was taken sick, and as there was now a little water in the river, I concluded to put my canoe in, and try to descend in it. His young horse, the night after I gave it up to him, was stolen by the Po-ta-wato-mies. He was seized with the bloody flux, but as he had a young man with him, I rendered him what assistance I could in starting, and let him go back. My Frenchman had deserted from me soon after I left Chikago, and I had now no person to assist me except an old Indian, called Gos-so-kwaw-waw, (the smoker.)* We put the canoe in the water, but we could not get into it ourselves, only sometimes the children were put in, and we took them down, one walking at the bow, the other at the stern of the canoe. We had proceeded no more than three miles, when I found that this method was likely to prove so laborious and slow, that I thought best to engage a Po-ta-wato-mie, whom I met there, and who agreed for a blanket and a pair of leggins, to take my baggage and my children on his horses to the mouth of the An-num-mun-ne Se-be, or Yellow Ochre River, a distance of sixty miles. The An-num-mun-ne comes from towards the Mississippi, and below it there is always, in the Illinois, water enough for canoes. I felt somewhat afraid to trust the Po-ta-wato-mie with my children, and the baggage, which contained some valuable property, but old Gos-so-kwaw-waw was of opinion that he would prove honest. When he put the children on the horses, he said, " In three days I shall be at the mouth of the An-num-mun-ne River, and shall wait for you there."

Without any farther words, we parted, and the old Smoker and myself continued our laborious and difficult route along the bed of the Illinois. Most of the country, on both sides the route, from Chikago to the Yellow Ochre River, are prairie, in which horses and carts can be driven without any difficulty. On our arrival at the place appointed, we found the Po-ta-wato-mie there, and all safe.

We now embarked every thing together in the canoe, and went down to Fort Clark, which is on a narrow neck of land, between two lakes, and is thence called by the Indians Ka-gah-gum-ming,† (the isthmus.) Here I found some acquaintances, or rather those who claimed relationship in consequence of their

* Sag-gus-swaw-waw—the Smoker, in Ojibbeway.
† Ka-gah-gum-ming, almost water.

having been in some measure connected with the family that I belonged to among the Indians. Here was a Taw-ga-we-nin-ne, a son of him that had been the husband of Net-no-kwa, and some of the relatives of one of my wives. One of these, an old woman, gave me a sack of Wiskobimmenuk, or that sort of corn which is plucked green, boiled, and then dried. Two or three miles beyond this, as I went on my way, I saw a man standing on the bank, who, as I came opposite to him, called out, "my friend, do you love venison?" When I told him I did, and had put my canoe in shore, he lifted a large and fat deer into it, saying, "perhaps you will like to eat some of this, which I have just now killed." He was going to turn away, when I called him back, and though he refused any compensation for the deer, I gave him a little powder and shot, and some flints, for which he appeared very thankful.

About this time, when I was one day warm at work, I shot a crane, and got into the water to take it up. Shortly after I felt somewhat unwell, but not reflecting on the cause of my illness, I went again into the water to get something I had shot, when immediately I fell down, and was unable to get up. My fever returned upon me with such violence, that being in immediate expectation of death, I gave the Old Smoker directions to take my children to Governor Clark, who, I was confident, would assist them in reaching my relatives. But contrary to my expectation, I became gradually better, and after some days was able to go on my journey. We passed great numbers of Potawattomies, their lodges standing many together, in almost every bend of the river. Some of them started out in their canoes occasionally, and accompanied me some distance on my way. One day a man came running from his lodge to the bank of the river, and asked me who I was. When I had told him, he inquired if my children could eat honey; and when I told him I believed they could, he sent two young men, each with a large wooden bowl full, which they brought wading into the water, and handed to me.

In this manner I descended the Illinois River, killing plenty of game, and having at all times enough to eat; my health, also, gradually improving, until I came to St. Louis. Here Governor Clark showed his wonted kindness, not only to me and my children, but to the Old Smoker, who had been so serviceable to me in my journey. After giving the old man a handsome present, he provided for his return to his own country, and dismissed him. I was detained longer at St. Louis than I had wished, as new clothes were to be made for my children. Some of these not having been completed in time for me to take with me, the Governor sent them afterwards to Kentucky. From St. Louis, I went to Cape Guirardeau, in my birch bark canoe, having a letter from Governor Clark to the Indian agent at that place.

At Cape Guirardeau, where I left my canoe, and where I remained but a very short time, I saw some of the gentlemen of Major Long's party, then on their return from the Rocky Mountains. This was in the fall of the year 1820, and was about one year after my first arrival on the Ohio, in 1819. From the time of my capture by Manito-o-geezhik and Gish-kaw-ko, just thirty years had elapsed, before I started in the spring of 1819, from the Lake of the Woods. So that it must have been in the spring of the year 1789, that I was taken prisoner. I am now forty-seven years old.

Four months I remained with my sisters at Jackson, fifteen miles from Cape Guirardeau; then I went to Kentucky, and the next fall I returned to St. Louis, to see Governor Clark; but he was not at home, and as many people were then dying in St. Louis of fevers, I made but a short stay. On my way home, I fell sick of a violent fever at the Grand Prairie, which is eighty miles from the place where I had left my children. Fortunately I fell into the hands of a woman who treated me with much humanity and kindness, and I soon began to recover. I now heard that my children were dying with the fever which prevailed so generally throughout the country, and notwithstanding my own miserable and debilitated condition, I hastened home. Only one of my children died. The others, though very sick, at last recovered. But I was not alone in this affliction. Seven died out of the circle of my near relatives, with whom I then lived, and an alarming mortality prevailed throughout that part of the state.

On the ensuing spring, an attempt was made to recover something for my benefit, from the estate of my father; but my stepmother sent several of the negroes, which it was thought might fall to me, to the island of Cuba, where they were sold. This business is yet unsettled, and remains in the hands of the lawyers.

In the spring of 1822, I started to go again to the north, not finding that I was content among my friends in Kentucky. I went by the way of the Grand Prairie, and having given my canoe to my brother, I took horses, and putting my children on them, I came to St. Louis, thence by way of the Illinois, towards Chikago.

The Indian agent for Fort Clark lived at this time at a place called Elk Heart, some distance below. He, as well as most of the people on this route, had been kind, and had shown a disposition to assist me whenever I needed any thing. On this journey I stopped at Elk Heart, at the house of the agent, and though he was not himself at home, I had my horses fed, and was supplied with what refreshment I needed for myself and children, free of expense. On the following day, I met the agent on his way home from Fort Clark, and told him of the reception I had met at his house in his absence. He was glad to hear of this, and he told me that I should soon come to a bad river to cross; " but," said he, " there is a boat now on this side, in which I have just crossed. The man to whom it belongs, lives on the other side. You must use the boat to cross, and then tell him to take it around to the other river, which is beyond his house, and help you to cross that, and I will pay him for his trouble." We crossed accordingly, but my daughter Martha being now sick, we stopped all day near the house of the man to whom the canoe belonged. I had one very handsome horse, which had been given me by my brother, and which this man said he was determined to have from me. He offered to buy it; but I told him the horse was necessary to my journey, and I could by no means part with it. Still he insisted, and said, unless I would let him have the horse, I should not have his canoe to cross the other river. He cursed and abused me, but all the means he could use, did not induce me to give up the horse. The canoe had been taken around to the river I had to cross, for the use of some other person, and when I was ready to go I started, expecting to find it there. But on my way to the ferry, I met the man on horseback, who said to me, " I have taken away the canoe, and you cannot cross." Without regarding this, I went on, and when I arrived, I found the canoe was indeed gone, and that there were no logs, or other materials to make a raft. Fearing to endanger the children, by swimming them across on the horse's backs, I stood for some time in doubt what to do. At last I recollected, that if he had hid the canoe, as was most probably the case, his track would lead me to it. Then going back to the road, a considerable distance from the river, I found his track coming into it. This I followed, until I found the canoe hid in thick bushes, about a mile below the ferry. Taking it up to the crossing place, I carried my children, and led the horses over; then giving the canoe a push into the stream, I said to it, "go, and stay where your master hides you."

At Chikago, I was compelled to sell my horses for much less than their value, to Captain Bradley and a Mr. Kenzie, who was then agent in place of Dr. Wolcott, as they told me I could not get them taken to Mackinac. One old horse, which I left as being of little or no value, I afterwards received fifteen dollars for, from some gentlemen who wished to make use of him, but who might have had him for nothing. When Captain Keith, in the schooner Jackson, arrived, he told me, on seeing the paper given me by Governor Clark, that he would have taken my horses to Mackinac for nothing; but it was now too late, as they were sold.

A principal part of my design in returning to Mackinac, was to engage myself to Col. Boyd, the Indian agent there, as an interpreter; he having very often expressed a wish that I should do so, whenever I had acquired such a knowledge of the English language, as would qualify me to discharge the duties of that station. It was now, therefore, a disappointment to me, to be informed that I had come too late, an interpreter having recently been hired to fill the place. He informed me, however, that an agent to be stationed at the Saut De St. Mary, would probably arrive in the steam boat which was expected immediately, and Col. Boyd thought I might obtain the situation of interpreter for him. When Mr. Schoolcraft, the gentleman expected, arrived at Mackinac, he readily accepted my proposal. But as he was to stay but an hour or two on the island, he directed me to make my preparations and follow him, allowing me four days after his arrival at the Saut, before it was necessary for me to be there. I made my preparations accordingly, and was nearly ready to start, when a letter came from Mr. Schoolcraft, stating that he had found an interpreter at the Saut, and therefore did not wish me to join him. I carried back to the traders the furniture and other articles which I had purchased with the expectation of residing at the Saut, and they willingly restored me my money.

CHAPTER XV.

Transactions of the agents and clerks of the American Fur Company, in the country about the Lake of the Woods—treachery of an Indian woman—misfortunes attendant on an attempt to bring my children from the Indian country.

BEING now destitute of employment, I engaged to Mr. Stewart, the agent of the American Fur Company, to go with the traders into the Indian country. This I preferred to remaining with the Indian agent, though he again proposed to hire me for a striker in his smith's shop. For my services with the people of the American Fur Company, I was to receive two hundred and twenty-five dollars per year, and a suit of clothes.

My children I placed at school at Mackinac, and went to the Saut De St. Marie with Mr. Morrison, one of the company's principal clerks. Thence they sent me, in a boat, with some Frenchmen, to Fond Du Lac. I was unacquainted with the manners of these people, and should have suffered, and perhaps perished for want of provisions, had I not purchased some occasionally from the crew. From Fond Du Lac I went to Rainy Lake with Mr. Cote; but my ignorance of the business in which I had embarked, exposed me to much inconvenience. I had still some of my traps with me, with which I took a considerable number of musk rats on this journey, and I was not less surprised than displeased, to be told that the skins did not belong to me. But I was not only compelled to give these up; I was made to paddle by myself a canoe, heavily loaded with wild rice, and to submit to various other laborious employments, which I did very reluctantly.

When we arrived at Rainy Lake, I went to hunt, but killed nothing. Soon afterwards, they sent me to the rapids of Rainy

Lake River; and before the ice had formed so as to put an end to the fishing, I had taken one hundred and fifty sturgeons. The winter had now commenced, and Mr. Cote sent me, with one clerk, four Frenchmen, and a small outfit of goods, equal to one hundred and sixty dollars in value, to trade among the Indians. We were furnished with no other food than wild rice, at the rate of eighteen quarts per man, and instructed not to return until we should have exchanged for peltries all our goods. As I knew we should be compelled to travel far before we found the Indians, I requested of Mr. Cote permission to remain while I could prepare a train and harness for two good dogs which belonged to me; also snow shoes for ourselves; but he would not hear of a moment's delay.

Four days after we started, a heavy snow fell, and our wild rice being all expended, the clerk and three of the Frenchmen left me and returned to the Fort. There was now only myself and one Frenchman named Veiage, who however was a hardy, patient, and most excellent man, and we struggled through the snow with our heavy loads as we might.

After some days, and when we were extremely reduced through want of provisions, we found some lodges of Indians, but they also were in a starving condition. With these I left Veiage, and with a few goods, went to visit another encampment at some distance; these also I found perishing of hunger. On my return to the place where I had left my companion, the lodges were removed, and no person remained. Here my strength failed entirely, and I sat down expecting to perish, as the night was very cold; but an Indian who had come back to look at his traps, found me, made a fire, and after he had raised me up, assisted me to his lodge. He had taken one beaver, and this was now to be divided among twenty persons, not one of whom had eaten a mouthful in two days, and all were in a starving condition.

Soon after this, as I continued on my journey according to my strength, I found the lodge of my friend Oto-pun-ne-be, the man who had taken my part in the affair with Waw-bebe-nais-sa. His wife began to cry when she saw the extreme misery of my condition, so much was I reduced and changed in appearance by hunger and fatigue. About this time eight starving Frenchmen came upon us, who had been sent by Mr. Cote, he supposing that I had found buffaloe, and must by this time have meat in great abundance. One of my dogs died, and we ate him. We were travelling on the old trail of the Indians, but a deep snow had fallen since they passed. Under this snow we found several dead dogs, and other things thrown away or left by the Indians, such as bones, worn out moccasins, and pieces of leather. With these we were able to sustain life. We killed also, and ate my last dog; but we had yet a long distance to travel before we could reach the buffaloe, and as we were all rapidly failing, we consulted together, and determined to kill one of the Fur Company's dogs. We did so, and this enabled us to reach the buffaloe, when our distress was for the present at an end.

After I had killed many buffaloes, and meat had for some time been plenty in our camp, the Frenchmen became lazy and insolent, and refused to go for meat, to carry packs, or render me any assistance whatever. When we were ready to return to the trading house, every one of these men refused to take any load but his own blanket and provisions, except Veiage, and with him I divided our peltries, which in all weighed six hundred pounds. We were of course a considerable time in carrying these heavy loads to the Fort.

When I arrived, I accounted for my whole outfit; having the peltries I had purchased in exchange for every article, except some powder and shot, which we had ourselves expended in hunting. The price of this was deducted from my pay, in my final settlement with the agent of the American Fur Company; then ten dollars, the price of the dog we had killed in the extremity of our hunger, and which had been the means of saving, not my life only, but that of the nine Frenchmen that were with me. But Mr. Cote did not consider my return* a good one, and complained of me for having refused to take whiskey with my outfit. I told him that if I had taken whiskey, I could certainly have obtained a much greater quantity of peltries, but I was averse to trading with the Indians when intoxicated, and did not wish to be one, on any occasion, to introduce whiskey among them. But as he had determined on sending me out

* This word, in the language of the fur traders, signifies not the coming back of the clerk or person sent out but the peltries acquired by the outfit, and is equally used if the trader never returns in person to his employer.

again, and insisted I should take whiskey, I told him I would for once, conform entirely to his instructions, which were "to use every method to procure the greatest possible quantity of skins, at the lowest price." This time I went to the country about the Lake of the Woods, and with an outfit valued at two hundred dollars, I purchased, by means of whiskey, more than double the amount of peltries I had before brought in. Now Mr. Cote expressed the highest satisfaction at my success; but I told him, if he wished to have his goods sold in that way, he must employ some other person, as I could not consent to be the instrument of such fraud and injustice. I had been so long among the Indians, that many of them were personally my friends, and having seen the extent of the mischiefs occasioned by the introduction of intoxicating liquors, I had become desirous of preventing it, as far as in my power, at least; I was not willing to be myself active in spreading such poison among them; nor was I willing to use the advantage, their unconquerable appetite for spirits might give me, in bargaining with them, as I knew, that though they might easily be defrauded, any fraud thus practised must be known to them, and they would feel resentment and dislike, in proportion as they were made to suffer; more particularly against me, whom they looked upon as one of their own number.

I remained fifteen months in the American Fur Company's employ, during all which time, I slept only thirteen nights in the house, so active and laborious were my occupations. It had been an item in my agreement with Mr. Stewart, that I should be allowed to go to Red River to see my children, and make an attempt to bring them out with me. Accordingly, when the traders were about to make their yearly visit to Mackinac, I was allowed to go by myself; but having been disappointed of moccasins and other articles that had been promised me by Mr. Cote, I suffered much inconvenience, travelling as I did by myself in a small canoe. My children were three in number, two daughters and one son, and had been a long time separated from me, even before I first left the Indian country.

Mr. Clark, of the Hudson's Bay Company, who was now stationed at Red River, and to whom I had a letter, refused to give me any assistance in recovering my children. In the morning, when I arrived there, I had left my blanket in his house, expecting, at least, that I should sleep there; but when at the approach of night I was about to go in, he sent the blanket out to me. From the manner in which this was done, I knew if I went in again, it would only be to be driven out, and I went immediately to select a place to sleep in the woods at a little distance. But Mr. Bruce, the interpreter whom I have before mentioned, saw me, and calling me into his lodge, invited me to remain, and while I did so, treated me in the most friendly and hospitable manner. Knowing that I had no reason to expect any assistance from Mr. Clark, who was soon to leave the country, I went to Captain Bulger, the military commandant, to state my business, and received from him a most attentive and friendly hearing. Immediately on my calling to see him, he asked me where I had slept, as he knew that I had arrived the day before. When he heard that I had been refused a lodging in the trading house, he invited me to come and eat with him, and sleep in his house as long as I should remain there. He knew of my business to the country, and asked me if I could tell where my children were. I had ascertained that they were with the Indians about the Prairie Portage.

Some Indians about the Fort, told me that those of the band with whom my children were, had heard of my arrival, and were determined to kill me if I should attempt to take my children from them. Nevertheless, I visited that band as soon as I could make the journey, and went into the lodge of the principal chief, who treated me kindly. I remained some time, always staying in the lodge with my children, who appeared pleased to see me; but I easily discovered that it was by no means the intention of the Indians to suffer me to take them away. Giah-ge-wa-go-mo, the man who had long before stolen away my son, and whom I had been compelled to beat, as well as to kill his horse, now treated me with some insolence, and threatened even to take my life. I said to him, "if you had been a man, you would have killed me long ago, instead of now threatening me. I have no fear of you." But being entirely alone, I could accomplish no more at present, than to induce the band to remove, and encamp near the fort at Red River. This was a considerable journey, and on all of it, my children and myself were made to carry heavy burthens, and were treated like slaves. They did not indeed give me a load to carry, but they were careful so far to overload my children, that when I had taken as much as I could move under, there were heavy loads left for them. After they had encamped near the fort, I asked them for my children, but they utterly refused to give them up. Giah-ge-wa-go-mo was the principal man who was active in resisting me, and with him the dispute had grown to so open a quarrel, that I was about to proceed to violent measures, but I bethought me that I should do wrong to attempt to shed blood without first making my intention known to Captain Bulger, who had expressed so much friendly feeling towards me. I went accordingly, and told him my situation, and that I was now convinced I could not take my children without using violent measures with Giah-ge-wa-go-mo. He approved of my having told him what I was about to do, and immediately sent Mr. Bruce to call my children into the fort. They came accordingly, and stood before his house, but with ten or twelve Indians accompanying them, and who were careful to stand near by on each side of them. Having pointed out my children to him, the captain directed his servant to feed them. Something was accordingly brought from his own table, he having just then eaten, and given to them; but the Indians immediately snatched it away, leaving them not a mouthful. A loaf of bread was then brought, but it went in the same way, not a particle of it being left to them. Captain Bulger now directed a store house to be opened, and told me to go in and get them something to eat. Finding there some bags of pemmican, I took the half of one, about twenty pounds, and making them sit down, all partook of it.

The Indians refused the children to the demand of Capt. Bulger, as they had done to me; but next day he called all the principal men, and among others Giah-ge-wa-go-mo, to come and council with him. The chief man of the band was very willing that I should take away the children, and when we all went into the council room, he took a seat with Captain Bulger and myself, thereby placing the four men who were principally active in detaining them, in the situation of persons who were acting in open contravention to his wishes.

Presents to the amount of about one hundred dollars in value, were brought in, and placed on the floor between the two parties. Captain Bulger then said to the Indians:

"My children, I have caused to be placed before you here, a pipe full of tobacco, not because I am willing to have you suppose I would purchase from you a right for this man to come and take what is his own, but to signify to you, that I still hold you by the hand, as long as you are ready to listen attentively to my words. As for this man, he comes to you not in his own name only, and speaking his own words; but he speaks the words of your great father who is beyond the waters, and of the Great Spirit, in whose hand we all are, and who gave these children to be his. You must, therefore, without venturing to give him any farther trouble, deliver to him his children, and take these presents, as a memorial of the good will that subsists between us."

The Indians began to deliberate, and were about to make a reply, when they saw a considerable armed force brought and paraded before the door of the council house, and finding themselves completely surrounded, they accepted the presents, and promised to surrender the children.

The mother of these children was now an old woman, and as she said she wished to accompany them, I readily consented. The boy, who was of age to act for himself, preferred to remain among the Indians, and as the time for giving him an education, and fitting him to live in any other manner than as the Indians do, had passed, I consented he should act as he thought best. Several Indians accompanied us four days' journey on our return, then all went back, except my two daughters and their mother.

I did not return to the Lake of the Woods by the way of the Be-gwi-o-nus-ko Se-be, but chose another route, in which I had to travel a part of the way by water, a part by land. In ascending the Bad River, there is a short road by what is called Sturgeon River, and a portage to come again into the principal river. Not far from the mouth of Sturgeon River was, at this time, an encampment, or village, of six or seven lodges. A young man belonging to that band, and whose name was Ome-zhuh-gwut-oons, had not long previous to this been whipped by Mr. Cote, for some real or alleged misconduct about the trading-house, and feeling dissatisfied, he, when he heard I had passed up Sturgeon River, started after me in his little canoe, and soon overtook me. After he had joined me, he showed, I thought, an unusual disposition to talk to me, and claimed to be, in some manner, related to me. He encamped with us that night, and the next morning we started on together. This day, when we stopped, and were resting on shore, I noticed that he took an opportunity to meet one of my daughters in the bushes; but she returned immediately, somewhat agitated. Her mother, also, was several times, in the course of the day, in close conversation with her; but the young woman continued sad, and was several times crying.

At night, after we stopped to encamp, the young man very soon left us; but as he remained at a little distance, apparently much busied about something, I went and found him with his medicines all opened about him, and he was inserting a thong of deer's sinew, about five inches in length, into a bullet. I said to him, " My brother," [for this was the name he had himself given me,] " if you want powder, or balls, or flints, I have plenty, and will give you as much as you wish." He said that he also had plenty, and I left him and returned to camp. It was some time before he came in; when at last he made his appearance, he was dressed and ornamented as a warrior for battle. He continued, during the first part of the night, to watch me much too closely, and my suspicions, which had been already excited, were now more and more confirmed. But he continued to be as talkative, and to seem as friendly as ever. He asked me for my knife, as he said, to cut some tobacco, and instead of returning it to me, slipped it into his own belt; but I thought, perhaps he would return it to me in the morning.

I laid myself down at about the usual time, as I would not appear to suspect his intentions. I had not put up my tent, having only the little shelter afforded by a piece of painted cloth that had been given me at Red River. When I lay down, I chose such a position as would enable me to watch the young man's motions. I could see, as he sat opposite the fire, that his eyes were open and watchful, and that he felt not the least inclination to sleep. When at length a thunder shower commenced, he appeared more anxious and restless than before. When the rain began to fall, I asked him to come and place himself near me, so as to enjoy the benefit of my shelter, and he did so. The shower was very heavy, and entirely extinguished our fire; but soon after it had ceased, the mosquitoes becoming very troublesome, Ome-zhuh-gwut-oons rekindled it, and breaking off a branch of a bush, he sat and drove them away from me. I was conscious that I ought not to sleep; but drowsiness was gaining some hold on me, when another thunder shower, more violent than the first, arose. In the interval of the showers, I lay as one sleeping, but almost without moving or opening my eyes. I watched the motions of the young man; at one time, when an unusually loud clap of thunder alarmed him, he would throw a little tobacco into the fire, as an offering; at another, when he seemed to suppose me asleep, I saw him watching me like a cat about to spring on its prey; but I did not suffer myself to sleep.

He breakfasted with us as usual, then started by himself, before I was quite ready. My daughter, whom he had met in the bushes, was now apparently more alarmed than before, and absolutely refused to enter the canoe; but her mother was very anxious to quiet her agitation, and apparently very desirous to prevent my paying any particular attention to her. At last, she was induced to get into the canoe, and we went on. The young man kept along before us, and at a little distance, until about ten o'clock, when, at turning a point in a difficult and rapid part of the river, and gaining a view of a considerable reach above, I was surprised that I could see neither him nor his canoe. At this place the river is about eighty yards wide, and there is, about ten yards from the point before mentioned, a small island of naked rock. I had taken off my coat, and I was, with great effort, pushing up my canoe against the powerful current, which compelled me to keep very near the shore, when the discharge of a gun at my side arrested my progress. I heard a bullet whistle past my head, and felt my side touched, at the same instant that the paddle fell from my right hand, and the hand itself dropped powerless to my side. The bushes were obscured by the smoke of the gun, but at a second look I saw Ome-zhuh-gwut-oons escaping. At that time the screams of my children drew my attention to the canoe, and I found every part of it was becoming covered with blood. I endeavoured, with my left hand, to push the canoe in shore, that I might pursue after him; but the current being too powerful for me, took my canoe on the other side, and threw it against the small rocky island before mentioned. I now got out, pulled the canoe a little on to the rock, with my left hand, and then made an attempt to load my gun. Before I could finish loading I fainted, and fell on the rock. When I came to myself again, I was alone on the island, and the canoe, with my daughters, was just going out of sight in the river below. Soon after it disappeared, I fainted a second time; but consciousness at length returned.

As I believed that the man who had shot me was still watching from his concealment, I examined my wounds, and finding my situation desperate, my right arm being much shattered, and the ball having entered my body, in the direction to reach my lungs, and not having passed out, I called to him, requesting him to come, and by putting an immediate end to my life, to release me from the protracted suffering I had in prospect. "You have killed me," said I; "but though the hurt you have given me must be mortal, I fear it may be some time before I shall die. Come, therefore, if you are a man, and shoot me again." Many times I called to him, but he returned me no answer. My body was now almost naked, as I had on, when shot, beside my pantaloons, only a very old and ragged shirt, and much of this had been torn off in the course of the morning. I lay exposed to the sun, and the black and green headed flies, on a naked rock, the greater part of a day in July or August, and saw no prospect before me, but that of a lingering death; but as the sun went down, my hope and strength began to revive, and plunging into the river, I swam across to the other side. When I reached the shore, I could stand on my feet, and I raised the sas-sah-kwi, or war whoop, as a cry of exultation and defiance to my enemy. But the additional loss of blood, occasioned by the exertion in swimming the river, caused me another fainting fit, from which, when I recovered, I concealed myself near the bank, to watch for him. Presently I saw Ome-zhuh-gwut-oons come from his hiding place, put his canoe into the water, embark, and begin to descend the river. He came very near my hiding place, and I felt tempted to make a spring, and endeavour to seize and strangle him in the water; but fearing that my strength might not be sufficient, I let him pass without discovering myself.

I was now tormented with the most excessive thirst, and as the bank was steep and rocky, I could not, with my wounded arm, lie down to drink. I was therefore compelled to go into the water, and let my body down into it, until I brought my mouth to a level with the surface, and thus I was able to drink. By this time, the evening growing somewhat cooler, my strength was, in part, restored; but the blood seemed to flow more freely. I now applied myself to dressing the wound in my arms. I endeavoured, though the flesh was already much swollen, to replace the fragments of the bone; to accomplish which, I tore in strips the remainder of my shirt, and with my teeth and my left hand I contrived to tie these around my arm, at first loosely, but by degrees tighter and tighter, until I thought it had assumed, as nearly as I could give it, the proper form. I then tied on small sticks, which I broke from the branches of trees, to serve as splints, and then suspended my hand in a string, which passed around my neck. After this was completed, I took some of the bark of a choke cherry bush, which I observed there, and chewing it fine applied it to the wounds, hoping thus to check the flowing of the blood. The bushes about me, and for all the distance between me and the river, were covered with blood. As night came on, I chose a place where was plenty of moss, to lie down on, with the trunk of a fallen tree for my pillow. I was careful to select a place near the river, that I might have a chance of seeing any thing that might pass; also, to be near the water in case my thirst should again become urgent. I knew that one trader's canoe was expected, about this time, to pass this place, on the way towards Red River, and it was this canoe from which I expected relief and assistance. There were no Indians nearer than the village from which Ome-zhuh-gwut-oons had followed me, and he, with my wife and daughters, were the only persons that I had any reason to suppose were within many miles of me.

I laid myself down, and prayed to the Great Spirit, that he would see and pity my condition, and send help to me, now in the time of my distress. As I continued praying, the musquitoes, which had settled on my naked body in vast numbers, and were, by their stings, adding greatly to the torment I suffered, began to rise, and after hovering at a little distance above and around me, disappeared entirely. I did not attribute this, which was so great a relief, to the immediate interposition of a Superior Power, in answer to my prayer, as the evening was, at that time, becoming something cool, and I knew it was entirely the effect of change of temperature. Nevertheless, I was conscious, as I have ever been in times of distress and of danger, that the Master of my life, though invisible, was yet near, and was looking upon me. I slept easily and quietly, but not without interruption. Every time I awoke, I remembered to have seen, in my dream, a canoe with white men, in the river before me.

It was late in the night, probably after midnight, when I heard female voices, which I supposed to be those of my daughters, not more than two hundred yards from me, but partly across the river. I believed that Ome-zhuh-gwut-oons had discovered their hiding place, and was, perhaps, offering them some violence, as the cry was that of distress; but so great was my weakness, that the attempt to afford them any relief seemed wholly beyond my power. I learned afterwards, that my children, as soon as I fainted and fell on the rock, supposing me dead, had been influenced by their mother to turn the canoe down the river, and exert themselves to make their escape. They had not proceeded far, when the woman steered the canoe into a low point of bushes, and threw out my coat, and some other articles. They then ran on a considerable distance, and concealed themselves; but here it occurred to the woman, that she might have done better to have kept the property belonging to me, and accordingly returned to get it. It was when they came to see these things lying on the shore, that the children burst out crying, and it was at this time that I heard them.

Before ten o'clock next morning, I heard human voices on the river above me, and from the situation I had chosen, I could see a canoe coming, like that I had seen in my dream, loaded with white men. They landed at a little distance above me, and began to make preparations for breakfast. I knew that this was the canoe belonging to Mr. Stewart, of the Hudson's Bay Company, who, together with Mr. Grant, was expected about this time; and being conscious that my appearance would make a painful impression upon them, I determined to wait until they had breakfasted, before I showed myself to them. After they had eaten, and put their canoe again in the water, I waded out a little distance into the river, to attract their attention. As soon as they saw me, the Frenchmen ceased paddling, and they all gazed at me, as if in doubt and amazement. As the current of the river was carrying them rapidly past me, and my repeated calls, in the Indian language, seemed to produce no effect, I called Mr. Stewart by name, and spoke a few words of English, which I could command, requesting them to come and take me. In a moment their paddles were in the water, and they brought the canoe so near where I stood, that I was able to get into it.

No one in the canoe recognised me, though Mr. Stewart and Mr. Grant were both well known to me. I had not been able to wash the blood off my body, and it is probable that the suffering I had undergone, had much changed my appearance. They were very eager and rapid in their inquiries, and soon ascertained who I was, and also became acquainted with the principal facts I have related. They made a bed for me in the canoe, and at my urgent request went to search for my children, in the direction where I had heard them crying, and where I told them I feared we should find they had been murdered; but we sought here, and in other places, to no purpose.

Having ascertained who it was that had wounded me, these two traders agreed to take me immediately to the village of Ome-zhuh-gwut-oons, and they were determined, in case of discovering and taking him, to aid me in taking my revenge, by putting him immediately to death. They therefore concealed me in the canoe, and on landing near the lodges, an old man came down to the shore, and asked them, " what was the news in the country they came from?" " All is well there," answered Mr. Stewart; " we have no other news." " This is the manner," said the old man, " in which white people always treat us. I know very well something has happened in the country you have come from, but you will not tell us of it. Ome-zhuh-gwut-oons, one of our young men, has been up the river two or three days, and he tells us that the Long Knife, called Shaw-shaw-wa-ne-ba-se, (the falcon,) who passed here a few days since, with his wife and children, has murdered them all; but I am fearful that he himself has been doing something wrong, for he is watchful and restless, and has just fled from this place before you arrived." Mr. Stewart and Mr.

Grant, notwithstanding this representation, sought for him in all the lodges, and when convinced that he had indeed gone, said to the old man, "It is very true that mischief has been done in the country we come from; but the man whom Ome-zhuh-gwut-oons attempted to kill, is in our canoe with us; we do not yet know whether he will live or die." They then showed me to the Indians, who had gathered on the shore.

We now took a little time to refresh ourselves, and to examine my wounds. Finding that the ball had entered my body, immediately under the broken part of my arm, and gone forward and lodged against the breast bone, I tried to persuade Mr. Grant to cut it out; but neither he nor Mr. Stewart being willing to make the attempt, I was compelled to do it myself, as well as I could, with my left hand. A lancet, which Mr. Grant lent me, was broken immediately, as was a pen knife, the flesh of that part of the body being very hard and tough. They next brought me a large white handled razor, and with this I succeeded in extracting the ball. It was very much flattened, and the thong of deer's sinew, as well as the medicines Ome-zhuh-gwut-oons had inserted in it, were left in my body. Notwithstanding this, when I found that it had not passed under my ribs, I began to hope that I should finally recover, though I had reason to suppose, that the wound being poisoned, it would be long in healing.

After this was done, and the wound in my breast taken care of, we went on to Ah-kee-ko-bow-we-tig, (the Kettle Fall,) to the village of the chief Waw-wish-e-gah-bo, the brother of Ome-zhuh-gwut-oons. Here Mr. Stewart used the same precaution of hiding me in the canoe, and then giving tobacco. which he called every man in the village, by name, to receive; but when there appeared no prospect of finding him, they made me again stand up in the canoe, and one of them told the chief that it was his own brother who had attempted to kill me. The chief hung his head, and to their inquiries about Ome-zhuh-gwut-oons he would make no answer. We, however, ascertained from other Indians, that my daughters and their mother had stopped here a moment, in their way towards Rainy Lake.

When we arrived at the North West Company's house, at Rainy Lake, we found that my daughters and their mother had been detained by the traders, on account of suspicions arising from their manifest agitation and terror, and from the knowledge that I had passed up with them but a few days before. Now, when I first came in sight of the fort, the old woman fled to the woods, taking the two girls with her. But the Company's people sent out and brought them in again. Mr. Stewart and Mr. Grant now left it to me to say what punishment should be inflicted on this woman, who, as we all very well knew, had been guilty of aiding in an attempt to kill me. They said they considered her equally criminal with Ome-zhuh-gwut-oons, and thought her deserving of death, or any other punishment I might wish to see inflicted. But I told them I wished she might be sent immediately, and without any provisions, away from the fort, and never allowed to return to it. As she was the mother of my children, I did not wish to see her hung, or beaten to death by the labourers, as they proposed; but as the sight of her had become hateful to me, I wished she might be removed, and they accordingly dismissed her without any punishment.

Mr. Stewart left me at the Rainy Lake trading house, in the care of Simon M'Gillevray, a son of him who many years ago was so important a partner in the North West Company. He gave me a small room, where my daughters cooked for me, and dressed my wounds. I was very weak, and my arm badly swollen, fragments of bone coming out from time to time. I had lain here twenty-eight days, when Major Delafield, the United States commissioner for the boundary, came to the trading house, and having heard something of my history, proposed to bring me in his canoe to Mackinac. But I was too weak to undertake such a journey, though I wished to have accompanied him. Finding that this was the case, Major Delafield gave me a large supply of excellent provisions, two pounds of tea, some sugar and other articles, a tent, nd some clothing, and left me.

Two days after this, I pulled out of my arm the thong of deer's sinew which had been attached, as I have before stated, to the bullet. It was still about five inches long, but nearly as large as my finger, and of a green colour. Ome-zhuh-gwut-oons had two balls in his gun at the time he shot me; one had passed near my head.

Immediately after the departure of Major Delafield, the unfriendly disposition of Mr. M'Gillevray made itself manifest; it had been only fear of Major Delafield that had induced him hitherto to treat me with some attention. Insults and abuses were heaped upon me, and at last I was forcibly turned out of the house. But some of the Frenchmen had so much compassion as to steal out at night, and without Mr. M'Gillevray's knowledge, furnish tent poles, and set up my tent. Thanks to the bounty of Major Delafield, I had a supply of every thing needful, and my daughters still remained with me, though Mr. M'Gillevray repeatedly threatened that he would remove them. His persecutions did not abate when I left the fort, and he went so far as to take my daughters from me, and send them to sleep in the quarters of the men; but they escaped, and fled to the house of an old Frenchman, near by, who was Mr. M'Gillevray's father-in-law, and with whose daughters mine had become intimate.

Forty-three days I had lain in and near this trading house, and was now in a most miserable condition, having been for some time entirely deprived of the assistance of my daughters, when my former acquaintance and friend, Mr. Bruce, unexpectedly entered my tent late in the evening. He was with Major Long, and a party of gentlemen then returning from Lake Winnipeg, who, as Mr. Bruce thought, would be willing and able to afford me some assistance in taking my daughters out of the hands of Mr. M'Gillevray, and perhaps in getting out to Mackinac.

Three times I visited Major Long at his camp, at that late hour of the night, though I was scarce able to walk, and each time he told me that his canoes were full, and that he could do nothing for me; but at length becoming a little acquainted with my history, he seemed to take more interest in me, and when he saw the papers I had from Governor Clark and others, he told me I was a fool not to have shown him these before. He had, he said, taken me for one of those worthless white men, who remain in the Indian country from indolence, and for the sake of marrying squaws; but now that he understood who I was, he would try to do something for me. He went himself, with several men, and sought in the trading house for my daughters. He had intended to start early the next morning after his arrival; but having been stirring nearly all night in my affairs, he determined to remain over the next day, and make farther exertions for the recovery of my children. All the search we could make for my daughters, at and about the trading house, resulted in the conviction, that through the agency of Mr. M'Gillevray, and the family of his father-in-law, they had fallen into the hands of Kaw-been-tush-kwaw-naw, a chief of our village at Me-nau-zhe-tau-naung. This being the case, I was compelled to relinquish the hope of bringing them out the present year, and miserably as I was situated, I was anxious to come to my own people, and to my three children at Mackinac, to spend the winter.

I knew the character of Mr. M'Gillevray, and also that the traders of the North West Company generally, had less cause to feel friendly towards me, than they might have had, if I had not concerned myself with Lord Selkirk's party, in the capture of their post at Red River. I knew, also, that my peculiar situation with respect to the Indians, would make it very difficult for me to gain permission to remain at or near either of the houses of the North West, or of the American Fur Company. I had been severely and dangerously wounded by an Indian, and according to their customs, I was bound, or at least expected, to avenge myself on any of the same band that might fall in my way; and should it be known that I was at either of the trading houses, very few Indians would venture to visit it. Taking these things into consideration, I determined to accept the friendly offer of Major Long, to bring me to the States, and accordingly took a place in one of his canoes. But after proceeding on our way an hour or two, I became convinced, as did Major Long and the gentlemen with him, that I could not safely undertake so long and difficult a journey in my present situation. Accordingly they put me in charge of some people belonging to the traders, and sent me back to the fort.

I knew that the doors of the North West Company's house would be closed against me, and accordingly made application to my late employers, the American Fur Company. Young Mr. Davenport, in whose care the house then was, granted a ready compliance with my request, and gave me a room; but as provisions were scarce on that side, I was supplied daily by Dr. M'Laughlin, of the North West, who had now taken the place of Mr. M'Gillevray. He sent every day as much as sufficed to feed me and Mr. Davenport, together with his wife.

I had not been long here, when Mr. Cote arrived, and took

charge of the house in place of Mr. Davenport. Mr. Cote came to my room, and seeing me on the bed, only remarked, "well, you have been making a war by yourself." That night he allowed my supper to be brought me, and early next morning turned me out of doors. But he was not content with driving me from the house; he forbade me to remain on the United States side of the boundary; and all my entreaties, together with the interference of Dr. M'Laughlin, could not influence Mr. Cote to change his determination. In this emergency, Dr. M'Laughlin, though he knew that the success of his post in the winter's trade, must be injured by the measure, consented to receive me on the British side, where he fed and took care of me. Early in the winter, my wounds had so far healed, that I could hunt a little, holding my gun in my left hand. But about new-years, I went out one evening to bring water, slipped and fell on the ice, and not only broke my arm in the old place, but also my collar bone. Dr. M'Laughlin now took the management of my case into his own hands, it having been left entirely to my own treatment before, and I was now confined as long as I had been in the fall.

In the spring, I was again able to hunt. I killed considerable numbers of rabbits, and some other animals, for the skins of which the Doctor paid me in money, a very liberal price. As the time approached for the traders to leave the wintering grounds, he told me, the North West had no boats going to Mackinac, but that he would oblige Mr. Cote to carry me out. It was accordingly so arranged, and Mr. Cote promised to take me to Fond Du Lac in his own canoe. But instead of this, he sent me in a boat with some Frenchmen. In the route from Fond Du Lac to the Saut De St. Marie, I was dependent upon Mr. Morrison; but the treatment I received from the boatmen was so rough, that I induced them to put me on shore, to walk thirty-five miles to the Saut. Mr. Schoolcraft now wished to engage me as an interpreter, but as I heard that the little property I had left at Mackinac had been seized to pay my children's board, and as I knew their situation required my presence, I went thither accordingly, and was engaged by Col. Boyd as Indian interpreter, in which situation I continued till the summer of 1828, when being dissatisfied with his treatment, I left Mackinac, and proceeded to New-York, for the purpose of making arrangements for the publication of my narrative; and upon my return to the north, was employed by Mr. Schoolcraft, Indian agent at the Saut De St. Marie, as his interpreter; to which place I took my family, and have since resided there.

Three of my children are still among the Indians in the north. The two daughters would, as I am informed, gladly join me, if it were in their power to escape. The son is older, and is attached to the life he has so long led as a hunter. I have some hope that I may yet be able to go and make another effort to bring away my daughters.

PART II.

PART II.

CHAPTER I.

Of feasts—of fasts and dreaming—their idea of the human soul, and of a future existence—customs of burial—of their knowledge of astronomy—traditions concerning the sun and moon—of totems—of their acquaintance with plants, animals, and minerals.

OF INDIAN FEASTS.

Among the Indians, the man who gives many feasts, or who, in the language of their songs, " causes the people to walk about continually," is accounted great. In times, therefore, when game is abundant, feasts are multiplied. Before the whites introduced among them intoxicating drinks, it is probable the assembling together for feasts, was their principal and most favourite source of excitement in times of peace, and comparative inactivity. They have several kinds of feasts:—

1st. METAI-WE-KOON-DE-WIN—Medicine feast, or that feasting which forms a part of their great religious ceremony, the Metai. This is under the direction of some old men, who are called chiefs for the Metai,* and the initiated only are admitted. The guests are invited by a Me-zhin-no-way, or chief's man of business, who delivers to each of the guests a small stick. In the

---

* Some discussion has heretofore taken place concerning the existence of a priesthood among the Indians. A little inquiry will convince any one, that the medicine men are a set of crafty impostors, who subsist, in a great measure, by practising on their credulity; by selling them medicines, or charms, for ensuring success in hunting, for enticing the females, and for other purposes. When one of these has been so fortunate as to gain an ascendance over their superstitious and credulous minds, he sometimes sets up for a prophet, and claims intercourse with superior and invisible beings.

other feasts, by being held commonly in the night time, and the showing off of many tricks with fire.

7th. JE-BI NAW-KA-WIN—Feast with the dead. This feast is eaten at the graves of their deceased friends. They kindle a fire, and each person, before he begins to eat, cuts off a small piece of meat, which he casts into the fire. The smoke and smell of this, they say, attracts the Je-bi to come and eat with them.

8th. CHE-BAH-KOO-CHE-GA-WIN—Feast for his medicine. During one whole day in spring, and another in autumn, every good hunter spreads out the contents of his medicine bag in the back part of his lodge, and feasts his neighbours, in honour of his medicine. This is considered a solemn and important feast, like that of the Metai.

9th. O-SKIN-NE-GE-TAH-GA-WIN—Boy's feast. This might be called the feast of the first fruits, as it is made on occasion of a boy, or a young hunter, killing his first animal, of any particular kind. From the smallest bird, or a fish, to a moose, or buffaloe, they are careful to observe it. Numerous instances of it occur in the foregoing narrative, therefore it need not be dwelt upon.

OF FASTS AND DREAMING.

RIGOROUS and long continued fasting is enjoined upon young and unmarried persons, of both sexes, and they begin at a very early age. The parent, in the morning, offers the child the usual breakfast in one hand, and charcoals in the other; if the latter is accepted, the parent is gratified, and some commendations, or marks of favour, are bestowed on the child. To be able to continue long fasting, confers an enviable distinction. They, therefore, inculcate upon their children the necessity of remaining long without food. Sometimes the children fast three, five, seven, and some, as is said, even ten days; in all of which time they take only a little water, and that at very distant intervals. During these fasts, they pay very particular attention to their dreams, and from the character of these, their parents, to whom they relate them, form an opinion of the future life of the child.

Dreaming of things above, as birds, clouds, the sky, &c. is considered favourable; and when the child begins to relate any thing of this kind, the parent interrupts him, saying, "it is well, my child; say no more of it." In these dreams, also, the children receive impressions, which continue to influence their character through life. A man, an old and very distinguished warrior, who was some years ago at Red River, dreamed, when fasting in his childhood, that a bat came to him, and this little animal he chose for his medicine. To all the costly medicines for war or hunting, used by other Indians, he paid no attention. Throughout his life he wore the skin of a bat tied to the crown of his head, and in his numerous war excursions, he went into battle exulting in the confidence, that the Sioux, who could not hit a bat on the wing, would never be able to hit him. He distinguished himself in many battles, and killed many of his enemies; but throughout his long life, no bullet ever touched him, all of which he attributed to the protecting influence of his medicine, revealed to him, in answer to his fasting, in boyhood. Of Net-no-kwa, his foster mother, the author of the foregoing narrative relates, that at about twelve years of age, she fasted ten successive days. In her dream, a man came down and stood before her, and after speaking of many things, he gave her two sticks, saying, " I give you these to walk upon, and your hair I give it to be like snow." In all her subsequent life, this excellent woman retained the confident assurance, that she should live to extreme old age, and often, in times of the greatest distress from hunger, and of apparent danger from other causes, she cheered her family by the assurance, that it was given to her to crawl on two sticks, and to have her head like the snow, and roused them to exertion by infusing some part of her own confident reliance upon the protection of a superior and invisible Power.

The belief, that communications take place in dreams from superior beings to men, is not peculiar to this people, or this age of the world. Men, particularly, when their minds are little cultivated, are ever ready to believe themselves objects of particular attention, and the subjects of especial solicitude to their divinities. Among the Indians of the Algonkin stock, many, and perhaps all, believe that not only their prayers, in times of distress, are heard and answered, but they think, that to some among them, are communicated in dreams intimations of things which are to happen in remote times, and even after death. It is probable their traditional belief of a future state, and of the circumstances attending it, have made so strong an impression on the minds of children, that they may often dream of it, and continue to do so, at intervals during life. Accordingly, several may be found among them, who, having in extreme sickness had their thoughts particularly directed to this subject, and having, perhaps, been reduced so low as to be considered in a desperate condition—[of a person in which situation they speak as of one dead]—may have dreamed, or imagined the impressions of their early childhood to have been realized. Hence, we hear them relating, with confidence, that such and such persons have been dead, and have travelled along the path of the dead, till they have come to the great strawberry, which lies by the road, this side the river; they have seen the river itself, some have even passed over it, and arrived in the villages of the dead. Dreams of this kind seem to have been frequent among them. But they have, most commonly, to tell of vexation, annoyance, and disappointment. They have come to the great strawberry, at which the Je-bi-ug refresh themselves, on their journey; but on taking up the spoon, and attempting to separate a part of it, the berry has become a rock, (which, with the people about Lake Superior, is a soft, red sand rock, because the type exists in their country.) They have then gone on, have been much alarmed at the Me-tig-ush-o-po-kit, (the swinging log,) on which they have to cross, or at the great dog, who stands beyond it. They have received taunts, and gibes, and insults, among their friends; have been sneered at, and called Je-bi! have had ashes and water given them, in place of Mun-dah-min aw-bo, or corn broth, bark for dried meat, and O-zhush-kwa-to-wuk, or the large puckwi, called puff balls, for squashes. Some men have commonly seen, in that country, only squaws, numbers of whom have competed for them, as an husband, and the dreams of all have been tinged with some shade of colour, drawn from their own peculiar situation. How these people came first in possession of their opinions respecting the country of the dead, cannot, perhaps, be known; but having it, we should not be surprised that it influences their dreams.

In connexion with this subject, we may devote a moment to the consideration of their idea of the human soul, or as they call it, the shadow.* They think this becomes unsettled, or as it were detached from the body in violent sickness; and they look upon a person who is very low, as one already dead. Hence it is not unusual to hear them speak of such and such a person, as being now dying, and yet to find him survive, not only many days, but years; and when told of this, they seem conscious of no impropriety in the expression: on the contrary, they often say of a person, he *died* at such a time, but *came again*. I have also heard them reproach a sick person, for what they considered imprudent exposure in convalescence; telling him that his shadow was not well settled down in him, and that therefore he was in danger of losing it. It would seem, however, that although they believe the soul leaves the body previous to the commencement of dissolution in the former, yet that it is not removed far from it until long after death. This is manifest from their usage in the feast of Che-bah-koo-che-ga-win, and from some of the ceremonies of interment, particularly in the case of women, when their husbands are buried.

In the spring of the year 1826, a man of the Menomonies died and was buried, very near the encampment of a part of the fifth regiment of United States infantry, on the high prairie in the rear of the village of Prairie Du Chein, on the Mississippi. The body was attended to the grave by a considerable number of the friends and relatives, and when it was let down into the shallow grave, the wife of the deceased approached the brink, and after looking down on the rude coffin, she stepped upon it, and immediately across, taking her course over the plains, towards the bluffs there, about a mile distant. This is a common practice of the women of that tribe; and the mourner is careful, if she contemplates a second marriage, never to look back towards the grave she has left, but returns to her lodge by some devious and circuitous route. It is done, as they say, that the Cha-pi (Je-bi of the Ojibbeways,) or the dead person, may not be able to follow them af-

* *O-jee-chau-go-man*—Schoolcraft. This is the substantive without any inseparable pronoun. It is commonly used in combination, as *ne-tah-chuk*, my shadow; *ke-tah-chuk*, thy shadow; *o-tah-chuk*, his shadow, among the Menomonies.

terwards. If the woman should look back, they believe she would either fall dead immediately, or become insane, and remain so ever after. On some occasions, but rarely, another person accompanies the mourner, carrying a handful of small twigs, and following immediately after her, flourishes it about her head, as if driving away flies. The verb applicable to this action, is in the third person singular, Wai-whai-na-how, the more general one applicable to the whole ceremony, Ah-neuk-kun-new.

In the instance above mentioned, the woman walked rapidly, and without looking back, across the wide prairie, in a direction almost opposite that leading to her lodge; but her loud and bitter lamentings could be heard at a great distance, seeming to contradict the action by which she professed to seek an everlasting separation from the deceased.

The more common and well known observances paid to the dead by these people, seem not to indicate such a destitution of affection as the ceremony just described. In many of their customs relating to the treatment of the dead, we can discover, not only the traces of kind feeling, but a strong confidence in a future existence, and the belief that their departed friends can know and estimate the value of friendly offices rendered them after their departure. At the time of the great council at Prairie Du Chein, in 1825, a Sioux chief, of the remote band of the Sissitong, sickened and died of a bilious fever. He had been a distinguished man among his own people, and, as he had come a great distance from his own country, in obedience to the call of our government, the military commandant at that post, was induced to bury him with the honours of war. The men of his band were gathered around his body, in the lodge where he died, and when the escort arrived, they raised him upon his bier, a hundred manly voices at the same time chanting forth a requiem, thus rendered by a person well acquainted with their language:

> Grieve not, our brother! the path thou art walking
> Is that in which we, and all men must follow.

And this they continued to repeat, until they reached the grave. There is something impressive and affecting in their habit of preserving and dressing up the je-bi, or memorial of the dead, which, like our weeds and crapes, finds a place in many a dwelling where little of mourning is visible. Yet, though the place which death had made vacant in their hearts, may have been filled; they seem never to forget the supply they consider due the wants of the departed. Whenever they eat or drink, a portion is carefully set apart for the je-bi, and this observance continues for years, should they not, in the mean time, have an opportunity to send out this memorial with some war party; when, if it be thrown down on the field of battle, as they aim always to do, then their obligation to the departed ceases.

Of the Chippewyans, the Sarcees, the Strong Bows, and other tribes inhabiting those dreary regions which border on the arctic circle, it is related, that they in many instances omit to bury their dead, and that they frequently desert their relatives and friends, whenever, from sickness or old age, they become unable to endure the ordinary fatigues of their manner of life. There is no more reason to question the accuracy of these statements, than of those in relation to the cannibalism, sodomy, and other shocking vices of more southern tribes. But as the destitution of natural affection manifested in the conduct of many of the American tribes, towards their relatives in sickness and decrepitude, is undoubtedly that among their vices, which is most abhorrent to the feelings of civilized men, so we shall find the instances of rare occurrence, except where the rigour of the climate, or other natural causes, impose on them a necessity, to which we ourselves, in the same circumstances, should probably yield, as they do. The horrible practices to which men of all races have been driven in besieged cities, in cases of shipwreck, and other similar emergencies, should admonish us that the Indians, as a race, deserve no peculiar detestation for crimes growing unavoidably out of their situation.

CATALOGUE OF PLANTS AND ANIMALS

Found in the country of the Ojibbeways; with English names, as far as these could be ascertained.

METIK-GOAG—*Trees.*
SHIN-GO-BEEK—*Ever greens, or cone bearing trees.*

Ma-ni-hik—Norway pine.
A-nee-naun-duk—Balsam fir.
Kik-kaun-dug—Spruce. The black pheasant feeds on the leaves.
Mus-keeg-wah-tick—Hackmatack, swamp wood.
Kaw-waun-duk—Single spruce.
Mis-kwaw-wauk—Red cedar.
Ke-zhik—White cedar.
Kaw-waw-zheek—Juniper bushes.
Kaw-waw-zheen-sha, or Ah-kaw-wtm-je—Yew.
Kaw-kaw-ge-wingz—Hemlock spruce.
Puk-gwun-nah-ga-muk—White pine, (peeling bark.)
Shin-gwawk—Yellow pine.

NE-BISH-UN—*Trees with broad leaves.*

Nin-au-tik—Sugar maple, (our own tree.)
She-she-gum-maw-wis—River maple, (sap flows fast.)
Shah-shah-go-be-muk—Low-ground maple.
Moo-is-oo-ais—Striped maple, (moose wood.)
Shah-shah-go-be-muk-oons—Spiked maple, (little shah-shah-go-be-muk.)
We-gwos—White birch.
Ween-es-sik—Black birch.
Buh-wi-e-me-nin aw-gaw-wunje—Red Cherry, (the wood of the shaken down fruit, or berry.)
Sus-suh-way-meen ah-ga-wunje—Choke cherry.
Buh-wi-me-nah-ne-gah-wunje—Black Cherry.
Nai-go-wim-me-nah gaw-we-zheen—Sand-cherry bushes.

Me-tik-o-meesh, (Mait-e-ko-ma, Menomonie)—Black oak, (wood cup.)
Meesh-a-mish—White oak.
Ah-sah-tia—White poplar.
Mah-nu-sah-tia—Balsam poplar, (ugly poplar.) Mat-heh metoos—Cree. Franklin's narrative, p. 78.
Be-zhew-au-tik—Coffee bean tree, (wild cat tree.) Found only 'n the south.
Way-miche-ge-meen-ah-ga-wunje—Honey locust, southern.
Uz-zhuh-way-mish—Beech; none northward of Mackinac.
Me-tig-wawb-awk—Smooth hickory, (smooth wood bow tree.)
Nas-kun-nuk-a-koosit Me-teg-wawb-awk—Hickory, (rough bark bow tree.)
A-neeb—Elm, white.
O-shah-she-go-pe—Red elm, two varieties: the bark of one only used for sacks.
Wa-go-be-mish—Linn, (bark tree.)
Bug-gaun-awk—Black walnut.
Ke-no-sha bug-gaun-awk—Butternut, (long walnut.)
Ahn-za bug-gaun-awk—Pecan, southern.
Suz-zuh-wuh-ko-mist—Hackberry.
As-seme-nun—Pawpaw.
Boo-e-auk—White ash.
We-sug-auk—Black ash.
Bug-gaun-ne-me-zeesh-ah—Hazle bush.
Waw-bun wah-ko-meezh—White arrow wood.
We-ah-ko-meezh—Arrow wood.
Mus-kwaw be-muk—Red ozier.
O-to-pe—Alder. O-to-peen—Alders.
Sis-se-go-be-mish—Willow.
Bug-ga-sah-ne-mish—Plum tree.
Mish-she-min-nuh ga-wunje—Crab apple tree.
Mish-she-min au-tik—Crab apple wood, or tree.
Ne-be-min-ah-ga-wunje—High craneberry bush.
Tah-tah-te-mun-ah-ga-wunje—Black haw bush.
Ke-teg-ge-manito—New-Jersey tea, (red root.)
Koose-gwaw-ko-mizhe-ga-wunje—High blue berry bush.
O-zhusk-ko-mi-zheen—Musk rat berries.
Be-mah-gwut—Grape.

We-gwos-be-mah-gwut—Birch grape.

Manito-be-mah-gwut, or manito-meen-a-gah-wunje—Cissus, a climbing vine, with scattered berries, somewhat like grapes.

Mus-ke-ge-min*—Cranberry, crane berries, (swamp berries.)

Sa-zah-ko-me-nah gah-wah-zheen, pl.—Saccacommis, or arbutus. The leaves of this plant, the *uva ursa* of the shops, are commonly used by the Ojibbeways, in whose country it abounds, to mix with their tobacco.

Waw-be-ko-meen-ah-ga-wunje—Nine bark, or spiraw.

Wis-seg-ge-bug, sing. wis-seg-ge-bug-goon, pl.—Bitter leaf; an andromeda, very highly esteemed by the Indians, as a remedy, and by them said to grow only about the Grand Traverse, in Lake Huron.

Ne-kim-me-nun—Swamp whortle berries.

Shug-gus-kim-me-nun—Thimble berries, or flowering raspberries.

Kaw-waw-be-ga-koo-zit—White bark, a small tree at Lake Traverse.

Ut-tuh-be-ga-zhin-nah-gook—A shrub said to be found only in the north.

Pah-posh-geshe-gun-au-tik—Red elder, (popgun wood,) very common about Me-nau-zhe-taun-naug, and the islands in the Lake of the Woods.

Bwoi-jim-me-nah-ga-wunje—Whortleberry bush.

Ne-kim-me-nah-ga-wunje—High blue berry bush.

Mus-keeg o-bug-goan—Labrador tea, (swamp leaves,) one of the most esteemed of the products of cold and swampy regions; used in decoction as tea.

Pe-boan-meen-ah-gaw-wunje—Winter berry bush, a prinos.

Mun-no-mun-ne-chee-beeg†—Red paint root.

Me-nais-sa gaw-wunje—Thorn apple.

Buz-zuk-ko-me-nais, sing., buz-zuk-ko-me-nais-ug, pl.—A kind of thorn apple growing in the north, which sometimes kill bears

---

* Mas-ge-kwi-min-all—Zeis. p. 83.

† A substance is brought by the Indians from a place called Na-kaw-wudj, on the shores of Lake Superior, which, when bruised, imparts a bright carnation colour. It is a small root, probably that of a species of Chenopodium, which is sometimes met with on the borders of swamps about St. Marks.

when they eat them in large quantities. The Indians suppose that it is in consequence of the strongly adhesive quality of the pulp, that they have this deleterious property.

Meen—Blue berry; meen-un—Blue berries, (fruit.) This is a word that enters into the composition of almost all which are used as the names of fruits or berries of any kind; as me-she-min, or me-she-meen, an apple, o-da-e-min, a strawberry, or heart berry, &c. The word ga-wunje, added to the name of any fruit or berry, indicates the wood or bush.

Meen-ah-ga-wunje—Blue berry, or whortle berry bush.

Ma-ko-meen-ah-ga-wunje—Black currant bush.

Mish-e-je-min-ga-wunje—This is a bush growing at and about the Lake of the Woods, which bears red currants, like those of the gardens; but the currants are beset thickly with hairs.

Shah-bo-min-nun—Goose berries; Shah-bo-min ga-wunje—the bushes.

Mis-kwa-min—Raspberry; mis-kwa-min-nug—Raspberries.

Gaw-waw-ko-meesh—Black raspberries.

O-dah-tah-gah-go-min—Blackberry; O-dah-tah-gah-go-me-nug—Blackberries.

Muk-kwo-me-nug, or muk-kwaw-me-nug—Bear berries; Muk-ko-me-nah-ga-wunje—The mountain ash, or American service tree.

O-gin-ne-mee-nah-ga-wunje—Rose bush. The fruit is much eaten in winter by the starving Indians in the north.

All these are called Mè-tik-goag, or woody plants.

WEAH-GUSH-KOAN*—*Weeds, or herbaceous plants.*

Me-zhus-keen, (Ma-zhus-koon of the Menomonies)—Grasses.

Na-bug-us-koan—Coarse swamp Grass.

Anah-kun-us-koan—Bull rush; (matt grass.)

Be-gwa-wun-us-koan—Soft coarse grass. The name of the Be-wi-o-nus-ko River and Lake, called Rush River on some of the maps, is from this word. This word seems, in some districts, to be used as the name of the cow parsley.

* Probably from *Weah-gush-ke*, dust; or that which is mixed together.

As-ah-gu-nus-koan—Bug-gusk—Iris.
Puk-kwi-usk-oge—Flags.
O-zhusk-gwut-te-beeg—Muskrat root, (a grass.)

The following are not called Me-zhus-keen.

Muz-zha-nush-koan—Nettles.
Skib-waw-we-gusk—Artichoke, a species of sun flower.
Ke-zhe-bun-ush-koan—Rushes.
O-kun-dum-moge—Pond lilies.
Ma-ko-pin, Ma-ko-pin-eeg, sin. and pl.—Chinkapin, or cyamus.
Waw-be-ze-pin-neeg—Arrow head, (swan potatoes.) The roots of the common saggittaria, as well as the bulbs of some of the crest flowering lilies, which are eaten by the Indians, receive this name.
Mus-ko-ti-pe-neeg—Lily, (prairie potatoes.)
Sah-sah-way-suk—Turkey potatoes.
O-kah-tahk—Cicuta.
Ma-ni-to O-kah-tahk—Sison? heracleum?
O-saw-wus-kwun-wees—Green small balls.
Sug-gut-ta-bo-way—Sticking burs; hounds tongues, &c.
Nah-ma-wusk—Spear mint, (sturgeon medicine.)
Wis-se-giche-bik—Indian's physic, (bitter root; Callistachia.)
Mis-kwe-wis-che-be-kug-guk—Blood root.
A-zhush-a-way-skuk—Square stem scrophularia.
Be-zhew-wusk—Wild cat medicine.
Ke-na-beek-o-me-nun—Snake berries; Dracaena borealis.
Main-wake—Angelica, or cow parsley.
Me-tush-koo-se-min—Apple of the Prairie of the Canadians, (Psoralia,) much eaten by the Crees and Assinneboins, in whose country it abounds.
Mah-nom-o-ne gah-wah-zheen, pl.—Wild rice, (the grass.)
Muk-koose-e-mee-nun—Young bear's berries.
We-nis-se-bug-goon—Wintergreen.
Mus-kee-go-bug-goon—Swamp winter green; perhaps the little rough wintergreen.
Be-na-bug-goon—Partridge flower.
Mus-ke-gway-me-taus—Side saddle flower, (swamp bottles, in allusion to the pitcher shaped leaves.)*

---

* More probably compounded of Mus-keeg, (a swamp,) and Me-taus, (a leggin,) from its resemblance to the leggins worn by the Indians.

Muk-kud-da-we-che-be-kug-guk—Black roots.
Ta-ta-sis-koo-see-men—The flower that follows the sun.
Pe-zhe-ke-wusk—Buffaloe medicine.   Wild carrot?
She-wa-bug-goon—Sweet cicely, (sour leaf.)
A-nich-e-me-nun—Wild pea vine.
O-da-na-me-na-gaw-wun-zheen, pl.—Strawberry vines.
Se-bwoi-gun-nuk—Corn stalks, (chaw sweet.)
O-pin—Potatoe.   O-pin-neeg.—Potatoes.
O-guis-e-maun—Squashes.   O-zaw-waw-o-guis-se-maun—Yellow squashes.
Mis-kwo-de-se-min—Bean.   Mis-kwo-de-se-me-nug—Beans.
As-ke-tum-moong—Melons.
Gitche-un-ne-beesh—Cabbage, (big leaf.)   Gitche-ne-beesh-un—great leaves.
Skush-kun-dah-min-ne-kwi-uk—Plantain; the leaves of this are particularly observed by hunter, as they show, better than any thing else, the age of the tracks of game.
Shig-gau-ga-win-zheeg,* pl.—Onions, (skunk weeds.)
O-kau-tauk—carrots.
Kitche-mus-ke-ke-meen—Red pepper, (great medicine berry.)
Ba-se-kwunk—This is a red astringent root, much valued by the Indians, as an application to wounds.   Avens root?
Shah-bo-ze-gun—Milkweed.   The Ojibbeway word signifies *purgative.*
Waw-be-no-wusk—Yarrow, (Wawbeno medicine.)
Ke-zhe-bun-ush-kon-sun—Small rushes, in prairie.
Nah-nah-gun-e-wushk—Fern.   Nah-nah-gun-ne-wush-koan—Ferns.
We-se-bain-jah-ko-nun—Usnaco.
Wah-ko-nug—Lichens; the edible gyrophora.
Ween-de-go-wah-ko-nug—Gyrophora inedible.
Waw-bah-sah-ko-nick—Sphagnun, used by the women to make a bed for young children.
Ah-sah-ko-mik—Marchantia, and green mosses, on the shady sides of trees.
O-zhusk-kwa-toan-suk—Reindeer moss, citrariac, &c.

* From *Shig-gau-gu-winje*, this word, in the singular number, some derive the name Chikago, which is commonly pronounced by the Indians *Shig-gau-go*—*Shig-gau-go-ong*, at Chikago.

O-zhush-kwa-to-wug—*Fungi.*

Waw-but-to—Pine touch-wood.
Me-tik-o-mish O-zhusk-kwa-to-wug—White oak touch-woods much used to burn mortars for pounding corn.
Sug-guh-tah-gun—Spunk.
Je-bi-e-push-kwa-e-gun—Xylostroma; dead people's moccasin leather, is the literal meaning of this word, which is applied to the leather-like substance in the fissures of old trees.
O-je-bi-e-muk-ke-zin—Ghost or spirit moccasin; puff ball; dead man's shoe; sometimes called Anung-wug—stars.

Ah-wes-sie-ug*—*Animals.*

The diminutive termination is used for the young of animals, and is, in the Ottawwaw dialect, generally in the sound of *ns*, or *nce*, when the noun ends with a vowel. Thus, *Gwin-gwaw-ah-ga*, a wolverene; *Gwin-gwaw-ah-gaince*, a young wolverene; the *a*, in the last syllable, retaining the same sound as in the word without the diminutive termination. When any distinction of sex is made, it is commonly by prefixing the words *i-ah-ba* and *no-zha*, very similar in signification to our *male* and *female*; thus *I-ah-ba Gwin-gwaw-ah-ga*, is a male wolverene; *No-zha Gwin-gwaw-ah-ga*, a female wolverene.

Gwin-gwaw-ah-ga—Wolverene, (tough beast.) Carcajou, French, *northern glutton*, a very sagacious and mischievous animal, but not of common occurrence; now principally found among the lakes.

Na-nah-pah-je-ne-ka-se—A mole? (foot wrong way.)
Bo-taich-che-pin-gwis-sa—Gopher, (blow up the ground.)
Manito Muk-kwaw—Great grizzly bear, always found in the prairie.
Ma-mis-ko-gah-zhe-muk-kwaw—Red nail bear; very fierce and dangerous, more feared by the Indians than the former, who very rarely attacks a man, unless wounded; but the red nailed bear attacks when unprovoked, and pursues with great speed. He lives in rocky places in woods.

---

* *A-wes-sis-sac*, Del. Zeisb. 2d ed. p. 46.

Muk-kwaw—Common bear; *Ou-wash-ah*, of the Menomonies.

Muk-koons, or Muk-koonce—Cub; *Ou-wa-sha-sha*, of the Menomonies.

I-aw-ba-koons and *No-zha-koons*, are used by the Ottawwaws and Ojibbeways to distinguish the male and female bear, where the Menomonies would use *Ou-wa-shah E-nai-ne-wow* and *Ou-wa-shah Ma-tai-mo-shuh.*

Me-tun-nusk, Ojib.—Toothless,
Mish-she-mo-nah-na, Ott.—Great burrower, } Badger.

Mus-ko-tai Chit-ta-mo—Prairie squirrel.

Mus-ko-tai Ah-gwin-gwoos—Prairie striped squirrel; small squirrel, with stripes and spots, burrowing in the prairie, sometimes with the *chittamo.*

Ah-gwin-gwoos—Chipping squirrel.

Atch-e-dah-mo—Red squirrel.

O-zhug-gus-kon-dah-wa—Flying squirrel, (strikes flat on a tree.)

Sun-nah-go, and Muk-kud-da As-sun-nah-go, and Mis-kwaw-sun-nah-go—The grey, black, and fox squirrels, not found in the country north of Lake Superior.

Uk-kuk-koo-jees—Ground hog, smaller than in the states.

Me-sau-boos—Hare, white in winter.

Waw-boos—Rabbit. Meezh-way, Meezh-way-ug, sin. and pl.—Southern rabbit.

Pish-tah-te-koosh—Antelope. This is reckoned the fleetest animal in the prairie country, about the Assinneboin.

Pe-zhe-ke—Buffaloe. No-zha-zha-pe-zhe-ke—A cow that has a young calf following her. O-neen-jah-nis-pe-zhe-ke—Farrow cow.

Jah-ba-pe-zhe-ke—Bull. Pe-zhe-keence—A young calf. O-saw-waw Koo-shance—A calf, while the hair is red. Poo-nah-koosh—Calf, a year old. Ah-ne-ka-boo-nah-koosh—Two years old.

Gitche-pe-zhe-ke—Fossil mammoth.

Ma-nah-tik—Big horn.

Gitche-mah-nish-tah-nish—Rocky mountain sheep.

AN-NE-MOO-SHUG—*Dogs.*

Na-ne-mo-why, Ott. } Small wolf, in prairie countries.
Mish-tah-tah-si, Ojib. }
Mi-een-gun-nug—Common wolves.
Mi-een-gun—Common wolf.
Muk-hud-da-mi-een-gun—Black wolf.
Waw-be-mi-een-gun—White wolf.
Shoon-sho—Long eared hound.
An-ne-moosh—Common dog.
Ta-tah-koo-gaut-ta-was-sim—Short leg dog.
Be-gwi-wa-was-sim—Long haired dog; Newfoundland.
Ke-wis-kwa-mi-een-gun-nug—Mad wolves, sometimes seen, but rarely bite, unless attacked.

WAW-GOO-SHUG—*Foxes.*

O-saw-waw-goosh—Common red fox.
Muk-kud-da-waw-goosh—Black fox.
Muk-kud-da-waw-goo-shug—Black foxes.
Wa-whaw-goosh—White fox, fur long, but of no value.
Ne-ke-kwa-tug-gah-wa-waw-goosh—Grey fox.
Pis-tat-te-moosh—Swift fox, (small dog.)

Kah-zhe-gainse—Common house cat, (little glutton.)
Pe-zhew—Wild cat.
Ke-tah-gah-pe-zhew—Lynx, (spotted wild cat.)
Me-she-pe-zhew—Panther, (big wild cat.)
Ah-meek—Beaver. Naub-ah-meek—Male beaver. Noash-ah-meek—Female beaver. Ah-meek-keanse—Young beaver.
Kin-waw-no-wish-shug, Cree, } Black tailed deer.
Muk-kud-da-waw-wash-gais, Ojib. }
Waw-wash-gais—Red or Virginian deer.
O-mush-keons, Ojib.   } Elk. On Red River, Mouse River,
Me-sha-way, Ottaw.   } the Saskawjawun, &c.
Waw-was-kesh, Cree,   }
Ah-dik—Reindeer. Ca-ri-bou, French. The feet very large and broad, fitting the animal to travel over smooth ice, or deep snow; found on all the shores of Lake Superior, and sometimes

at the upper end of Lake Huron; but most frequent farther north.

Mooze, or Moonce, Ojib. ⎫ Moose. The nasal sound, at the
Moon-swah, Cree, ⎭ end of this word, is common in these dialects; but it is difficult to represent, by the letters of our alphabet.

I-aw-ba-mooze—Buck moose. No-zha-mooze—Deer moose. Moonze-aince—Little moose, &c.

A-yance—Opossum, only in the south. The word a-yance, means *crafty*.

Shin-goos—Weasel, two kinds.
Shin-goo-sug—Weasels.
Ne-gik—Otter. Ne-gik-wug—Otters.
Kwaush-kwaush-ko-tah-be-ko-sheezh.
Keen-waw-no-wa waw-waw-be-gun-o-je—Long tail leaping mouse.
Waw-waw-be-gun-o-je—Mouse.
Ah-mik-waw-waw-be-gun-o-je—Beaver, or diving mouse.
Kah-ge-bin-gwaw-kwa—Shrew. Two species are common about St. Maries, in winter.
Kahg—Porcupine.* Kahg-wug—Porcupines.
Shong-gwa-she—Mink.
Wah-be-zha-she—Marten. *Woapchees*, Z. p. 18.
A-se-bun—Raccoon.
She-gahg—Skunk.
O-zhusk—Muskrat.
Ah-puk-kwon-ah-je—Bat.
O-jeeg—Fisher weasel, a very stupid animal, easy to kill.

* The young of this animal, if taken out of the uterus with care immediately on killing the dam, and put upon a tree, will cling to it, and often live. The Indians relate, that the porcupines, in the prairie countries of the north, pass the winters on oak trees, where they oftentimes have no hole, or any other protection from the weather, than is afforded by the trunk of the tree. They strip all the bark off one tree, before they go to search for another, and one may pass the greater part of the winter on a single tree, if it happens to be a large one. They also pretend to fatten the porcupine in the summer, whenever they can find him in some hole, where he has constructed his nest, which is of his own excrement. This, they say, he eats, and never fails, when thus confined, to become very fat. The porcupine is not disposed to make any other resistance, when attacked by a man, than his spiny skin affords, and the Indians have a saying of this animal, and of the rabbit, that those whom they bite will live to a great age.

BA-BAH-MO-TA-JEEG—*Reptiles.*

Nau-to-way—Thick, short rattle snake. [Sha-no-we-naw—The rattler?]

She-she-gwa—Common rattle snake. Both these are occasionally kept tame by the Indians. They sometimes make feasts to them, and they are said to be very docile and intelligent.

Me-tik-o-she-she-gwa—Adder.

Na-wa—Moccasin snake.

Pih-kun—Prairie snake. At the head of Mouse River, and in the prairies towards the Missouri, these snakes are more than six feet long, and proportionably large. Pih-kun-un are common snakes, but never half so large as the above.

Mis-kwan-dib—Red head; copper snake?

O-zha-wus-ko Ke-na-beek—Green snake.

Muk-kud-da Ke-na-beek—Black snake.

O-mus-sun-dum-mo—Water snake.

Wa-in-je-tah Ke-na-beek—Garter snake, (right or true ge-na-bik.)

O-kaute Ke-na-beek—Lizzard, (legged snake.)

Gee-kut-tau-nating—Lizzard of some kind.

Que-we-zains—Little boy, (also a lizzard.)

Nib-be-ke O-muh-kuk-ke—Orbicular lizzard? (medicine frog.)

Wain-je-tah O-muh-kuk-ke—Right frogs, or common frog.

Dain-da—Bull frog, *and hannie,* Z. 19.

Mis-ko-muh-kuk-ke—Red toad.*

Be-go-muh-kuk-ke—Common toads. These two last, at the approach of winter, place themselves erect on the surface of the ground, on their hams, and by turning themselves round and round, they sink into the ground, which closes over them, and they keep below the frost. They are often found, several within two or three feet of each other, buried deep in the earth, but keeping constantly their heads erect.

O-shaw-wus-ko-muh-kuk-ke—Tree frog.

Me-zhe-ka, Ottaw. } Large tortoise.
Me-kin-nauk, Ojib. }

Ta-ta-be-ko-nauk—Soft shelled tortoise.

---

* From *O-muh-kuk-ke,* (toad,) and *Ak-koo-se-win,* (sickness,) is probably derived the word *Mo-muk-ke-ze-win,* (the small pox.)

Boos-kut-ta-wish—A tortoise with round deep shells.
Mis-kwaw-tais-sa—Terrapin.
Sug-gus-kwaw-ge-ma—Leech.

BE-NAIS-SE-WUG—*Birds.*

Ke-neu—War eagle; the master of all birds.
Me-giz-ze—White headed eagle. Me-giz-ze-wug, plural.
Ka-kaik—Spotted hawk.
Be-bo-ne-sa, Ottaw. ⎱ Winter hawk.
Ke-bu-nuz-ze, Ojib. ⎰
No-je-ke-na-beek-we-zis-se—Marsh hawk, (snake eating.)
Wa-be-no-je Ke-na-beek-we-zis-se—White marsh hawk.
Mis-ko-na-ne-sa—Red tail hawk.
Pish-ke-neu—Black tail hawk.
Muk-kud-da-ke-neu—Black hawk.
Bub-be-nug-go—Spotted tail hawk.
Be-na-seeh's—Small pheasant hawk.
Cha-een-sa—A small hawk, so named from its cry.
Pe-pe-ge-wiz-zain's—Smallest hawk.
We-nong-ga—Turkey buzzard.
Kah-gah-ge, Ojib. ⎱ Raven. Kah-gah-ge-wug—Ravens.
Gau-gau-ge-she, Ott. ⎰
On-daig—Crow. On-daig-wug—Crows.
As-sig-ge-nawk—Black bird.
Mis-ko-min-gwe-gun-nah Sig-ge-nauk—Red wing black bird.
O-pish-kah-gah-ge—Magpie. O-pish-kah-gah-ge-wug—Magpies.
Gween-gwe-sha—Similar in habits and locality to the former, and closely resembling, in size and colour, the following.*
Teen-de-se—Blue jay. These begin to lay their eggs before the snow is off the ground in the spring.
Be-gwuk-ko-kwa o-wais-sa—Thrush.

---

* The Gween-gwe-sha is met with about the Saut De St. Marie, in the winter season. It is a little smaller than the blue jay, and of a leaden colour on the back, the lower part of the neck, and the wings; a few of the feathers about the belly are a dirty white above, but plumbeous below; as are those on the forward part of the neck, and about the insertion of the beak. It appears to be the *Corvus Canadensis* of Rees' Cyclop. It is said to have been found as far south in the United States, as the Little Falls of the Mohawk.

Ah-luk—Similar to the thrush in habits.

Ween-de-go be-nais-sa—King bird, (the bird that eats his own kind.)

O-pe-che*—Robin.

Ma-mah-twa—Cat bird.

Chaum-ma-wais-she—Another of the same size.

Kos-kos-ko-na-ching—Ground bird? A small bird so named from its note.

Put-tas-se-wis.

Waw-be-ning-ko-se—Snow birds.

Che-ki-che-gau-na-sa—A very small lively bird, peculiar to the north.

Mis-kobe-na-sa—Red bird.

Sa-ga-bun-wau-nis-sa—Waxen chatterer.

---

* This social little bird seems to be not less the favourite and companion of the Indian than of the white man. They relate, that long ago, soon after Nanabush had made the ground, there was an old chief, a great and good man, who, with his wife, had one son. But this young man disregarded the advice and admonitions of his parents; particularly he neglected to fast and pray, as all young men and women are enjoined to do. For many successive days, had his father presented him his breakfast in one hand, and in the other offered charcoals with which to paint his face; but the ungracious son had steadily preferred the venison, or the broth, to the coals. One morning he directed the old woman to make a choice kettle of Mun-dah-min-aw-bo, or corn broth, and taking a bowl full of it in one hand, and as usual some coals in the other, he presented them both to his son. The young man choosing the broth, the father returned to the fire place, and taking a handful of ashes, threw it into the bowl. The young man then took the coals, and rubbing them in his hands, painted his face, and retired to the bushes near by. After he had lain three or four days, his father offered him something to eat, but he would not accept it. This was repeated from time to time, until the tenth day; then the young man still remaining in the bushes, called his father, and his mother, and his relatives, and addressed them thus: "My friends, it has been unpleasant to you to see me eat so much as I have eaten; hereafter I shall eat less; but although I can no longer live with you in the lodge, I shall remain near you, and it shall be my business to forwarn you when any stranger is approaching." He then took some red paint, and put it on his face and his breast, to signify that his fast was finished, and was immediately changed to a bird called O-pe-che. Still he delights to live near the lodges of those who were his relatives; and oftentimes taking a stand on the highest branch of a tree, he cries out p'doan-watch-e-go, p'doan-watch-e-go, to foretel that some one is coming. But having found that his prediction often proves false, he is ashamed as soon as he has uttered it, and flying down, he hides himself in thick bushes, or on the ground, crying out che! che! che! che!

O-zhah-wus-kobe-na-sa—Green bird.
O-zaw-we-be-na-sa—Yellow bird.
Ma-ma—Red headed wood pecker.
Paw-paw-sa—Spotted wood pecker.
Muk-kud-da paw-paw-sa—Black pawpawsa. The male of this kind, has a bright yellow spot on the top of the head. They are found about Lake Superior in winter.
Mo-ning-gwun-na—Yarril, (highhold.)
Ke-ke-ba-na—small spotted wood pecker.
Che-gaun-do-wais-sa—Brown wood pecker, confined to cedar countries.
Shin-go-beek-ai-sa—Cedar bird.
Gitche-o-gish-ke-mun-ne-sa—Great king fisher.
O-gish-ke-mun-ne-sa*—Common king fisher.
Shaw-shaw-wa-ne-bais-sa—Swallow.
O-ge-bun-ge-gush.
O-kun-is-sa—Loxia enudeator, found at Lake Superior in February.
Pe, sing. Pe-ug, pl.—A fringilla, smaller than the waxen chatterer. The female has a spot of red on the top of the head; the male, the whole head and neck of the same colour. The tail feathers are bent outwards near the ends. Found about Lake Superior in the winter.
Mam-mah-twa.
Bosh-kun-dum-moan—Parakeet, (croch perons.)
Moash-kah-o-se We-kum-mo, (Menomonie)—Stake driver, (bittern.)
Kun-nuh waw-be-mokee-zhis wais-sa—Fly up the creek, (sun gazer.)
Me-mom-i-ne-ka-she—Rail, (rice bird.)
Pud-dush-kon-zhe—Snipe.
Gitche-pud-dush-kon-zhe—Wood cock.

CHE-CHEES-CHE-ME-UK—*Waders.*

Mo-voke—Curliew, [a foreign word.]
Mus-ko-da che-chees-ke-wa—Upland plover.

* Zichemenig Zein, 66.

PLANTS AND ANIMALS.

Wain-je-tah che-chees-ke-wa—Yellow leg plover.
Che-to-waik—Bull head plover.
Che-chees-ke-wais—Tern.
Wawb-uh-che-chawk—White Crane.
O-saw-waw-che-chawk—Sand hill crane.
Me-zis-sa—Turkey.
Be-na—Pheasant.
Mush-ko-da-sa—Grouse; confined to pine and cedar countries.
Ah-gusk, (Ojib.) Ke-waw-ne, (Ott.)—Prairie hen.
O-me-me—Pigeon; o-me-meeg—Pigeons. Amemi, Z. 19.

Ko-ko-ko-oge*—*Owls*.

Waw-wain-je gun-no—Great horned owl.
Wain-je-tah koko-koho—Right owl.
Koko-oanse—Little owl; gokhotit, Z. 18.
Bo-dah-wah doam-ba—Size of a pigeon, (membrum virile.)
Kaw-kaw-be-sha—Brown owl.
Waw-be-ko-ko—Snow owl, very large.
Waw-o-nais-sa—Whippoorwill.
Baish-kwa—Night hawk.

She-she-bug—*Ducks*.

Waw-be-zee—Great Swan.
Mah-nah-be-zee—Smaller swan, not common. Their cry resembles the voice of a man. The word means ugly or ill looking swan.
Ne-kuh—Brant; ne-kug, pl.
Pish-ne-kuh—A smaller brant.
Wa-wa—Goose; Wa-waig—Geese; Waw-be-wa-wa—White goose; Waw-be-wa-waig—White geese.
An-ne-nish-sheeb—Duck and mallard.
Tah-gwaw-ge she-sheeb—Fall duck, red neck.
Mah-to-gun she-sheeb—Scraper bill duck.
Scah-mo—Wood duck.
Wa-weeb-ge-won-ga—Blue wing teal, (swift winged.)

* Gok-hos, Z. 11.

Ke-nis-te-no-kwa sheeb—Cree woman duck.
Muk-kud-da sheeb—Black duck.
Kitche-waw-we-big-wa-wya—Large blue wing duck.
Pe-gwuk-o-she sheeb—Large bill, or blunt arrow duck; from pe-gwuk, the blunt or unbarbed arrow. This species has a large bill, and head of a leaden colour. They are found throughout the winter, in the rapids between Lakes Superior and Huron.
Ma-muh-tway-ah-ga—Whistling wing.
Kee-no-gwaw-o-wa sheeb—Long neck duck.
A-ha-wa—House duck.
Wab-ka-we sheeb—White duck.
Gaw-waw-zhe-koos—Shell duck.
Ah-zig-wuk—Fishing duck.
Sah-gah-ta—Mud hen.
Shin-ge-bis—Greebe; Gitche-shin-ge-bis—Large greebe.
Mahng—Loon.
A-sha-mahng—Small loon.
Gau-gau-geshe sheeb—Cormorant.
Sha-da—Pelican; sha-daig—Pelicans.
Shuh-shuh-gah—Blue heron.

Gi-aushk-wug—*Gulls.*

Gitche-gi-aushk—Great gull. Gi-as-koo-sha of the Ottawwaws.
Paush-kaw gi-aushk—Black headed gull.
Nas-so-waw-gwun-nus-kitte-kwah-gi-aushk—Fork tailed gull.
Muk-kud-da gi-aushk—Black gull.

Man-e-toanse-sug*—*Insects.*

Bo-dush-kwon-e-she—Large dragon fly.
Bo-dus-kwon-e-sheense—Small dragon fly.
Gitche-me-ze-zauk†—Large horse fly.
Me-zauk—Common horse fly.
Me-zauk-oons—Nat fly.

---

* Man-e-toanse-sug, or man-e-toanse-ug, small spirits; not exactly synonymous in this application with our word insects, but used to designate, indiscriminately, all very small animals.
† Mesissachowak, Zeis. 84.

Wain-je-tah che-chees-ke-wa—Yellow leg plover.
Che-to-waik—Bull head plover.
Che-chees-ke-wais—Tern.
Wawb-uh-che-chawk—White Crane.
O-saw-waw-che-chawk—Sand hill crane.
Me-zis-sa—Turkey.
Be-na—Pheasant.
Mush-ko-da-sa—Grouse; confined to pine and cedar countries.
Ah-gusk, (Ojib.) Ke-waw-ne, (Ott.)—Prairie hen.
O-me-me—Pigeon; o-me-meeg—Pigeons. Amemi, Z. 19.

Ko-ko-ko-oge*—*Owls*.

Waw-wain-je gun-no—Great horned owl.
Wain-je-tah koko-koho—Right owl.
Koko-oanse—Little owl; gokhotit, Z. 18.
Bo-dah-wah doam-ba—Size of a pigeon, (membrum virile.)
Kaw-kaw-be-sha—Brown owl.
Waw-be-ko-ko—Snow owl, very large.
Waw-o-nais-sa—Whippoorwill.
Baish-kwa—Night hawk.

She-she-bug—*Ducks*.

Waw-be-zee—Great Swan.
Mah-nah-be-zee—Smaller swan, not common. Their cry resembles the voice of a man. The word means ugly or ill looking swan.
Ne-kuh—Brant; ne-kug, pl.
Pish-ne-kuh—A smaller brant.
Wa-wa—Goose; Wa-waig—Geese; Waw-be-wa-wa—White goose; Waw-be-wa-waig—White geese.
An-ne-nish-sheeb—Duck and mallard.
Tah-gwaw-ge she-sheeb—Fall duck, red neck.
Mah-to-gun she-sheeb—Scraper bill duck.
Scah-mo—Wood duck.
Wa-weeb-ge-won-ga—Blue wing teal, (swift winged.)

* Gok-hos, Z. 11.

Ke-nis-te-no-kwa sheeb—Cree woman duck.
Muk-kud-da sheeb—Black duck.
Kitche-waw-we-big-wa-wya—Large blue wing duck.
Pe-gwuk-o-she sheeb—Large bill, or blunt arrow duck; from pe-gwuk, the blunt or unbarbed arrow. This species has a large bill, and head of a leaden colour. They are found throughout the winter, in the rapids between Lakes Superior and Huron.
Ma-muh-tway-ah-ga—Whistling wing.
Kee-no-gwaw-o-wa sheeb—Long neck duck.
A-ha-wa—House duck.
Wah-ka-we sheeb—White duck.
Gaw-waw-zhe-koos—Shell duck.
Ah-zig-wuk—Fishing duck.
Sah-gah-ta—Mud hen.
Shin-ge-bis—Greebe; Gitche-shin-ge-bis—Large greebe.
Mahng—Loon.
A-sha-mahng—Small loon.
Gau-gau-geshe sheeb—Cormorant.
Sha-da—Pelican; sha-daig—Pelicans.
Shuh-shuh-gah—Blue heron.

GI-AUSHK-WUG—*Gulls.*

Gitche-gi-aushk—Great gull. Gi-as-koo-sha of the Ottawwaws.
Paush-kaw gi-aushk—Black headed gull.
Nas-so-waw-gwun-nus-kitte-kwah-gi-aushk—Fork tailed gull.
Muk-kud-da gi-aushk—Black gull.

MAN-E-TOANSE-SUG*—*Insects.*

Bo-dush-kwon-e-she—Large dragon fly.
Bo-dus-kwon-e-sheense—Small dragon fly.
Gitche-me-ze-zauk†—Large horse fly.
Me-zauk—Common horse fly.
Me-zauk-oons—Nat fly.

---

* Man-e-toanse-sug, or man-e-toanse-ug, small spirits; not exactly synonymous in this application with our word insects, but used to designate, indiscriminately, all very small animals.
† Messachowak, Zeis. 84.

Gitche-ah-mo—Humble bee. Amoe, a bee, Z. 19.
Ah-mo, sing., ah-maag, pl.—Wasps, hornets, &c.
Waw-waw-tais-sa—Lightning bug.
An-ne-me-ke wid-de-koam*—Miller, sphinx, thunder's louse.
Pah-puk-ke-na—Grasshopper.
Ad-de-sah-wa-a-she—Locust.
Mow-wytch-e-ka-se—Beetle, (dung worker.)
Gitche-o-mis-kose—Great water bugs.
O-mis—Common water bug.
Ma-maing-gwah—Butterfly.
Metig-onishe-moan-ka-she—(He that sleeps in a stick.) Found in the bottom of springs.
Sha-bo-e-ya-sa—Rowing water bug.
Man-e-toanse o-ke-te-beeg pe-me-but-toan—Literally, the little [creature or] spirit that runs on the water.
O-mush-ko-se-se-wug—Grass bugs.
O-o-chug—Blowing flies and house flies.
Sug-ge-ma—Musquito.
Pin-goosh, pin-goosh-ains-sug—Gnats and sand flies.
Mat-wa-nuh-kai-moag—Swarming flies.
Sub-be-ka-she—Spider, (net worker.) A-a-be-ko—Large black spider.
An-e-go—Ant.†
Mis-ko-manetoanse—A little red bug common in the north.
Me-nah-koo-sit manetoanse—Strawberry bug.
Puh-beeg—Flea; Puh-beeg-wug—Fleas.
Eze-gaug—Tick.
E-kwuh—Louse; E-kwug—Lice.

Mo-saig—*Worms.*

O-zah-wash-ko-mo-sah—Green worm.
Way-muk-kwah-na—Great catterpillar, (bear skin.)

---

* This is one of those clumsy sphinxes, or moths, that are found on the ground in damp weather, or after showers of rain, and the Indians imagine that they fall from the *Animikeeg,* the beings whose voice is the thunder.

† The Nawdoway Indians have a fable, of an old man and woman who watched an ant heap until they saw the little insects changed to white men, and the eggs which they carry in their mouths, to bales of merchandise.

Gitcha-mo-sa—Great white grub; gitche-mo-saig, plural.
Me-shin-no-kau-tait-mo-sa—Millipede.
Pe-mis-koo-de-seence—Snail.

Ke-goi-yug—*Fishes.*

Nah-ma—Sturgeon.
Mas-ke-no-zha—Maskenonge, or pike.
O-zhaw-wush-ko ke-no-zha—Green pickerel, only found in the north.
Ke-no-zha—Pickerel; from kenose, long.
Nah-ma-goosh—Trout.
Na-zhum-ma-goosh—Brook trout.
Ne-git-che—Buffaloe fish.
Bush-she-to—Sheeps head; bush-she-toag, plural.
Mon-nuh-she-gun—Black bass.
Ad-dik-kum-aig, (attai-kum-meeg, Menom.)—White fish, or rein-deer fish; from ad-dik, rein-deer, and gum-maig, water.
Buh-pug-ga-sa—Large sucker.
Mis-kwaw-zhe-gun-no—Red horse.
Nah-ma-bin—Sucker; Mis-kwun nah-ma-bin—Red sucker.
Ug-gud-dwawsh—Sun fish.
Sah-wa—Perch, (yellow.) Sah-waig, pl.
O-ka-ah-wis—Fresh water herring.
We-be-chee—A flat fish larger than herring; only found in Red River.
Mon-num-maig—Great cat fish.
Ah-wa-sis-sie—Little catfish. The Indians say this fish hatches its young in a hole in the mud, and that they accompany her for some time afterwards.
Ke-na-beek gwum-maig—Eel, (water snake.)
O-da-che-gah-oon—Gar.
Shig-gwum-maig—Shovel nose; only in the Mississippi.
Kuk-kun-naun-gwi—Little toad fish; Lake Huron.
O-gah-suk—Little dories; Lake Huron.
O-gah—Dory.
Bag-gwut-tum-mo-goon-suk—These are small fishes, that make their appearance in ponds having no connexion with rivers or lakes, and which are sometimes quite dry. But though they

all perish in times of drought, they re-appear when the ponds are filled.

Shaw-ga-she—Craw fish.
Ais—Clam; Ais-sug—Clams.
Ais-ainse—Little clam.
Mis-koan-sug—Red clams.

MINERALS.

That the Indians are less observant of inanimate substances than of organized beings, will be manifest from the following meagre catalogue of minerals.

Bin-gwaw-beek—Lime stone, (ashes stone.)
Mat-toat-wah-nah-beek—Granite.
Muk-kud-dah-waw-beek—Black stone.
Mik-kwum-me-waw-beek—White Flint, (ice stone.)
Pish-ah-beek—Sulphuret of iron. They often find this passing into sulphate of iron, and make use of it for dying black.
O-poih-gun-us-sin—Pipe stone; farther distinguished according to colour.
O-skaw-shut-waw-beek—Gneiss, (vein stone.)
Mis-kwaw-sin—Red sand stone.
Gaw-gaw-wusk—Gypsum.
Waw-be-gun—White clay.
O-num-un—Ochre.
Mis-kwaw-be-gun—Red earth.
O-saw-waw-be-gun—Yellow earth.
Muk-kud-da-wuk-kum-mik—Black mould.
Waw-be-gun-uk-kaw—Clay ground.

OF TOTEMS.

Among the Indians of the Algonkin stock, every man receives from his father a *totem*, or family name. They affirm that no man is, by their customs, allowed to change his totem; and as this distinctive mark descends to all the children a man may have, as well as to all the prisoners he may take and adopt, it is manifest that, like the genealogies of the Hebrews, these totems should afford a complete enumeration of the stocks from which all the families have been derived. It differs not from our institution of surnames, except that the obligations of friendship and hospitality, and the restraint upon intermarriage, which it imposes, are more scrupulously regarded. They profess to consider it highly criminal for a man to marry a woman whose totem is the same as his own; and they relate instances where young men, for a violation of this rule, have been put to death by their nearest relatives. They say, also, that those having the same totem are bound, under whatever circumstances, as they meet, even though they should be of different and hostile bands, to treat each other not only as friends, but as brethren, sisters, and relatives of the same family.

Of the origin of this institution, and of the obligation to its strict observance, the Indians profess to know nothing. They say they suppose the totem was given them in the beginning, by their creator. Like surnames among us, these marks are now numerous; and, as in the case of our surnames, it is difficult to account for their multiplicity, without supposing a time when they might have been changed, or new ones adopted, more easily than at present.

It is not, as yet, well ascertained that any of the North American Indians, except those of the Algonkin family, have these peculiar genealogical marks. Those of the great Chippewyan family, in the north, we are well assured, have them not. From long acquaintance with the Dahcotah bands of the Mississippi and St. Peters, in which designation we include the Hoochawgenah, or Winnebagoes, and the Ioways, and from a more transient sojourning among the Otoes, the Kansas, the Omawhawes, the

Pawnees, and other western tribes, we have, with careful inquiry and search, been able to collect no intimation of such a custom among them. But of the western Indians we cannot speak with entire confidence, as we recollect to have heard Renville, an interpreter for the Sioux, after much puzzling and cross-examination, admit that something of the kind might exist among that people. It may be observed, that the Algonkins believe all other Indians to have totems, though, from the necessity they are in general under, of remaining ignorant of those of hostile bands, the omission of the totem in their picture writing, serves to designate an enemy. Thus, those bands of Ojibbeways who border on the country of the Dahcotah, or Sioux, always understand the figure of a man without totem, to mean one of that people.

CATALOGUE OF TOTEMS
Among the Ottawwaws and Ojibbeways, with the names of some to whom they belong.

Muk-kwaw—Bear, the totem of Pe-ga-gun, O-shaw-wa-no, and O-ka-taw, chiefs of Waw-gun-nuk-kiz-ze.

Ke-no-zha—Pickerel, of A-ke-win-de-ba.

Ad-dik-kun-maig—White fish, of Wawb-o-jeeg, (the white fisher.)

Moons—Moose, of Naw-o-gee-zhik, (in the middle of the sky.) This is said to be the original totem of the Ottawwaws; having received many accessions of people from other bands, many other totems have been derived from them, and are now intermixed with the original stock.

Ad-dik—Rein deer, of Ma-má-ah-jun, (he that goes.)

Mahng—A loon, of Too-beesh.

Me-giz-ze—White headed eagle, of Me-zhuk-kwun-na-no.

Ka-kaik—Henhawk, of O-ge-mah-we-hin-ne.

Pe-pe-ge-wiz-zains—Sparrow hawk, of Muk-kud-da-be-na-sa.

Ah-meek—Beaver, of Wa-me-gon-a-biew and Net-no-kwa.

Mus-sun-dum-mo—Water snake, of O-kin-je-wun-no, Sin-ne-way, &c.

————Forked tree, of Ke-me-wun, O-jeeg, &c.
Gi-oshk—Gull, of Puh-koo-se-gun.
Ad-je-jawk—Crane, of Au-da-mene.
Nah-ma-bin—Sucker, of Nain-noh-we-ton.
Pe-zhew—Wild cat; common totem among the Muskegoes.
Ah-wa-sis-se—Small cat fish, of Matche-kwe-we-zainse. Sometimes they call the people of this totem, "those who carry their young," from the habits of the small cat fish.
She-she-gwun—Rattle snake; the totem of Gish-kaw-ko, Manito-o-geezhik, &c. and by them given to Tanner.

Many more might be enumerated, but these are sufficient to give an idea of the kinds of objects from which they choose to derive their names. The trivial or common name of a man may be, and often is, changed on his going to war, or at the occurrence of any remarkable event; but the totem is never changed. It is not true, that they have, in all instances, the figure of whatever may be their totem always tattooed on some part of their body, nor that they carry about them a skin, or any other mark, by which it may be immediately recognised. Though they may sometimes do this, they are, in other instances, when they meet as strangers, compelled to inquire of each other their respective totems.*

---

* The tribes known to the Ottawwaws, are by them denominated as follows:—
1. Ottawwawwug, Ottawwaws,
2. Ojibbewaig, Ojibbeways, } Close allies in all past times, and their dialects very similar.
3. Potiwattimeeg, Potiwattomies,
4. Kekaupoag, Kickapoos.
5. Oshawanoag, Shawneese, or southern people.
6. Wawbuniukkeeg, Stockbridge, or white tops.
7. Muskotanje, Muskantins of the early French writers; formerly lived at Wawkwunkizze, whence they were driven by the Ottawwaws, and the latter now consider them as lost. By some they are supposed to have been a band of Potiwattomies; but the Ottawwaws enumerate them as a distinct people.
8. Osaugeeg, Sankewi.
9. Mahnomoneeg, Menomonies, (wild rice people.)
10. Kneeistenoag, Crees. They are said to call themselves Nahhahwuk.
11. Muskegoag, Muskegoes, (swamp people.)
12. Muskegoag, Nopemit Axhinneneeg, or Nopemetus Anineeg, (back woods people,) a second relationship of Muskegoes.
13. Sheshebug, Ducks.
14. Bowwetegoweninnewug, Fall Indians.

The word *totem* is of the Ojibbeway language, and, like almost all others, is readily moulded into the form of a verb, as will appear from the following examples:—

Ah-neen en-dah che-un-net, O-to-tem-e-waun maun-dah-pe?
How many   are these   are totems   here?
How many are the totems of this band?

Wa-nain way-gi-osh-kun wa-to-ta-met?
What   the gull   is his totem?
What is the gull's totem?

KNOWLEDGE OF ASTRONOMY.

OF the opinions of the Indians respecting the heavenly bodies, little need be said. An extensive acquaintance with the motions, figures, distances, &c. of these bodies, could not have been expected from people situated as they are, and deprived altogether

15. Tuskwawgomeeg, Uskwawgomees; near Montreal.

The above fifteen tribes are thought to speak languages which resemble Ottawwaw.

16. Nautowaig, Naudowaya, (rattle snakes.)
17. Mat-che-naw-to-waig, Bad Naudoways.
18. Ioewaig, Ioways.
19. Nabuggindebaig, Flat heads; said to have lived below the Illinois River.
20. Winnebagoag, Winnebagoes, or Puants.
21. Bwoinug, Sioux; Naudowesseeg, Ott., Roasters.
22. Ussinebwoinug, Assinneboins, (stone roasters.)
23. Agutchaninnewug, Minnetahrees, (settled people.)
24. Kwowahtewug, Mandans.
25. Ahmeekkwun Eninnewug, Beaver People; among the Fall Indians.
26. Mukkudda Ozituhnug, Black Feet.
27. Ussinnewadj Eninnewug, Rocky Mountain Indians.
28. Pahneug, Pawnees.
29. Wamussonewug.
30. Kokoakeeg.
31. Aguskemaig, Esquimaux, (those who eat their food raw.)
32. Weendegoag, Cannibals. This last is an imaginary race, said to inhabit an island in Hudson's Bay. They are of gigantic dimension, and extremely given to cannibalism. The Mnskegoes, who inhabit the low and cheerless swamps on the borders of Hudson's Bay, and are themselves reproached by the other tribes as cannibals, are said to live in constant fear of the Weendegoag.
33. Ojeeg Wyahnug, Fisher Skins.

of the aids of instruments, and a written language. They pretend to no more knowledge on these subjects than they possess.

Au-do-me-ne, an intelligent Ottawwaw of Wawgunukkizze, in answer to my inquiries concerning their opinion of the sun and moon, related to me the following fable:—

Long ago, an old Ojibbeway chief, and his wife, who lived on the shore of Lake Huron, had one son, a very beautiful boy. His name was Ono-wut-to-kwut-to, (he that catches clouds,) and his totem, after that of his father, a beaver. He would have been a great favourite with them, for he was, in the main, affectionate and dutiful, except that they could never persuade him to fast. Though they gave him charcoal, in place of his usual breakfast, he would never blacken his face, and if he could find fish eggs, or the head of a fish, he would roast them, and have something to eat. Once they took from him what he had thus cooked in place of his accustomed breakfast, and threw him some coals instead of it. But this was the last of many attempts to compel him to fast. He took up the coals, blackened his face, went out, and lay down. At night, he did not return into the lodge of his parents, but slept without. In his dream he saw a very beautiful woman come down from above, and stand at his feet. She said, "Ono-wut-to-kwut-to, I am come for you; see that you step in my tracks." The lad obeyed without hesitation, and stepping carefully in her steps, he presently found himself ascending above the tops of the trees, through the air, and beyond the clouds. His guide at length passed through a small round hole, and he following her, found himself standing on a beautiful and extensive prairie.

They followed the path, which led them to a large and rich looking lodge; entering here, they saw on one side pipes and war clubs, bows, arrows, and spears, with the various implements and ornaments of men. At the other end of the lodge were the things belonging to women. Here was the home of the beautiful girl who had been his companion, and she had, on the sticks, a belt she had not finished weaving. She said to him, " My brother is coming, and I must conceal you." So putting him in one corner, she spread the belt over him. Ono-wut-to-kwut-to, however, watched what passed without, from his concealment, and saw the brother of the young woman come in, most splendidly dressed, and take down a pipe from the wall. After he had smoked, he laid aside his pipe, and the sack containing his pah-koo-se-gun, and said, "When, my sister, will you cease from these practices? Have you forgotten that the Greatest of the Spirits has forbidden you to steal the children of those who live below? You suppose you have concealed this that you have now brought, but do I not know that he is here in the lodge? If you would not incur my displeasure, you must send him immediately down to his friends." But she would not. He then said to the boy, when he found that his sister was determined not to dismiss him, "You may as well come out from that place, where you are not concealed from me, and walk about, for you will be lonesome and hungry if you remain there." He took down a bow and arrows, and a pipe of red stone, richly ornamented, to give him. So the boy came out from under the belt, and amused himself with the bow and pipe the man gave him, and he became the husband of the young woman who had brought him up from the woods near his father's lodge.

He went abroad in the open prairie, but in all this fair and ample country, he found no inhabitants, except his wife and her brother. The plains were adorned with flowers, and garnished with bright and sparkling streams, but the animals were not like those he had been accustomed to see. Night followed day, as on the earth, but with the first appearance of light, the brother-in-law of Ono-wut-to-kwut-to began to make his preparations to leave the lodge. All day, and every day, he was absent, and returned in the evening; his wife, also, though not so regular in the time of her departure and return, was often absent great part of the night.

He was curious to know where they spent all the time of their absence, and he obtained from his brother-in-law permission to accompany him in one of his daily journeys. They went on in a smooth and open path, through prairies, to which they could see no boundary, until Ono-wut-to-kwut-to, becoming hungry, asked his companion if he did not think he should find any game. "Be patient, my brother," said he; "this is my road in which I walk every day, and at no great distance is the place where I constantly eat my dinner. When we arrive there you shall see how I am supplied with food."

They came at length to a place where were many fine mats to sit down upon, and a hole through which to look down upon the earth. Ono-wut-to-kwut-to, at the bidding of his companion, looked down through this hole, and saw far beneath him the great lakes, and the villages, not of the Ojibbeways only, but of all the red skins. In one place he saw a war party, stealing silently along toward the hunting camp of their enemies, and his companion told him what would be the result of the attack they were about to make. In another place he saw people feasting and dancing: young men were engaged at their sports, and here and there women were labouring at their accustomed avocations. The companion of Ono-wut-to-kwut-to called his attention to a group of children playing beside a lodge. "Do you see," said he, "that active and beautiful boy?" at the same time throwing a very small stone, which hit the child, who immediately fell to the ground, and presently they saw him carried into the lodge. Then they saw people running about, and heard the she-she-gwun, and the song and prayer of the medicine man, entreating that the child's life might be spared. To this request his companion made answer, "Send me up the white dog." Then they could distinguish the hurry and bustle of preparation for a feast, a white dog killed and singed, and the people, who were called, assembling at the lodge. While these things were passing, he addressed himself to Ono-wut-to-kwut-to, saying, "There are, among you in the lower world, some whom you call great medicine men; but it is because their ears are open, and they hear my voice, when I have struck any one, that they are able to give relief to the sick. They direct the people to send me whatever I call for, and when they have sent it, I remove my hand from those I had made sick." When he had said this, the white dog was parcelled out in dishes, for those that were at the feast; then the medicine man, when they were about to begin to eat, said, "We send thee this, Great Manito;" and immediately they saw the dog, cooked, and ready to be eaten, rising to them through the air. After they had dined, they returned home by another path.

In this manner they lived for some time, but Ono-wut-to-kwut-to had not forgotten his friends, and the many pleasant things he had left in his father's village, and he longed to return to the earth. At last, his wife consented to his request. "Since," said she, "you are better pleased with the poverty, the cares, and the miseries of the world beneath, than with the peaceful and permanent delights of these prairies, go. I give you permission to depart; not only so, but since I brought you hither, I shall carry you back to the place where I found you, near your father's lodge; but remember, you are still my husband, and that my power over you is in no manner diminished. You may return to your relatives, and live to the common age of man, by observing what I now say to you. Beware how you venture to take a wife among men. Whenever you do so, you shall feel my displeasure; and if you marry the second time, it is then you will be called to return to me."

Then Ono-wut-to-kwut-to awoke, and found himself on the ground, near the door of his father's lodge. Instead of the bright beings of his vision, he saw about him his aged mother, and his relatives, who told him he had been absent about a year. For some time he was serious and abstracted; but, by degrees, the impression of his visit to the upper world wore off. He began to doubt the reality of what he had heard and seen. At length, forgetful of the admonitions of his spouse, he married a beautiful young woman of his own tribe. Four days afterwards she was a corpse. But even the effect of this fearful admonition was not permanent. He again ventured to marry, and soon afterwards, going out of his lodge one night, to listen to some unusual noise, he disappeared, to return no more. It was believed that his wife from the upper world came to recall him, according to her threat, and that he still remains in those upper regions, and has taken the place of his brother-in-law, in overlooking the affairs of men.

It appears from this tradition, that worship, or sacrifices, are, among the Ottawwaws, sometimes made to the sun and moon; and they acknowledge that these luminaries, or rather the man in the sun, and the woman in the moon, keep watch over all our actions.

The various changes of the moon afford them a method of measuring time, very definite as to the periods, but variable in the names they give them. Their old men have many disputes about the number of moons in each year, and they give different names to each of these. Some of the names in common use are the following. The first words are in the Ottawwaw, and the second in the Menomonie dialect.

O-ta-ha-mene kee-zis—O-tai-hai-min ka-zho—Strawberry moon.

Me-nes kee-zis—Main ka-zho—Whortleberry moon.

Menomonie-ka-we kee-zis—Pohia-kun ka-zho—Wild rice gathering moon.

Be-nah-kwaw-we kee-zis—Paw-we-pe-muk ka-zho—Leaves falling moon.

Gush-kut-te-ne kee-zis—Wun-nai ka-zho—Ice moon.

Ah-gim-me-ka-we kee-zis—Wa-si-ko-si ka-zho—Snow shoes, Ojib.; bright night, Menom.

Mah-ko kee-zis—Wa-mun-nus-so ka-zho—[Manito o-kee-zis, Ojib.]—Bear moon, Ott.; dear rutting moon, Men.; [Spirit moon, Ojib.]

Kitche-manito o-kee-zis—Ma-cha-ti-wuk wa-mun-nuz-so-wuk—Longest moon, good for hunting.*

Me-giz-ze-we kee-zis—Na-ma-pin ka-zho—[Na-ma-bin kee-zis, Ott.]—Sucker moon.

Ne-ke kee-zis—Sho-be-maw-kun ka-zho—Brant moon, Ojib.; Sugar moon, Men.

Maung-o kee-zis—As-sa-bun ka-zho—Loon's moon, Ojib.; raccoon moon, Men.

Sah-ge-bug-ah-we kee-zis—Pe-ke-pe-muk ka-zho—Leaves moon.

Another moon spoken of by the Menomonies, is Wai-to-ke Ka-zho, the snake moon, which belongs to the spring season.

The following short catalogue of stars and constellations, will show that they pay some attention to the more remote of the heavenly bodies. Some few of their old men, it is said, have many more names.

Waw-bun-an-nung—The morning star.

Ke-wa-din an-nung—The north star.

Muk-koo-ste-gwon—The bear's head. Three stars in the triangle.

Muh-koo-zhe-gwun—Bear's rump. Seven stars.

* A person born in this moon, (January,) will be long lived.

Oj-eeg an-nung-wug—Fisher stars. The bright stars in ursa major, and one beyond, which forms the point of the fisher's nose.

Mah-to-te-sun—The sweating lodge. One of the poles of this lodge is removed. They say the man whom they point out near by, was so overcome with the heat of the Mah-to-te-sun, that in his hurried attempt to escape, he pulled up this pole.

Mahng—A loon.

Nau-ge-maun-gwait—Man in a canoe hunting the loon.

Ah-wah-to-wuh o-moag—The companions sailing.

An-nung-o-skun-na—Comet. They have the opinion common among ignorant white people, that the appearance of a comet is an indication that war is to follow. The Ojibbeway An-nung-o-skun-na, seems to signify blazing star. The Menomonies call them Sko-tie-nah-mo-kin, the seeing fire. Some of the Ojibbeways, also, Wa-ween-e-zis-e-mah-guk Ish-koo-da, fire that has hair.

Of the true cause of the increase and decrease of the moon, of eclipses, and of other phenomena which depend upon the motions of the heavenly bodies, they have no correct conceptions. When the moon is in eclipse, they say it is dying, and they load and discharge their guns at it; and when they perceive the bright part becoming a little larger, they imagine they have aided to drive away the sickness which was overpowering it. Of the milky way, they sometimes say, that a turtle has been swimming along the bottom of the sky, and disturbed the mud. Of the aurora borealis, which they call the dance of the dead, their opinion, though a little more poetic, is equally childish. Several meteoric phenomena they distinguish from those remoter appearances which are beyond our atmosphere, and of the former they sometimes say, "they belong to us."

What was long ago stated by Roger Williams, of the mythology of the Indians of Rhode Island, agrees but in part with the opinions of the present day among the Ottawwaws. Of Cau-tan-to-wit, "the great south-west god," we hear nothing. Ning-gah-be-an-nong Manito, the western god, the younger brother of Na-na-bou-jou, the god of the country of the dead, has taken his place. In his Saw-waw-nand, we recognize the Shaw-wun-noug Manito, the southern god of the Ottawwaws. But all these, Waw-bun-ong Manito, the god of the morning, or of the east, Ke-way-tin-ong Manito, the god of the north, with Ka-no-waw-bum-min-uk, " he that sees us," whose place is in the sun, are inferior in power to many others; even to the Ke-zhe-ko-we-nin-ne-wug, the sky people; a race of small, but benevolent and watchful beings, who are ever ready to do good to mankind.

CHAPTER II.

COMPARISON OF NUMERALS, TO TEN, IN SEVERAL AMERICAN DIALECTS.

1. *Oto—From Say.*

Yon-ka	Sha-gua
No-wa	Shah-a-muh
Tah-ne	Kra-rah-ba-na
To-wa	Shan-ka
Sah-tah	Kra-ba-nuh

2. *Konza.*

Meakh-che	Shahp-peh
Nom-pah	Pa-om-bah
Yah-ber-re	Pa-yah-ber-re
To-pah	Shank-kuh
Sah-tah	Ker-ab-bu-rah

3. *Omawhaw.*

Meach-che	Shap-pa
Nom-bah	Pa-noom-ba
Ra-bene	Pa-rah-bene
To-bah	Shoon-kah
Sah-tah	Kra-ba-rah

4. *Yauktong.*

Wan-chah	Shah-kah-pe
No-pah	Shah-ko-e
Yah-me-ne	Sha-kun-do-ah
To-pah	Nuh-pet-che-wun-bah
Zah-pe-tah	Week-che-min-nuh

NUMERALS.

5. Dahkotah—Of Upper Mississippi.

Wau-zhe-tah
No-a-pah
Yah-min-ne
To-a-pah
Zah-pe-tah

Shah-kah-pe
Shah-koan
Shah-han-doah
Neep-chew-wun-kah
Week-chim-mah-ne

6. Minnetahse.

Le-mois-so
No-o-pah
Nah-me
To-pah
Cheh-hoh

A-cah-me
Chap-po
No-pup-pe
No-was-sap-pa
Pe-sah-gas

7. Pawnee.

As-ko
Pet-ko
Tou-wet
Shke-tiksh
She-oksh

Shek-shah-bish
Pet-ko-shek-sha-bish
Tou-wet-sha-bish
Tok-shere-wa
Tok-shere

8. Choktaw.

Chaf-fah
To-ko-lo
To-cha-nah
Osh-tah
Tath-lah-pe

Han-nah-la
Oon-to-ko-lo
Oon-to-che-nah
Chak-ah-ta
Po-ko-la

9. Ojibbeway.

Ning-gooj-waw, or Ba-zhik
Neezh-waw, or Neezh
Nis-swaw, or Nis-swe
Ne-win
Nah-nun

Ning-good-waw-swe
Neezh-zhwaw-swe
Shwaw-swe
Shong-gus-swe, or shong
Me-dos-swe, or kwaitch

10. Muskwake.

Ne kot
Neesh

Nee-swa
Ne-o

Ne-on-en				Neesh-waus-eek
Ne-kot-waus-keek		Shaunk
Ne-kot-wau-swa			Me-to-swa

11. *Minsi—From Heckewelder.*

Gut-ti			Gut-tasch
Nis-cha			Nis-choasch
Na-cha			Cha-asch
Ne-wa			No-we-li
Na-lan			Wim-bat

12. *Algonkin—From Heckweelder.*

Pe-gik			Nin-gon-ten-as-sou
Ninch			Nin-chou-as-sou
Nis-soue		Nis-sou-as-sou
Neou			Chan-gas-sou
Na-sau			Mil-las-sou

13. *Delaware—From Heckewelder.*

Ni-gut-ti		Gut-tasch
Nis-cha			Nis-chash
Na-cha			Chasch
Ne-wo			Pes-chonk
Pa-le-nach		Tel-len

14. *Mahnomonie.*

Ne-kotes		Ne-kot-was-sa-tah
Neesh			No-ha-kun
Nah-new			Suah-sek
Ne-ew			Shaw-ka-waw
Nean-nun		Me-tah-tah

15. *Cree—From Say.*

Paynk			Ne-go-to-ah-sek
Ne-shuh			Ta-pa-coh
Nesh-to			Aa-na-nes
Na-a-wo			Ta-ka-to
Nean-nun		Me-ta-ta

NUMERALS.

16. *Winnebago.*

Zhunk-he-rah
Noam-pee-wee
Tah-nee-wee
Kho-a-pee-wee
Saut-shah
Ah-ka-a-way
Shau-kōa
Ar-waw-oank
Zhunke-schoonk-schoone
Kar-ra-pun-na-nah

17. *Adage—From Duponceau.*

Nan-cas
Nass
Colle
Cac-ca-che
Sep-pa-can
Pa-ca-nan-cus
Pa-can-oss
Pa-ca-lon
Sic-kin-ish
Neus-ne

18. *Muskogee—From Adair.*

Hom-mai
Hok-kole
Too-che-na
Osh-ta
Cha-ka-pe
E-pah-ghe
Ho-loo-pha-ge
Chee-ne-pa
Oh-sta-pe
Pa-ko-le

19. *Choktah and Chiksah—From Adair.*

Cheph-pho
Too-ga-lo
Toot-che-na
Oos-ta
Tath-la-be
Han-nah-le
Un-too-ga-lo
Un-too-che-na
Chak-ka-le
Po-koo-le

20. *Cherokee—From Adair.*

So-guo
Tah-ne
Choch
Nauk-ke
Ish-ke
Soo-tare
Ka-re-koge
Sah-nay-ra
Soh-nay-ra
Skoeh
So-at-too (11)
Ta-ra-too (12)

21. *Quoddies, [Maine.]—From Duponceau.*

Nai-get
Nes
Ni-hi
Na-he

NUMERALS.

Nane
Ga-mat-chine
A-lo-he-gan-nah

Ok-muh-hine
As-kwi-nan-dak
Ney-dinsk

22. *Quawpaw—From Duponceau's MS.*

Milch-tih
Non-ne-pah
Dag-he-nig
Tu-ah
Sat-ton

Schap-peh
Pen-na-pah
Pe-dag-he-nih
Schunk-kah
Ge-deh-bo-nah

23. *Penobscot—From Duponceau's MS.*

Pe-suok
Neise
Nhas
Yeuf
Pa-le-neusg

Neuk-tansg
Ta-boos
San-suk
No-cle
Ma-ta-ta

24. *Miami—From Duponceau's MS.*

Ng-goo-teh
Nii-ju-eh
Nisth-ueh
Nu-ueh
Ilaan-ueh

Ka-kat-sueh
Sueh-tet-sueh
Po-laa-neh
Ngo-te-me-neh-kek
Mo-taat-sueh

25. *Shawnese—From Duponceau's MS.*

In-gut-i, or, n'gut-i
Nis-chwe
N'swe
Ni-wi
Nia-lan-wi

Ka-kat-swi
Swach-tet-swy
Pal-la-ni
N'gut-ti-me-pech-gi
Mat-tat-swy

26. *Unachog—From Duponceau's MS.*

Na-gwut
Nees
Nos
Yaut
Pa, or, na-paa

Na-cut-tah, or, cut-tah
Tum-po-wa
Swat
Neone
Pay-ac

NUMERALS.

27. *Natick—From Elliot's Bib.*

Ne-gunt Ne-kwut-ta-tah-she
Neese Ne-sau-suk-tah-she
Nish Shwo-suk-tah-she
Yau Pa-skoo-gun-tah-she
Na-pan-na-tah-she Pi-uk

28. *Nousaghauset—From Elliot's Bib. in MS.*

Ne-guit Kwut-ta
Nase E-na-da
Nish Shwo-suk
Yoh Pas-ku-git
Na-pau-na Pi-uk

29. *Sourikwosiorum.—From John De Laet.*

Ne-gout Ka-ma-chin
Ta-bo E-roe-kwe-sink
Chicht Meg-on-ma-chin
Ne-ou Egh-ko-na-deck
Nau Me-tun

30. *Canadenses, Ib.—From Auct. Lescarbot.*

Be-gou Con-tou-sai-hin
Ni-chou Ne-o-va-chin
Nich-toa Nes-to-va-chin
Rau Pes-co-va-det
A-pa-te-ta Me-tun

31. *Saukikani—From J. D. Laet, Auct. Johan. Smith.*

Cotte Cot-tash
Nysse Nys-sas
Na-cha Ge-chas
Wy-we Pes-chon
Pa-re-nagh Ter-ren

32. *Algonkin—From J. Long.*

Pay-jik Nis-soo
Ninch Neoo

NUMERALS.

Na-ran Nis-so-was-so
Nin-goot-was-soo Shon-gas-soo
Nin-cho-was-soo Ni-tas-soo

33. *Chippeway—From J. Long.*

Pay-shik Ne-gut-wos-swoy
Neesh Swos-swoy
Nees-swoy Shau-gos-swoy
Ni-on Me-tos-swoy
Na-ran

34. *New Stockbridge—From Kao-no-mut, a woman who had been living on Fox River, 1827.*

N'got-tah N'ko-taus
Ne-shah To-pau-wus
Nah-hah Khous-so
Nah-wah Nah-ne-we
No-nun N'tan-net

35. *Mohegan.*

Ug-wit-toh Ug-wit-tus
Nes-oh Tu-pou-wus
Nogh-hoh Ghu-sooh
Nau-woh Nau-ne-weh
Nu-non Ne-tau-nit

36. *Monsee—From an Indian at Buffaloe.*

N'got-tah N'got-waws
Ne-shah Nush-waus
N'hah N'haus
Na-ah No-wa-lah
Naw-bun Wim-bat

37. *Naudoway—From Tanner.*

Wis-ka-ut Yah-gah
Tik-ke-ne Shah-tuk
Os-sah Sah-ta-gah
Kia-nec Te-unk-teuh
Whisk We-go-ne

NUMERALS.

38. Seneca—From an Indian at Buffaloe, 1827.

Skaut   Yah-eh
Tik-thnee   Chah-duk
Snu-ah   Ta-ke-oh
Ka-ae   Teu-tohn
Weish   Wus-han

39. Potiwattomie—From an Indian at Detroit, 1827.

Ne-got   Ne-got-waut-so
Neesh   No-okt-so
Nees-wa   Su-aut-so
Na-ow   Shah-kah
Na-nun   Kwetch

40. Ottawwaw—From Tanner.

Ne-goch-waw   Nin-got-wau-swa
Neesh-waw   Neesh-wau-swa
Nis-waw   Nis-wau-swa
Ne-win   Shaunk
Nah-nun   Kwetch

41. Chippewyan—From a German Interpreter.

Ish-li-a   I-ka-lah-rah
Nuh-ka   I-ka-taing-ha
Tah-sha   Ish-lah-in-ding-ga
Taing-a   Kas-ka-koo-un-nee-rah
Sah-zhun-lah-ha Koo-un-nu-ah

42. Chippewyan—From M'Kenzie.

Sta-chy   Al-ke-tar-hy-y
Na-ghur   Al-ki-deing-hy
Tagh-y   Ca-ki-na-ha-noth-na
Dengk-y   Ca-noth-na
Sas-sou-la-chee

43. Chippewyan—From a woman, a native of Churchill.

Ith-lia   Ting-he
Nuk-ka   Sah-zun-lah-ha
Krah-ha, or tah-rhe   Il-ket-tah-rah

Shah-zet-te   Kah-kin-ho-en-er-nah
Il-ket-ting   Ho-en-er-nah

44. *Anglo Saxon.*

Aen   Six
Twe-gen, or, twa   Se-o-fou
Threo, or, thry   Eaghta
Feo-ther, or, feo-wer   Ni-gone
                         Tyn

45. *Cree—From M'Kenzie.*

Pey-ac   Ne-gou-ta-woe-sic
Ni-sheu   Nish-wi-o-sic
Nish-tou   Jan-na-new
Ne-way   Shack
Ni-an-nan   Mi-ta-tat

46. *Algokin—From M'Kenzie.*

Pe-cheik   Ni-gou-ta-wa-swois
Nije   Ni-gi-was-wois
Nis-wois   She-was-wois
Neau   Shan-gwos-wois
Na-nan   Mit-as-swois

47. *Chippewyan—From a Chippewyan.*

Eth-li-ah   El-kat-har-ri
Nuk-kur   Slus-ing-ding-he
Tor-ri   El-ket-ding-he
Ding-he   Kutch-e-no-ner-re
Sos-su-li-he   Ho-ner-ne-nuh

48. *Winnebago—From a Winnebago.*

Zhunk-kaid   Har-ker-ra
Noamp   Shar-goan
Tarn   Kad-do-unk
T'joab   Yunk-ked-joos-koon
Sarj   Ker-reb-hon-na

49. *Cree—From a native.*

Pe-ak   Ne-su

Nees-to   Ta-be-ko
Ne-o   E-nah-ne
Ne-ah-nun   Kam-me-tah-tat
Ning-good-waw-sik   Me-tah-tat

50. *Mahnesheet, (slow-tongues,) residing on the St. Johns, N. B. From a native.*

Na-koot   Kah-mutch-in
Tah-bo   Lo-he-gin-nuk
Sheist   O-go-mul-chin
Na-oo   Aish-ko-nah-daig
Nahn   Ko-dainsk

CHAPTER III.

MUSIC AND POETRY OF THE INDIANS.

HERE, it must be acknowledged, we enter a barren field, offering little to excite industry, or to reward inquiry. Without literature to give perpetuity to the creations of genius, or to bear to succeeding times the record of remarkable events, the Americans have no store house of ancient learning to open to the curiosity of the European race. They have probably never thought like the Arabs, that the cultivation of their language was an object of importance; and though the orator must at times have experienced the effect of a happy choice of expression, he must always have been confined to a narrow range, by the necessity of keeping within the comprehension of his hearers. Hence their public speakers appear to depend more on a certain vehemence and earnestness of manner, which is intelligible without words, than upon any elegance of thought, or refinement of diction.

Their songs, whether of war or devotion, consist, for the most, of a few words or short phrases many times repeated; and in their speeches, they dwell long and vehemently on the same idea. One who hears an Indian orator without comprehending his language, would confidently suppose that his discourse abounded with meaning; but these speeches, like their tedious and monotonous chants, when clearly understood, appear so poor and jejune, that few white men would listen to either, were it not with the hope of extracting information, of which the speaker, or the singer himself, must be wholly unconscious. But after all is heard and explained, and carefully examined in all its bearings, it must be principally the business of a quick and fertile imagination, to find in them moral instruction or historical information. If we find among the American Indians traditional items, bearing manifest and strong resemblance to those of the great Asiatic family, from whom we have adopted many of our religious opinions, this can only be considered as indicating what needed no proof; namely: That this people, as well as ourselves, have descended from that primeval stock, which, planted somewhere upon the mountains of Asia, has sent forth its branches into all parts of the earth. Thither, we are taught by the most ancient human records, and by the concurrent deductions of all sound philosophy, and honest inquiry, to look for the great fountain of the human race: and if some of the streams, in descending thence, have been concealed in swamps, or sunk beneath sands, we ought not therefore to doubt that their origin is to be thence deduced. But that existing or retrieveable monuments or resemblances, will ever enable the curious satisfactorily to trace the American branch to its origin, need not now be expected. Nevertheless, this part of the subject may have interest for those who love to trace the human character through all situations and exposures, and to contemplate the effect of revolutions in external circumstances, on manners, language, and metaphysical opinions.

Sufficient evidence probably exists, to convince many, that the natives of the central regions of North America, whatever diversities of dialect may now exist, are essentially of the same race with the Peruvians, the Mexicans, and the Natchez; between whom and the ancient inhabitants of Greece and Italy, and that portion of the present population of India who worship Brama, Boudd, Ganesa, Iswara, &c. a near relationship has already been ascertained. In the metamorphoses which the Indian traditions assign to many trees, plants, animals, and other things, we are strongly reminded of the similar superstitions preserved by the Roman poets. We find, also, in the American traditions, distinct allusions to a general deluge, and to several other particulars which we are accustomed to consider as resting solely on the authority of the Mosaic history. But when we reflect on the almost universal distribution of these opinions, in some shape or other, among all known races of men, we may admit a doubt whether they have been derived from the historical books of the Hebrews, or whether they are not rather the glimmerings of that primitive light, which, at the first great division after the flood, into the families of Shem, Ham, and Japhet, and more recently at the dispersion of Babel, must have been in possession of all mankind. We find in the Mosaic history, written, as it was,

Nane.   Ok-muh-hine
Ga-mat-chine   As-kwi-nan-dak
A-lo-he-gan-nah   Ney-dinsk

22. *Quawpaw—From Duponceau's MS.*

Milch-tih   Schap-peh
Non-ne-pah   Pen-na-pah
Dag-he-nig   Pe-dag-he-nih
Tu-ah   Schunk-kah
Sat-ton   Ge-deh-bo-nah

23. *Penobscot—From Duponceau's MS.*

Pe-suok   Neuk-tansg
Neise   Ta-boos
Nhas   San-suk
Yeuf   No-cle
Pa-le-neusg   Ma-ta-ta

24. *Miami—From Duponceau's MS.*

Ng-goo-teh   Ka-kat-sueh
Nii-ju-eh   Sueh-tet-sueh
Nisth-ueh   Po-laa-neh
Nu-ueh   Ngo-te-me-neh-kek
Ilaan-ueh   Mo-taat-sueh

25. *Shawnese—From Duponceau's MS.*

In-gut-i, or, n'gut-i   Ka-kat-swi
Nis-chwe   Swach-tet-swy
N'swe   Pal-la-ni
Ni-wi   N'gut-ti-me-pech-gi
Nia-lan-wi   Mat-tat-swy

26. *Unachog—From Duponceau's MS.*

Na-gwut   Na-cut-tah, or, cut-tah
Nees   Tum-po-wa
Nos   Swat
Yaut   Neone
Pa, or, na-paa   Pay-ac

NUMERALS. 329

27. *Natick—From Elliot's Bib.*

Ne-gunt			Ne-kwut-ta-tah-she
Neese			Ne-sau-suk-tah-she
Nish			Shwo-suk-tah-she
Yau			Pa-skoo-gun-tah-she
Na-pan-na-tah-she	Pi-uk

28. *Nousaghauset—From Elliot's Bib. in MS.*

Ne-guit		Kwut-ta
Nase		E-na-da
Nish		Shwo-suk
Yoh		Pas-ku-git
Na-pau-na	Pi-uk

29. *Sourikwosiorum.—From John De Laet.*

Ne-gout		Ka-ma-chin
Ta-bo		E-roe-kwe-sink
Chicht		Meg-on-ma-chin
Ne-ou		Egh-ko-na-deck
Nau		Me-tun

30. *Canadenses, Ib.—From Auct. Lescarbot.*

Be-gou		Con-tou-sai-hin
Ni-chou		Ne-o-va-chin
Nich-toa	Nes-to-va-chin
Rau		Pes-co-va-det
A-pa-te-ta	Me-tun

31. *Saukikani—From J. D. Laet, Auct. Johan. Smith.*

Cotte		Cot-tash
Nysse		Nys-sas
Na-cha		Ge-chas
Wy-we		Pes-chon
Pa-re-nagh	Ter-ren

32. *Algonkin—From J. Long.*

Pay-jik		Nis-soo
Ninch		Neoo

42

NUMERALS.

Na-ran	Nis-so-was-so
Nin-goot-was-soo	Shon-gas-soo
Nin-cho-was-soo	Ni-tas-soo

33. *Chippeway—From J. Long.*

Pay-shik	Ne-gut-wos-swoy
Neesh	Swos-swoy
Nees-swoy	Shau-gos-swoy
Ni-on	Me-tos-swoy
Na-ran	

34. *New Stockbridge—From Kao-no-mut, a woman who had been living on Fox River, 1827.*

N'got-tah	N'ko-taus
Ne-shah	To-pau-wus
Nah-hah	Khous-so
Nah-wah	Nah-ne-we
No-nun	N'tan-net

35. *Mohegan.*

Ug-wit-toh	Ug-wit-tus
Nes-oh	Tu-pou-wus
Nogh-hoh	Ghu-sooh
Nau-woh	Nau-ne-weh
Nu-nqn	Ne-tau-nit

36. *Monsee—From an Indian at Buffaloe.*

N'got-tah	N'got-waws
Ne-shah	Nush-waus
N'hah	N'haus
Na-ah	No-wa-lah
Naw-bun	Wim-bat

37. *Naudoway—From Tanner.*

Wis-ka-ut	Yah-gah
Tik-ke-ne	Shah-tuk
Os-sah	Sah-ta-gah
Kia-nec	Te-unk-teuh
Whisk	We-go-ne

NUMERALS.

38. Seneca—From an Indian at Buffaloe, 1827.

Skaut Yah-eh
Tik-thnee Chah-duk
Snu-ah Ta-ke-oh
Ka-ae Teu-tohn
Weish Wus-han

39. Potiwattomie—From an Indian at Detroit, 1827.

Ne-got Ne-got-waut-so
Neesh No-okt-so
Nees-wa Su-aut-so
Na-ow Shah-kah
Na-nun Kwetch

40. Ottawwaw—From Tanner.

Ne-goch-waw Nin-got-wau-swa
Neesh-waw Neesh-wau-swa
Nis-waw Nis-wau-swa
Ne-win Shaunk
Nah-nun Kwetch

41. Chippewyan—From a German Interpreter.

Ish-li-a I-ka-lah-rah
Nuh-ka I-ka-taing-ha
Tah-sha Ish-lah-in-ding-ga
Taing-a Kas-ka-koo-un-nee-rah
Sah-zhun-lah-ha Koo-un-nu-ah

42. Chippewyan—From M'Kenzie.

Sta-chy Al-ke-tar-hy-y
Na-ghur Al-ki-deing-hy
Tagh-y Ca-ki-na-ha-noth-na
Dengk-y Ca-noth-na
Sas-sou-la-chee

43. Chippewyan—From a woman, a native of Churchill.

Ith-lia Ting-he
Nuk-ka Sah-zun-lah-ha
Krah-ha, or tah-rha Il-ket-tah-rah

NUMERALS.

Shah-zet-te   Kah-kin-ho-en-er-nah
Il-ket-ting   Ho-en-er-nah

44. Anglo Saxon.

Aen   Six
Twe-gen, or, twa   Se-o-fou
Threo, or, thry   Eaghta
Feo-ther, or, feo-wer   Ni-gone
                            Tyn

45. Cree—From M'Kenzie.

Pey-ac   Ne-gou-ta-woe-sic
Ni-sheu   Nish-wi-o-sic
Nish-tou   Jan-na-new
Ne-way   Shack
Ni-an-nan   Mi-ta-tat

46. Algokin—From M'Kenzie.

Pe-cheik   Ni-gou-ta-wa-swois
Nije   Ni-gi-was-wois
Nis-wois   She-was-wois
Neau   Shan-gwos-wois
Na-nan   Mit-as-swois

47. Chippewyan—From a Chippewyan.

Eth-li-ah   El-kat-har-ri
Nuk-kur   Slus-ing-ding-he
Tor-ri   El-ket-ding-he
Ding-he   Kutch-e-no-ner-re
Sos-su-li-he   Ho-ner-ne-nuh

48. Winnebago—From a Winnebago.

Zhunk-kaid   Har-ker-ra
Noamp   Shar-goan
Tarn   Kad-do-unk
T'joab   Yunk-ked-joos-koon
Sarj   Ker-reb-hon-na

49. Cree—From a native.

Pe-ak   Ne-su

Nees-to	Ta-be-ko
Ne-o	E-nah-ne
Ne-ah-nun	Kam-me-tah-tat
Ning-good-waw-sik	Me-tah-tat

50. *Mahnesheet, (slow-tongues,) residing on the St. Johns, N. B. From a native.*

Na-koot	Kah-mutch-in
Tah-bo	Lo-he-gin-nuk
Sheist	O-go-mul-chin
Na-oo	Aish-ko-nah-daig
Nahn	Ko-dainsk

CHAPTER III.

MUSIC AND POETRY OF THE INDIANS.

Here, it must be acknowledged, we enter a barren field, offering little to excite industry, or to reward inquiry. Without literature to give perpetuity to the creations of genius, or to bear to succeeding times the record of remarkable events, the Americans have no store house of ancient learning to open to the curiosity of the European race. They have probably never thought like the Arabs, that the cultivation of their language was an object of importance; and though the orator must at times have experienced the effect of a happy choice of expression, he must always have been confined to a narrow range, by the necessity of keeping within the comprehension of his hearers. Hence their public speakers appear to depend more on a certain vehemence and earnestness of manner, which is intelligible without words, than upon any elegance of thought, or refinement of diction.

Their songs, whether of war or devotion, consist, for the most, of a few words or short phrases many times repeated; and in their speeches, they dwell long and vehemently on the same idea. One who hears an Indian orator without comprehending his language, would confidently suppose that his discourse abounded with meaning; but these speeches, like their tedious and monotonous chants, when clearly understood, appear so poor and jejune, that few white men would listen to either, were it not with the hope of extracting information, of which the speaker, or the singer himself, must be wholly unconscious. But after all is heard and explained, and carefully examined in all its bearings, it must be principally the business of a quick and fertile imagination, to find in them moral instruction or historical information. If we find among the American Indians traditional items, bearing manifest and strong resemblance to those of the great Asiatic family, from whom we have adopted many of our religious opinions, this can only be considered as indicating what needed no proof; namely: That this people, as well as ourselves, have descended from that primeval stock, which, planted somewhere upon the mountains of Asia, has sent forth its branches into all parts of the earth. Thither, we are taught by the most ancient human records, and by the concurrent deductions of all sound philosophy, and honest inquiry, to look for the great fountain of the human race: and if some of the streams, in descending thence, have been concealed in swamps, or sunk beneath sands, we ought not therefore to doubt that their origin is to be thence deduced. But that existing or retrieveable monuments or resemblances, will ever enable the curious satisfactorily to trace the American branch to its origin, need not now be expected. Nevertheless, this part of the subject may have interest for those who love to trace the human character through all situations and exposures, and to contemplate the effect of revolutions in external circumstances, on manners, language, and metaphysical opinions.

Sufficient evidence probably exists, to convince many, that the natives of the central regions of North America, whatever diversities of dialect may now exist, are essentially of the same race with the Peruvians, the Mexicans, and the Natchez; between whom and the ancient inhabitants of Greece and Italy, and that portion of the present population of India who worship Brama, Boudd, Ganesa, Iswara, &c. a near relationship has already been ascertained. In the metamorphoses which the Indian traditions assign to many trees, plants, animals, and other things, we are strongly reminded of the similar superstitions preserved by the Roman poets. We find, also, in the American traditions, distinct allusions to a general deluge, and to several other particulars which we are accustomed to consider as resting solely on the authority of the Mosaic history. But when we reflect on the almost universal distribution of these opinions, in some shape or other, among all known races of men, we may admit a doubt whether they have been derived from the historical books of the Hebrews, or whether they are not rather the glimmerings of that primitive light, which, at the first great division after the flood, into the families of Shem, Ham, and Japhet, and more recently at the dispersion of Babel, must have been in possession of all mankind. We find in the Mosaic history, written, as it was, long after the period here spoken of, abundant evidence, not only that traditional remembrance of the deluge, and other great events in the early history of mankind, was still preserved; but that direct revelations of the mind and will of the Creator had been, and were still made to men, at sundry times, and in divers places. Within two or three hundred years of the deluge, some knowledge of the mechanic arts, at least ship building and masonry, must have remained, or so many men would not have been found ready to undertake the erection of a tower whose top should reach *unto heaven*. At this time, Noah, the second father of mankind, and his three sons, who, as well as himself, had known the "world before the flood," were still alive. Any branch, therefore, of the family of either of the three sons of Noah, removed at this time to "the isles of the gentiles," or to whatever remote part of the earth their knowledge of navigation and other arts might enable them to reach, would retain at least a traditional cosmogony and theogony, which, after ever so many years, or ever so wide and devious a wandering, must probably have preserved resemblance, in some particulars, to the originals. Hence it will, we think, be evident, that although we may find a strong resemblance between some of the observances of the Indians and the Hebrews, we are by no means to infer, that one of these races must have descended from the other. All that they have in common, will probably be found to have grown out of similarity of circumstances; or may be traced to times long previous to the calling of Abraham.

But let us leave this profitless discussion, which has long since received more attention than it deserves, and return to the subject before us.

The poetry of the Indians, if they can properly be said to have any, is the language of excitement, and the expression of passion; and if whatever has this character, and is at the same time raised above the tone and style of ordinary conversation, and is or may be sung to music, is poetry, it cannot be denied that they have among them poetry and poets in abundance. Excitement of whatever kind, calls forth a peculiar manner of expression; and though measure and rythm, polished and artificial structure, equally balanced and harmonious periods, may be wanting, they commonly accompany the utterance of their words by some modulation of the voice, like what we call singing. In all their religious feasts and solemnities, they address their prayers and praises to superior beings in song. In all times of distress and danger, or when suffering under the apprehension of immediate starvation, or awaiting the approach of death in some more horrid form, the Indian expresses his anxiety, offers up his petition, or perhaps recals some favourite and cherished idea, his boast in life, and his consolation in death, by a measured and monotonous chant, in which the ear of the stranger distinguishes principally the frequent repetition of the same word.

Nor is it on the serious and momentous occasions of life only, that we witness these rude efforts at poetry and music. Love, in its disappointment, or in its success; sorrow, hope, and intoxication, choose the same method of utterance. When in a state of intoxication, as they often are, the men, and more particularly the women of some tribes, are heard by night, and often almost throughout the night, singing in a plaintive and melancholy tone of the death of their friends, or of other misfortunes. One who listens to these lamentations, while darkness and distance interpose to conceal the too often disgusting objects who utter them, and to soften down and mellow the tone of high pitched voices, will often find something affecting in their honest and unpremeditated complaints. Their voices are often fine, and the sentences they utter, are the language, most commonly, of real suffering, devested of affectation or art. From the great frequency with which these melancholy chantings, and the profuse flow of tears occur, as the consequences of intoxication among them, one might infer, either that their condition has in it a greater share of sorrow and of suffering than that of some other races, or that the excitement of strong drink affects them in a different manner. A fair inference, at least, is, that in their sober moments, they, like other men, wear a mask. Indeed, those who best know the Indians, are best acquainted with the constant efforts they make at concealment, and how well they at length teach the outward aspect to conceal or misrepresent the internal emotions. But for these unpremeditated effusions, particularly for the whining and drivelling of intoxication, the most enthusiastic admirer of the Indians will not claim the appellation of poetry. If any thing among them deserves this name, we must search for it among those traditionary songs which descend from father to son, and are transferred from man to man by purchase, to be used in their feasts, in the administration of remedies to the sick, and above all, in medicine hunting. That some of the songs thus preserved have considerable antiquity, we do not doubt; that they have much merit as poetical compositions, we are not disposed to assert. The poetry of the Indians, like their eloquence, requires the assistance of able translators, and those not too scrupulous to draw only from the materials of the original.

The method of delineation, by which they aid the memory in retaining and recalling, on occasion, these compositions, exhibits, perhaps, one of the earliest steps towards a written language. Yet, from its existence among them, in the present form, one would not hastily infer, that had they never been intruded upon by men of another race, learning or arts would finally have flourished among them. There are but too many evidences, that the aboriginal Americans are, by temperament, by some peculiarity of physical structure, or moral propensity, a more sluggish race, than the European; consequently, destined to a slow advance, or, perhaps, like most of the Asiatics, to be for ages stationary, or retrogradent, in the journey of improvement. We would not risk the assertion, that the Americans are an inferior race; the barrier to their improvement appears to be, that indolence which is not less a habit of their minds than of their bodies, and which disqualifies them for spontaneous and long continued and laborious thinking. Hunger may, and does, overcome the habit of bodily indolence, or, at least, sometimes interrupts it; but, in the Indian character, the tendency is always to quiescence. Instances are infinitely rare, among them, of that restlessness of mind so common in the European race, which is ever in quest of something beyond the complete gratification of the wants of the body, and which has been the true source of so many great and ennobling actions. The past history of this race of men, is not wanting in instances of the manifestation of that inherent sluggishness of disposition, which has kept them back from the knowledge, the improvements, and the civilization, which have been so long urged upon them. Let it be granted, as doubtless it should be, that the Jesuits, and, to some extent, at least the Moravian, and other protestant missionaries, commenced their labours where they should have ended them, by offering to the benighted minds of the Indians, the stupendous, and, to them, totally incomprehensible doctrines of the christian religion; and that they, in a great measure, neglected to teach them those arts, which, by ensuring an abundance of means for the sustenance of life, might enable them, first of all, to fix in settled habitations, and afterwards gradually to adopt those habits and opinions which have ever been found indispensable in preparing the wilderness for the reception of the good seed. Yet, must we not acknowledge, that the descendants of those who were early received into intimate association with the whites, and learned from them the mechanical, and all the common arts of life, are, at this time, lamentably deficient in the virtues, as well as the knowledge we might have expected from them?

It is no part of the design of these remarks, to discourage any attempts that may be made to introduce the christian religion among these people; on the contrary, we look upon these efforts as always, in a greater or less degree, useful to the Indians; they originate as well in a diffusive and amiable benevolence, as a feeling of justice, and severe, though tardy compunction, which would seek, at this late day, to render to the starved and shivering remnant of the people who received us to their country in our day of small things, some recompense for the fair inheritance which we have wrested from their forefathers. The example of the Cherokees, and some others in the south, has been sufficient to prove, that under the influence of a mild climate, and a fertile soil, these people can be taught habits of settled, if not of persevering industry. From this condition of things, we can already see how, among that people, habits of mental enterprise and industry are to spring up, and we look forward with confidence to a source of continued improvement. That all the other bands and tribes, under similar auspices, and similar influences, would pursue a similar course, cannot be doubted. Philologists and speculative theorists may divide and class as they please; to the patient and industrious observer, who has mingled intimately with this race, in the low and fertile districts of the Mississippi, in the broad and smiling plains of Arkansaw and Red River, in the forests of the Upper Mississippi, and among the pines and the mosses of the upper lakes, it will be evident that the aboriginal people of the United States Territory, are all of one family, not by physical constitution and habit only, but by the structure and temperament of their minds; their modes of thinking and acting; and, indeed, in all physical and mental peculiarities, which set them apart from the remainder of the human family, as a peculiar people. Whatever course has, in one situation, proved in any measure effectual, to reclaim them from their vague and idle habits, will certainly succeed in another situation, though perhaps more slowly, as they may be influenced by a less genial climate, or a more barren soil.

SONG FOR THE METAI, OR FOR MEDICINE HUNTING.

Fig. 1. 2. 3. 4. 5.

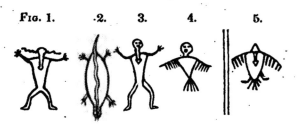

Fig. 1. Shi-e-gwuh ne-no-no-nen-dum ah-me, Me-tai we-nin-ne-wug, ne-kạu-nug ane-mub-be-un-neh.*

Now I hear it, my friends, of the Metai, who are sitting about me.

This, and the three following, are sung by the principal chief of the Metai, to the beat of his bwoin ah-keek, or drum. The lines from the sides of the head of the figure indicate hearing.

2. O-wa-nain ba-me-je-waun-ga ? Man-i-to O-ba-me-je-wa-un-ga.

Who makes this river flow? The Spirit, he makes this river flow.

The second figure is intended to represent a river, and a beaver swimming down it.

3. Ka-weh-whau-bo-me-tai, ka-weh-whau-bo-me-tai neh-kau-nuk neej-huh nish-a-nau-ba ka-ke-ka-ne-me-kwain neh-kau-nuk.

Look at me well, my friends; examine me, and let us understand that we are all companions.

This translation is by no means literal. The words express the boastful claims of a man, who sets himself up for the best and most skilful in the fraternity.

* These rude pictures are carved on a flat piece of wood, and serve to suggest to the minds of those who have learned the songs, the ideas, and their order of succession; the words are not variable, but a man must be taught them, otherwise, though from an inspection of the figure he might comprehend the idea, he would not know what to sing.

4. O-wa-nain ba-bah-mis-sa-haht, weej-huh nish-a-nau-ba? Be-nais-se-wah ba-bah-mo-sa-haht, weej-huh nish-a-nau-ba.

Who maketh to walk about, the social people? A bird maketh to walk about the social people.

By the bird, the medicine man means himself; he says, that his voice has called the people together. Weej-huh nish-a-nau-ba, or weej-a nish-a-nau-ba, seems to have the first syllable from the verb, which means, to accompany. The two lines drawn across, between this figure and the next, indicate that here the dancing is to commence.

5. Neen ba-pah-mis-sa-gahn ne-goche ah-wes-sie neen-gah-kwa-tin ah-waw.

I fly about, and if any where I see an animal, I can shoot him.

This figure of a bird, (probably an eagle or hawk,) seems intended to indicate the wakefulness of the senses, and the activity required to ensure success in hunting. The figure of the moose, which immediately follows, reminding the singer of the cunning and extreme shyness of that animal, the most difficult of all to kill.

6. 7. 8. 9.

6. Neen-go-te-naun ke-da-ne,* ne-miz-zho-taun ke-da-ne, ah-wis-sie ke-da-ne, ne-miz-zho-taun ke-da-ne.

I shoot your heart; I hit your heart, oh animal, your heart, I hit your heart.

This apostrophe is mere boasting, and is sung with much gesticulation and grimace.

7. A-zhe-nahng gwit-to iah-na ish-ko-tang a-zhe-nahng gwit-to iah-na.

I make myself look like fire.

* Ke-da-ne, ke-da, (thy heart;) but a syllable is added in singing.

This is a medicine man, disguised in the skin of a bear. The small parallelogram, under the bear, signifies fire, and they, by some composition of gunpowder, or other means, contrive to give the appearance of fire to the mouth and eyes of the bear skin, in which they go about the village late at night, bent on deeds of mischief, oftentimes of blood. We learn how mischievous are these superstitions, when we are informed, that they are the principal men of the Metai, who thus wander about the villages, in the disguise of a bear, to wreak their hatred on a sleeping rival, or their malice on an unsuspecting adversary. But the customs of the Indians require of any one who may see a medicine man on one of these excursions, to take his life immediately, and whoever does so is accounted guiltless.

8. Ga-tah e-no-tum mau-na ne-be-way me-ze-ween, ne-be-way neen-dai, gin-no-tah mau-na.

I am able to call water from above, from beneath, and from around.

Here the medicine man boasts of his power over the elements, and his ability to do injury or benefit. The segment of a circle with dots in it, represents water, and the two short lines touching the head of the figure, indicate that he can draw it to him.

9. Yah-nah-we nah-gwe-hah-ga e-nai-ne-wah, kin-ne-nah.
Yah-nah-we nah-gwe-hah-ga ma-tai-mo-sah, kin-ne-nah.
Yah-nah-we nah-gwe-hah-ga o-ba-no-sah, kin-ne-nah.

I cause to look like the dead, a man I did.
I cause to look like the dead, a woman I did.
I cause to look like the dead, a child I did.

The lines drawn across the face of this figure, indicate poverty, distress, and sickness; the person is supposed to have suffered from the displeasure of the medicine man. Such is the religion of the Indians! Its boast is to put into the hands of the devout, supernatural means, by which he may wreak vengeance on his enemies, whether weak or powerful, whether they be found among the foes of his tribe, or the people of his own village. This Metai, so much valued and revered by them, seems to be only the instrument, in the hands of the crafty, for keeping in subjection the weak and the credulous, which may readily be supposed to be the greater part of the people.

10.

10. Ain-de-aun, ain-de-aun, ne-kau-neh ; ah-wes-sie, an-wes-sie, ne-kau-neh, ne-mah-meek ko-naw-waw, ne-kau-neh.

I am such, I am such, my friends ;. any animal, any animal, my friends, I hit him right, my friends.

This boast of certain success in hunting, is another method by which he hopes to elevate himself in the estimation of his hearers. Having told them that he has the power to put them all to death, he goes on to speak of his infallible success in hunting, which will always enable him to be a valuable friend to such as are careful to secure his good will.

SONG FOR THE METAI ONLY.

Fig. 1. 2. 3.

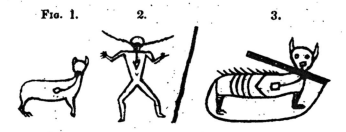

Fig. 1. Nah-ne-bah o-sa aun neen-no ne-mah-che oos-sa ya-ah-ne-no. [Twice.]
I walk about in the night time.

This first figure represents the wild cat, to whom, on account of his vigilance, the medicines for the cure of diseases were committed. The meaning probably is, that to those who have the shrewdness, the watchfulness, and intelligence of the wild cat, is entrusted the knowledge of those powerful remedies, which, in the opinion of the Indians, not only control life, and avail to the restoration of health, but give an almost unlimited power over animals and birds.

2. Neen-none-da-aun ke-to-ne-a, ma-ni-to we-un-ne.
I hear your mouth, you are an ill [or evil] spirit.

The wild cat, (or the sensible and intelligent medicine man,) is always awake; or if he seems to sleep, by means of the supernatural powers of his medicine, he becomes acquainted with all that passes around him. If one man speaks evil of another, to bring sickness upon him, the wild cat hears and knows it; but confident in his own superior strength, he disregards it. At the bar they begin to dance. The lines from the mouth of the human figure, represent the speeches of the evil minded and malicious.

3. Shi-a ne-mo-kin-nuh-we, be-zhe-wa-wah* neah-wa. [Twice.]
Now I come up out of the ground; I am wild cat.

* The sound of *b* and *p* are used indiscriminately in many words, thus: *bena*, *pena*, for the word meaning a pheasant.

I am the master of the wild cats; and having heard your talk, I come up out of the ground to see what you do. This man, it appears, claims superiority over other medicine men, and now rouses himself to attend to what is passing. The bar across the neck of the figure representing the wild cat, indicates that he is just coming out of the earth.

4. Bin-nah! neen be-zhe-wa-wah ke-meen-waw-bum-me-na.
Behold! I am wild cat; I am glad to see you all wild cats.

This figure, with open eyes and erect ears, denotes earnestness and attention. [The word ke-meen-waw-bum-me-na, affords a strong instance of what has been called the synthetic character of this language; *ke*, the inseparable pronoun, in the accusative plural, *meen*, from ne-mee-noan-dun, (I love, or am pleased,) and waw-bum from ne-waw-bo-maw, (I see.)]

5. Ne-man-i-to, o-wa-she-na a-ai-gah nee-na ketto-we goh-we-ke-na.

I am a spirit; what I have I give to you in your body.

This is the figure of a medicine man, with his pah-gah-ko-gua-un, or the instrument with which he beats his drum, in his hand. He appears to be boasting of his own powers.

6. Ah-ne ah-gah, kah-neen-na ke-taus-saw-wa-unna ke-nis-se-go-na.

Your own tongue kills you; you have too much tongue.

This is addressed to the malicious man, and the slanderer, one who speaks evil of others. His crooked and double speech goes out of his mouth, but is changed to an arrow in his hand, and turned against himself; his own body bears the marks of the injuries he would have inflicted on others. The lines across the chest are tne traces of misfortune, brought on him by the indulgence of his own malicious disposition. In the songs and addresses of some of the most esteemed chiefs, or persons, who may be considered in some measure set apart for the Metai, are many attempts to convey and enforce moral instruction, or rather the inculcation of those opinions and actions which constitute the virtues of savage life.

SONG FOR BEAVER HUNTING AND THE METAL.

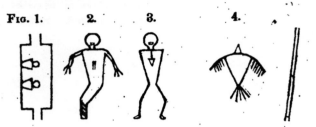

Fig. 1. O-nub-be-tum-maun, Metai-we-gaun, Manito-we-ga-un.

I sit down in the lodge of the Metai, the lodge of the Spirit.

This figure is intended to represent the area of the Metai-we-gaun, or medicine lodge, which is called also the lodge of the Manito, and two men have taken their seats in it. The matter of the song seems to be merely introductory.

2. Neezh-o-go-na we-tah-bim mah-kum-ma ne-kaun; ne-o-go-na we-tah-bim mah-kum-ma ne-ka-un.

Two days must you sit fast, my friend; four days must you sit fast, my friend.

The two perpendicular lines on the breast of this figure, are read ne-o-gone, (two days,) but are understood to mean two years; so of the four lines drawn obliquely across the legs, these are four years. The heart must be given to this business for two years, and the constrained attitude of the legs indicates the rigid attention, and serious consideration, which the subject requires.

3. Wha-be-nia, Meen-de-mo-sah, ke-ko-nia wha-be-nia.

Throw off, woman, thy garments, throw off.

The power of their medicines, and the incantations of the Metai, are not confined in their effect to animals of the chase, to the lives and the health of men; they control, also, the minds of all, and overcome the modesty, as well as the antipathies of women. The Indians firmly believe that many a woman, who has been unsuccessfully solicited by a man, is not only, by the power of the Metai, made to yield, but even, in a state of madness,

MUSIC AND POETRY. 349

to tear off her garments, and pursue after the man she before despised. These charms have greater power than those in the times of superstition among the English, ascribed to the fairies, and they need not, like the plant used by Puck, be applied to the person of the unfortunate being who is to be transformed; they operate at a distance, through the medium of the Miz-zin-ne-neens.

4. Na-wy-o-kun-ne-nah wun-nah he-nun-ne-wah ba-mo-sa keen-nah-na.

Who makes the people walk about? It is I that calls you.

This is in praise of the virtue of hospitality, that man being most esteemed among them, who most frequently calls his neighbours to his feast.

5.   6.   7.   8.   9.

5. He-o-win-nah ha-ne-mo-we-tah neen-ge-te-mah-hah bo-che-ga-ha-ne Mo-e-tah neen-ge-te-mah hah-nah.

Any thing I can shoot with it, (this medicine,) even a dog I can kill with it.

6. Nin-goo-te-naun ke-ta-he, e-nah-ne-wah ke-ta-he.

I shoot thy heart, man, thy heart.

He means, perhaps, a buck moose by the word e-nah-ne-wah, or man.

7. Neen ne-na-sah waw-be-maung neen-ne-na-sah.

I can kill a white loon, I can kill.

The white loon, *rara avis nigroque simillino cygno*, is certainly a rare and most difficult bird to kill; so we may infer, that this boaster can kill any thing, which is the amount of the meaning intended in that part of his song, recorded by the five last figures. Success in hunting they look upon as a virtue of a higher character, if we may judge from this song, than the patience under suffering, or the rakishness among women, or even the hospitality recommended in the former part.

8. Ne-kau-nah-ga. * * *

My friends. * * *

This seems to be an attempt to delineate a man sitting with his hands raised to address his friends; but the remainder of his speech is not remembered. This is sufficient to show that the meaning of the characters in this kind of picture writing, is not well settled, and requires a traditional interpretation, to render it intelligible.

9. Shah-bwo-ah-hah-mah ne-mow-why-waw-ne-no ah-buh-hah-mah ge-we-na-she-mah-ga.

I open my wolf skin, and the death struggle must follow.

This is a wolf skin, used as a medicine bag, and he boasts, that whenever he opens it, something must die in consequence.

SONG FOR MEDICINE HUNTING—RARELY FOR THE METAI.

Fig. 1. 2. 3. 4. 5. 6. 7. 8.

Fig. 1. Waw-ne-ge-ah-na gah-ne-geah-na Manito-wah-ga gah-ge-zhe-hah-gwaw gah-ne-ge-ah-na.

I wished to be born, I was born, and after I was born I made all spirits.

2. Gee-she-hah-ga manito-whah-ga.

I created the spirits.

The figures in the commencement of this long and much esteemed religious song, represent Na-na-bush, the intercessor, the nephew of mankind. They seem designed to carry back the thoughts towards the beginning of time, and have a manifest allusion to a period when this mysterious and powerful being exercised a wish to assume the form of a man. In the second figure he is represented as holding a rattle snake in his hand, and he calls himself the creator of the mani-toge. The Indians calling invisible and spiritual beings by the same name which they give to the lowest class of reptiles, it is doubtful whether Na-na-bush here claims to have created intelligences superior to man, or only reptiles, insects, and other small creatures, which they commonly call Mani-toag.

3. Na-hah-be-ah-na na-nah-boo-shoo, o-tish-ko-tahn ma-jhe-ke-sha.

He sat down Na-na-bush; his fire burns forever

This figure appears to be descriptive of the first assumption by Na-na-bush of his office, as the friend and patron of men. He is represented as taking a seat on the ground. Fire, with the northern Indians, is the emblem of peace, happiness, and abundance. When one band goes against another, they go, according to their language, to put out the fire of their enemies; therefore, it is probable that in speaking of the perpetual fire of Na-na-bush, it is only intended to allude to his great power, and the permanence of his independence and happiness.*

* In the sitting figures of Na-na-bush, as rudely delineated by the Indians, there is some resemblance to the Asiatic *Iswara*, or *Satyavrata*, who, in the eastern mythology, is connected with one of their deluges. Like Noah, like Saturn, and like Iswara, Na-na-bush preserved, during the inundation, those animals and plants, which were afterwards to be useful to mankind; and his addresses to the animals, which the Indians often repeat, remind us of the age when one language was common to men and brutes. (Tooke's Pantheon, p. 118. Am. ed.) It is true, that, like the Ovidian Deucalion, Na-na-bush reproduced men, the old stock having been entirely destroyed; but it is to be remembered, that any resemblance, however strong, between these traditions, have had ample time to be obliterated. Instead of complaining that the similarity in the opinions of these people to ancient fables, is no stronger, we ought, perhaps, to be surprised that any resemblance exists. If any one would attempt a comparison between the opinions of the Americans and the Pagans of former ages, or of any other race, he should bear in mind how vague and mutable must be all such traditions, in an unwritten language. He must not be surprised to find, on close examination, that the characters of all pagan deities, male and female, melt into each other, and, at last, into one or two, for it seems a well founded opinion, that the whole crowd of gods and goddesses of ancient *Rome*, the modern *Váránes* of the east, and *Mani-toag* of the west, mean, originally, only the powers of nature, and principally those of the sun, expressed in a variety of ways, and by a number of fanciful names. (Asiatic Researches, Vol. I. p. 267, Lond. ed.)

The resemblance between the Algonkin deity, (Na-na-bush,) and Saturn and *Satyavrata*, or *Iswara*, of the Sanscrit, may be farther traced in each being figured with a serpent, sometimes held in the hand, and in other instances, as in many of the Roman figures of Saturn, in the mouth. This resemblance is, perhaps, the more worthy of remark, as the Americans seem not to have retained any very satisfactory explanation of this circumstance.

It will not be supposed that these vague resemblances in religious opinions, if they may be so called, afford the means of tracing the American tribes to their origin. That these people have customs and opinions closely resembling those of the Asiatics, particularly of the Hebrews, previous to the christian dispensation, will not be denied; but the final result of all inquiries into this subject will, perhaps, be the adoption of the opinion of *Bryant*, of Sir *William Jones*, and other men of profound research, that Egyptians, Greeks, and Italians, Persians, Ethiopians, Phenecians, Celts, and Tuscans, proceeded, originally, from one central place, and that the same people carried their religion and sciences into Chi-

4. Tah-gwa ne-mah-go-so-me-go, ne-ah-ge-zhe-we ne-kaun, ne-kaun.

Notwithstanding you speak evil of me, from above are my friends, my friends.

The fourth figure, which, in the original, is a priapus, indicates that a man takes up the discourse. The circle about his head but descending no lower than his shoulders, shows that his help and his protection are from above, and in the strength thus derived he is able to defy those who speak evil of him, or seek, by the power of their medicines, to break his life.

5. Chaw-gaw ko-no mau-na se-maun-duk waw-wan-o-sa-wah.

I can use many kinds of wood to make a bear unable to walk.

The business of hunting is one of the first importance to the Indians, consequently, it finds a place in his devotions; indeed, devotion itself having apparently no object beyond the wants and weaknesses of this life, relief in times of hunger, is one of the most important blessings they ever ask for in their prayers. Accordingly, their young men are directed never to use these songs, or to have recourse to the medicine hunt, except in times of the extremest need.

6. Ke-te-na-ne-me-na we-nis-ze-bug-go-na an-no-kau-tum-mau-na, ke-te-na-ne-me-na.

Of you I think, that you use the We-nis-ze-bug-gone, I think this of you.

The common spicy wintergreen, a stalk of which this figure is intended to represent, is much valued as a medicine by the Indians. It is called *we-nis-se-bug-goon*, from *we-ne-sik*, the spicy birch, and *bug-goon*, which in composition means leaf.

---

na and Japan, to Mexico and Peru, and, we may add, to the banks of the Mississippi, and the coasts of Hudson's Bay.

Some of the arguments adduced in support of the favourite opinion, that the American tribes are the long lost remnant of the children of Israel, certainly require no answer. An intimate acquaintance with many languages is now so widely diffused, as to supercede the necessity of remarking, or of proving, that a strong similarity in the sound of some few words of different languages, even though they should be found similar in meaning, does not establish the fact of community of origin; and the wide dissimilarity between the American and the Hebrew, and its cognate dialects, in the one particular, of the compounding of words, is probably, to the learned, conclusive proof that our tribes are, in no sort, derived from the Hebrew stock.

7. Ma-mo-yah-na, mis-kwe, ma-mo-yah-na.

That which I take [is] blood, that which I take.

Here is the figure of a bear lying dead on the ground, and a hand is thrust into the body, to take out some of the blood. The instruction communicated probably is, that when the prayers offered in the preparation for the medicine hunt, have been answered, and an animal killed, offerings should be immediately made, by taking some of the blood in the hand, and pouring it on the ground; or, as is more commonly done, by throwing a handful of it towards each of the four cardinal points.

8. Hi-a-gwo ne-ma-nah-ho-gahn nah-we-he-a! whe-e-ya!

Now I have something to eat.

The two last words seem to have no very definite meaning; they are repeated at the end of some of the sentences, apparently only to lengthen out the sound. This figure is that of a lean and hungry man, who, having asked for food, has been heard, and is now proceeding to allay his hunger.

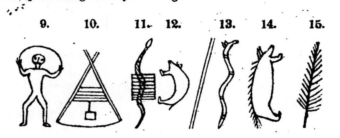

9. We-wah-kwa be-gah-na mani-to-ga.

I cover my head, sitting down to sleep, ye spirits.

The figure is that of a man, probably designed to be represented in a recumbent position, and drawing his blanket over him. His prayer having been answered, his wants supplied, he declares to the spirits his intention to take repose.

10. Moosh-kin a-guh-wah man-i-to-whah, whah-he-yah! whe-ha-ya! &c.

I fill my kettle for the spirit.

This is the hunter's lodge, and the kettle hanging in it contains the heart of the animal killed in the medicine hunt, of which none but a man and a hunter must venture to taste. Should a woman or a dog even touch this heart, or the blood of the animal, sudden death, or lingering sickness, would follow it. This effect, as well as the dark colour which the Indians say the skin of the females assumes, in instances of the violation of this rule, they attribute to the effect of the medicine applied by the hunter to the heart of the Me-ze-nin-ne-shah. They point out instances of women, formerly distinguished among them for beauty, and particularly for the fairness of the skin, who, by eating of the heart, or touching the blood of an animal killed in medicine hunting, have not only lost that enviable distinction, but have become disgusting and frightful objects, the skin being blackened and covered with ulcers.

11. Nah-nah-wa-kum-me-ga wa-nuk-ke-she nah-neh keen-o-wah man-i-to-whah.

Long ago, in the old time, since I laid myself down, ye are spirits.

This is the figure of a snake running over the ground ç but some are of opinion that the delineation should be different, namely, an old woman lying down in the middle of the ground. A new speaker is here introduced, which is the mythological personage called Me-suk-kum-me-go-kwa, the grand mother of mankind, to whom Na-na-bush gave in keeping, for the use of his uncles and aunts, all roots and plants, and other medicines, derived from the earth. She received, at the same time, especial direction never to leave home, and always to surrender to men the treasures deposited in her bosom, when they should be, in a suitable manner, demanded of her. Hence it is, that the medicine men make an address to Me-suk-kum-me-go-kwa, whenever they take any thing from the earth, which is to be used as medicine.

12. Ne-mo-kin-nen-naun she-maun-duk kwun-ne-no nuh-pe-mo-ke-ne-naun.

I open you for a bear, I open you.

Me-suk-kum-me-go-kwa speaks to one of the medicines whose power she had just acknowledged, by calling them spirits, and says, I disclose, or reveal you for a bear, or to enable the hunter to kill a bear.

13. Me-too-ga man-i-to-too-ga, heo-yeo-yah-yoh! he-ge-tah-waw-kum-me-ga wy-oan do-sa-jeek me-to-ga-nah, *whe-i-ah! whe-i-ah!*

That is a Spirit which comes both from above and below. [Here they begin to dance.]

14. Whain-je-neen-da su-mah-ga chah-ge-mah-ni-to-whah-ga. [Twice.]

Neen-nis-sah ween-neen-dah so-mah-we-neen-nah chah-ga-to man-i-to whah-ga, *yah-we-he-ya! whe-ge-a!* [Twice.]

I am he that giveth success, because all spirits help me.

15. Me-ge-ne-nah me-ge-ne-nah me-gwun-nah-ga me-ge-ne-nah, *whe-he-ya!* [Twice.]

The feather, the feather; it is the thing, the feather.

It sometimes happens that the hunter has wandered far from his lodge, and has neither birch bark on which to delineate his Me-zen-ne-neens, nor o-num-nu, or other powerful medicine, to apply to its heart. In these cases he takes some of the ashes of his fire, and spreading it on a smooth place, he traces in it the figure of the animal; he then takes a feather and sticks it in the heart, then applies fire until it is consumed to the surface of the ashes, and on this he places the same reliance as on the more common method of treating the Me-zen-ne-neens.

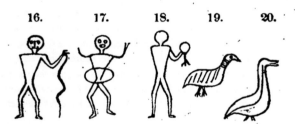

16. 17. 18. 19. 20.

16. Wha o-man-i-to-whah? *he-ah-e-whe-ya!* ma-she-ge-na pe-po-sa-jeek wha-in-je man-i-to-whah, ah-keeng pa-mo-sah *hah-he-whe-ya!*

Who is a spirit? He that walketh with the serpent, walking on the ground; he is a spirit.

This figure is nearly the same as is given to Na-na-bush, in the beginning of the song, and an allusion is probably intended to the time when this interpreter between mankind and the Supreme Spirit, the Creator of all things, was driven from the presence of his father, to dwell with the meanest things of this world.

The allusions in the traditionary fables of the Algonkins, to the quarrel between Na-na-bush and the Great Spirit, are frequent, and cannot fail to remind any one of the most important of the doctrines of the christian religion. It can scarce be doubted that, from some source or other, these people have derived some obscure conceptions of the incarnation and mediatorial office of the second person in the Divine Trinity.*

* In Mr. M'Kenney's "Tour to the Lakes," p. 202, 205, some account is given of *Na-na-bou-jou*, and the renovation of the earth after the deluge, which agrees, in most particulars, very closely with the traditions among the Ottawwaws and Menomonies. But these last relate it with the following addition: " When the earth, which was found in the claws and in the mouth of the muskrat, began to expand itself upon the surface of the water, Na-na-bou-jou sat, day after day, watching its enlargement. When he was no longer able to see the extent of it, he sent out a wolf, and told him to run round all the ground, and then return to him, that he might thus know how large it had become. The wolf was absent only a short time, and returned. After sometime he sent him out the second time, with similar directions, and he was gone two years. Again, after this, he sent him out, and he returned no more. Then Na-na-bou-jou gave the animals, all of whom he called Ne-she-mah, (my younger brother,) each his own peculiar kind of food. He also told such of them as were to be for food for men, that he had given them to his uncles, and they must expect, from time to time, to be hunted and killed; he also enjoined it upon them, that as long as men should choose a speedy and merciful method of killing them, they should make no resistance; but, in cases of wanton and cruel injury, they might turn to resist.".

It is also to be observed, that this renovation of the earth is clearly distinguished, in the traditions of the Ottawwaws, from the original creation, which was long previous. How much of the instructions of the Jesuits, and of other whites, may now be combined in these legends, it is difficult to say. But they relate that men, before the flood, though they had been long before upright and good, had now become exceedingly degenerate; but they do not assign this as the cause for which the deluge was brought upon the earth. They say that the younger brother of Na-na-bou-jou was slain by the Great Spirit, the father of both, and it was in grief and in anger that Na-na-bou-jou himself caused the earth to be overwhelmed. To so great an extent did he carry his resentment against the Great Spirit, and the other Spirits, that they, with the hope of appeasing him, restored his brother to life. But Na-na-bou-jou said, "No, my brother, this cannot be, that any should die and come again to live here as before; return again to the place to which they had sent you; it is there that many of my uncles and aunts must come every year. You shall be the friend and the protector of those, as I am of the living, who are here on this earth." He returned accordingly, and it is this brother of Na-na-bou-jou, who is now spoken of as NING-GAH-BE-AR-NONG MAN-I-TO, (the western god,) though this is not his name, by which he was known to his brother. He is the god of the country of the dead, the towns of the Je-bi-ug, which are always towards the setting sun.

17. He-ah gut-tah wees-sene, wun-no-kwa neen-nah neen-de-kwa-wug-ge-ga ween-dum mah-wah neen-nah-hah neen-nah whe-he-ya!

Now they will eat something, my women; now I tell them they will eat.

This figure, with open mouth and distended belly, seems to speak the language of human thanksgiving, and gratitude for favours conferred by a superior power.

18. O-num-mun-nah nin-go-che-we-nah. [Twice.]

This yellow ochre, I will try it.

The o-num-mun, a yellowish earth, which they find in many places, and which is particularly abundant on one of the branches of the Illinois River, thence called O-num-mun-ne See-be, when roasted in the fire, becomes red, and is a medicine to which they attribute great power. It is a little sack of this which is disproportionately represented in the hand of the figure.

19. Yah-hah nin-go-che-we-nah whe-he-ya-ha! be-nais-se-waw yah-hah nin-go-tin-non-gay nin-go-che-hah-hah, yah-hah nin-go-te-non-ga.

Now I wish to try my bird; sometimes I used to try, and sometimes it used to be something.

The figure is that of a bird's skin, in which his medicine is contained, and it is that, and not the skin itself, he wishes to try.

20. Ah-wes-sie nees-sah neen-no, ka-she-e-way ke-kaun-ne-nah; ah-wis-sie nees-sah neen-no, whe-he-ya! he-whe-ya!

I can kill any animal, because the loud-speaking thunder helps me; I can kill any animal.

This large bird, whose open mouth indicates the power of his voice, is not one who inhabits the earth, or is ever seen; he lives in the clouds, and his voice is the thunder. He is more commonly called a-nim-me-kee, but here ke-kaun; our loud sounding medicine is strong to give us wind or rain, or whatever state of the air may be needful to ensure success in the hunt.

MUSIC AND POETRY.

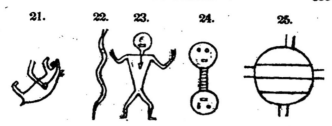

21.   22.   23.   24.   25.

21. Mah-mo-yah-na hah-che-maun-duk hah-yo-ta-he mah-mo-yah-na.

I take a bear, his heart I take.

The allusion is here to the observances respecting the heart and blood of animals killed in medicine hunting, and the sacrifices to be made in the event of success.

22. O-she-she-gwa-waw tun-wa-we-tun-ga neen-dah buh-zheen-ga tun-wa-we-tun-ga, whe-he-ya!

A rattle snake makes a noise on the poles of my lodge; he makes a noise.

The jealousy of rival hunters is a frequent cause of quarrels and troubles among the Indians. This man boasts that the rattle snake, which always gives notice when danger is near, is on the poles of his lodge, and no evil can come near him without his being informed of it. His life is guarded by a superior power, and he fears not what his enemies can do to him.

23. O-shaw-wah-no nah-o-bah-guh-he gun-nun-na, ho-kah-mik a-no-gweh, whe-he-ya! Neen-da-bwa-wa se-to nah-na, whe-he! ya-ha!

To a Shawnee, the four sticks used in this song belonged. When struck together they were heard all over the country.

This is the figure of a man holding in his left hand the four nah-o-bah-e-gun-nun, or sticks, on which this song was recorded, and the authorship is claimed by a Shawnee, from whom the Ojibbeways acknowledge to have received it; and here, it is probable, the performance originally concluded. The remaining figures appear to have been added from other songs.

24. Hi-ah shah-we mah-mo-ke-ah-na Man-i-to ne-whaw-baw-maw ah-mik-kwug ne-whaw-baw-maig, whe-ha-ya!

I come up from below; I come down from above; I see the spirit; I see beavers.

The design of this figure is to suggest to the mind, that the spirit, to whom the prayers in the medicine hunting are addressed, not only knows where animals are on the surface of the ground, but that so great is his power, he can create them where they did not before exist, to supply the wants of those that pray unto him, and can cause them to come up out of the earth.

25. We-waw-bun o-kah-tawn neen-gah-beah no-kwa-nah we-waw-bun o-kah-tawn, we-he-ha-ya!

I can make an east wind come and pass over the ground.

This is sung four times, the north, the west, and the south winds being each, in turn, substituted for the east wind here spoken of. The meaning is, that the spirit has power to give a wind in any direction that may be necessary for the success of the hunter; that he controls all the changes of the atmosphere, and will overrule them in such a manner as to ensure the success of those whose medicine is strong; in other words, whose prayer is effectual. They must therefore neither regard the wind nor the sky, but go forward in confidence of success. The idea of the circle in this figure, into which the winds are represented as rushing, is derived from the apparent form of the visible horizon; the Indians neither know, nor will they believe that the form of the earth is globular.

26.   27.

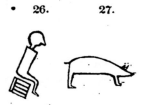

26. Na-nah nub-be-gah-ne-na ha-ge-tah wah-kum-me-ga uk-ke-ko-no-dah go-na, neen-na-nah nah-be-yahn-ne-na, ke-na-nah nub-be-ah neen-na, whe-he-yah! we-he-ya!

Thus have I sat down, and the earth above and below has listened to me sitting here.

This is again the figure of Na-na-bush, sitting on the earth, in the same attitude in which he is represented in the first part of the performance. The meaning is, that all who join in these devotional exercises must, throughout their continuance, which is for the greater part of the night, retain immoveably the same attitude, and give a serious attention to the performer, who must observe the same rule; and when all is finished, he, without uttering a word to any of those about him, rises and walks out of the lodge.

27. Pa-mo-ta-yah-na che-maun duh-kwa pa-mo-ta-yah-ga, whe-he-ya-ha!

I make to crawl, a bear, I make to crawl.

Probably the meaning is, that by these observances, and by this prayer, the hunter may cause to crawl [kill] a bear, or any animal. It is to be observed, that a bear is never, in these songs, called by the common name, but always che-mahn-duk.

It requires two years of attentive study, in the intervals of leisure that occur in the life of a hunter, to learn this song, and he must pay his instructor the value of many beaver skins. It was first introduced into the band to which Mr. Tanner belonged, by an Ojibbeway of the village of Was-waw-gun-nink. Our narrator, as well as his foster brother, Wa-me-gon-a-biew, had paid this man, whose name was Ke-zha-shoosh, great sums for his medicines, and it was a quarrel originating in this subject, which ended in his assassination by Wa-me-gon-a-biew, as related in the preceding narrative. The Ojibbeways of Red River relate, and *some of them believe*, that very wonderful effects have been produced by this song, and the medicine belonging to it, such as, that after using it for four days one man succeeded in bringing a live moose into the midst of the village at Was-waw-gun-nink in such a state of fatuity, that he made, though uninjured, no effort to escape. These extravagant fables remind us of the powers attributed by the ancients to the music of Orpheus, and others of the earliest poets.

One of the established customs of the Indians, in relation to hunting, though not immediately connected with the subject of the preceding song, may be here mentioned. As in the case of many other customs, its origin is unknown, but its tendency seems to be to encourage the spirit of generous hospitality, and to render the proceeds of the chase the common property of the band to which the hunter belongs. The custom is, that if any man, in returning from his hunt, no matter how long and laborious it may have been, or how great may be the necessities of his own family, meet another just starting out to hunt, or even a little boy walking from the camp or village, he is bound to throw down at his feet, and give him whatever he may have brought. It is partly to avoid the effect of this custom, that the men oftentimes leave their game on the spot where they killed it, and the women are sent to bring in the meat. In other instances the hunter carries the animal on his back as far as he thinks he can without the risk of meeting men, then conceals it, and goes home. No difference is said to be made when game is taken which is not needed in the village for food; beavers, otters, martins, or whatever the hunter may have taken, he is expected to relinquish to the person who meets him.

ISWARA *of India, the* SATURN *of Italy, the* NANABUSH *of the Algonkins.*

[*See Asiatic Researches, Vol.* I. *p.* 249.]

SONG FOR THE MEDICINE HUNTING, PARTICULARLY FOR BEAVERS.

Fig. 1.   2.   3.   4.

Fig. 1. Che-mahn-duk-kwa ne-muh-kwi-o-sa ne-ah-hah-wa, ne-an-hah-wa, ne-muh-kwi-o-sa, *he-ah-whe-he-ah!*

A bear, I walk like a bear myself; myself, I walk like a bear.

The medicine man here speaks in his disguise of a bear skin. Ne-muh-kwi-o-sa might be more literally translated "I walk a bear;" it is the compound of neen-muk-kwaw and pa-pah-mo-sa, or ba-bah-mo-sa. Che-mahn-duk is commonly used, in these songs, for a bear.

2. Ah-wes-sie hi-ah-wa-nah bah-twa-we-tahng-gah? Waw-wash-kesh e-wah bah-twa-we-tahng-gah.

A beast, what beast comes calling? It is a deer comes calling.

The word bah-twa-we-tahng-gah is expressive not only of the peculiar call of the male deer, at the rutting season, but also of the circumstance that the animal is approaching the speaker: were he going the other way, or even standing still, the word would be different.

3. O-num-mun-nah nin-go-che-we-nah. [Twice.]

This yellow ochre, I will try it.

This is the same, in all respects, as No. 18, in the preceding song to Na-na-bush.

4. Wun-ne ho-i-yahn, wun-ne ho-i-ah-na nah-we-he-a he-o-ge-mah-wah ka-be-waw-bum-me-kwain wun-ne-hoi-yah nah-we-ne-a.

I disguise myself to cheat you, so that only a chief, if he sees me, can know who I am.

The hunter, to deceive the animal he wishes to kill, puts on the dress of a white man, or assumes the appearance of some harmless creature, and he boasts that his disguise is so perfect as to deceive any but a chief medicine man, or a great hunter. It should be remembered, that the language of these songs is commonly that of distant allusion, rather than direct figure; hence, though the words may seem unmeaning to us, they always convey much signification to the Indians. Thus, in this instance, though the hunter says he puts on the appearance of a white man, it is probable he means that he disguises himself as a bear, or some other animal, equally harmless with a man who wears a hat, or a white man. That the Indians should think little of the white man's skill in hunting, is by no means surprising.

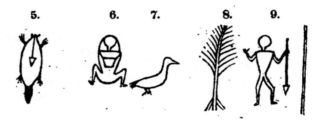

5. I-ah-ne-wah-ho go-mo-yaun, i-ah-ne-wah-ho go-mo-yaun? i-am-mik-gung-ga-nah; i-ah-ne-wah-ho go-mo-yaun.

Can any one remain longer under water than me? I am beaver, and I can remain longer than any under water.

This language, descriptive of the difficulties in taking beaver, is put into the mouth of the animal himself.

6. I-an-we-be-ah-ne ne-hub-be-ah-na be-ah-na. [Many times repeated.]

I am well loaded; I sit down to rest; I am loaded.

The hunter hears, but he regards not the boasting language of the beaver. The evidence of his skill and success is on his back, suspended by a strap passing round his forehead; and to signify that his load is heavy, he sits down to rest.

7. Mah-mo-ke-hea hi-ah-maung-wug-e-he-a man-i-to-we-he-tah.

He must come up, even the loon, though he is Manito.

This is another answer of the hunter to the boast of the beaver. Are you a greater diver than the loon? Yet even he must rise to the surface after a certain time. The country of the Ojibbeways abounding in small lakes, which sometimes lie very near each other, without any visible communication, they have taken up the idea that communications exist under ground, and they believe a loon can dive down in one, and come up in another of them. They think, also, that the beaver can carry down so much air entangled in his coat, that if left undisturbed at the bottom, he can thrust his nose into his fur, and breathe for some time.

8. Whe-gah ween-ah-waw sah-ge-mah-tik-o-waw, hio-ge-mah-waw, sah-ge-mah-tik-o-waw.

I can cut down that chief tree, though it be the tree of a chief.

The beaver says he can cut down any tree. Though a great hunter, and a man of medicine, may claim the tree, though he may have placed it there, the beaver can cut it down. Sah-gem-ah-tik reminds us of the word Sa-chem, derived from some of the eastern dialects of the Algonkin.

9. Neen-dah no-je-ah we-ah-wing man-i-to-we-tah we-ah-wing, &c.

Though he is Manito, I can work to take his body.

This is the hunter, cutting open the ice, or breaking up the beaver's lodge, in pursuit of him. [At the bar they begin to dance.]

10. 11. 12. 13. 14.

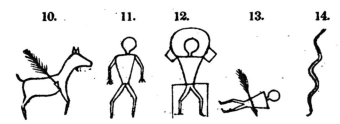

10. N'whe-go-tin-no-waw a-zhe-un-na chaw-gaw-wais-sie a-zhe-un-na.

I would shoot, as you told me, any animal; as you told me.

This is addressed to Na-na-bush, and the hunter professes his desire to follow his advice in every thing, that he may be assured success in hunting. Na-na-bush is particularly the hunter's god, and from him his best skill is derived.

11. Neen n'buh-we-hah he-na-ne-whaw, na-ne-buh-we-hah.
Neen n'buh-we-hah meen-da-mo-sah, na-ne-buh-we-hah.

I make to stand, a man, I make him stand.

The words e-na-ne-wah and meen-da-mo-sah, mean here the male or female of the animals hunted; and as, at some seasons, only the males are fat, and at others only the females, the one line or the other is sung first, according to the season. The word n'buh-we-hah is more commonly spoken, particularly by the Mississippi Indians, n'po-we-ah.

12. Ne-ah-wa een-da-be-to-na ne-ah-how.

Myself, I do good to myself.

It is certainly politic for the medicine men, who receive extravagant fees not only for teaching their songs, but for the medicines used conjointly with them, to remind their employers that all the expenditures they make are not unavailing. Here, then, is a figure which seems to be that of a female, covered profusely with the clothing purchased from the proceeds of the medicine hunts; over the head of the figure are blankets and cloth, and around the waist is suspended an ample garment, belonging to a woman.

13. Ne-kaun-naw nin-go-che-hah ne-kaun-naw.

My friends, I will try, my friends.

Prosperity, as among other men, leads to insolence and the abuse of power. This man, who, in imagination, has been successful in his pursuits, whose medicine has made him rich, and clothed his family, now proposes to turn its power against his fellows. The victim of his malice lies on the ground, transfixed with an enormous arrow.

14. Na-wi-ahn, na-wi-ah-na, o-ho-o wun-nah he-na-ne-waw we-gah-be-waw bum-me-kwi-a-ne.

A moccasin snake; a moccasin snake's skin is my medicine bag; let any man come to see me that will.

If any man is jealous of my success in hunting, let him know that a moccasin snake skin is my medicine bag; let him know that he cannot, without danger, come in my way.

15.   16.   17.   18.   19. 20.   21.

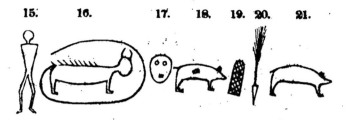

15. Ne-ah-we-na, ne-ah-we-na, waw-bun-dum-mo a-zhe-nah-gwuk ne-ah-we-na.

Myself, myself, behold me, and see that I look like myself.

This is some great medicine man, probably the author of the song, who shows himself to the people.

16. Che-be-gau-ze-naung gwit-to-i-ah-na maun-dah-ween ah-kee-ge neen-wa-nah gua-kwaik ke-nah gwit-to-i-ah-na.

I come to change the appearance of the ground, this ground; I make it look different in each season.

This is a Manito, who, on account of his immensity of tail, and other peculiarities, has no prototype. He claims to be the ruler over the seasons. He is probably Gitche-a-nah-mi-e-be-zhew, (great under-ground wild cat.)

17. Ka-whaw-bum-me-ta he-ah ne-haun-na che-mo-ke-ah-na he-ah ne-haun-na.

You may see me, my friends; I have risen, my friends.

This is the Manito of the ground, who puts only his head above the surface to speak; but in this figure his horns are omitted, perhaps by mistake.

18. Muk-ko-we-tah-wa neen-dah-nees-sah e-kwuh-e-tah-wa.

Were he a bear, I could kill him, were he a louse.

Thus aided by the Manito of the seasons, or of the weather, and by him of the ground, as is expressed by the two preceding figures, the hunter says he could find and kill whatever was a bear, though it were no bigger than a louse. The figure is that of a bear, with a louse on it.

19. O-ta-nuh we-yo che-mahn-duk o-ta-nuh-we-yo.

His tongue, a bear, his tongue.

The tongue, like the heart and blood in the other song, is now to be kept from the profane touch of a woman or a dog.

20. Man-i-to uh-we-she-nah-na io-kun-na man-i-to we-she-nah-na.

A spirit is what I use; a spirit do thou use.

The speaker, in this instance, is Na-na-bush, who gave mankind an arrow; that is, all those arms which give man dominion over the brutes. He used these things before us, and we must use them agreeably to his instruction and example.

21. We-ah-hah muk-ko-we-e-tah yah nah-mah kummig, ain-dah-zheesh she-no-gwain muh-ko-we-tah.

Although it were a bear concealed under the ground, I could find him.

Thus aided by the Manitoag, and armed with the weapons of Na-na-bush, what animal shall be able to escape from the hunter!

MEDICINE SONG, FOR HUNTING, AND SOMETIMES FOR MAKING LOVE.

Fig. 1.   2.   3.   4.

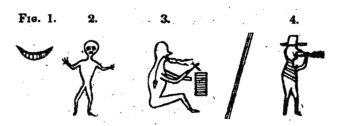

Fig. 1. Neen-nah-hah ah-ne-an-do-gwain ga-no-zei wain-je man-i-to whe-gwain, we-hi-yah, we-he-ya!

What I know not makes ga-no-zhe (the long moon) Manito.

One of the winter moons, commonly called Gitche-manito-o-gee-zis, (the Great Spirit's moon,) which corresponds to our month January, is considered particularly favourable for hunting. Children born in that month are reckoned long lived.

2. He-ah neen-gwi-o-ho o-ho man-i-to-we-tah-hah gah-neen-gwi-o we-i-ah-nah we-he-a!

My painting, that makes me a Manito.

One of the particular kinds of medicine to be used with this song, is mixed with o-num-un, and used in painting the face. The Indians attribute to it the greatest efficacy in giving immediate success; but many of them fear to use it, from a belief that it will have an injurious effect on them after death. A man who has used it will, they say, in the country to which we go after death, have no flesh upon those parts of his face where the medicine has touched. It is rare to observe, among the Indians, any ideas which would lead to the belief, that they look upon a future state as one of retribution. The innocent are those who fail to reach the villages of the dead; and the unfortunate are those who, when they arrive there, are distinguished from others, by being compelled to dance on their heads. As might be expected from a people in such profound ignorance, it is not to those actions which are pernicious to happiness, and the true well being of the society, or the individual here, that the idea of future punishment is attached.

3. [The words belonging to this figure are lost. He seems to be beating the Me-tig-waw-keek, or metai drum, and is doubtless boasting of his great medicine.]

4. Yah-hah-ween-gah we-ah-hah ye-hi-ah-yah we-he-a? yah-hah o-ge-mah-waw goan-dum-mo-nah o-ge-mah-waw.

I am able to make a chief swallow an arrow.

This has allusion to the thrusting of arrows, and similar instruments, into the stomach, by the medicine men. The words are put, perhaps, into the mouth of the medicine. Tricks of this kind are often exhibited in the Metai, as well as several miserable sleight of hand tricks, which all the initiated, at least, seem willing to look upon as miracles. A common performance is that of suffering one's self to be shot at with a marked bullet, which had previously been shown to all the persons sitting in the lodge. The medicine man stands at one end of the lodge, with a small wooden bowl in his hand, and his companion, after having exhibited the bullet, loads the gun in the sight of all present; then dancing and singing backwards and forwards, discharges the piece, apparently at the head, but taking particular care not to hit him. As soon as the smoke is dispersed, the one who had stood to receive the fire is seen with a ball in his dish, marked accurately like the one which had been put in the gun. With this he dances, exulting and shouting, three or four times around the lodge. Other tricks are played with little puppets of wood and feathers moved by strings, but kept concealed in sacks, or otherwise. Many of these things, too childish and trifling to be minutely described, are the standing wonders of the boasted ceremonies of the Metai, or grand medicine, the principal religious ceremony of the Indians.

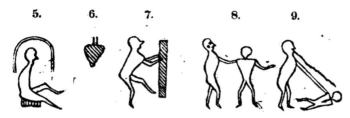

5. Wuh-we-kwa-be-yah neen-na neen-go-che meen-da-mo-sah nei-an dun-nub be-ah-neen-na.

I cover over myself, sitting down in a secret place with a woman.

6. Hug-ge-ta a-a-ho ke-ta-nee-na ke-ta-nee-na.

I speak of your heart; [to a moose.]

7. Do-je-teem mam-mo-e-yahn ween-e-se mam-mo-e-yahn o-nah-ge-che mam-mo-e-yahn.

Your tripe, I take your melt, I take; your straight gut I take.

These are the choice parts of a moose; the attitude of the hunter is expressive of his exultation; it is the o-nah-ge-che which he holds in his hands. It is this part of which those delicious sausages, called *hunter's puddings*, are made.

8. Neen-dai-yah gutche-hah hi-e-kwa-waw-hah, neen-noan-dah-waw sah-ween a-ye-ke-tote whe-i-ah-hah whe-he-ya!

I can make her ashamed, because I hear what she says of me.

9. Waus-suh wa-kum-me-ga na-bah-gwaim, whe-ah whe-he-e yag-gah-ming-go na-bah-gwa.

Though you slept very far off, though you slept on the other side.

He boasts of his success with women. If his mistress slept ever so far off, even across a lake, his arm is long enough to reach her, and she will hear his voice.

MUSIC AND POETRY.

10. 11. 12. 13.

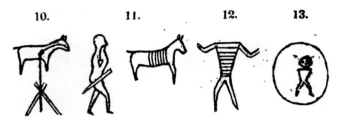

10. Neen-nah-mah neen-nah-je-ta-ha zwaw-ga, neen-nah-mah n'do-to waw-wha-to-ga n'do-to waw-wa-we-hia-ah, ya-we-he-a!

I draw your heart up, that is what I do to you.

It is intended here to represent a moose at a distance; and the line from his heart to the lodge of the Indian, indicates that he draws it, or by means of the power of his medicine controls the inclination of the animal, and brings him to a situation where he can easily be found.

11. Ne-we-nah neezh-wah neen-nah hi-ah-wa-sah [a-wes-sie,] ne-wa neezh-wah neen-nah.

I can kill any animal, I can kill.

His large knife seems intended to represent his confidence of success, and the animal is before him which he cannot only kill, but cut up.

12. O-jee-bi-yahn man-i-to, yeo-wah-ne-he-e-nah, yeo-wah-ha o-jee-bi-yahn man-i-to, whe-he-ya!

A dead man's skin is Manito.

Sometimes they use sacks of human skin to contain their medicines, and they fancy that something is thus added to their efficacy.

13. Me-nee-sing, a-be-gwain neen-ge-wun-naijh che-hah-ga-to-ga me-nee-sing a-be-gwain, whe-he-ya!

Were she on a distant island, I can make her crazy to swim over, were she on a distant island.

Here he again boasts of the power of his medicine over the inclinations of females. This song seems to present a fair view of the state of the *passion of love* among the Ojibbeways.

SONG OF A MEDICINE MAN, AT THE GIVING OF MEDICINE TO A SICK PERSON.

Fig. 1.   2.   3.   4.

Fig. 1. Neen-gaw-gaw wain-e-me-ko o-ho-i-ah a-nish-a-nau-ba.

I say some person has injured your life.

Among the Indians, when a doctor is called for the sick, it is usual to present him, on his entering the lodge of his patient, a kettle of the best food they are able to procure; and it is probable he commonly commences his treatment, as in this instance, by assuring his patient that he is suffering from the malice of some enemy, who has *shot medicine at him,* or practised upon his *me-zin-ne-neens,* to make him a victim of disease. Complaints of whatever kind, are commonly among them, if not always, attributed to *bad medicine,* under which comprehensive term they include every thing, except open violence, which can be the consequence of human malice and envy. The medicine man will generally go much farther than to tell his patient that he is under the influence of the incantations of somebody; he will name some person, either his own or his patient's enemy, as he may think most for his interest. This point is fully illustrated in the history of Ais-kaw-ba-wis, in the preceding narrative. The figure has a little sack of medicine, and his song is represented by the two lines coming out of his mouth.

2. Bin-nah neen-ne-kaun, ne-mah-tah-ho-ne-go-ka. [Twice.]
Behold me, my friends, I distribute.

He directs his Me-zhin-no-way, or attendant, to distribute to his friends, and whatever persons may have assembled in the lodge on this occasion, the kettle which he holds in his hand, and which is a part of his fee.

3. Hah-we-yah be-zin-duh-wug-ga ha-be-zin-duh-wug-ga neej-a-nish-a-nau-ba nin-gat-tum-me-ga.

There is talking, there is talking, but I will eat my people.

Many diseases the Indians suppose to exist within the body, in form of a worm, or something similar, and it is a being of this kind who now speaks from the stomach of the sick person. He says, " I hear your threatening and confident words ; but it is not in your power to displace me. I will devour my own, or those people that belong to me." The medicines which this song is intended to accompany, are often given in cases of a malady, to which white men are rarely subject. It commences by a swelling of a toe, or on some part of the foot, sometimes of the knee, and this at length comes to suppuration. An indolent and tumid ulcer gradually takes possession of the whole foot, extending to the ancle and leg, and life at length yields to it, though usually after many years. Two distinguished men of the Sioux, namely, the son of the Red Wing, of the village at Lake Pepin, and Tah-tunk-ah-nah-zhe, a chief from the plains, were suffering with this complaint in 1825. The latter, who had lately been attacked, found some benefit from the application, in various forms, of the nitro-muriatic acid. The Indians look upon the complaint as incurable, except by the extirpation of the diseased bone ; and the author of the foregoing narrative has know one successful instance of this treatment. The Indian himself amputated the bone both above and below the knee joint, preserving the muscles of the leg. He survived and recovered, but his leg was of course useless. [At the bar they begin to dance.]

4. Hah-go-way ke-new-wug-ga ki-ah-ga ga-to-che-ga ki-ah-go ga-to-che-ga.

This is the gray eagle talking ; he will talk.

Here the doctor speaks in his own person. He compares himself to the gray eagle, whom the Ojibbeways consider undisputed sovereign among the birds.

MUSIC AND POETRY.

5. This figure represents the sun, but the song is lost.

6. Ka-moke-yah-hah ka-moke-yah waw-be-gaw-gaw-ge waw-ga.

Come ye up, come ye up, white crows.

7. Ka-kaik koi-ah-na bub-bah mis-sa-wuh.

Mv henhawk's skin will fly about.

SONG OF CHI-AH-BA, A CELEBRATED OJIBBEWAY MEDICINE MAN, AT THE ADMINISTRATION OF HIS REMEDIES.

Fig. 1.   2.   3   4.   5.

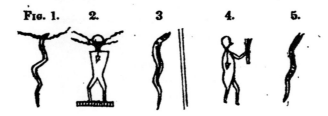

Fig. 1. Ah-way-ah noan-dah-wug-ga muk-kud-da ge-na-beek goo-we-ah-we-aun ne-kaun.

Some one, I hear him; but I make myself black snake, my friend.

The medicine man speaks in his own person. He hears some one; he knows who it is that has used bad medicine to break his patient's life; but he brings, to oppose it, the power and craftiness of the black snake.

2. Ain-dun wa-we-tum-maun o-ge-tah-kum-maig ke-he-a.
Ain-dun wa-we-tum-maun, &c.
I myself speak, standing here on the ground.
He takes a bold and open stand against his enemies, and those of his employer.

3. Wa-go-nain-wa-we-ow we-he-naun? O-ge-na-beek-o-ga wa-we-yah we-he-nah.

What is this I put in your body? Snake skins I put in your body.

The two first verses are sung on entering the lodge, and before he commences giving his medicine. The third accompanies the exhibition of the first dose, which consists either of eight snake skins tied together, and the foremost having a small frog fastened to the head of it, as in the figure, or of eight fathoms of a small cord, or thong of leather, and eight wild cat's claws fastened at equal intervals. Difficult as the swallowing of this prescription may appear to us, and as it doubtless is, the patient receives and swallows it, all the time on his knees, and the doctor stands by singing the above song, and occasionally aiding with his finger, or a little water, in the inglutition of his formidable remedy. After this has remained a shorter or longer time in the stomach, according to the inclination of the medicine man, it is to be withdrawn; and it is in this operation, particularly when the cat's claws are used, that the patient suffers the most excruciating torture. The end which is first given up is put into the hand of some of the attendants, and they dance and sing with it about the lodge, as the remainder is gradually given back. Then the medicine man sings the following, while the dance becomes general.

4. Ne-man-i-to-we-tah hi-ye-che-be-kun-na on-je-man-i-to-wee-yaun we-ug-usk.
I am Manito, the roots of shrubs and weeds make me Manito.
5. O-ge-na-beek-o-ga ne-kau-naug.
Snakes [are] my friends.

6.

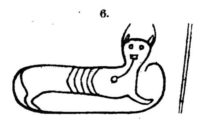

6. A-nah-me be-zhe ne-kau-naw.
Under-ground wild cat, is my friend.

At the fourth verse, he exhibits his medicines, which he says are the roots of shrubs, and of We-ug-gusk-oan, or herbs, and from these he derives his power, at least in part; but lest his claim, founded on a knowledge of these, should not be considered of sufficient importance, he proceeds to say, in the fifth and sixth verses, that the snakes and the under-ground wild cat are among his helpers and friends. The ferocity and cunning, as well as the activity of the feline animals, have not escaped the notice of the Indians, and very commonly they give the form of animals of this family to those imaginary beings whose attributes bear, in their opinion, some resemblance to the qualities of these animals. Most of them have heard of the lion, the largest of the cats known to white men, and all have heard of the devil; they consider them the same. The wild cat here figured has horns, and his residence is under the ground; but he has a master, Gitche-a-nah-mi-e-be-zhew, (the great under-ground wild cat,) who is, as some think, Matche-Manito himself, their evil spirit, or devil. Of this last they speak but rarely. Gitche-a-nah-mi-e is a compound epithet, and in this application can scarce fail to remind the Greek scholar of many similarly compounded words in that language. The English reader will perceive the resemblance in the following " most heroic" line, preserved by Cowper:—

"To whom rephéd the Devil yard-long-tailed."

There was never any thing more truly Grecian, says the learned translator of the Iliad, than this triple epithet.

WAR MEDICINE SONG.

Fig. 1.   2.   3.   4.

Fig. 1. Che-be-moke sa-aun.

I am rising.

This figure represents the rising sun, and intimates to the warrior the vigilance and activity required in the business on which he goes.

2. Ma-mo-yah-na ge-zhik ma-mo-yah-na.
Ma-mo-yah-na ah-ke ma-mo-yah-na.

I take the sky, I take.
I take the earth, I take.

This is all grasping ambition; with one hand he seizes the earth, with the other the sky, or the sun, for ge-zhik means either. He thinks

> it were an easy leap
> To pluck bright honour from the pale faced moon;

but this effervescence of valour is apt to be of short duration, showing itself more in words than in deeds.

3. Ba-mo-sa-yah-na kee-zhik-onk ba-mo-sah-yah-na.

I walk through the sky, I walk.

This figure is to represent the moon, and may be designed to intimate to the warrior that his business is principally to be done in the night time.

4. Waw-bun-oank tuz-zhe-kwa* ne-waw-ween ne-go-ho-ga.

The eastern woman calls me.

This is, perhaps, some local allusion, or it may have been ap-

---

* Waw-bun-oank-tus-e-kwa.

pended to the song in those times when the idea of taking prisoners of white women may have been a spur to the valour and enterprise of the Indian warrior. Admiration of the beauty of white women, on the part of the Indians, is not exclusively confined to the narratives of romance writers.

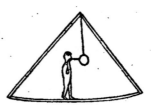

5. This figure, the words for which are lost, or purposely withheld, represents a lodge, a kettle, and a boy, who is a prisoner. The line from his heart to the kettle, indicates too plainly the meaning of the song. I know not whether any still doubt that the North American Indians are cannibals; if so, they are only those who have taken little pains to be correctly informed. The author of the preceding narrative had spent the best years of his life among the Ojibbeways; a woman of that tribe was, as he somewhere says, " the mother of his children;" and we need not wonder that, after becoming aware of the strong feeling of white men on this subject, he should be reluctant in speaking of it. Yet he makes no hesitation in saying, that the Sioux eat their enemies, and he once admitted, that in the large Ottawwaw settlement of Waw-gun-uk-ke-zie, he believed there were few, if any, persons living in the late war, who did not, at some time or other, eat the flesh of some people belonging to the United States. I see no reason why we should disbelieve the assertions of the Indians, and those who know them best, on this subject, or why we should expect from this race a degree of refinement and humanity, which we, and all who possess it, owe to a state of advanced civilization, and the influence of the christian religion. We doubt not that our pagan forefathers, in the wilds of Scotland, Ireland, or Hungary, ate the flesh, and particularly the hearts, of their enemies slain in battle. Why should we not believe this of the savages of our own continent?

SONG OF THE WARRIORS ABOUT TO START ON A WAR PARTY.

1. Ka-go sah-ween mow-we me-zhe-kain e-kwa-we-un-na ne-boi-ah-na mow-we me-zhe-ka.

Do not mourn, my women, for me, who am about to die.

2. Hah-me-ge-neen a-na-ne-mo-e-yahn a-bitche e-nin-neeng a-na-ne-mo-kwain ah-me-ge-neen a-na-ne-mo-e-yahn.

If any man thinks himself a great warrior, I think myself the same.

[This song has been published, and illustrated, by Mr. Schoolcraft.]

CHAPTER IV.

LANGUAGES OF THE NORTH AMERICAN INDIANS.

Of a subject so imperfectly understood as that now before us, little can be said, without some risk of falling into error. It is probable that the threefold division, long since made by Mr. Heckewelder, of the Indian languages, spoken within the territory of the United States, may be well founded; and every advance of discovery has but confirmed the views respecting the character of these languages, which were long since elicited and announced in the correspondence between Heckewelder and Mr. Duponceau. We may speak with confidence in relation to all the dialects of the Algonkin, or Lenni Lennape, by which we mean all those having a manifest resemblance to the Delaware, or the Ojibbeway, not only in all the principal peculiarities of structure and idiom, but also in the sound of words. But whenever assertions, founded on an acquaintance with the languages of this family, are, without careful examination, extended to other branches of the American race, they should doubtless be received with caution. It may very probably be true, that the American languages, from one extremity of the continent to the other, have the family resemblance which is so manifest in the physical peculiarities of the race; but this should neither be assumed nor admitted until it has been proved.

That etymology has been of some use in historical inquiries, no one will doubt; but the evidence it affords is commonly fallacious, and where it elucidates one fact, it obscures a thousand. We know, says Sir William Jones, *a posteriori*, that *fitz* and *hijo*, by the nature of two several dialects, are derived from *ji-lius*; that *uncle* comes from *avus*, and *stranger* from *extra*; that *jour* is deducible, through the Italian, from *dies*, and *rossignol* from *luscinia*, or the *singer in groves*; that *sciuro écureuil*, and *squirrel*, are compounded of two Greek words, descriptive of the animal; which etymologies, though they could not have been demonstrated *a priori*, might serve to confirm, if any such confirmation were necessary, the proofs of a connexion between the members of one great empire.

Philologists, on the ground solely of etymology, or rather of similarity and dissimilarity of sound, assign to the limited territory of the United States, many different languages; and if they are content to assign these different languages, as they are pleased to call them, a common origin, and that at no very remote period, it is matter of indifference how many stocks they enumerate. But if they would claim for each stock a different origin, the sober inquirer will certainly receive their opinions with caution.

It has been stated, that the languages of North America are not only etymologically different from those of Europe and Asia, but that their grammatical forms are also essentially unlike. Either to support or to controvert this assertion, would require a more extensive acquaintance both with American and European languages, than it falls to the lot of many to possess. We may remark, however, that the *synthetic*, or *agglutinated* structure, is met with in many other languages. *Riggajuhsamat'haroa*, according to GOVERDHAN CAUL, is a compound word in the Sanscrit, made up of *Rich, yajush, saman;* and *At'harvan, Gauripituriswarendraciranaihpushyat-sitimnogireh*, is a word in the same language, which may challenge comparison with any of the long and unutterable compounds in the Indian tongues; and at page 361, Vol. I. of the Asiatic Researches, we have the translation of a word which reaches *one hundred and fifty-two syllables*. Some of the compound words in the Greek and Latin, as well as in the English, seem to be formed in a manner precisely analogous to corresponding words in the American dialects. Resemblances and disagreements of this kind, as well as those purely etymological, doubtless may be traced between all languages. *Awight*, the Saxon word equivalent to *Aliquid*, has certainly an etymological resemblance to *Ahwao*, the same word in the Menomonie dialect; but it will not be inferred from this, or many similar instances, that the Menomonies are of Saxon origin. When we read the conjectures of the most learned and sagacious etymologists, that not only *qualis* and *talis*, but τηλικος, and τηλιος, have been supposed to come from the Moeso-Gothic *leiks*, and immediately from *guhdeiks* and *thalik*, whence came also the Anglo-

Saxon *thylic, lic, like.* We shall scarce wish to base upon such a foundation our opinions concerning the early history, or the subsequent migrations of nations. It is admitted that many of the American languages are similar in construction and general outline, and when we see how wide and devious have been the wanderings of the *roots*, even in written languages, we shall cease to expect uniformity of sound, or similar etymology in the various members of a race exposed to numberless and diversified influences in the widely separated parts of our vast continent.

Of two great families of Asiatic languages, or dialects, one abounds in polysyllabic and compound words, and inflected verbs, like the more commonly known American tongues. This family includes the *Persian, Sanscrit,* and many others. The second, to use the language of the learned President of the Asiatic Society, *abhors the composition of words,* and also the inflection of verbs. To the latter class belong the Hebrew, the Arabic, and some others; and between these and our dialects strong resemblances have been pointed out, or may be easily discovered From the Hebrew, or some of its kindred idioms, from the Sanscrit, or from the Tartar stock, it is probable the American languages must originally have been derived. But when we have good reason to believe that a rude and wholly illiterate people, removed from a low and fertile, to a cold and mountainous country, will, in the course of a few centuries, entirely change their language, why should we hope to be able to trace the dialects of our Indians satisfactorily to their parent stock?

In a great measure, if not equally vague, must be all conjectures based on mythological opinions and traditionary customs. We believe that those who have been extensively acquainted with our Indians, and have witnessed the variety of forms and dresses in which the same tradition appears, when related in different dialects, will place little reliance on opinions concerning remote history, deduced from such traditions.

One species of relicks, found westward of the Mississippi, and perhaps elsewhere, may be thought to afford more conclusive evidence than all derived from language and customs, that the race of Ham have, for immemorial ages, inhabited our country. I allude to those rocks bearing very distinct and deeply indented figures, resembling the impressions of human feet. That these are works of art, is unquestionable, and being found in mountainous and scarce accessible parts of the country, remote from any of the present seats of population, or routes of communication, they afford, by their aspect of undoubted antiquity, conclusive evidence, that in ages long since elapsed, regions now desolate were tenanted, and that a wandering and hunter-population, has succeeded to one whose habits of settled industry enabled them to leave such durable monuments. I am satisfied that a person, in any measure familiar with the valuable records of the Asiatic Society, cannot visit a locality of these ancient relicks, without being reminded of a passage in the *Puranes*, where King *Sravana* is described " on the *White Mountains*, meditating on the traces of the *Divine foot*." We are assured, by credible travellers, that this language is not understood figuratively, but that the people of the east boast of stones in their country, on which footsteps are discernible, which they assert are those of *Vishnu*. What is more probable, on the supposition that a branch of this race early found their way to America, than that crafty priests, or persons still possessing some of the arts of the east, should have engraved these figures from the same motives that have supplied similar memorials for the worshippers of *Vishnu* and *Satyavrata* ?

But though we cannot reasonably hope to derive from the study of the American languages and dialects, any very important assistance to aid inquiries into the remote history and connexions of the various tribes who speak them, yet there is one view in which these languages will always excite a degree of interest. In them we have an authentic record of a portion of the history of the human mind. To the inquirer of any age, or any nation, who would enlarge his acquaintance with the powers and properties, the capabilities and the propensities of the minds of men, this field can never be entirely uninviting. Human language, it is probable, must ever vary with the degree of refinement, the various revolutions in the manner of thinking, and the endless variations of external influence, to which, in progress of time, they must be exposed. It is well known to every one conversant with the subject of languages generally, that, viewed summarily and superficially, language presents a great, not to say an infinite number of families and dialects. But the Mosaic account of creation, as well as the conclusions of the more sane of the physiologists and natural historians, assure us that all mankind are descended from a single pair, who could consequently have spoken but one language. It is by many supposed that some of the existing dialects spoken as mother tongues at the present day, must have been in being in the ages immediately succeeding the general deluge. At the time of this great catastrophe, it may perhaps be safely supposed, that among the eight persons saved in the ark, but one dialect was commonly spoken, as we have the positive assurance of the inspired historian, that until some time after the deluge, all the earth was of one speech and of one language; according to the computation commonly received in Europe, it is not more than four thousand years since all men spoke a common language. The inquiry which naturally presents itself is, whether the existing ramifications can be satisfactorily traced through any common branches, or directly to their union with the primeval trunk. It may be difficult to clear up this question, as the investigation presupposes a more extensive acquaintance with ancient and modern languages, than falls to the share of many to possess. Yet if, upon careful examination, we find a part, or all the dialects of the American race agreeing, not in the sound of words, but in certain grammatical peculiarities, which have an intimate and inseparable connexion with the structure and genius of the language, as some of the physical peculiarities of the race depend unalterably on temperament and peculiarity of structure, co-extensive with the race, we shall then be compelled to adopt one or the other of these conclusions, namely, that all these dialects, or languages, have been derived from the same stock; or, secondly, if, with Malte Brun and others, we admit a number of different emigrations from remote parts of the world, we must then conclude that not only language, but physical conformation, is modified, moulded, and revolutionized by the influence of situation and external causes. If we admit the latter conclusion, and believe that our American race are the descendants of people who came at different and remote periods, from Asia, from Africa, and from Europe, we may then dismiss the inquiry at once. Having admitted the position, that the American languages are now all of the same family, that is, that they resemble each other as much as the men of the different bands and tribes, in external aspect, physical constitution, and moral character, resemble each other, we may cease to inquire whence they derive the peculiarities of person and language, by which they are distinguished from all other men. But we believe that an hypothesis of this kind will gain few advocates among considerate and well-informed inquirers. We believe there will be found in the languages, manners, traditions, as well as in the physical conformation and character of our Indians, proofs sufficient to satisfy the candid inquirer, that they are derived from the Asiatic stock, but not from that branch of it to which belonged the haughty, the noble, the unconquered race of Ishmael; or to that race, more interesting by their history, but less pleasing in person, manners, and character, to which were committed the promises, and from which, according to the flesh, sprang the Saviour of the world. The idea has been a favourite one with many ingenious and pious men, that in our native Americans we see the long lost tribes of Israel. Ingenuity and argument, as far as they can be carried, unsupported by a firm basis of facts, have been exhausted in the discussion of this question. We propose not to enter the field of argument. We admit that several of the usages of the Indians, such as their rigid separation of females during menstruation, the care with which they, in certain feasts or sacrifices, watch that no bone of the victim shall be broken, and many others, form points of strong resemblance between this race and the Hebrews. Yet the one fact, that their languages all delight in the composition of words, sufficiently satisfies us that they cannot have been derived from that stock to which belongs the Hebrew, the Chaldaic, and the Arabic. Other arguments, which, to many minds, will not appear equally conclusive, may be derived from their total ignorance of the rite of circumcision, their considering the flesh of dogs as acceptable, in sacrifice, to their deities, &c. &c. The two facts last mentioned may be allowed to have as much weight in an argument against Hebrew original, as the separation of females, and the practice of preserving entire the bones of animals eaten in war feasts, can have for it. And thus would it be easy to bring some countervailing objection to answer every one of the arguments founded on the customs and opinions of the Indians. It is not, I believe, at this time considered necessary to meet such proofs as those of Adair, which never had any other existence than in his own fancy, nor need we take into consideration the multiplied arguments, and the ingenious speculations of others, who, without sufficient acquaintance with the habits, languages, and opinions, either of the remote Hebrews or of our own Indians, have gone about to establish the belief of a strong similarity between them. In the way of a summary answer to all the arguments of these men, we may be allowed to state, that in language, rather than in any other character, would the descendants of a people retain some resemblance to their remote ancestors. Religious ceremonies, civil and domestic customs, in the exposed and wandering life of barbarians, all whose thoughts must often, and perhaps for a greater part of the time, be absorbed in the necessary, and sometimes painful and laborious struggle for self-preservation, often would be intermitted and dispensed with. Previous usages would change to suit the new and ever varying condition of the people. So might language. But being indispensable to the intercourse of every day and every moment, in all situations and emergencies, and unlike religious observances of such a nature, that what is spoken to day may, under any circumstances, with equal convenience, be spoken to-morrow, and with infinitely more facility than new signs can be invented or understood, is it not reasonable that language, of all those things pertaining to men, by which their family identity might be marked, should change slowest and last?

No extensive acquaintance with our Indians, and their languages, is required to perceive, that in all emergencies of necessity, as in those instances where they are compelled to exchange ideas with foreigners, they readily adopt any terms in a foreign idiom, for which they may not find a corresponding sign in their own; and words thus adopted becoming parts of their own language, are subject to all the inflections and modifications of sound of those which appertain orginally to their tongue. Hence that diversity in sound of words in the various dialects, which bids defiance to etymological, or rather phonological investigation. But though sounds, which, for the sake of illustration, may be compared to planks on the frame of a vessel, or shingles on the roof of a house, may be, one by one, removed and substituted by new ones, still the original frame of the language, the grammatical construction, the idiomatic forms, remaining the same, the language certainly remains the same language, though altogether changed in sound, as a vessel, covered with new planks of a different colour and aspect, would still be the same vessel. Therefore, we think that if the American languages can be proved closely and entirely to resemble each other in grammatical forms and general arrangement, we may safely consider them all as dialects of the same stock, though they should now present wide and apparently unaccountable diversities in the sounds of words. How much more easily the sounds of words, standing for the ideas we have in our minds, may be changed, than the grammatical structure and idiom of language, we may every day observe in foreigners, who, though they may ever so carefully and perfectly have learned our language, rarely, if ever, attain to some of the niceties peculiar to our tongue, or ever lay entirely aside some of the characteristic peculiarities of their own. If we reflect on the habits of the life the Indians lead, their frequent migrations, intermarriages with distant bands, their conquests, the numbers of prisoners they adopt, and, more than all, the want of any written characters to represent sounds, we shall not be surprised to find such wide diversity in the sound of what are acknowledged to be the same words in different dialects of the same tongue; nor shall we hastily, on the foundation of mere diversity of sound, attempt to establish a multiplicity of different stocks. It is to be remembered, that the Americans have never, like the ancient Arabs, made the improvement of their idiom a common, or, in any shape, a general or public concern; they have never appointed solemn assemblies for the purpose of exercising their poetical talents, or held it a duty to make their children acquainted with traditionary compositions of any sort, which measures, even had they been adopted, could not have effectually secured their languages against mutations of sound or structure.

But although we can by no means pretend either to trace the American languages to the remote parent stock, or to assert that they have or have not been derived from existing and known languages, we may easily groupe together those which have manifest resemblance, equally in structure and in the sound of words, and the groupes thus formed will always be found to bring together assemblages of people, showing strong family resemblance to each other. The threefold division which was long since made by Mr. Heckewelder, of the languages within the United States' territory, is probably founded in correct observation of the district at that time known. The Lenni Lennape, or Algonkin, the Iroquois, and the Floridian, presenting each numerous and widely dissimilar dialects, occupy all the country from the Gulf of St. Lawrence to Cape Florida, and westward to and beyond the Mississippi. Of the languages spoken in the remote and almost unexplored countries about the Rocky Mountains, too little information has been obtained, to enable us to indicate to what extent the dialects of either of the above mentioned groupes may prevail in that direction. Toward the north the Iroquois seem to be limited to a few remaining in the settled parts of Canada, and to the Dahcotah bands extending northward, in the direction of the upper branches of the Mississippi, but scarce reaching the parallel of forty degrees north. Beyond this the Algonkin dialects, particularly the Ojibbeway and Cree, and the Muskegoe, expand through all the country, from near the base of the Rocky Mountains to the south western shores of Hudson's Bay, and even in the vast peninsula of Labrador.

Westward of Hudson's Bay, from the Churchill River to the Pacific coast, and northward to the country of the Esquimaux, are found the languages of the Chip-pe-wi-yan* groupe, including the people commonly called Chippewyans, the Sarcess, the Beaver, Red Knife, Strong Bow Indians, and many other tribes. Here we meet with a language far more monosyllabic than any hitherto known among the North Americans; one possessing a dual termination for substantives, but no plural, and whose verbs are nearly or quite incapable of inflection. Yet in the circum-

---

* Of the origin of the name Chip-pe-wi-yan, by which, since Hearne and M'Kenzie, these people have been called, it may now be difficult to give any satisfactory account. A very intelligent person among the Ojibbeways asserts, that the name is derived from that language, and is only a vicious pronunciation of the compound word *O-jee-gwi-yan*, which means the skin of the fisher weasel. But the Chi-pe-wi-yans, in their own country, have no knowledge of the animal, and it is not easy to imagine how the name of its skin should have been fixed upon by them as a distinctive appellation. They are called by the Canadians, and many white men residing in the Athavasca country, "Mountaineers," which appellation they derive from the country of bleak and snowy rocks, which they inhabit. Tanner thinks the name *O-jee-gwi-yah-nug* may be derived from a word which means, " *to pierce with an awl a fold of skin.*"

stance of a tendency to compounding, we find it not unlike other dialects. The peculiarities of these languages are as yet too little understood to enable the philologist to pronounce with confidence that they have any nearer resemblance to the Algonkin or the Iroquois, than to the Erse or German. Yet the people who speak them have, in their persons, all the prominent peculiarities of the American race.

Of all the remaining parts of North America, information is too scanty to justify any attempt to class the dialects.

In the present state of information on these subjects, more important service will be rendered to philology, by adding to the mass of materials, than by any vague and general discussions; we shall therefore devote the remainder of this chapter to such specimens of Indian languages as have fallen in our way, premising that our aim has been to conform, as nearly as possible, to the orthography of the English language.* This orthography is liable to many objections; so also would be any other that could be devised. The sounds of letters must always be somewhat arbitrary, inasmuch as there is no manner of resemblance between the sign and the thing signified.

* *A* is to be sounded as in fate; *ah* as in father; the still broader sound is marked by *aw*, or *au*. The other English vowels are less ambiguous. C only used before *h*, and the sound thus indicated is never to be compounded with that of *k*. G is always hard, as in *go*; *j* always soft, as in *June*. At the end of words it has the sound of the English *dge*, as in knowledge; *zh* sounds as *s* in pleasure.

Several of the consonant sounds are used interchangeably, not only in different dialects, but even in the same, and by people of the same band: thus, *m* for *n*, *g* for *k*, or *t* for either, *b* for *p*, *d* for *t*, *l* for *n*, and *r* for either of these. In the Cree dialect, for example, the word *e-rin-ne* signifies man; in the Ojibbeway it is *e-nin-ne*; in some other dialect approaching the Delaware, it is *il-len-ni*; in the Delaware, according to Zeisberger, *len-no*; in the Menomonie *e-nain*, or *e-nai-new*, when the meaning of the verb substantive is combined. This observation should be borne in mind by all who take the trouble to compare and examine the written words of any Indian language. To many of the Algonkin dialects the sound of *b* is entirely foreign; others have no *r*. Many of the guttural and nondescript sounds of the Chippewyan, as well as several of those in the Winnebago, and the nasal in the Algonkin, cannot be represented by our alphabet.

COMPARISON OF WORDS AND SENTENCES IN THE DIALECTS OF THE OTTAWWAWS AND MENOMONIES.

Ottawwaw. Menomonie. English. Free translation, &c.

Me-notch-pun-gee—Me-na-wutch—A little.
O-ta-me-ne-kwain—Kut-tai-me-no—He will drink. He will drink a little.
Tun-ish-win—Tah-tah-we-nah—Wherefore.
Mow-wy-un?—Us-moke?—Doth he cry?
Ka-gaw-pung-ge-zhe-moke—Ka-zho-nieut—Near sun set. Almost sun set.
Kaw-ween—Kun—Not.
Neen-dah-koose-se—Ne-wa-suk-ko-si-nun—I was not sick.
Ke-tah-koose-nah?—Ke-wa-suk-ko-si-met?—Art thou sick?
Kuh-kish-pin-at-tone-nah?—Kau-to-te-pai-hai-met?—Wilt thou buy? For substances inanimate, or animals not entire, except a stone is spoken of. In the case of entire, or living bodies, Kuh-kish-pin-a-nah-nah, &c.
Ke-pe-nu-gin-nah—Ke-pe-now-wuk-ket—Dost thou bring She she-buk?—Sha-shai-puk?—ducks?
Ke-pe-nau-nah—Ke-pe-now—Dost thou bring She-sheeb?—Sha-shaip?—a duck? More commonly the order of arrangement is the reverse; Sha-shaip-ke-pe-now, &c.
En-to-kwain—Nin-nauk—I know not.
Ga-get-nah—Kat-ten-nah—Indeed [is]
O-ke-mah-ow?—O-ko-mow-waw-wew?—he is a chief? Is he indeed a chief? or, doth he chief? The resemblance to the Greek Βασιλευω, and the Latin *Regno*, both in composition and signification, need not be pointed out to the philologist.
O-wa-nain—Wah-ne—Who
Gos-kitche-ah-na-pwa-ot?—Skesh-suk-ke-poutch?—bit his nose off?
Nish-a-nau-ba—Ma-cha-ti (adj.?)—An Indian
We-ko-mi-ko-onk—We-ko-mik-ko—at the lodge

| Ottawwaw. | Menomonie. | English. | Free translation, &c. |

We-tush-e—Owa—he will be
Ke-wus-kwa-be—Ke-wus-ke-pe-nun—drunk. He will be drunk at the Indian lodge.
Een-gah-ke-way—Nuh-ke-waim—I will go home. For the ideas of fitness, propriety, personal beauty, and fine quality, as of a blanket, &c. they commonly use the same word.
Bo-zin—Po-she-nun—Embark, (imper.)
Kitche-kwi-naitch—Na-sha-wis-ke-wuh—it is very well.
Bo-au-zi-un—Us-hub-po-ai-un—that you embark.
O-wa-nain-waw-te-ga-mut?—Wah-wia-ke-mut?*—With whom lives he?
Ke-wus-ahiz-ze-wuk—Ka-wis-so-wuk ah-wuk—They are orphans.
Ke-we-ah-m'woi-gin-nah—Push-ke-mwow-wuk-ket?—Will you eat
Me-she-min-ug?—Me-she-min-uk?—apples?
Maung—Mouk—A loon,
Ma-za-tah-go-zit—Kou-ke-to—he yells. A loon yells.
We'metai-we-wug—Kut-tai-metai-we-wuk—They will have metai
A-gaw-mink—A-gaw-me—on the other side. They are about to have a medicine dance and feast on the other side the river.
Kitche—Ketch—Very much
Ke-te-mah-ki-zhe—Ka-ti-mok-ka-zhit—he is poor. He is very poor.
A-gaw-mink—A-gaw-me-um—From the other side
Ne-to-an-je-bah—Ne-to-pe-um—I came. I came across, or from the other side.
Win-ne-ba-go-kwi—Win-ne-ba-go-ke-wun—A Winnebago woman
Mi-uk-e-kway-wan—Wa-wa—he wives;
Pun-gee Ome-nom-o-ne-wew—*Me-na-wutch* ah-wew.—a little, he Menomonies. A Winnebago woman is his wife, himself is a sort of a Menomonie. The arrangement of the words differs in the two dialects. The termination *ah-wew*, which marks the verb, being separated in the Menomonie.

---

* *Wah-wia-ke-mut?* With whom doth he we-ge-wam? This is similar to the Greek in John i. 14. "*The word was made flesh, and dwelt among us;* εσκηνωσεν εν ημιν, literally, *tabernacled among us.*

| *Ottawwaw.* | *Menomonie.* | *English.* | *Free translation, &c.* |

Ah-gwut-ching—A-guat-chew—Without. Out side of the lodge.
Nish-a-nau-baig—Ma-cha-ti-wuk—Indians
Ta-kosh-in-oag—Pe-wuk—they come,
Che-to-wug—Ah-wauk—they say. Indians are coming, they
    say; or, it is said, Indians are coming.
Ke-ke-waw-nem—Ke-ka-no-kim—Thou liest,
Ke-sa-ah-gis-in-nah?—Ke-ko-ti-met?—dost thou fear?
Nah-wutch—Ko-kai-win-ne-ko—More
Ke-zhe-kah—Ke-she-ah—he is swift. He is swifter.
U-ne-shaw—Na-shup-naip—Without cause,
Tah-neen-a-ke-toi-un?—Kis-ke-zha-met?—what sayest thou?
    Εμισησαν με δωρεαν, John xvi. 25. "They hated me,
    without cause," is a form of expression similar to this in
    the dialect of the Menomonies. *Nas-kup-nai* ke-pe-um-
    met? *Without cause, or for nothing,* didst thou come?
Tah-neen a-ke-tote?—Kus-ha-wat-to?—What saith he?
Kub-ba—Ko-pai—Throughout
Ke-zhik—Ka-zhik—the day.
Kom-ma-cee, or, kaw-ma-cie—Kun-ne-mah-shew—Not yet
Ne-we-she-ne-se—Ne-meet-che-shim—I eat. I have not yet
    eaten, or, it is before I have eaten.
No-pe-mik*—No-pa-ma—Back
Pe-po-nish-she—Kin-nuh-pe-po-nup-pa—thou wilt winter. The
    Ottawwaw is in the imperative mood; the Menomonie, in
    the future, used as imperative.
Tau-ne-pe—Ko-pai-pe-pone—All winter,
Ke-pe-po-ne-sheak?—*Tæs*-kesh-pe-po-na-piak?—when did ye
    winter? There is here some difference in the arrange-
    ment of the words.
Pe-po-nunk?—Winters.
Tau-ne-pe—Tas—Where
Ke-ne-bin-e-she?—O-e-at-ne-bin ah-kwo?—didst thou summer?
    Where didst thou remain throughout the summer? is the
    translation of the sentence in Menomonie.

---

* This word, which means, as here used, *back,* or off the routes of communication, has been translated, or rather paraphrased by the traders, *in the lands.*
No-pe-mik means, also, at the back side of a house, &c.

| Ottawwaw. | Menomonie. | English. | Free translation, &c. |

Pe-kwut-tinn-onk—Pe-kwut-ti-no—At Peguttino
Ko-pa-een-je-tah—Ne-kes-kim-me-no ko-pa-ne-bin—I remained all summer.
Tau-ne-pe ke-pe-po-ne-shit—Tas-kesh-pe-po-nup-pet—Where did he winter,
Ke-si-ah?—Ka-sha—thy elder brother? Where did thy elder brother pass the winter?
Tau-ne-pe as-hi-at—Tas-e-et—Where remains
Non-gum—Muh-no-nah-new—now
Ke-si-ah?—Ka-sha?—thy elder brother? Where is now your elder brother?
Shi-a—Sha—Soon
Neen-gah-waw-bo-maw—Nuh-nah-wow—I shall see
Ne-si-ah—Na-sha—my elder brother.
Paw-ne-maw—Kun-new—By and by
Neen-gah—Nuh—I shall
Kus-kau-dum—Kus-kai-ne-tum—sorrow. By and by I shall be sorry.
No-pe-mik—No-pa-ma—From back
Nee'toan-je-bah—Ne-to-pe-um—I came. I came from *the lands,* or from the interior.
Ke-ke-pe-mish kaw-nah?—Oos-ke-pish o-met-us-pe-um?—Didst thou paddle? Didst thou come by water? The expressions are not similar in the two dialects.
Kaw-ween—Kun—No;
Pazh-ko-ka-she—Pazh-ko-ka-she—a horse
Neen-pe-pa-mo-mik—Ne-pish-nio-nik—me did bring. No; I came on horse back.
Pah-ti-e-no-wug—Ma-sha—Many
In-nah.
Kah-pe-we-je-wuh-jik?—Pish-we-je-waw-wuk-ket?—did they accompany thee? Did many persons come with thee? *Ket,* at the end of the Menomonie verb, has the force of *in-nah,* or *nah,* which is the mark of interrogation in the Ottawwaw.
Nah-nun—Ne-an-nun—Five
Neen-ge-pe-we-je-wauk—Pish-we-je-waw-wuk—accompanied. Five persons came with me.

Ottawwaw.   Menomonie.   English.   Free translation, &c.

'Nin-ne' wi-gun—Match-o-to o-kau-nun—Man's bones

Neen-ge-me-kah-nun—Ne-mah-kun-un—I found. I found human bones, or, the bones of a man.

Tau-ne-pe-ke-ke muh-kum-un—Tas-kesh mak-kaw-mun—Where didst find

O-kun-nun?*—O-kau-nun?—bones? Where did you find bones?

Pe-guh-kum-me-gah-sink—Spaw-ke-uh—On a mound

Neen-ge-me-kaw-nun—Ne-mah-kun—I found

O-kun-nun—O-kau-nun—bones. *Ne-nah-kun*, in the Menomonie, appears to be in past time, without the usual syllable to mark it.

Puk-kau-nun—Puk-kau-nuk—Nuts,

Ne-kish-pin-at-to-nun—Ne-kesh-tah-pah-hak-wuk—I bought them. These examples are not entirely similar; the verb used in the Menomonie being found also in the other dialect, and in both meaning *to pay*, though it is commonly thus used by the Menomonies.

Gau-gwug—Ke-ti-me-wuk—Porcupines,

Me-na-sun—Me-na-sun—thorn apples

Tumm-wow-waun—Ke-me-wuk—they eat. Porcupines eat thorn apples.

Maung—Mouk—A loon

Wi-e-buh be-che-sa—Os-ke-pew—comes early—A loon comes early in spring.

Mau-na-sheens—Mau-na-sha-sha—A fawn

Nah.

Ke-pe-nau?—Ke-pe-now?—dost thou bring? Have you brought a fawn?

Mau-na-sheen-suk—Mau-na-sha-shuk—Fawns

Nah-ke-pe-naug?—Ke-pe-now-wuk-ket?—dost thou bring? Have you brought fawns?

We-yaus-in-nah—Ma-ja-ma-sha—Meat

Ke-pe-tone?—Ke-pe-to-met?—dost thou bring? Do you bring meat?

---

* From this example compared with the preceding, we may see how flexible are the words in these dialects, when used in combination; *nin-no-wy-gun* instead of *a-nin-ne o-kun-nun*.

COMPARISON OF WORDS.

Ottawwaw. Menomonie. English. Free translation, &c.

O-pe-neeg in-nah—O-pai-neuk—Potatoes
Ke-pe-naug?—Ke-pe-now-wuk-ket?—dost thou bring? Do you bring potatoes?
Waw-was-kesh—Pah-zhus—Red deer.
Ka-go—Poan—Do not.
Gi-as-koo-sha—Pas-ke—A gull.
O-nu-mun—O-nah-mun—Red paint.
Min-ne-kwain—Me-nai-nun—Drink thou.
Kok-kin-nah—Mow-wo—All.
O-way-o—Way-uk—Some one
Ne-ke-me-nik—Ne-kesh-ma-nik—me did give. Some one gave it me.
Mok-kut-ti-wah—Op-pa-je—Black.
Wah-ne—Wah—Who
Wa-che-mau-net?—O-tos-hiah-wik?*—is that canoe? Whose canoe is that?
Neesh o-ke-maig—Neesh o-ka-mow-wuk—Two chiefs
Che-mau-ne-wah—O-to-now—it is their canoe. It is the canoe of two chiefs.
Bo-che-kwet—Bo-che-kwet-to—To Green Bay
We-shaw-wuk—Kut-tai we-she-wuk—they will go. They will go to Green Bay, or, Bo-che-kwet.
O-wus-he-mah—Ko-kai-win-ne-ko—More
At-ta o-nis-he-shin—Pus ne-ma-no—could I well
Ne-tai-pe-mah-te-ze—Pa-mah-ta-shim—live
Je-ba-gom-mi-gonk—Je-pi me-ne-kaw-ne—in the town of the dead. I could be more happy to die; or, in the village of the dead I could live better.

* *Wah-o-tos-hi-ah-wik?* is pronounced by the Menomonies as one word; it is probable that the interrogative pronoun *wah* should be considered separate. Of the remaining syllables, the prefix *o* seems used to indicate the third person; the next syllable, *to*, pronounced *toe*, is the word *oos*, meaning canoe; and *iahwik* implies possession. The whole sentence is similar in form and signification to what we often hear from Canadians, or persons very imperfectly acquainted with the English language. " Who belongs that canoe?" The word *neen-di-ah*, which has by some been thought to afford an affirmative answer to the question, whether these languages have the verb substantive, to me appears to correspond very accurately with the Latin *habeo, Iche iah't, habere*, and like that verb, it may be used for the true verb substantive.

| Ottawwaw. | Menomonie. | English. Free translation, &c. |

Kee-ta-ne-mo-siew-nah ?—A-na-mo-neen ke-tai-wim-met ?—Art thou a dog?

Ah neet-ane-moose—On-kah'a-nam ne-tai-wim—Yes, I am a dog.

Je-bu-ka-nong—Je-pi e-mik-kun—Road of the dead.

OJIBBEWAY WORDS AND PHRASES.

Fire—Ish-koo-da. Fires—Ish-koo-daig.
Smoke of a distant fire—Puk-kwa-na.
Water—Nee-be.
Ice—Mik-kwun.
Earth—Ah-ke.
Land—Ah-ke.
A little ground—Pun-ge-sha-ah-ke.
Big, big lake—Gitche-gitche-gum-me.*
Wave—Te-go. Waves—Te-go-wug.
Lake—Sah-gi-e-gun.
Shore—Tid-e-ba.
On the shore—Cheeg-a-beeg.
Island—Me-nis. Islands—Me-nis-un.
River—Se-be. Rivers—Se-be-wun.
Dirty pond—Pe-to-beeg. Small clear pond—Ne-bis.
Rivulet—Se-bo-wis-sha.
Rivulet, or small River—Se-be-ainse.
Up the river—O-ge-tah-je-wun.
Down the river—Nees-sah-je-wun.
Falls—Bow-we-tig.
Rapids—Sah-sah-je-wun.
Boiling spring—Mo-kid-je-wun ne-beeg.
Crossing place—Ah-zhug-ga-win

---

* Gitche-gitche-gum-me, (far, far across.) This seems to be the only word the western Indians have for the ocean, a circumstance which would induce one to believe, (could any reliance be placed upon a language preserved only by the memories, and consequently depending on the external circumstances of a few rude men,) that these tribes are not the remains of those formerly driven west, but have long occupied their present position. The manner of expressing the superlative degree appears similar to that in the Hebrew, where we are informed the degrees of comparison are made sometimes by prefixing certain syllables, or by repeating the word expressing quality, whether substantive or adjective. By some the word Gitche-gum-me is considered a compound of *Gitche*, (great,) and *gum-maig*, (water.)

Banks of a river—Kish-kut-te-naunk.
Forks—Saw-waw-koo-te-kwi-aig.
Left hand side—Mum-mun-je-nik e-nuh-kuh-ka-yah.
Right hand—Gitche-nik.
Portage—One-gum.
Hill—Pe-kwut-te-naw.
Mountain—Wud-ju. Mountains—Mud-ju-wun.
Valley—Nas-sah-wut-te-naug.
Valley—Tah-wut-te-naug.
Path—Me-kun-nuh.
War road—Nun-do-bun-ne me-kun-nuh.
Stone—Us-sin. Stones—Us-sin-neeg.
Rock—Ah-zhe-beek.
Sand—Na-gow.
Clay—Waw-be-gun.
Dirt of houses—We-ah-gus-se.
Mud—Uz-zish-ke.
Cavern in rock—Ween-bah-zho-ke-kah.
Cavern, or hole in ground—Weem-baiah.
Salt—She-we-tau-gun.
Salt spring—She-we-tau-gun e-mo-gitche-wun-ne-beeg.
Deer lick—Om-waush ke-wa-wa.
Metal—Pe-waw-be-ko.
Gold—O-zaw-waw-sho-neah.
Silver—Sho-neah.
Copper—Mis-kwaw-beek.
Lead—Os-ke-ko-maung.
Iron—Pe-waw-beek.
Brass—O-saw-waw-beek.
Pewter—Waw-bush-ke-ko-mah.
Birth—Mah-chees-kunk pe-mah-te-se-win.
Death—Skwaw-be-mah-te-se-win.
Love—Meen-oo-neen-de-win.
Hatred—Sheen-ga-neen-de-win.
Marriage—We-te-kun-de-win.
Hunger—Buk-kud-da-win.
Blacking, or fasting—Muk-kud-da ka-win.
Sickness—Ah-koo-se-win.
Pain—Suc-kum-mun-dum-mo-win.

A word—Ke-ke-to-win.
Name—Ah-no-zo-win.
Cold—Kis-se-nah-win.
Heat—Ke-zhe-ta-win.
Dampness—Shuk-kiz-ze-win.
Length—Uh-kwaw-win.
Breadth—Mun-kwut-tia-ah-win.
Height, or tallness—Ke-no-ze-win.
Depth—Keen-ween-du-mah-win.
Shortness—Tuh-ko-ze-win.
Circle—Waw-we-a-ah.
Roundness—Waw-wi-a-ze-win.
Square—Shush-shuh-wao.
Squareness—Shush-shuh-wa-ze-win.
A measure—Te-bi-e-gun.
A hole—No-ko-na-ah.
Calamity, *bad look*—Mah-nah-bo-wa-wis.
Harmony—Bup-pe-she-ko-way-win.
Playfulness—Paw-pe-niz-ze-win.
Mind—Gaun-nug-gus-ke wa-shie.
Trouble—Sun-nug-ge-ze-win.
Work—Ah-no-ke-win.
Laziness—Gitche-mish-ke-win.
Strength—Mus-kaw-we-ze-win.
Shape—E-zhe-ke-win.
Breath—Puk-ke-tah-nah-mo-win.
Sleep—Ne-pah-win.
A person—Ah-we-ah.
A thing—Ka-go-shis.
Nothing—Kah-ka-go.
Noise—Be-giz-ze-win.
A shriek—We-suk-wa-win.
Howling—Wah-o-no-win.
Voice—Mus-se-tah-goo-se-win.
White (animate)—Waw-biz-ze.
White (in)—Waw-bish-kaw.
Black—Muk-kud-da-waw
Red—Mis-kwaw.
Blue—Me-zhuh-kwod-oong; a-zhe-nah-guwt, like the sky.

Yellow—O-saw-waw.
Green—O-saw-wus-kwaw.
Great—Mit-chaw, *animate*.
Greater—Nah-wud mit-chaw.
Greatest—Mi-ah-mo mit-chaw.
Small—Ah-gah-saw.
Smaller—Nah-wuj ah-gah-saw.
Smallest—Mi-ah-ma ah-gah-saw.
Strong—Soang-gun [tough.]
Hard—Mush-kaw-waw.
Heavy—Ko-se-gwun.
Light—Nahn-gun.
High—Ish-pah.
Low—Tup-pus-sah.
Damp—Tip-pah.
Thick—Kip-pug-gah, as a board.
Thick—Pus-sug-gwaw-gum-me, thick as mush.
Thick—Kip-pug-ge-gut, as cloth.
Thick—Kip-pug-ga-big-gut, as iron.
Sharp—Ke-nah.
Weak—Sha-wiz-ze.
Brave—Soan-ge-ta-ha; *strong hearted*.
Brave—Mahn-go-ta-sie; *loon heart*.
Coward—Shah-go-ta-a; *weak heart*.
Old—Ke-kaw.
Young—O-ske-ne-ge.
Good—O-nish-e-shin.
Bad—Mah-nah-tut, *inanimate*.
Bad—Mah-nah-diz-ze, *animate*.
Wicked—Mutche-e-pe-wa-tize.
Handsome—Kwo-nahdj.
Ugly—Mah-nah-diz-ze.
Healthy—Me-no-pe-mah-diz-ze.
Sick—Ah-koo-ze.
Alive—Pe-mah-diz-ze.
Dead—Ne-po.
Sensible—Ne-bwaw-kah.
Cunning—Kuk-ki-a-ne-ze.
Foolish—Ke-pah-te-ze.

Happy—Pau-pin-an-ne-mo.
Cool—Tuk-ka-yah.
Cold—Kis-se-nah.
Warm—Ke-zho-ze, *animate;* Ke-zho-yah, *inanimate.*
Hot—Ke-zhau-ta,
Thirsty—Kos-kun-nah-pah-kwa.
Hungry—Buk-kut-ta.
First—Neet-tum, [*wy-aizsh-kut.*]
Second—A-ko-nee-shink.
Long—Keen-waw; *keen-waizh,* long in time.
Wide—Mun-gut-ta-yah.
Deep—Keen-ween-dum-mo, [*as water.*]
I—Neen.
Thou—Keen.
He—Ween.
She—Ween.
It—E-eu.
We—Neen-ah-wind, (excluding the person addressed.)
We—Keen-ah-wind, (including the person addressed.)
They—E-gieu, or, ween-ah-waw.
Them—E-gieu, [to persons;] e-nieu, [to things.]
My—Our, ⎫
Thy—Your, ⎪
His—Their, ⎬ [None.]
Its, ⎭
That—E-eu, *animate.* That—Wah-ow, *inanimate.*
This—Mahn-dun, or, O-o, [to things.]
This—Wah-ow, or Mah-bum, [to persons.]
This person—Mah-bum, if near.
This person—Ah-weh, if far off.
These—Ah-noon-dah, if near.
These—An-ne-weh, if far off.
Who—Wa-nain.
Which—Tah-neen-e-eu.
Both—I-eezhe.
Either—Wa-go-to-gwain.
Other—[None,] ah-ne-we, [nearly.]
All—Kok-kin-nuh.
Many—Bah-ti-eem.

Much—Ne-be-waw.
Few—Pun-ge.
A little—[The same.]
More—Min-o-waw.
Some—Ga-go.
Several—Ne-be-waw.
Where—Ah-neen-de.
When—Ah-nuh-pe.
Here—O-mah.
There—E-wid-de.
At—[Inseparable.]
Above—Ish-pe-ming.
Below—Tub-bush-shish.
Over—Gitche-i-e.
Under—A-nah-mi-e-e.
Within—Peenj-i-e.
Near—Ba-sho.
Far—Waw-saw.
Now—Noang-goom.
Soon—Wi-e-buh.
Then—Me-ah-pe.
Always—Mo-zhuk.
Never—Kah-we-kaw, or kaw-ween-we-kaw.
To-day—Nong-gum-ge-zhe-guk.
Yesterday—Pitch-e-nah-go.
To-morrow—Waw-bunk.
Long ago—Shah-shiah.
Hereafter—Pon-ne-mah.
Before—Bwoi.
After—Kah-esh-kwaw.
Once—Ah-be-ding.
Twice—Ne-zhing.
How—Ah-neen.
Well—Kwi-uk, strait.
Ill—Kaw'gwi-uk.
Quickly—Wa-weeb.
Slowly—Ba-kah-diz-ze.
Why—Ah-nish-win.
With—A-i-yeesh.

Without—[None.]
From—Wain-je.
Towards—[None.] Ah-che-waw?
Yes—Uh. Certainly—Me-nung-ga-hah
No—Kaw.
If—Keesh-pin.
And—Gi-a.
Or—[None.]
Also—[None.]
Perhaps—Go-ne-mah, or, kah-nah-butch.
One—Ning-gooj-waw.
Two—Neezh-waw.
Three—Nis-swaw.
Four—Ne-win.
Five—Nah-nun.
Six—Nin-good-waw-swe.
Seven—Neezh-waw-swe.
Eight—Shwaw-swe.
Nine—Shong-gus-swe.
Ten—Me-dos-we.
To eat—Che-we-sin-it.
To be hungry—Che-we-buk-kud-dit.
To drink—Che-min-ne-kwait.
To walk—Che-pe-mo-sait.
To run—Che-pe-me-bat-toan.
To sit down—Che-nam-mad-a-bit.*
To lie down—Che-shin-ge-skink.
To stand—Che-ne-bo-wit.

---

* Lemattachpin, Del. Zeisb. 51, second edition. Pom-mis-so-wak, (they walk,) Ib. 62. All these words here given as infinitives, have not a form and termination analogous to those of the Delaware infinitives, as given in Zeisberger's Grammar, but they resemble very closely those of the Massachusetts language, as represented by Mr. Elliot. Infinitives appear not to be used with great frequency by the Chippeways; some examples, however, occur, in which we can scarce suppose ourselves mistaken respecting the mood of the verb; such as this, *n'noan-do-waw a-ne-moose-me-gid*, (I hear a dog bark.) The preposition *to* appears to have no other signification than our *to*, with infinitives, their *local case*, as it has been called, affording a substitute for it, in all cases where we should prefix *to* to a substantive, as, *to the house, to the town, to the substantive*, &c. if they had any such words.

To stay—Cha-ah-bit.*
To dance—Cha-ne-mit.
To go—Cha-mah-chaht
To come—Cha-tah-ko-shink.
To ride—Che-me-zhug-gaut.
To ride—Che-pe-mah-bi-o-goat.
To hunt—Che-ke-o-sait.
To fight—Che-me-kwa-zoat.
To smoke—Che-sug-gus-swawt.
To sing—Che-nug-gah-moat.
To smoke—Che-been-dah-kwait.
To sleep—Che-ne-baht.
To die—Che-ne-bote.
To say—Che-e-ke-doat.
To speak—Che-keke-doat.
To treat—Che-to-to-waut.
To marry—Che-we-wit.
To think—Che-nain-dunk.
To know—Che-ke-ken-dunk.
To wish—[This is not a regular verb, in the Ottawwaw.]
To see—Che-wau-bit.
To hear—Che-non-dunk.
To taste—Che-ko-tun-dunk.
To smell—Che-me-non-dunk.
To touch—Che-tahn-je-nunk.
To love—Che-san-gi-unk.
To hate—Che-shin-ga-ne-maut.
To kill—Che-nis-saut.

* The final *t* in many of these words would, to many, appear more closely to resemble our consonant sound *d*; but so unsteady is the practice of the Indians themselves in this particular, that the ear must be far nicer than ordinary, that can distinguish, in the language of the best speakers, any steady and invariable usage in pronouncing the same word. It is allowable, in attempting to give a written form to any language, to decide a little arbitrarily in such cases. We may, perhaps, have been influenced to give preference, in some instances, to the sound of *t*, as the termination for this mood, by the example of Mr. Elliot, who steadily gives it in the infinitive forms of the Massachusetts dialect; and we are convinced that no Chippeway will ever mistake any word, on account of its having the final sound *t*, instead of *d*. They are, in the main, perfectly interchangeable.

To scalp—Che-mah-miz-zhwaut.
To give—Che-me-naut.
To take—Che-o-tau-pe-naut.
To bring—Che-be-naut.
To carry—Che-mah-che-naht.
To cut—Che-kis-ke-shunk.
To stick—Che-wa-po-to-waut
To plant—Che-ke-te-gait.
To burn—Che-chau-ge-zung.
To bury—Che-ning-wo-waut.
To sow—Che-kus-ke-gaw-saut.
To blow—Che-pe-me-bo-tote.
To hide—Che-guk-ket-tote.
To cook—Che-che-bah-kwait.
To melt—Che-nin-ge-taik.
To subdue—Che-muk-dwait.
To have—Che-iaht.
To be—Che-iaht.
He is—Ween-sah.
I am—Neen-sah.
I am cold—Neen-ge-kudj.
I am warm—Neen-ge-zho-se.
I am young—Neen-do-ske-neeg
I am old—Neen-ge-kaw.
I am good—Ne-meen-no-zhe-wa-bis.
I am strong—Ne-mush-kaw-wees.
I am hungry—Ne-buk-kud-da.
I am sick—Neen-dah-kooz.
It rains—Ke-me-wun.
It is cold—Kis-se-nah.
Go—Mah-jon.
Stay—Ah-bin.
Bring—Pe-toan.
Give—Meezh.
Give me—Me-zhe-shin.
Take him—O-tah-pin.
Take it—O-tah-pe-nun.
He drinks—Ween-min-ne-kwa.
He runs—Ween-pe-me-bat-to.

He sings—Ween-nug-gah-mo.
I sing—Neen-nug-gah-mo.
We eat—We-sin-ne.
I eat—Ne-wee-sin.
I came—Neen-ge-tuh-koo-shin.
He came—Ween-ge-tuh-koo-shin.
We came—Neen-ge-tuh-koo-shin-noam.
I have eat—Ne-ke-we-sin.
Thou hast eat—Ke-ke-we-sin.
He has eat—O-ke-we-sinne.
He saw—O-ke-waw-bo-maun.
He is dead—Ween-ke-ne-bo.
He has been seen—Ke-waw-bo-maw.
He shall speak—Oan-jit-tah kah-ge-e-ke-to, (I make.)
He shall go—Oan-jit-tah tah-mah-jah, (I make, &c.)
He may go—Tah-mah-jah.
We may go—Tah-mah-jah-men.
This dog—Maw-buh-an-ne-moosh.
These dogs—Ah-goon-dah-an-ne-moag.
This is mine—Neen-een-di-eem, [mine it remains.]
That is thine—Keen-ke-ti-eme, [it belongs to thee.]
Whose dog is this?—Wha-nain-wha-ti-et?
What is thy name?—Ah-neen-a-zhe-ne-kah-so-yun.
What do you call this?—Ah-neen-a-zhe-ne-kah-dah-mun?
To whom shall he speak?—O-wa-na-nan ka-kun-no-nah-jit?
Which of us shall go?—O-wa-nain ka-e-shaut?
Who shall go?—Tah-neen-a-ow-ka-e-shaut?
Either of us shall go—Ne-got-wa-hi-ao o-tai-a-shon.
Who saw these?—Wa-ne-wi-ah-bo-mik?
He—Ween.
My father—Nos-a.
My brother—Ne-kau-nis; n'dah-wa-mah, by the women.
Elder—Nesiah.
Younger—Ne-she-ma.
My sister—N'dah-wa-mah.
Elder—Ne-mis-sah.
Younger—Ne-she-mah.
My son—Ne-gwis.
My daughter—Ne-dan-nis.

My child—Ne-en-jah-nis.
My head—Ne-o-ste-gwon.
My feet—Ne-o-zit-tun.
My dog—Neen-di.
My shoes—Ne-muk-ke-zin-nun.
I saw you—Nee-ke-waw-bo-min.
I love you—Ke-zaw-gè-in; to a woman only, ne-ma-ne-ne-min.
I will marry thee, [a man to a woman]—Neen-gah-we-te-ga-mah; [a woman to a man,] kuh-we-te-ge-min.
He is taller than me—Nah-wudj-ween ke-nose-a-ko-zeaun.
He is a stranger in the village—Mi-ah-mah-mush-kaw-e-zeet o-da-nin-nong.
My wife is called handsomer—Ne-wish nah-wuj kwo-nahj a-zhe-nah-ko-zi-ian.
Your wife is younger than mine—Ke-wis nah-wudj os-ke ne-ge neen-a-pe-te-zit.
My brother is with his wife—Ne-kaun-nis o-we-je-waun we-wun.
My hatchet is in there—Ne-waw-gaw-kwut-peen-dig at-ta.
Where is he?—To-ne-e-peezh at-taik?
I am here—Maun-di-pe een-di-ah.
I am a man—Een-da-nin-ne-ne-ew.
I am a good man—Ne-min-no a-nin-ew.
Thou art a woman—Keet-e-kwa-o.
There is a God—Man-i-to sah-iah.
I am that I am—Neen-goo-sah-neen.*
He sings well—Ne-tah-nug-gah-mo.
He sings ill—Kaw'nit-tah nug-gah-mo-se.
He sings slow—Se-bis-kautch e-nug-gah-mo.
He sings quick—Ka-tah-tub-buh-um.
He sings his death song—O-be-mah-tuh-se-win e-nug-gah-mo-toan.
I see him—Ne-waw-bo-maw.
I see a man—E-nin-ne ne-waw-bo-maw.

---

* Neither *i-ah* nor *goo-sah*, are thought to be the verb substantive in these examples. The former seems to approach, in signification, very closely to the Latin *habeo*.

I see near—Pa-show n'duk-wawb.
I see far off—Was-saw n'duk-wawb.
He came on foot—Ke-bim-me-to-sa.
He came on horseback—Ke-be-pe-mom-mi-co.
You came on horseback—Ke-ke-be-pe-mo-mik.
He came by land—Ah-keeng ke-pe-e-zhaw.
He came by water—Ke-be-pe-mish-kaw-nah.
He came before me—Ke-be-ne-kaune.
He came last—Skwi-ahtch ke-ta-koo-shin.
He came without me—Kaw'neen-ge-we-je-we-goo-se.
I struck him—Neen-ge-wa-po-to-waw.
I struck him with my foot—Neen-ge-tan-gish-ko-waw; (I kicked him.)
I struck him with a stone—Us-sin neen-ge-wa-po-to-waw.
I struck him with a hatchet—Waw-gaw-kwut neen-ge-wa-po-to-waw.
I gave it to him—Neen-ge-me-nah.
I did not give it to thee—Ka-ween-keen ke-ke-me-nis-se-noan.
He gave it to me—Neen-neen-ge-me-nik.
What I gave him—Wa-go-to-gwain e-to-ge-gaw-me-nuk.
What he gave me—Wa-go-to-gwain e-to-ge-gaw-me-zhit.
And did he give it to thee?—Ke-ge-me-nik-in-nah?
Hast thou given it to him?—Ke-ge-me-nah-nah? (Didst thou give?)
Wilt thou give it to me?—Ke-kah-me-shin-nah?
May I give it to him?—Kaw-nuh neen-dah-me-nah-se?
I wish to go with thee and catch his horse—Op-pa-tus we-je-win-naun che-tah-ko-nuk o-ba-zheek-o-guh zhe-mun.
Give me some venison to put in his kettle—Me-she-shin we-yos, che-po-tah kwi-aun o-tah-ke-koonk.
We conquered our country by our bravery, we will defend it with our strength—Ne-munk-kund-wa-min ain-dun-uk-ke-ung, e-zhin-ne-ne-wi-aung, [our manliness,] or, ne-mahn-go tah-se-we-win-ne-naun, [our loon heartedness,] ne-kah-ko-no-ain-dah-men ne-mus-kaw wiz-ze-win-ne-naun.
Good morning—Me-gwaitch wi-ah-bah-me-non; [I am glad to see you.]
How is it with thee?—Tah-neen keen-o-waw aiz-zhe-be-mah-te-

ze-aik?—[If two or more, ke-me-no be-nah te-ze-nah?—how dost thou live?]

He is a good man—Me-no-pa-mah-tiz-ze e-nin-ne.
Dost thou live well?—Ke-men-no-pe-mah-tiz-ze-nah!
What news?—Ah-heen ain e-kum-me-guk?
I know him—Ne-ke-ken-ne-maw.
I understand—Ne-ke-kèn-dum; [weeds and small things; of a tree, or a large stone, they say, ne-ke-ken-ne-maw.]
She is a good woman—Men-no-pa-mah-te-se.
It is a large tree—Gitche-me-tik: [large tree.]
I see it—Ne-waw-bo-maw, if a man, a tree, or a large stone; Ne-waw bun-daun, if inanimate, or a very small animate object.
I give you this canoe—Ke-me-nin* maun-dun che-maun.
Take it—O-tau-pe-nun.
I give you this deer—Ke-me-nin maw-buh waw-waw-wash-gais.
Take him—O-tau-pin.
Give me meat—Me-zhe-shinwe-yos; give or hand to me, pe-doah.
Give me that dog—Me-zhe-shin owan-e-moose.
Bring water—Ne-beesh nah-din.
Bring the prisoners—Beesh a-wuh-kau-nug.
This is my father's canoe—No-si-ah maun-dun o-che-maun.
I gave corn to my father—Mun-dah-me-nun neen-ge-me-nah noas.
I planted corn for my father—Neen-ge ke-te-go-waw noas.
I love my father—Ne-sah-ge-ah noas.
I took corn from my father—Neen-ge o-tah-pe-nun-no-waw noas mun-dah-min.
I came with my father—Ne-pe-we je-waw noas. [I accompanied my father.]
I saw a deer—Neen-ge-waw-bo-mo waw-wash-gais.
I saw two deer—Neesh-waw-wash-gais-e-wug ne-waw-bo-maig.
I killed a deer—Waw-wash-gais neen-ge-ne-sah.
I killed him with my hatchet—Ne-waw-gaw-kwut-ne-ko oonjin-nee-sah.
I took the skin from the deer—Neen-ge puk-ko-nah, (if he saved the meat;) neen-ge-gitche ke-zwo-ah, (if he threw it away.)

---

* *Gemilelen*, Del. Zeib. 2d ed. p. 46.

CONJUGATION OF A VERB.

To tie—Tah-ko-pitche ga-wing.*
Tie him—Tah-ko-pish.
Tie them—Tah-ko-bish ah-giew.
I tie—N'tah-ko-pe-toon.
Thou tiest—Ke-ta-ko-pe-toon in-a-nim.
He ties—O-tah-ko-pe-toon.
We (two) tie—Neen-dah-ko-pe-do-men.
We tie—(The same.)
You (two) tie—Ke-tah-ko-pe-toan-ah-waw.
They tie—O-tuh-ko-pe-toan-ah-waw.
He ties me—Neen-dah-ko-be-nik.
He ties thee—Ke-tah-ko-be-nik.
He ties him—O-tah-ko-be-naun.
He ties her—(The same.)
He ties us (two)—Ke-tah-ko-be-nik o-naun.
He ties us (all)—(The same.)
He ties you (two)—Ke-tah-ko-be-nik-o-waw.
He ties you (all)—(The same.)
He ties them—O-tah-ko-bin-naun.
They tie me—Ne-dah-ko-bin-ne-goag.
They tie thee—Ke-tah-ko-bin-ne-goag.
They tie him—O-tah-ko-bin-ah-waun.

---

* *Tah-ko-bitche-gun*, (prisoner string,) *Tah-ko-bitche-gun-un*, (prisoner strings.) These cords are made of the bark of the elm tree, by boiling, and then immersing it in cold water; they are from twenty-five to fifty feet in length, and though less than half an inch in diameter, strong enough to hold the stoutest man. They are commonly ornamented with porcupine quills; and *se-bas-kwi-a-gun-un*, or rattles are attached at each end, not only for ornament, but to give notice of any attempt the prisoner may make to escape. The leader of a war-party commonly carries several *Tah-ko-bitche-gun-un's* fastened about his waist, and, if in the course of the fight any one of his young men takes a prisoner, it is his duty to bring him immediately to the chief, to be tied, and the latter is responsible for his safe keeping.

They tie her—(The same.)
They tie us (two)—Ke-tah-ko-bin-ne-ko-nah-nik.
They tie us (all)—(The same.)
They tie you (two)—Ke-tah-ko-bin-ne-go-waug.
They tie you (all)—(The same.)
They tie them—O-tah-ko-bin-nah-waun, (the same as one.)
I tie thee—Ke-tah-ko-be-nin.
I tie him—Neen-dah-ko-be-naun.
I tie you (two)—Ke-tah-ko-be-ne-nim.
I tie you (all)—(The same.)
I tie them—Neen-dah-ko-be-naug.
We (two) tie thee—Ke-tah-ko-bin-ne ne-nin-ne-min.
We (two) tie him—Ne-dah-ko-be nah-naun.
We (two) tie you (two)—Ke-tah-ko-bin-ne nin-ne-min.
We (two) tie you (all)—(The same.)
We (all) tie them—Ke-tah-ko-bin-nah-nah-nik.
Thou tiest me—Ke-tah-ko-bish.
Thou tiest him—Ke-tah-ko-bin-nah.
Thou tiest us (two)—Ke-tah-ko-bish-e-min.
Thou tiest us (all)—(The same.)
Thou tiest them—Ke-tah-ko-bin-naug.
We (all) tie thee—Ke-tah-ko-be-nin-ne-min.
We (all) tie him—Neen-dah-ko-bin-nah-naun.
We (all) tie you (two)—Ke-tah-ko-bin-nun-ne-min.
We (all) tie you (all)—(The same.)
You (two) tie me—Ke-tah-ko-biz-zhim.
You (two) tie him—Ke-tah-ko-bin-nah-waw.
You (two) tie us (two)—Ke-tah-ko biz-zhe-min.
You (two) tie us (all)—(The same.)
You (two) tie them—Ke-tah-ko-bin-nah-waug.
You (two) tie me—Ke-tah-ko-be-zhim.
You (all) tie him—Ke-tah-ko-bin-ah-waw.
You (all) tie us—Ke-tah-ko-biz-zhe-min.
You (all) tie them—Ke-tah-ko-bin-nah-waug.
He has tied us—Een-ge-tah ko-bin-ne-ko-nahn.
He has tied thee—Ke-ke-tah-ko-be-nik.
He has tied him—O-ke-tah-ko-be-nahn.
He has tied us (two)—Een-ge-tah-ko-bin-ne-ko-nahn.
He has tied us (all)—(The same.)

He has tied you (two)—Ke-ke-tah-ko be-nik-o-waw.
He has tied you (all)—(The same.)
He has tied them—O-ke-tah-ko-be-naun.
They have tied me—Neen-ge-tah ko-bin-ne-goag.
They have tied him—O-ke-tah-ko-bin-nah-waun.
They have tied us (two)—Ke-ge-tah-ko-bin-nik o-nah-nik, or, neen-ge, if a third person is addressed.
They have tied us (all)—(The same.)
They have tied you (two)—Ke-ke-tah-ko-bin-mih-o-waug.
They have tied you (all)—(The same.)
They have tied them—O-ke-tah-ko-bin-nah-waun.
I have tied him—Neen-ge-tah-ko-bin-nah.
I have tied them—Neen-ge-tah-ko-bin-nahg.
Thou hast tied me—Ke-ke-tah-ko-bish.
Thou hast tied him—Ke-ke-tah-ko-be-nah.
Thou hast tied us (two)—Ke-ke-tah-ko-biz-zhe-min.
Thou has tied us (all)—(The same.)
Thou hast tied them—Ke-ke-tah-ko-be-nahg.
We have tied him—Neen-ge-tah ko-be-nah-nahn.
We (all) have tied him—(The same.)
You (two) have tied him—Ke-tah-ko-be-nah-waw.
You (all) have tied him—(The same.)
He will tie me—Neen-gah-tah-ko-be-nik.
He will tie thee—Ke-gah-tah-ko-be-nik.
He will tie him—O-gah-tah-ko-be-nahn.
He will tie us (all)—Ke-gah-tah-ko-be-nik-ah-nahn, to the second person; to a third, Nin-gah-tah-ko-bin-nik-ah-nahn.
He will tie them—O-kah-tah-ko-be-nahn.
They will tie me—Neen-gah-tah-ko-bin-ne-goag.
They will tie thee—Ke-gah-tah-ko-bin-ne-goag.
They will tie him—O-gah-tah-ko-hin-nah-waun.
They will tie us (two)—Ke-gah-tah-ko-bin-ne-ko-nah-nik, to the second person.
They will tie you (two)—Ke-gah-tah-ko-bin-ne-ko-waug.
They will tie them—O-gah-tah-ko-bin-nah-waun.
I will tie him—Neen-gah-tah-ko-bin-nah.
I will tie them—Neen-gah-tah-ko-bin-nahg.
Thou wilt tie me—Ke-gah-tah-ko-bish.
Thou wilt tie him—Ke-gah-tah-ko-be-nah.

Thou wilt tie them—Ke-gah-tah-ko-be-nahg.
We (two) will tie him—Neen-gah-tah-ko-be-nah-nahn, to the third person.
We (all) will tie him—(The same.)
You (two) will tie him—Ke-gah-tah-ko-be-nah-nahn.
You (all) will tie him—(The same.)
I would tie thee—Ke-tah-tah-ko-be-nin.
I would tie him—Neen-dah-tah-ko-be-nah.
I would tie them—Neen-dah-tah-ko-be-nahg
He would tie thee—Ke-tah-tah-ko-be-nik.
He would tie him—O-dah-tah-ko-be-nahn.
He would tie them—(The same.)
I might tie thee—Tah-ko-be-nin-naun.
I might tie him—Tah-ko-be-nug.
I might tie them—Tah-ko-bin-nug-waw.
He might tie thee—Tah-ko-bin-naut.
He might tie them—(The same.)
I ought to tie thee—Tah-ko-bin-ne-nahm-bahn.
I ought to tie him—Tah-ko-bin-nug-ge-bun.
He ought to tie thee—Tah-ko-bin-nik-e-bun.
He ought to tie them—Tah-ko-bin-nut-waw-bun.
That I may tie thee—Go-mah-tah-ko-be-nin-nahn.
That I may tie him—Go-mah-tah-ko-bin-nuk.
That I may tie them—Go-mah-tah-ko-bin-nuk-waw.
That he may tie thee—Go-mah-tah-ko-be-zhit.
That he may tie him—Go-mah-ween-tah-ko-be-naht.
That he may tie them—(The same.)
If I tie thee—Tah-ko-bin-ne-naun.
If I tie him—Tah-ko-be-nug.
If I tie them—Tah-ko-be-nug-waw.
If he tie thee—Tah-ko-be-nik-e-bun.
If he tie him—Tah-ko-be-nau-pun.
If he tie them—(The same.)
I make thee tie them—Oon-jit-tah ke-kah-tah-ko-bin-nahg.
I make him tie them—Oon-jit-tah o-kah-tah-ko-be-naun.
I make them tie thee—Oon-jit-tah ke-kah-tah-ko-bin-ne-goge.
He makes me tie them—Ne-kah-gau-zo-nick, tah-ko-be-nug-waw.
He does not tie me—Kaw'neen-dah-ko-bin-ne-ko-se.

He does not tie thee—Kaw'ke-tah-ko-bin-ne-ko-se.
He does not tie him—Kaw'o-tah-ko-bin-nah-zeen.
They do not tie me—Kaw'neen-dah-bo-bin-ne-ko-seeg.
They do not tie him—Kaw'o-tah-ko-bin-nah-se-waun.
He has not tied me—Kaw'neen-ge-tah-ko-bin-ne-ko-se.
He will not tie me—Kaw-ween nun-gah-tah-ko-bin-ne-ko-ze.
He shall not tie me—Kaw-pau-pish neen-dah-tah-ko-bin-ne-ko-se.
That he may not tie me—Ga-mah-tah-ko-biz-zhe-sik.
If he does not tie thee—Tah-ko-be-nis-se-nook.
I will make him tie you—Oon-jit-tah ke-kah-tuh-ko-be-nik.
I will not make him tie thee—Kaw'ne-kah-gah-gaw-zo-mah-se jit-tah-ko-be-nik.
He made me tie thee—Ne-ke-gah-gau-zo-mik ke-chah-tah-ko-be-ne-naun.
He did not make me tie thee—Kaw'neege-e-go-so jit-tah-ko be-ne-naun.
I am tied—Neen-dah-ko-bees.
Thou art tied—Ke-tah-ko-bees.
He is tied—Tah-ko-biz-zo.
We (two) are tied—Ke-tah-ko-biz-zo-min; to the second person, nee-dah-ko-biz-zo-min.
We (all) are tied—(The same.)
You (two) are tied—Ke-tah-ko-biz-zoom.
You (all) are tied—(The same.)
They are tied—Tah-ko-biz-zo-wug.
I was tied—Een-ge-tah-ko-bis.
I was tied by thee—Keen-gah oon-je-tah-ko-biz-zo-yahn.
I was tied by him—Ween-gah oon-je-tah-ko-biz-zo-yahn.
He shall be tied—Oon-jit-tah tah-tah-ko-be-zoo.
That he may be tied—Kut-tah tah-ko-be-zo.
I am not tied—Kaw'n'dah-ko-biz-zo-ze.
He is not tied—Kaw'tah-ko-biz-zo-ze.
I was not tied—Kaw'ne-ke-tah-ko-biz-zo-ze.
He shall not be tied—Kaw'tah tah-ko-biz-zo-ze.
He who is tying thee—Ai-neen a-piz-zoi-un.
We tie each other—Mah-ma-ash-kote guh-tah-ko-bin-ne-te-min.
You tie each other—Mah-ma-ash-kote tah-ko-bin-ne-tik.
They tie one another—Tah-ko-bin-ne-te-wug.

I tie myself—N'tah-ko-bin-ne-tis.
He ties himself—Tah-ko-bin-ne-tiz-zo.
We tie ourselves—Nind-dah-ko-bin-ne-tiz-zo-min.
They tie themselves—Tah-ko-bin-ne-tiz-zo-wug.
Does he tie thee?—Ke-tah-ko-bin-nik-in-nah?
Has he tied thee?—Ke-ke-tah-ko-bin-nik-in-nah?
Shall he tie thee?—Ke-kah-tah-ko-be-nik-in-nah?
Do they tie him?—O-tah-bo-bin-nah-waun-in-nah?
Have they tied him?—O-ke-tah-ko-bin-nah-waun-in-nah?
Will they tie him?—O-we-tah-ko-bin-nah-waun-in-nah?
Shall I tie them?—Een-gah-tah-ko-bin-nahg-in-nah?
Wilt thou tie them?—Ke-kah-tah-ko-bin-nahg-in-nah?
Will thou tie him?—Ke-kah-tah-ko-bin-nahm-nah?

LORD'S PRAYER, IN OJIBBEWAY AND ENGLISH.

Ko-se-naun, (our Father,) o-wa-nain, (who,) ish-pe-ming, (above,) ain-daut, (liveth,) mah-no-ti esh-she-wa-but, (what you wish to be done,) wah-e-she wa-be-to-e-yun, (let it be done,) Kaw-taw-paw-pish zhin-dah-zeem, (let us not play with thy name,) mah-no-be-zhe nah-zhi-yun nah-gah-muk sa-ne-guk, (let thy great power come,) me-zhe-shin-naung ka-me-je-yaun nong-goom ge-zhe-gut, (give us our food this day,) me-zhe-shin-naung o-ma-ze-naw-o-mon-aung, (give us our debts,) a-zhe-ko-te-bah-mah-tink, (as we give our debtors,) Ka-go e-zhe-wizh-zhis, zhe-kaun-gain mi-ah nah-tuk, (do not lead us into bad things,) kun-no-wa-no mish-she-naung mi-ah-nah-tuk, (keep us from bad things,) naw-gau-ne-zit ta-ba-ne-mut (power belongs to thee,) gia mash-kaw-e-zeet, (and strength,) kau-gin-neek, (for ever.)

LORD'S PRAYER, IN OJIBBEWAY.

Kosenaun owanain ishpeming aindaut mahnoti eshshewabut waheshewabetoeyun kawtawpawpish zhindahzheem mahnobezhe nahzhiyun nahgahmuk saneguk mezheshinnaung, kamejeyaun nonggoom gezhegut mezheshinnaung omazenawomonaung azbe-kotebahmahtink; Kago ezhewizhzhis zhekaungain miahnahtuk; kunnowano mishshenaung miahnahtuk; nawgaunezit tabanemut gia mashkawezeet, kauginneek.

COMPARISON OF THE LANGUAGE OF ELLIOT'S VERSION OF THE
BIBLE, WITH SOME OF THE DIALECTS OF THE PRESENT DAY.

Elliot.   *Ottawwaw.*

Ne-oh-ke-oo-ook*—Me-nik ka-oh-ko pe-mah-tuk ah-ke—As
   long as the ground lives,
Oh-ke-ko-nah-kah—O-pe-ga-to-gonk-gia—planting time and
Ke-pe-num-mun-at—O-pe-ina-matwg—gathering time,
Toh-koi-hah-kus-si-teau—Kis-se-nah-gia-ke-shaut-ta—cold and
   heat,
Ne-pun-nah—Ne-bin-gia—summer and
Po-pon—Pe-poan—winter,
Ke-su-kod-kah—Ke-zhi-kut-gia—day and
Nu-kon—Tib-bik-kut—night,
Mat-ta—Kaw-we-kaw—never
Jeish-ah-kwoh-ta-noo—Ta-pun-nah tis-se-noan—shall cease.

    While the earth remaineth, seed time and harvest, cold and
heat, summer and winter, day and night, shall not fail. Gen.
viii. 22.

Ne-tah-tup—E-she-way-buk—Even so
Nish-noh—Pa-pa-zhik—each
Wun-ne-gen ma-tug—Way-nish-she-shit-me-tik—good tree
Ad-tan-ne-gen—Wain-je-ne-tah-we-jink—produceth
Wun-ne-ge-nash mee-chum-mu-on-gash—Mo-zhe-ka-ko-mah-jink
   —every kind of food,
Gut-match-tit ma-tug—Koo-shah matche-me-tik—but a bad tree
Ad-tan-ne-gen *match-te-toash*—Na-tah-we-git—beareth
Me-chum-mu-on-gash—Mat-che-me-nun—bad berries.

    Even so every good tree bringeth forth good fruit, but a cor-
rupt tree evil fruit. Matt. vii. 17.

Kah o-moh-ku—Gia-pus-e-gwe—And he arose,
Kah *mon-chu-en* we-kit—Gia-we-ke-wa-mink *e-zhaw*—and to his
   house he went.

---

* Mr. Elliot seems to have used *oh-ke-oo-ook* as a verb, as if he had said, while
the earth *earth's*, or, " is the earth," which is perfectly in accordance with the
principles of these dialects.

And he arose and went to his house.   Matt. ix. 2.

Mat-ta-pish koo-mit-tam-wus-sis-su—Kaw-ween ke-kah-we-wis-sis-se—Not shalt thou wive,

Kah-mat-ta-pish koo-nau-mo-ni-yeu—Gia-kaw'ke-kah o-kwis-sis-se—and not shalt thou son,

A-suh-koo-taun-i-yeu—Kaw-ke-kah o-dau-nis-sis-se—not shalt thou daughter,

Yeu-ut-a-yeu-on-ga-nit*—Mgun-di-pe nuk-ka-kum-mik—here in the place.

Thou shalt not take thee a wife, neither shalt thou have sons or daughters in this place.   Jer. xvi. 2.

* These two examples will be found, in almost every respect, entirely similar, and they afford striking instances of the tendency of these dialects to crowd together, and to change all words to verbs. *Wun-au-mon*, in Eliot's Bible, means a son.

COMPARISON OF THE LANGUAGE OF SOME VERSIONS OF THE BIBLE, WITH THE OTTAWWAW OF THE PRESENT TIME.

Of two existing versions of the Bible, or parts of it, in dialects similar to the Ojibbeway, that of Mr. Elliot, made in 1661, would be most easily adapted to the use of the Ottawwaws and Ojibbeways, in the country about the lakes. The Delaware of Mr. Deuke's version, printed at New-York, 1818, whether owing to difference of orthography, or some other cause, seems widely unlike any of the Algonkin dialects we have heard spoken. The following comparison with the Ottawwaw of the present day, will perhaps scarce afford a single point of resemblance.

Ehoalachgik! jukwe metschi ktelli wundamemensineen Gelanitowitink; schuk neskwe majawii elsi jauktsch, schuk ktelli majaweten dameneen, nkwuttentsch woachkwake ktellitsch linanizeen elinaxit ktellilsch newoaneen elinaxit.—1 *John* iii. 2. *Deuche's version.*

Sah-git-te-wun-nun! (ye beloved!) gee-no-wind ([are] we) Gitche-Manito, (the great God,) o-gwis-sun (his sons) kaw-ween (not) ke-ke-ken-dun-se-min (ye understand) ka-iz-zhe-wa-biz-zhe-wunk (how we shall be) koo-shah (but) ke-ken-dah-min (we know) ope-che-waw-bu-muk (when he appeareth) ah-yeesh na-she-nah-koo-se-min (we shall resemble him) ke-kah-waw-bo-maw-naun (we shall see him) a-zhe-nah-koo-zit (what he is like.)—*Ottawwaw.*

Beloved, now are we the sons of God; and it doth not yet appear what we shall be, but we know that, when he shall appear we shall be like him, for we shall see him as he is.—*English version.*

The following are comparisons of passages from Mr. Elliot's Bible, with the same dialect.

 Elliot. *Ottawwaw.*
Onk-as-kook*—Gia-ke-na-beek—And the snake

---

* Many instances might be adduced, to show the close affinity between the language of Mr. Elliot's version of the Bible, and several of the dialects of the pre-

| Elliot. | Ottawwaw. |

Un-nan—O-ge-gah-no-naun—said to
Mit-tam-mo-sis-soh—E-kwa-wun—the woman,
Mat-ta—Kaw-ween—not
Woh-nup-poo-e ke-mup-poo—O-jit-tah-ke-kah-ne-boas*—shall you die.

And the serpent said unto the woman, thou shalt not surely die.—*Eng. ver. Gen.* iii. 4.

[Elliot, Cotton Mather, and other early protestant divines, thought it not best to attempt translating any of the names of the divinity into the Indian, for the obvious reason, that their language affords no word which would not awake associations in the minds of the natives, very inconsistent with the character of the true and holy God. They thought it better to retain the English appellations, and attempt gradually to elevate the conceptions of the Indians to our standard, than incur the risk of perpetuating their ideas of the characters attributed to their deities, by introducing their original names into the new version of the Scriptures.]

sent day. The termination in *wug* is found among the Crees, and, as in that translation, it is used in speaking of animate objects. *We-at-chim-me-nash*, (corn,) in the plural number, is the same in both, and the same forms of expression: as, No-wad-cha-num-un-neek, (*I keep my house,*) No-wad-cha-num-un-ash-noo-we-at chim-me-nash, (*I keep my corn.*) Gram. p. 10, precisely analagous to *n'ko-noán-dun new-ke-wam*, (I keep my house,) *n'ko-no-wa-ne-maug ne-man-dah-min-e-wug*, (I keep my corn of the harvest day.)

* Ojibbeway—Me-tus-uh ge-na-beek a-naut a-new-e-kwa-wun, kaw-ween-go sah ke-kah-ne-boas.—C. J.

COMPARISON OF A GREEK SENTENCE WITH THE DIALECT OF THE OTTAWWAWS.

αἱ ἀλωπικες, [The foxes]—Waw-goo-shug, [foxes]
φωλιους, [holes]—Waw-zhe-wug, [hole, v. a.]
ἐχουσι, [they possess,]—Gia-nun-nuh-ke-zhik, [and between sky adj.]
καιτα πετεινα, [and the birds]—Be-nais-se-wug, [birds]
του ουρανου, [of heaven]—O-wus-sis-so-ne-wug, [nest, v. a.]
κατασκηνωσεις· [nests,]—Koo-shah, [but]
ὁ δε υιος, [the but son]—O-nin-ne o-gwis, [man his son]
του ανθρωπου, [of man]—Kaw'nin-goo-che, [not any where]
ουκ εχει, {not possesseth]—In-ne-kwa-shin-she, [may lie down.]
που, [where]
την κεφαλην, [his head]
κλινη, [he may lay.]

The foxes have dens, and the birds of the air have neats, but the son of man hath not where to lay his head. Matt. viii. 20.

FIRST CHAPTER OF GENESIS, TRANSLATED INTO THE OJIBBEWAY LANGUAGE.

1. Wi-azh-kut Man-e-do wa-zhe-toan mahn-dun Ge-zhik gia Ak-ke.
2. Gia pa-bunk ak-ke at-tah go-bun gia kah-ga-go at-ta-sin o-go-bun, gia tib-be-kut o-kit-te-beeg, gia man-e-do o-pug-git-to nah-mo-win o-mam-mah-je-mug-gut o-kit-te-beeg.
3. Man-e-do ke-e-ke-do to-we-was-siah; gia ge-was-siah.
4. Gia man-e-do o-waw-ben-daun was-siah, ge-o-nish-she-shin gia man-e-do o-nah-nah-we-nahn was-siah gia tib-be-kut.
5. Gia ma-ne-do o-ke-shinne-kau-taun was-siah, Ge-zhe-gut gia tib-bik-nis-se o-ke-shinne-kau-taun tib-be-kut, Gia o-nah-koo-shig ke-ke-zhaib ne-tum ke-ge-zhe-guk.
6. Gia man-e-do ke-e-ke-do Kut-ti e-she-wa-bug mahn-dun nun-nuh ge-zeik nus-sow-wi-a-e ne-bish ush-uh-ko-taig, gia aut-taush-ke-no-mink e-toi'a-e, ne-bish e-toi-wi-a-e git-che, te-go-mug-guk ish-pe-ming gia-tub-bush-shish.
7. Gia man-e-do o-ke o-zhe-toan nun-nuh-ge-zhe-gut gia o-na-nah-we-naun ne-beesh ish-pe-ming gitche-tah-goak gia tub-bush-shish gitche-tah-goak, me-kah-e-she-e-wa-buk.
8. Gia man-e-do o-ge-zhin-ne-kau-taun nun-nuh-ge-zhik Ge-zhik a-nah-koo-zhik Ke-ke-zhaib wi-ah-ne-ka-ge-zhe-gut.
9. Gia man-e-do ke-e-ke-do mahn-dun-ne-beesh an-nah-mi-a-e at-taig tum-mah-wun dosh-kah ah-ke-kut tuh-bung-wun, me-kah e-zhe-wa-buk.
10. Gia man-e-do o-ke-zhin-ne-kau-taun ak-ke gia kaw-mow aun-dos-kaug ne-beesh o-ge-zhin-ne-kau-taun Gitche-gum-me gia man-e-do o-waw-ben-daun o-nish-e-shing.
11. Gia man-e-do ke-e-ke-do ak-ke kut-ti on-je-ne-tah-we-gin me-zhus-keen, gia me-zhus-keen tu-e-me-ne-kau-ne-wun-nong, gia me-tig mah-jink wain-je-we-tah-we-gi-uk me-ne-kaun me-tig-goank at-ta on-jit-tah-gum-mig me-kah e-she-wa-buk.

12. Gia shi-a ke-ne-tah we-gin-noan me-zhus-keen gia me-ne kaw-ne-wun-noan mo-zhuk-keen tib-bin-no-wa-go zhe-nah-gwut gia me-tig me-ne-ne kau-ne-we tib-bin-no-wa me-ne-kaw-ne-we tib-bin-no-wa o-ke-tah-kum-mig, Gia man-e-do o-ge-waw-bun-daun uz-zho nish-she-shing.

13. Gia an-nah-koo-zhik Ke-ge-zhaib me-nis-swo ge-zhe-guk.

14. Gia man-e-do ke-e-ke-do tuh-we wah-si-ahn nun-nuh-ge-zhik uh-ge-zhik-oank che-na-nah-we-num-ming ge-zhe-gud gia tib-be-kud, tuh-we ke-kin-no-wautch che-gau-ta gia ke-ke no-no-win-nun ge-zhe-gud gia pe-boan.

15. Gia tuh-we was-si-ahn nun-nuh-we ge-zhik o-ke-tah-kum-mik che-was-siag o-ke-tah-kum-mik, me-kàh e-she-wa-bug.

16. Gia man-e-do o-ge-o-zhe-toan neezh gitche was-si-ahn, gitche was-si-ah che-te-ban-dung ge-zhe-gut gia a-gaw-sing was-si-ah che-te-ban-dung tib-be-kut, gia o-ke-o-zhe-naun an-nung-wun.

17. Gia man-e-do puk-kit-te-naun was-si-ah nun-nuh ke-zhik. onk gitche was-si-aig o-ge-tah-kum-mig.

18. Gia che-mus-ko-kung ge-zhe-gut gia tib-be-kut, gia che-na-nau-we num-ming was-si-ah ge-zhe-gut gia tib-be-kut gia man-e-do o-waw-bun-daun o-nish-she-shing.

19. Gia an-nah-koo-zhik ke-ke-zhaib-ne-o-ko-ni-guk.

20. Gia man-e-do ke-e-ke-do, ne-beeng tuh-we oan-je ne-tah-we-ga ba-mah-de-zeet mah-nah-cheet gia be-nais-se-wug, ka-pa-ba-buh me-so-jig nun-nuh ke-zhik.

21. Gia man-e-do o-to-zheaun Gitche-mah-nuh-maig-wun, gia kok-kin-nuh ba-mah-de-zid ma-mah-cheet ne-beeng on-je ne-tah-we-kwug, gia ba-ba-zhik wa-nin-gwe kwun-nah-jik be-nais-se-wug, gia man-e-do o-waw-bun-daun o-nish-e-shing.

22. Gia man-e-do o-gug-guh-no-naun e-ke-tong, tuh-oan-je ne-gin gia gitche-ne-bin-nah moosh-kin-nah-toag, gitche-gum-me, tuh-we bah-te-no-wug be-nais-se-wug o-ge-tak kum-mig.

23. Gia an-nah-koo-zhig ke-ke-zhaib ni-ah-no ko-ni-guk.

24. Gia man-e-do ke-e-ke-do ak-ke tuh-we oan-je ne-ton-we-go-be mah-de-zit ah-wes-se-ug gia ba-bah-ma-to-jig ah-wes-se o-ke-tah-kum-mig me-gah esh-e-wa-buk.

25. Gia man-e-do o-ke-o-zhe-aun ah-wes-se-ug che-she-nah-koo-ze-nit, gia ba-me-nint ah-wes-se, gia kok-kin-nuh a-zhe-nah-

koo-zit ba-bah-mo-tait, gia man-e-do o-waw-ben-daun o-nish-she sheng.

26. Gia man-e-do ke-e-ke-do, gah o-zhe-ah-naun e-nin-ne, a-zhe-nah-koo-ze-unk che-me-nah-koo-zit, a-zhe kok-kin-nuh wautch-che-yah-zho-yunk che-she-nah-goo-zit, a-zhe-kok-ken-nuh wautch-che-yah-zho-yunk che-she-nah-goo-zit, gia o-kah te-ba-ne-mah-waun kok-kin-nuh ke-goi-yug gitche-gum-mig gia be-nais-se-wug nun-nuh he-zhik-koank, gia a-wes-se-yug, gia kok-kin-nuh ak-ke, gia kok-kin-nuh ba-bah-mo-ta-jig o-ke-tah-kum-mig.

27. Ge man-e-ko o-ke-o-zhe-aun e-nin-ne-wun a-zhe-nah-koos-nit, a-zhe-nah-ko-zit man-e-do o-ke-e-zhe-aun e-nin-ne-wun, e-kwa-wun o-zhe-naun.

28. Gia man-e-do o-gug-guh-no-naun gia, man-e-do o-din-naun tuh-oan-je ne-tah-we-gin, che-bah-ti-e-no-waud che-moosh-ke-naig ak-ke gi-Af-e-to-tum-mo-waut,-gia, te-be-ne-nah-waut ke-goi-yug, gia be-na-se-wug nun-nuh ke-zhik-koank, gia kok-kin-nuh ba-mah-ta-zit o-ke-tah-kum-mig.

29. Gia man-e-do ke-e-ke-do——ke-me-nin kok-kin-nuh maun-dun, na-tah-we-gi-uk o-ke-tah-kum-mig, gia pa-pa-zhik me-tig, wain-je ne-tah-we gwi-uk ka-ko mah-ji-uk, ke-nah-waw wain-je-ne-tah-we-gi-uk ke-me-je-aig.

30. Gia kok-kin-nuh a-wes-se-yug o-ke-tah-kum-mig, gia be-na-se-wug nun-nuh-ke-zhik, gia ba-bah-mo-ta-jig o-ke-tah-kum-mig, kok-kin-nuh ne-men-aug-we-ug o-me-zhuh-keen, che-nin-je-ga-waut, me-kah-e-she-e-wa-buk.

31. Gia man-e-do o-waw-bun-daun kok-kin-nuh maun-dun wa-zhe-to-te o-nish-she-she-shing, gia an-nah-koo-zhik ke-ke-zhaib ne-kot-wa-as-so-ko-ni guk.

THE END.

Lightning Source UK Ltd.
Milton Keynes UK
13 November 2009

146194UK00001B/77/A

9 781432 532376